JOURNEYS TO THE
HEART OF BALTIMORE

MICHAEL OLESKER

JOURNEYS TO THE HEART OF BALTIMORE

THE JOHNS HOPKINS UNIVERSITY PRESS ■ BALTIMORE AND LONDON

© 2001 The Johns Hopkins University Press
All rights reserved. Published 2001
Printed in the United States of America on acid-free paper
9 8 7 6 5 4 3 2 1

The Johns Hopkins University Press
2715 North Charles Street
Baltimore, Maryland 21218-4363
www.press.jhu.edu

Library of Congress Cataloging-in-Publication Data

Olesker, Michael.
Journeys to the heart of Baltimore / Michael Olesker.
        p.   cm.
ISBN 0-8018-6754-1 (hardback : alk. paper)
1. Baltimore (Md.)—Ethnic relations—Anecdotes.   2. Baltimore
(Md.)—Race relations—Anecdotes.   3. Baltimore (Md.)—Biography.
4. Pluralism (Social sciences)—Maryland—Baltimore—Anecdotes.
I. Title.
F189.B19 A28 2000
975.2′6043—dc21   2001000241

"I'm talking about all this grinding and screaming that's going on inside you—you're wearing yourself out for nothing, Phillip, absolutely nothing! I'll tell you a secret—I have all kinds coming into my office, and there's not one of them who one way or another is not persecuted. Yes. Everybody's persecuted. The poor by the rich, the rich by the poor, the black by the white, the white by the black, the men by the women, the women by the men, the Catholics by the Protestants, the Protestants by the Catholics—and of course all of them by the Jews. Everybody's persecuted. Sometimes I wonder, maybe that's what holds this country together! And what's really amazing is that you can't find anybody who's persecuting anybody else."

ARTHUR MILLER
Breaking Glass

To Suzy

And to Melanie and Sara and Erik,
So they will know where they came from

And in memory of Barry Director and John Steadman

CONTENTS

PREFACE AND ACKNOWLEDGMENTS

Think of this as a love letter sent across the generations.

I suppose I started to compose it years ago when I found an old photograph of a man from Latvia named Max Strull, sitting in a New York City sweatshop early in the twentieth century, with his sleeves rolled up and his head full of Yiddish. Then it began to take shape in the public schools of Baltimore where children from all backgrounds, black and white, Jewish and gentile, Italian and Greek, Polish and German, were thrown together because it was believed to be the American way. And it gained texture over years when I went into Baltimore neighborhoods such as Highlandtown and Pigtown and Park Heights, and Little Italy and Forest Park and Fells Point, where people wanted a sense of feeling fully American—but also held tenaciously to many of the old ways their forebears carried to this country from somewhere else.

And then it crystalized, over the last year, in a couple of places. There was a criminal courtroom where a Latino immigrant named Felix Guevara, robbed of his dishwasher earnings by a uniformed city policeman, reached for a measure of American justice.

And there was a room at the Johns Hopkins Hospital, where the sportswriter John Steadman fought cancer. John brought me into the newspaper business years ago. Now there were afternoons where old friends would gather at his bedside to help him pass the hours. His wife, Mary Lee, and his brother Tom were always there, of course. And there were old friends, such as Lou Grasmick and Bill Stetka, Lou Sleater and Bob Blatchley. And some of the old Baltimore Colts would drop in, such as Art Donovan and Jim Mutscheller, and John Unitas and Lenny Moore.

Steadman, lying in his hospital bed with tubes everywhere, picked up the telephone one time and said, "I don't want you coming down here."

"I don't have to listen to you," John Unitas said back.

It sounded like two old friends, in their oblique way, saying they loved each other.

One day at the hospital the talk got around to family stories. Steadman and Donovan were both proud Irish Catholics. Steadman said his people had worked with horses: "Steeds" evolved into Steadman, he said. Growing up in the city's old Tenth Ward, John's father was known as Irish Steadman. His mother's maiden name was Dolan.

"Had she been a boy," John said, "her name was to have been James Corbett Dolan, after the boxer. The reason being, John L. Sullivan was a swashbuckling drunk who went into every saloon and said, 'I can lick any man in the house.' The Irish felt they were being embarrassed by him. So now, along comes a bank teller, Gentleman Jim Corbett, and it gave the Irish a little bit of stature at a time when they were striving for any kind of a grip. Everybody heard those stories about the signs: 'No Irish need apply.' I guess a lot of them couldn't even get pick and shovel jobs, the way it worked."

Steadman's father became a fireman in Baltimore; Donovan, growing up in the Bronx, had family and friends moving up in the New York City police ranks. In Steadman's hospital room that afternoon, Donovan told the story about the legendary 1958 Sudden Death championship game, when the Colts defeated the New York Giants.

"John Brady, a captain on the New York Police Department," Donovan said. "I knew him from the neighborhood. He decides he's sittin' on our bench. It's Yankee Stadium, and we're playing the biggest game of our lives. And he's got a bottle, and he's drinking, and I'm coming off the field and he's telling me how to play my position. I'm going, 'John, Jesus, what are you doing?' And Weeb sees him."

Weeb was Weeb Ewbank, the Colts' head coach.

"He didn't know who he was," Donovan says. "All he knows is he's got a New York City cop sittin' on our bench with a bottle in his hand, telling me how to play football. And Weeb sees another cop, and he tells him, 'Get rid of this guy.' Meaning Brady. And the cop says, 'Coach, you go before he goes. Because he's Jesus Christ.'"

Everybody in the hospital room laughed at the story. It didn't matter that some of us had heard Donovan tell it before; in fact, that was part of the joy. We were already in on the joke. We were part of a community of shared histories.

Assimilation is always reciprocal. We overlap—or else, what's the point of America? We compromise, we shed the garments of the past. But we simultaneously strain to hold onto yesterdays. It is the hunger of memory.

America is the voice of the crowd, the sound coming out of the car radio, the streetcorner riff, the fashions in the department store window, the lunch table in the school cafeteria, the newest pop music hit, the baseball box score in the morning paper, the political race, the Fourth of July fireworks. It is the air we breathe.

But it should also be a place where we know we have differences, and can celebrate them—and not just tolerate them, or find them suspicious or threatening because they are different. That is what I have tried to write about here: the journey from various backgrounds, as it was lived in people's homes, in their neighborhoods, in schools and in the wars we fought—and how all these things became part of our full citizenship and our sense of belonging.

I am indebted to those people who opened up their lives and their hearts: Bob Blatchley, Michele Boyd, Vince Culotta, Tommy D'Alesandro III, Art Donovan, Nick Filipides, Felix Guevara, Al Isella, Toni Keane, Joel Kruh, Gary Levin, Joan Levin, Marvin Mandel, Barbara Mikulski, Lenny Moore, Jake Oliver, Martin O'Malley, John Pica, Maria Pica, John Prevas, Turhan Robinson, Dutch Ruppersberger, Ron Sallow, the Reverend Father Constantine Sitaris, Dolores Snyder, Angelo Solera, John Steadman, Ted Venetoulis.

Also, my gratitude to my mother, Selma Olesker, and my uncle, Dr. Richard Loebman, for long afternoon talks around a kitchen table.

And to my wife, Suzy, for her insights and her encouragement along the way.

In researching conditions in pre–World War II Baltimore, I was aided by two remarkable books: *Baltimore: The Building of an American City,* by Sherry H. Olson; and *The Baltimore Book: New Views of Local History,* edited by Elizabeth Fee, Linda Shopes, and Linda Zeidman.

And I thank the writers of a song called "The House I Live In," which I believe to be the American hymn.

JOURNEYS TO THE HEART OF BALTIMORE

ONE

"DON'T GIVE IN
TO THE BASTARDS"

On the morning of November 30, 1999, Felix Guevara squeezed his flinty little body into the bend of a fourth-floor courthouse corridor and said he wanted to go home again. Home was El Salvador, where police made people disappear in the middle of the night. Guevara resided in America, where such things were not supposed to happen. But a policeman in uniform had taken all his money one miserable night in America, right there on a public sidewalk of the city of Baltimore, and now El Salvador did not look so bad.

"I want to go back," Guevara said in Spanish. He seemed to shrink inside a cluster of people whose faces he did not recognize. He wore a white sweatshirt with letters printed in a circle across the front. "United States of America," it said. He stood in the dreary corridor next to a tiny woman named Dorothy Katzenstein, who was his court-appointed translator.

"Don't give in to the bastards," a man named Angelo Solera said to Guevara.

Solera said this in English. Dorothy Katzenstein turned the words into Spanish for Guevara. Angelo Solera was from Salamanca, Spain, but he spoke to Guevara in English now because he wanted to be heard by everyone who might find this story infuriating and connect it to something larger in the American experience.

In Baltimore, in the closing months of the 1900s, those who followed Guevara's troubles recalled kitchen-table stories passed through the generations of their own families. They knew tales of grandparents who arrived with tags around their necks and tried to figure out the journey from the immigration pier to the heartland. They knew about immigrants who handed over their children to the public schools and the streetcorners as potential citizens, and as personal offerings to the America of their imaginations. They knew that not every newcomer is mugged by a policeman, but that the journey to the full America has its perils.

At century's turn, the city of Baltimore had about 30,000 Latinos in a population of about 600,000 citizens. Many wondered: Where do we fit in? A generation earlier, American blacks organized en masse to ask the same question, and before that were the millions of former Europeans. *Where is our place?*

It is America's constant echo. My people came from Eastern Europe at the start of the twentieth century and stayed inside the *Yiddishkeit* womb for a generation. They spoke the language, held on to the old rituals, felt most comfortable with others who were newly arrived, and passed down to their children many of their carefully cultivated traditions and their newest anxieties. But not all. Their children instinctively tested the waters. The children's homeland was not some vanished place on the far side of an ocean, but America.

"I'm a *Yenkee*," my seventy-five-year-old grandmother once exclaimed in an accent that arrived out of parents who spoke Yiddish by way of Minsk and Latvia. A Yankee; an American.

And if, in the course of becoming a Yankee, and of mixing with strangers in the new country and sometimes getting their feelings hurt or their noses bloodied, at least it was becoming a fairer fight for these newcomers. Each generation became more American.

The Felix Guevara case touched something in me, and in many who watched it up close. It was an affront to our image of the country, of what it meant to be a "Yenkee"—and yet it made us wonder: What, exactly, was that image?

My generation, born in the afterglow of World War II, was raised on the language of assimilation. Our elders said the country was a melting pot and told us we should be color-blind. They said we should be tolerant of people's differences.

But sometimes it sounded like a parent telling a child that it isn't nice to stare at that poor man over there, it's not his fault he has a deformity. It hadn't quite occurred to us that we could enjoy our differences, and our idiosyncrasies, and in the good cheer take ourselves to a new kind of friendship; that we should enjoy our own special delicacies and not just toss them into the melting pot and hope they got lost in the blend.

When my generation read history books that said Franklin Roosevelt had once been considered a traitor to his class because he brought outsiders, scruffy ethnic Americans, into the political process, we found this ludicrous and mocked the very notion. *Who are you calling an outsider, buddy?* Our parents had survived the Depression and World War II, each a dreadful era in its own way. But the experiences made them a part of the American process, for better or worse, and the paying of those dues gave them a fuller citizenship than their own parents ever felt.

And yet, into each new era, certain anxieties are inevitably passed on. My generation heard stories from our parents' generation about their own parents' woes. *The others didn't like us, they tried to keep us out. There were housing codes, there were quotas, there were unspoken winks. They called us names.* We heard about signs: No Irish Need Apply. We knew about a swim club: No Jews, Blacks or Dogs. We thought, yes, but such things don't happen in our own time, do they? And yet we wondered why we sometimes felt a little estranged, a little cut off from that fully American feeling that others—Which others?—seemed to possess by birth.

We wanted to be mainstream Americans, but later we wondered: If we reach for the mainstream, do we lose the texture that makes us who we are? How much do we have to give up before we qualify as fully American? Our real names? The memory of a language spoken by those who came before us? We want to take part in the life of America, but not give up everything we came from—and we want to know: Is the journey worth it, when America seems to extract such a price?

Felix Guevara came to America with his wife, Elena. They left behind family members who lived in a village of about 600 people in El Salvador's San Luis Valley. Guevara had friends there who were shot by police and hanged from bridges the next day. His home had no running water and his family wore clothes stitched together over the years. He earned two dollars a day at farm labor.

In America he washed dishes in a kitchen and made six dollars an hour. He had never seen so much money before, and so he counted it several times a day, spreading it across bedspreads and tablecloths. For a brief while, he imagined himself marvelously wealthy. He sent two hundred dollars a month home to his parents and wrote them a letter about a trip to Washington, D.C., where he bought the United States of America sweatshirt that he would wear to criminal court in Baltimore.

The trip was part of his American journey. In the schoolroom the teacher speaks of George Washington, the father of our country. The child hears this repeated until it becomes part of him: *Our* country—until it no longer matters that the child arrived from Minsk. The television displays handsome young members of the polyglot sharing friendly laughter, and even those who cling to the family tales of San Juan are gradually absorbed by America's charms. They want to be in on the joke, to belong to that happy crowd.

But the crowd gives and it takes. In America Felix Guevara passed corner taverns and steamy little storefront restaurants on his way home from his jobs. Working-class East Baltimore has such places on almost every rowhouse block, each not only a neighborhood gathering place but sometimes an ethnic enclave. They are the city's working-class equivalent of suburbia's country clubs. For those such as Guevara, here was America with the conversational overlay of El Salvador, where a jukebox played salsa music while a television high on a wall showed the Orioles playing major league baseball games.

Outside one of those places, on Gough Street, Guevara was snatched up by a Baltimore policeman for the crime of not speaking English. He had never imagined such a thing when he left El Salvador for America. And now, seven years after his arrival, in November of 1999, he stood at the bend of this courthouse hallway with fearful confusion in his eyes. Strangers pressed in against him, including reporters, asking questions in a language he did not comprehend.

Watching him, he seemed a figure out of distant memory to me—but from where?

"I want to go back," he said in Spanish.

"Don't give in," said Angelo Solera in English.

"I don't want to stay," said Guevara through the interpreter Katzenstein.

Which distant memory was it? Squeezed against the wall he seemed like somebody I had known, some fragment of an incident long ago. And it began to haunt me.

"Why do you want to go home?" a voice called.

"I don't feel I'm gonna be safe here," Guevara said in Spanish. "I got nobody behind me. If this man is let go, maybe he sees me on the street again. Maybe this time he don't take my money. Maybe he shoots me this time. I am always thinking about this."

"Don't give in," Angelo Solera said again, more firmly this time.

Solera had been saying this for nearly a year, until it sounded like a mantra. He was crewcut and swarthy and passionate. He was a middle man between the mayor's office and the Latino community. On the evening of December 28, 1998, the day after Guevara had his money taken away, Solera ate a quick dinner at the Caribbean Food Restaurant, a tiny East Baltimore place with a steamed-over front window and half a dozen tables. This is how the newly arrived begin a mercantile class: Rent a store front, put up some tables and chairs, cook the food that smells like home.

Baltimore's Latino community had begun arriving in the 1960s. There were Central Americans and anti-Castro Cubans, middle-class professional people. Then came middle-class Mexicans, Guatemalans, Argentines, Peruvians, and Puerto Ricans. In 1980 another influx of Cubans arrived: Fidel Castro's outcasts, mostly poor and uneducated, many of them former prisoners. By the middle of the decade, they were joined by thousands fleeing civil war in Guatemala and El Salvador.

Felix Guevara had fled the uniformed soldiers of El Salvador, only to find his uniformed policeman in Baltimore.

Now, on a wall of the Caribbean Food Restaurant, Angelo Solera saw a notice written in Spanish. It said a policeman had held up a Latino who could not speak English. At first Solera thought it was a poem. When he realized it was not, he walked out of the restaurant, furious, and looked for this man named Guevara.

It was not so easy to find him. Guevara worked three menial jobs so he could send money home to El Salvador. By the winter of 1998 he had discovered that six dollars an hour was not a king's fortune. So he washed dishes and cleaned tables at a restaurant called the Baltimore Brewing Co. At Victor's Café, he washed more dishes. At the Fleet Street Grille, he washed dishes and cut salads and potatoes. He had no car. He still counted his money each day and still sent money home to El Salvador. After seven years in America his parents had used this money to buy a small plot of farmland, and five cows and a bull.

Exhausted, Guevara walked home from his job at the Baltimore Brewing Co. that winter night when the city policeman spotted him on Gough Street. The policeman was Dorian Martin, a twenty-seven-year-old black man built like a municipal statue. Guevara was forty-seven and scrawny. Martin was a six-year veteran who wore his uniform and drove a police van that night. Guevara was clothed in his vulnerability.

Martin quickly found that Guevara spoke almost no English. He motioned for him to put his hands on his head, and then he reached into Guevara's pants pocket. Guevara thought he was looking for immigration papers. He was not yet a citizen. Martin took a wad of money from him, about three hundred dollars, and turned to walk away.

"*Dame mi moneda,*" Guevara said. "Give me my money."

Instead, Martin climbed into his police van and drove into the night, imagining Guevara would be too intimidated to complain to authorities. He was almost right. When Guevara arrived home that night, he told Elena what had happened.

"Why did you have all that money in your pocket?" she asked.

"I was going to pay some bills," Guevara said.

Then he repeated the story to a few Latino friends. They insisted he go to the police. Guevara, remembering El Salvador, said no. But the friends prevailed. By the time Dorian Martin finished his police shift that night and reported back to the city's Southeastern District, his commanding officer, Major George Klein Jr., had been roused from bed and awaited him.

"We have a complaint," Klein said.

Martin feigned ignorance. Klein, trying to hold his temper, offered details. Three hundred dollars, he said. He asked if Martin had cash in his pockets. Slowly, Martin pulled out money: about three hundred dollars—including the specific denominations Guevara said had been taken.

A coincidence, Martin said. Nobody bought the story. Martin resigned from the force minutes later in what was taken as implicit admission of guilt. Felix Guevara imagined quick punishment and justice. But, instead of arrest and jail, Martin simply went home. His case went to a grand jury but, within weeks, seemed to disappear in the maze of a huge downtown courthouse.

In the Latino community many asked why Martin had never been arrested. They were suspicious of the secret grand jury process and thought the officer's quick resignation looked like a fix to protect the police department's image. They suspected a system of justice designed only to aid the politically connected.

One month after the incident, on an icy night inside the Enoch Pratt Public Library branch at Broadway and Fayette Street, less than a mile from the block where Guevara's money was taken, nearly a hundred people gathered to thrash out his story and two more. It turned out Guevara's was not an isolated case. Two weeks before his money was taken, a twenty-three-year-old named Hector Portillo, formerly of El Salvador, was stopped on the street.

Portillo spoke no English. He was robbed of five hundred dollars by a uniformed city policeman who imagined—correctly—that Portillo would be too frightened to complain. The policeman was the same Dorian Martin. Six months earlier, this happened to James Garcillia Roy. The amount was one hundred dollars; the policeman was Dorian Martin. Guevara came to the Pratt Library that night, and so did Portillo and Roy, finally emboldened to come forth. And so did officers from the Baltimore Police.

There would be no cover-up, they said. This was an embarrassment to the police department. This was Baltimore and not El Salvador. The investigation would take time, but justice would be done. Guevara and the other victims seemed assured by the racially mixed crowd, and by each placating word spoken by those in power and translated into Spanish for their benefit.

Covering the meeting for the *Baltimore Sun,* I looked around the gathering and felt like a citizen. I am descended from the immigrants of Russia and Germany and Poland and Austria who knew persecution and came to this country feeling marginalized. They wished to become part of the happy American crowd—but how does such a thing occur? This is the question asked across the generations by millions of families in this country, including Felix Guevara's.

The gathering at the library felt like a dream my great-grandparents might have had. I sensed the same emotion on the edge of everything spoken by law enforcement people that night: We will show these immigrants how America works, and one rogue cop will not taint the country; we have histories of our own.

I thought about people I had known through the years, the children and grandchildren of minorities who had to find their own version of America. Inevitably, a price was paid along the way. They felt like outsiders and wanted to get in. But they also wondered about giving up too much of their souls, of losing the ethnic identity that made them who they were. That, too, is the American way.

I went through school with John Jacob "Jake" Oliver, who was now publisher of the *Afro-American* newspaper. We were classmates in the first wave of racially integrated public schools. But the tide had gone back out, the schools effectively resegregated, and Oliver now ran a newspaper whose mission wasn't so clear. Did his readers want integration, or merely equality? Could there be one without the other? Where were the new racial lines drawn?

I thought about Maria Pica. She had a father, John Pica Sr., who had grown up in the city's Little Italy and become a war hero, a city councilman, the closest of friends with Tommy D'Alesandro Jr., the three-time mayor of Baltimore. Also, Pica had a congenitally roguish sense of humor.

One day, Maria Pica told her father she was going to wed. But she'd been keeping a secret from her father. Her young man was Protestant, not Catholic.

"You can't do that," John Pica Sr. told his daughter. "You gotta marry in the faith. You gotta marry a Catholic or a Jew."

Later, when I asked Pica about the story, I mentioned a broader perspective, a sense of *sympatico* I saw between some Italians and Jews. "Why is that?" I asked. I had a little sense of historical perspective. I knew about the old garment workers' union hall, the Labor Lyceum, on East Baltimore Street where Russian Jews and Italians lived. Union activists were born in this setting, and women suffragists, too. But Pica's sense of ethnic ties was more emotional.

"'Cause the Jews were the only ones who would have us," he said.

I thought about Ted Venetoulis, whose parents had come here from Greece and tried to teach their children the old ways. Venetoulis, reaching for mainstream America, had become Baltimore County executive only a few years after Spiro Agnew. When Venetoulis ran for office, in the shadow of the disgraced Agnew, he heard voices cry, "We don't need another Greek in Baltimore County."

When do we become fully American, and how much do we have to give up to get there? East Baltimore still had its Greektown and its Little Italy, and plenty of Jewish neighborhoods still blanketed the northwest corridor, and there were scores of neighborhoods solely African American.

In each of these places, families understood what it meant to feel like outsiders. The Guevara case stoked Baltimore ethnics' memories of feeling vulnerable. Guevara looked like someone out of familiar archives who dressed in *shmattes,* who filled tenement streets and sold rags off of pushcarts and horse-drawn wagons. Guevara worked for three different employers. Portillo worked as kitchen help. Garcillia Roy was a laborer. They were the newest variation of almost any immigrant family history.

"I know all police are not to blame for the actions of one," Guevara said through an interpreter as he left the library meeting that winter night.

"I am comforted by this gathering," said Portillo.

The two of them walked out of the building bundled against the frigid night, strangers in an intemperate zone. I left the library warmed by my emotions. Maybe these scrawny Salvadoran guys would give everyone an important reminder: of the justice system correcting itself, and of America attempting to welcome its newcomers instead of first alienating them. It felt like an unanticipated salute to a previous generation's arduous journey. Maybe we were learning to be nicer to each other.

I drove home through the city that night thinking about a great-grandfather of mine, Max Strull, who fled Latvia when he was fifteen and worked as a tailor on the Lower East Side of New York. He spoke Russian all his life, and Yiddish, and read the New York newspapers. He kept an English dictionary at his side, which became his second passport to America. This one was for him. I thought of a great-grandmother from Russia named Zlotte who changed her name. From Zlotte she became Jenny. She imagined this sounded more American, even when wrapped in the Yiddish inflections of a Zlotte. This one was for her. This was the country at its best, I thought, when it looks out for those who are struggling to find their way.

And then all good feeling disappeared. Weeks passed, and then months. Winter and spring faded to summer. Instead of Dorian Martin standing trial, there was now courthouse discussion of a plea bargain. Martin had reconcocted his story. He now recalled meeting Guevara that December night. He said the Latino man had come out of a Gough Street bar and cursed him and held a handful of bills aloft, and Martin had angrily snatched the money away. He meant to give it back, he said, but was distracted by other police business. When he went back to find Guevara, the Latino man was gone. A mistake, said Martin, but no crime was intended.

Never mind the lame, shifting alibis—prosecutors were prepared to take the easy way out. Despite using the power of the police badge to steal money from Guevara, Martin would simply pay a small fine, endure a brief period of probation, and then he would be permitted to fade away. And the cases involving Portillo and Roy would be dropped and then hopefully disappear from all collective memory.

And this would be the symbol of America embracing its newest citizens.

That summer I met Angelo Solera for lunch on Eastern Avenue in the Fells Point neighborhood of Southeast Baltimore, not far from the streets where the policeman Dorian Martin had confronted each of his Latino victims.

In the early years of the twentieth century, this neighborhood had been home to thousands of Europeans emigrating to America, mostly Germans and Poles, Lithuanians and Ukrainians, Italians and Greeks. They settled in Fells Point and the neighborhoods just east, such as Patterson Park and Highlandtown and Canton, and slightly to the west where it became Little Italy.

Fells Point had streets of cobblestone and seagulls fluttering over tugboats chugging through its gray harbor waters. Narrow blocks were lined with rowhouses where families could overhear each other whenever a voice was raised. Sailors and dockworkers found taverns all along Broadway, and boardinghouses, and noisy food markets where merchants hollered across the aisles in their Eastern European accents. It was America in its constant reinvigoration.

By the end of the twentieth century the neighborhood had another kind of eclectic blend: young professional people bored with bland suburbia, mixing with the surviving remnants of the old Eastern European ethnics and with the city's newest wave of Latino immigrants.

Solera and I lunched at the Caribbean Food Restaurant, on Eastern Avenue between Broadway and Ann Street. This was the place where he discovered the note about Felix Guevara's robbery. A small portable cassette player plugged into a wall socket played Spanish music, and a television showed a soap opera. The dialogue was Spanish, but the actors looked like any homogenized American young people wanting to feel like part of a tribe.

On this one little block of East Baltimore were establishments named Eltaquido Mexicano and the Bodega-Hispana Spanish-American Market, the Dios es Amor Iglesia Pentecostal Church and the Latin American Connection Travel Agency. The future was arriving with a Latin beat.

"Hispanics are the Pilgrims of the nineties," Solera said that day. He laughed when he said this, but he meant it. The nation was always embracing new immigrants, or holding them at arm's length, and Solera's point was simple: The city of Baltimore should welcome those arriving at its door and not cringe from a sense of impending trouble.

Each generation struggles to learn that lesson. Solera was seventeen years old when he arrived in Baltimore from Spain. It was 1981. He spoke no English. He did housework for two dollars an hour for German immigrants who spoke only broken English. They communicated with hand gestures and nods and mutual patience. Solera lived in a friend's apartment in the 2900 block of St. Paul Street, near Johns Hopkins University, and one day took the wrong bus home. He was lost and unable to ask where he was. He saw a street sign. It said "One Way." He thought it was the name of the street. For Solera, the story took on the quality of a metaphor: one way toward a sense of belonging.

Just blocks away from our lunch, where the policeman Dorian Martin found his victims, he had known his advantage: Their tongues were tied. I thought about the grandparents of Barbara Mikulski, of Poland and East Baltimore, and the father of Tommy D'Alesandro Jr., of Italy and East Baltimore. They had lived within walking distance of this street and had struggled to learn the English language. All saw their children become leaders of a community far beyond their own, but not without a struggle.

I thought about D'Alesandro, whose power base had been Little Italy, several blocks west of the restaurant, when the city's Italians were breaking through politically. D'Alesandro had been the crown prince of Little Italy. One of thirteen children of a laborer from Abruzzo, Italy, he was an eighth-grade dropout who became a congressman and then mayor of Baltimore, and produced a son, Tommy D'Alesandro III, who also became mayor, and a daughter, Nancy Pelosi, who became a U.S. congresswoman from California. When Tommy the elder went to Congress in 1938, he was befriended by Franklin Roosevelt, and then by Harry Truman and John Kennedy.

"Oh, my father adored Roosevelt," Tommy D'Alesandro III remembered years later. "Well, you know, FDR opened doors for people who never felt part of that political mainstream." A son, born the day FDR was sworn into office, was named Franklin Delano Roosevelt D'Alesandro.

D'Alesandro III remembered the first time his father had met Roosevelt, in 1938, when Tommy the elder was running for a congressional seat. Roosevelt was in Denton, on Maryland's Eastern Shore. D'Alesandro packed his wife and six children into the car and drove there because he wanted everyone to know he was a Roosevelt man, and he hoped some newspaper photographer would snap a picture.

"My father went over to meet him at his car, and I walked behind him," D'Alesandro said. "There was a big, massive convertible, and I see this guy, the president. He looked like a mountain. And the Secret Service guys opened the door and formed this basket—to carry him. And his pants, it was like there were no legs, they were just sticks. I'll never forget that. And even when they were carrying him, he never stopped smiling."

When D'Alesandro the candidate reached Roosevelt, no newspaper photographers were paying attention. D'Alesandro was nobody important to them. In his mind, he was reaching not only for the president's hand, but a piece of the political pie, a bridge between the immigrant risen from the working class and the president descended from the upper crust. And nobody was watching.

D'Alesandro spotted a little girl with a box camera nearby. He called over to her, "Take a picture, would you, please." The little girl looked at D'Alesandro. He took FDR's hand. "Glad to meet you, Mr. President," said D'Alesandro. The little girl did not move. "Snap the picture, snap the picture," D'Alesandro called to her. He kept shaking Roosevelt's hand. "Glad to meet you, Mr. President, glad to meet you."

The little girl finally snapped the picture. D'Alesandro dropped Roosevelt's hand and strode over to the little girl. "Will you take $20 for the camera?" he asked. She did. Then D'Alesandro piled his family back into the car and drove to Baltimore, where he took the roll of pictures to the *Baltimore Sun.* That was big-media politics in 1938; it was also a kind of passport snapshot.

After his election to Congress D'Alesandro met Roosevelt in the White House Oval Office and blurted, "Wow, Mr. President, if the boys in the old neighborhood could only see me now."

D'Alesandro reveled in the journey to America's mainstream. But sometimes he was infuriated by the prices he paid. In Congress he brought a young man from the neighborhood—John Pica. On occasion, D'Alesandro sent Pica to the Texas delegation, where a young Lyndon Johnson would tell him, "Yeah, Tony, okay, Tony, go back and tell Tony . . . " Johnson, the future president, the man who signed more civil rights legislation than any president, who showed such public empathy for those on America's political fringes, found the nickname amusing: *He's Italian, so he must be Tony.* Pica, ticked off, related everything to D'Alesandro.

"He keeps calling us 'Tony.' Everything's 'Tony.'"

"It's 'Tony,'" D'Alesandro the congressman said through tight lips, "'cause he don't have the guts to call you a fuckin' wop."

D'Alesandro the elder and Pica had each told me that story. I repeated it to Solera that day on Eastern Avenue, one ethnic minority telling another of a third outsider's travails. This much we have in common: We each stand just out of reach of some perceived mainstream, hoping to be accepted, wondering about that nagging little voice warning us that maybe we are not—and yet simultaneously wanting to hold onto those things that make us who we are instead of some bland homogenized soul without an identity to call our own.

I thought about Barbara Mikulski. Years earlier, when her parents arrived here from Poland, they initially settled in this Fells Point neighborhood before moving slightly east to Highlandtown. Mikulski was a U.S. senator now, and still nurtured the spirit of the hyphenated American. All politics were local —even when arriving from Warsaw. Mikulski was quick and pugnacious and impatient. You could imagine the nuns at school teaching her proper manners while she simultaneously discovered the instinct to make a fist.

One day years earlier, I mentioned to her a trip I'd taken to the immigration museum at Ellis Island. I assumed a mutual sentimental journey would follow. Instead, Mikulski rattled off American immigration quotas from half a century earlier.

"Sixty-five thousand Anglo-Saxons to three hundred Greeks," she snapped. "Now, what's that all about?"

She talked about ethnic communities that grew, and were reinforced, out of the need for emotional self-protection. In East Baltimore the Poles had their fraternal groups and their churches and their bowling leagues and the Polish Women's Alliance.

"An urban village," she called her old Highlandtown neighborhood.

But she knew the village had paid a price for its insularity. Outsiders made fun. They stereotyped her people as clods in sweatshirts. The Polish joke was a longtime slur that enraged her. The urge to settle in familiar clusters was balanced frustratingly against the desire to branch out and be seen as fully American.

"And this is the Latino community today," Angelo Solera said now, sitting in the little Eastern Avenue Caribbean restaurant, his voice rising. "We want to be accepted. We're a workforce. We work. You can look at the unemployment figures, and it doesn't matter what they say, we're working two jobs."

"Like Felix Guevara," I suggested.

"Like Guevara," Solera said, "except he works three jobs. We're a labor force. We're a market force. We embrace the family, which is the center of everything for us. And we bring diversity, which is America, right?"

His voice trailed off. It was America, but the country moved to selected rhythms. It was human nature to fear change, and to suspect those who are different, and to take advantage of the weak. Look at poor Guevara.

Solera sighed. He was now thirty-five years old, divorced, with a teenage son who attended a preppy private school whose graduates went to Ivy League universities. Solera had a municipal job with a title and a little bit of access to strands of power.

"And still," he said, "people hear my accent and ask for my green card. Now, what is that?"

Now, what is that?

They were Mikulski's words from years earlier: Why is my group the outsider? Again, the eternal American conflict, this desire to assimilate while harboring anxiety about others who seem already to have made the journey and appear to look strangely at us. Where do we reach compromise? And how do we fit in without committing cultural suicide?

And when do we decide we will not?

"I want to go back," Felix Guevara said on the morning of November 30, 1999.

"Don't give in to the bastards," said Angelo Solera.

Standing in the courthouse hallway, Guevara seemed overwhelmed by the small mob of reporters and courthouse hangers-on who crowded around him, his eyes dancing all over the place. I knew that look, I'd seen it against another wall years ago. I remembered a crowd of people, and voices rising, and someone frightened and looking for a way out. But I couldn't place the memory.

Now the interpreter Katzenstein said something into Guevara's ear as a courtroom door a few feet away swung open. A decision on Dorian Martin had now been made. Guevara took a deep breath and slowly came out of his little corner. I stood next to him and pointed to his sweatshirt: United States of America.

"That's a good shirt," I said.

Katzenstein the translator put this into Spanish. Guevara's expression said he wasn't so certain. America was not, after all, his country. These people in the courthouse were not his people. This was my country, and my city—and yet, as a religious minority, I thought I had some sense of his isolation.

I remembered growing up with mixed feelings: comfort and familiarity with my own people, the Jews, but a desire to feel part of something larger, something that connected to the country's avowed belief that there was room for all.

My family moved to Baltimore from the Bronx, New York, in 1949. My father was a college freshman who signed up for the Army Air Corps the day after Pearl Harbor. A few years after the war we moved to Baltimore so he could finish his schooling.

We lived in Abbott Court in the Latrobe Homes housing project, hemmed in on one side by the enormous Church of St. James directly across one street and, on the other side, hovering over us a few small streets away, by the Maryland Penitentiary. I went to P.S. 20. There were no Jewish children in my world. My parents never made an issue of this, nor do I recall ever hearing an anti-Semitic slur. But I knew there were differences. My friends and their parents walked across the street to St. James each Sunday morning, celebrated Christmas and Easter, and spoke on occasion of someone named Jesus Christ.

"Who is that?" I asked.

"One of our boys," my father said, glancing up momentarily from his morning newspaper.

"Huh?"

"Eat your breakfast."

Or a song would play on the radio: "White Christmas."

"One of ours," my father would declare with grand comic proprietorship.

"Irving Berlin," my mother explained. "He wrote this song. He's Jewish."

He was dreaming of a white Christmas, just like the ones he used to know.

"Why don't we have a Christmas tree like everybody else?" I asked in December.

One year we did. The tree was brought into the apartment the day before Christmas, looking malnourished and nothing like the glorious things I had seen in magazine photographs. My parents didn't want me to feel *different*. They decorated the tree in the living room after I went to sleep that night and then hustled it back out an evening or two later. But I managed to slip a few friends in before it was snatched away: Look, we have a tree, too.

It wasn't that I wanted to be gentile; I had no particular idea what a gentile was. I only wanted to be like everybody else, an American, and being gentile seemed to be an inextricable part of that identity. The country sent out all sorts of signals on such things, visible even to a child's eye. It was the holiday almost everybody celebrated, and a few people on the edges did not. It was a whole system of sweet family memories and the things that surrounded them: Santa Claus in all the advertisements, presents under the tree, miracles of the season at the movies. And "White Christmas" on the radio.

No one ever told me I wasn't fully American; no one had to. But no one ever told me that we are a nation of such people, feeling marginalized for any of a multitude of reasons, outsiders who come from the identical place: Somewhere Else. And the America we hear about, the country of myth and song—this is a place that is just out of reach, the grand party to which all newcomers await invitation.

Senator Barbara Mikulski was that outsider every time she remembered immigration quotas. So was Tommy D'Alesandro the elder, when he shook the hand of Franklin Roosevelt but returned to Congress to hear little jokes about "Tony." And so was Felix Guevara, standing in that courthouse hallway with a haunted look that arrived from somewhere in a distinctly American memory.

We are a nation of families with a history, somewhere along the line, of feeling left out. So we wrap ourselves in the things that are our own, we but reach out a hand and hope someone is reaching back. We are a nation of cultural mutts, trying to reconcile the normal human desire to fit in while holding on to the things that give us comfort and make us unique.

TWO

THE AMERICANIZATION
OF ZLOTTE

The great-grandmother on my mother's side of the family, Zlotte Gurion, arrived in New York City from Minsk at the beginning of the twentieth century and slowly created a new American self. First came the changing of the name: Zlotte into Charlotte, instigated by her daughters; and, when this did not feel sufficiently American, Charlotte into Jenny. Then, in time, Jenny invented a new history of America. From the greatest Protestant presidents of her life, she imagined instant Jews: Franklin Delano Rosenfeld, Harry S. Schuman, and Dwight D. Eisenberg.

It was not lost on the family that some of the nation's old-line gentry also accorded Roosevelt an imaginary Jewish surname, though this was said with a sneer by those who imagined him a traitor to his class. From Zlotte it was affectionate tribute, a way of embracing the nation's most important men, and maybe hoping they would embrace her back.

On the Lower East Side of the city, she met my great-grandfather, who left

Kiev in Czarist Russia as Max Strewl and, by the time he traversed U.S. Customs, had become someone known as Max Strull. He spoke no English and knew not a soul on the Lower East Side of New York, where at age fifteen he found work in a basement sweatshop and eventually met the girl then known as Zlotte, who worked in a clothing factory. They were part of a nation newly brimming with people such as themselves.

At the beginning of the twentieth century, one-third of all those living in the United States were immigrants, or the children of immigrants. The cities bulged with them. In 1900 alone 90,000 people arrived here from Russia and the Baltic states. From Italy 100,000 came and from Austria-Hungary 115,000. From Ireland and from Poland they came by the tens of thousands, and from Greece and Germany by the thousands. They packed their few pieces of clothing, and some pots and pans, and they made their way across the Atlantic. Most of them were crammed into steerage, where the air was fetid and the food dreadful and the voyage lasted as long as three weeks. Some of them paid as little as twelve dollars, and struggled to scrape together even that pitiful amount. They constituted a wave of nearly half a million people landing that year from all parts of the world because they heard quite correctly that here was the golden land. The average American worker at that time made twenty-two cents an hour. Such gold! There were nearly two million child laborers, some of whom earned twenty-five cents a day. Such opportunity! The average life expectancy was forty-seven years. Such a future awaiting everyone!

I have a brown photograph of Max Strull, which I liberated from a cardboard box in my mother's closet. My great-grandfather sits in this airless sweatshop on Hester Street on the Lower East Side with his sleeves rolled up and a mustache on his lip. Wariness crosses his face, as though he anticipates burly Cossacks crashing into the room if he foolishly lets his guard down. He will save his smiles for later. Other immigrant men surround him in long undershirts with the sleeves rolled up to their bony elbows, each at his own cramped sewing machine, with electrical wires dangling from a ceiling and swatches of cloth strewn haphazardly about.

The photograph was a curiosity when I first discovered it, an amusing artifact of odd-looking men who might have been from Chaplin's era, or the Paleozoic. The world moves too quickly for an adolescent boy to care too much about such ancient figures. But the photo was hung on a wall, and the

The author's great-grandfather (*third from left*), who had departed the Russian republic of Latvia as Max Strewl and, by the time he emerged from U.S. Customs, had become someone called Max Strull. He worked in this sweatshop on the Lower East Side of New York City.

vague curiosity became a reminder: This man's arrival was a precursor of my own. Without him there is no America for me.

In Kiev Max was a *Yeshiva bocher,* a scholar of the Torah. In the sweatshop of New York he was a mender of pants. Another man put pockets in them, another the crotch, another the seams. Ralph Lauren it was not. They spoke Russian and German and Polish and Yiddish and snatched up random pieces of the American patois here and there between the stitching and the sweating. They took comfort in their huddled Jewishness, because they came from places where to be Jewish was to feel ostracized. Some who came here took only the smallest tentative steps to the world outside their womb, intimidated by the sound of language not their own, and by the assumption that different still meant dangerous. Never mind Felix Guevara's oppressive policeman; to them, all police were intimidating.

At night in Max and Zlotte's apartment on Henry Street, where they raised their six children, my great-grandfather sat by a small gas lamp where he read the *Jewish Daily Forward* in Yiddish and the New York newspapers in English with a dictionary at his side to Americanize himself at his own pace. His children remembered notebooks in which he wrote English words with their pronunciations and their translations. And while he wrote, he hummed snatches of Russian melodies.

"Russian?" I asked when I heard the story.

"They reminded him of home," said his daughter, my grandmother Ruth Loebman, nearly three-quarters of a century after the fact. Nations wage political wars and send men to the moon whose names we forget the following week. The things that survive are tales told around kitchen tables. My grandmother was approaching seventy-seven when she mentioned her father's evening rituals. She wore a sunny yellow wig over her gray hair and dabbed at leaky eyes with a tissue kept beneath the band of her watch.

"My father was a scholar who mended pants," she said. "You would see him with the dictionary, with his writing, with the books and books of what he would write, and the corrections and the pronunciations. He would sit by the gaslight in this little apartment on Henry Street."

In tape-recorded conversations I had with her, my grandmother speaks in soft inflections reminiscent of Gracie Allen. In the years these tapes sat on a shelf, I had forgotten the sound of her voice and her quick sense of humor.

"And this was how he spent his free time?" I said. "Reading?"

"Well, he would take my mother to the movies," my grandmother said.

I imagined Chaplin to delight a generation of immigrants. I imagined Laurel and Hardy and Our Gang comedies showing scruffy American children at play and a man in an orchestra pit tinkling a piano over dialogue printed against a black background. Max and Charlotte were two diminutive pilgrims off to see the whole country on a movie screen.

"No, not *inside* the movies," my grandmother explained. She laughed so delightedly that it sounded like a sneeze. "Just *to* the movies. My mother would tell me, 'Your father treated me so nice. He took me to the theater. We got as far as the theater, and we looked at the marquee, and then we came home.' This was his idea of a night on the town."

My grandmother treasured the story because it showed her parents in their innocence, laughing their way past all monetary insufficiencies. *We don't have money? Big deal, we'll go to the theater anyway.* There were five daughters and a son living in their three-room apartment heated by a coal stove. They slept three to a bed. The apartment was additionally cramped because my great-grandparents reached for solvency by taking in boarders. Some slept in the living room, others in the kitchen. In the kitchen they might sleep three or four at a time, side by side across the bare floor. At the far end of a hallway outside was a toilet, shared at all hours of the murky night by other families in their building, and by all strangers who found an overnight shelter in some family's available apartment space.

"You got out of bed in the middle of the night," my grandmother said lightly, "and you hoped you didn't lose your spot. The bedroom was filled, the kitchen was filled. You needed a bath, you went to the public baths. You learned how to swim, they took you to the East River and they threw you in, and you were on your own."

She said this with a shrug instead of a chuckle. *You were on your own.* She had lived in New York until she was past fifty, moved to Miami Beach to live with a sister Lilly who had never married, and on this weekend had come to Baltimore to be with her son and daughter, her six grandchildren, and her two great-grandchildren. Sunlight filtered through a kitchen window onto her soft pleated skin. My grandmother was given to easy laughter, but she seemed to be tiring out from the slow business of trudging through old age. I sensed I was reaching for remnants of what was literally an exhausted culture.

"The sweatshop," I said, pointing to the old photograph of her father.

Saying the word—*sweatshop*—seemed to confer certain family credentials. Dues had been paid. America opened its door, but nothing was given. Someone sat in a miserable, cramped, smelly room, *shvitzing* through summers and threading sewing needles through winter cold, and thus did we begin to earn a place in this country. To Max Strull's great-grandson living three quarters of a century later in air-conditioned relief, this lent a texture, a sturdy, once-removed piece of the struggle, to one's own pale and puny life story.

"What kind of money did your father make in the sweatshop?" I asked.

"Three dollars," my grandmother remembered distinctly.

"A day?"

"A day, he should be so lucky." She laughed merrily at the preposterous ness of such a thought. "For a whole week, he made three dollars. In the evenings my mother and I would visit him there to bring him dinner, while he sat over a sewing machine in the heat. There was no air in the place, believe me. He was looking to make a few cents extra."

All over the country, such things were happening in the early years of the century. In Baltimore immigrant families would "follow the crops," migrating to farms to pick ripening fruits and vegetables in the spring, then returning to the city's packing houses to prepare the crops for canning. Children too small to work were held on mothers' laps. Women who worked twelve-hour days earned five dollars a week. Oyster shuckers earned a few cents for each quart they shucked. Children worked under squalid conditions in factories and packing houses.

In other cities men went into coal mines and corroded their lungs. They built bridges and tunnels and balanced themselves on steel girders at the tops of windy skyscrapers. They worked sixty-hour weeks. The women made dresses and worked telephone switchboards and taught children to whom English was an alien language. On the Lower East Side of New York, along the crowded, noisy outdoor markets of Hester Street and the Bowery, at double rows of pushcarts, bent little men wearing derby hats sold sour pickles, and chickens with the feathers not yet plucked and the *kishkas* not yet removed, and all manner of dishes redolent of the old world.

Eventually Max Strull escaped the sweatshop and ran a tiny grocery store on Montgomery Street, where my grandmother and her sisters helped out after school. "In the grocery store, we sold three pounds of onions for a nickel," my grandmother remembered, still marveling at the bargain. "And a customer comes into the store one afternoon, and she looks at the price, and she says, 'Every day, the cost goes up.'"

Such customers drove Max crazy. My grandmother remembered the place opening at dawn and closing long after dark. She remembered huge loaves of black bread, and women arriving in the morning who would tell her father they would return at day's end, so he should save the bread for them.

"And he would hold it," my grandmother said, "and they would come back and say, 'Let me have two cents worth of the bread.' And that's what you had to deal with in those days."

On Friday evenings, when Max Strull went to synagogue, the elders called him forward to seek his interpretation of law and tradition. He knew more than the rabbis, my grandmother boasted decades later. On the high holy days the family went to a grubby converted loft, where they would mount the stairs and sit on metal folding chairs set before a makeshift stage from which services were conducted.

They were far from home, but they carried their traditions with them. They were poor, but they valued learning. A daughter, Nina, graduated public high school at age fifteen and studied at the Sorbonne on scholarship. Two daughters, Vicky and Edith, became schoolteachers. At night Edith taught English classes to adults wishing to learn the language of the new world. One of them was her mother, the former Zlotte Gurion turned Jenny Strull.

So we reach for America.

We reach with this hand, and hold back with that one. The newly arrived pray to God in the language of the old world, and hope that this will translate in His new world. They hold onto the old music, and the comforting rituals, and their children dance to the new world's sprightly rhythms but leave a corner of the mind to wonder if their parents' ways are worth holding onto.

My grandmother Ruth went to Washington Irving High School, and one day she met a boy from Peter Stuyvesant High named Moe Loebman. Moe was born in Austria. He had a father, Willie, who smoked big cigars and sold insurance, and a mother, Elsie, who learned to speak English by going to the Boulevard Theatre to watch vaudeville shows on Saturday afternoons.

After school Ruth and Moe would meet in a little park so he could walk her home. Then they worked in the same shoe store, my grandmother as a bookkeeper and Moe as a salesman. When they dated, my great-grandfather Max Strull walked discreetly behind them. When it became nine o'clock, Max stretched to his full five-feet-five inches and declared to his daughter, "That's it. You have to go home now."

Moe Loebman was a muscular fellow more than six feet tall. He had olive skin and full lips and a broad forehead. He took my grandmother to movie theaters and then, breaking all family tradition, actually took her inside. They rode into the future in taxicabs. He bought her flowers and candy. My grandmother remembered a sense of formality, of traces of the old world having survived the journey to America.

"It was only after I was seeing Moe for two or three years, that we knew it was the real thing and he wouldn't hurt me in any way, that my father had confidence in him," my grandmother remembered. "But my mother didn't want me to marry him. She thought I was too pretty to settle for the first boy I fell in love with."

"Would anybody have been good enough for her?" I asked.

"No," my grandmother said firmly. "No. Never, never."

"So, how did Moe win you over?"

"By constant wooing. He says, 'I will go with you until you're engaged to someone else. And, when you're engaged, then I'll know there's no chance for me. Then I'll let you go.' It was such a lovely romance, and so beautiful, and so pure. And so well-meaning."

Ruth and Moe married in 1920, and then Moe went away. In the flush years of the twenties, he owned three little shoe stores, mom-and-pop operations but profitable. He was a man who seemed to be constructing a future. In July of 1924 there arrived a child, my mother, Selma, and in August of 1928 there arrived another, my Uncle Dick. Four weeks after my uncle's birth Moe died.

"What was it that took his life?" I asked my grandmother.

"I really don't know," she said. "Kidneys. I don't know."

It was half a century since Moe died, and it forever altered her life and the lives of her children, but she had successfully obscured from herself the facts concerning her husband's sudden death at age twenty-nine.

"Kidneys," she said softly. "I was too young to understand." She was twenty-six. "I get sick when I think of it."

Kidneys it was. An infection that came from who knows what, and it killed him. One shot of penicillin, and he's alive for the next hundred years, with shoe stores to outfit a whole city. But there was no penicillin, and when he left his hospital bed for a sweet glance at his new son pneumonia set in, and a few weeks later Moe Loebman was gone.

The Depression arrived in September of the following year, and by the next spring the three little shoe stores once owned by Moe were gone.

"Who had money for shoes?" my grandmother asked fifty years after the fact. "We sold galoshes out of the store for five cents a pair. We sold shoes for twenty-five cents or half a dollar. But nobody had half a dollar."

Everything was sold to a liquidator. In the thirties, unemployment reached 25 percent. My grandmother's schoolteacher sisters made twenty-two dollars a week. Moe Loebman's brother Dave became a doctor and made barely sixty dollars a week, and his brother Eddie was considered a great family success because he landed a job with the U.S. Post Office where, by the end of the 1930s, he had the security of a twenty-four-dollar weekly paycheck. There was also a brother Solly, who called himself Jack and joined the merchant marines, and a sister named Ann. She lived at home until she married. The process was complex. Each young man who arrived at her parents' apartment for a first date was quizzed by her father, Willie Loebman, on the young man's employment and financial prospects. When Ann finally complained that this process was chilling her prospects, the father eased up and merely tried to sell insurance to the unfortunate young men.

Meanwhile, my grandmother settled into a small apartment in Brooklyn's Canarsie section for a while, at Avenue K and Ninety-third Street where the streets hadn't yet been paved, in a couple of dingy rooms behind Moe's last remaining shoe store with two little children and no husband.

For my mother and my uncle, now began the first dawning of the separateness of American culture. My uncle opened a window and heard Christmas carolers in the street; the music they had previously known was the sound of Max Strull chanting Russian melodies or Sabbath prayers. In Canarsie they knew no other Jewish children. One day my mother was beaten up because she was a Jew, and another time she was not allowed in a friend's home at Christmas because she was a Jew. She always remembered standing on the family's front stoop, looking through a frosted window at a Christmas tree with toys on the floor.

"It was their holiday," my mother remembered years later. "And they just wouldn't let me come in."

The scene became a metaphor: the twinkly gentile holiday, and the Jewish child wishing to take part in it. Not because it is gentile, and not merely for its bright lights, but because it represents the way of the American majority. To be gentile, to celebrate Christ's life, is to be part of the American spirit. It says so in all the pop cultural artifacts each December.

And this, too, becomes part of the journey.

THREE

DANCING ON THE ROOF

One drizzly Saturday morning in the spring of 2000 I arrived for Shabbos services at the B'nai Israel Congregation, 27 Lloyd Street, only a few footsteps away from that strip of Lombard Street known for many years as Corned Beef Row and, to some souls in a less sensitive time, as Jewtown.

East Baltimore's Lombard Street had once been the closest thing I imagined to New York's Lower East Side, writ small. Nearly 10,000 Jews once crowded the area and attended any of thirty-five neighborhood synagogues. Behind every delicatessen counter was a slicer of corned beef who was an amateur philosophizer on the side. Every street peddler of second-hand clothing quoted Talmud to the evening attendant of the public baths, who responded in Hebrew or in Yiddish with wisdom of his own. They had no money, but they imagined themselves aristocrats of the intellect.

Now, from a second-floor sanctuary window of the synagogue, I could see the tattered remains of that hectic culture. Empty little buildings and vacant lots were interspersed with a couple of Asian grocery stores and Jewish delicatessens whose hearts beat mostly from memory. A public housing high-rise, newly cleared out, awaited municipal dynamiting. The block was an old man's smile with most of his teeth gone.

Someone whose life had spanned the century might have thought: After so much tumult, the city has simply exhausted itself. A few miles south of Lombard Street, in the years surrounding the turn of the previous century, hundreds of thousands of immigrants arrived at Locust Point and stumbled out of steerage onto American land. They found piers where Irish, German, and black men, stripped to the waist and covered in dust and sweat, worked as coal trimmers. They found Italians working construction on nearby railroad lines. They found a waterfront lined with smoking factories and a harbor filled with steamships. They rented rooms or moved in with friends or relatives in stifling little Federal Hill rowhouses from which they could walk to the inner harbor markets and warehouses and the bustling port. They found ferries to take them across the harbor to Fells Point, where they found apartments poorly lighted, barely ventilated, with no water or toilets, where three or four families shared space designed for one. They looked for work in the city's garment industry, or its canneries or packing houses. Some found work in shipbuilding or steel making. If they were skilled laborers who happened to be white males, they could make as much as three dollars a day.

To Federal Hill's west was Sharp-Leadenhall, where African Americans had lived since the eighteenth century. Beyond that was old West Baltimore where blacks moved into alley houses—literally, ramshackle little dwellings in grubby alleys—and the remains of rowhouses whose charms had faded years earlier. Such shabbiness among the colored was considered commonplace. White employers froze them out of jobs paying decent money. Housing codes boxed them in. Jim Crow laws crippled them politically. When they tried to find a collective voice, they found only a few with any muscle: their churches; a union of brickmakers, wagoners, grain trimmers, and stevedores known as the Knights of Labor; a newspaper called the *Afro-American.*

The city drew thousands of immigrants from southern Italy, who found work digging railroad tunnels and sewers, and built schools and bridges and emptied cargo from ships. They found low-cost housing near the harbor. So many clustered in one clump of about twelve square blocks that the Arch-diocese of Baltimore built the first Italian parish in the city—St. Leo's—and the neighborhood became known as Little Italy and produced a political dy-nasty named D'Alesandro.

East of Little Italy were Canton and Highlandtown, which would embrace Greeks named Venetoulis and Poles named Mikulski. Each group settled in distinct ethnic enclaves and created its own institutions. They grew out of a sense of pride and self-protection. Each produced astute politicians who spoke the language of the old country and organized, block by block, precinct by precinct, ward by ward.

And there was Lombard Street, around which clustered the Jews and Ital-ians from the fringes of nearby Little Italy. For generations the street had corned beef and pastrami in its ozone and chicken fat hanging from its fin-gers. Here would come not only the thick sandwich of the places such as Attman's Deli but the pasta at Pastore's Italian Grocery, and Stone's Bakery where customers found the bagel, the bobka, the strudel, and the fragrant challah. The street was also home to the second-hand clothing store, and the Turkish bath, and later the Depression-era flophouse where the blowtorch was used to drive out the bedbugs. On Lombard Street the housewife waited for the poultry plucker who did his business by a handmade sign reading, "Chickens Killed While You Relax."

I looked through the synagogue window on this overcast Saturday morn-ing and remembered David Yankelove standing by that sign years earlier at Yankelove's Poultry House, holding a couple of doomed chickens by the neck. Now there were three lean black kids on Lombard Street, ducking through the scattery morning raindrops. The sweat ran down Yankelove's face and beefy neck that long-ago day. These black kids snapped a basketball back and forth, past the abandoned public high-rise, as though launching a three-on-none fast break to nearby Exeter Street. Yankelove wore a little cow-boy hat over his bald head and blood over much of his white apron. He stood there in 1971, when the Jews of East Baltimore had long since moved to the suburban northwest, leaving behind the projects and the hungry black kids whose dream of basketball and cheering crowds was not dampened by sod-den mornings such as this. But the Yankeloves of the neighborhood were fad-ing away.

"My father was married in this house," Yankelove said that day, gesturing behind him. "His children were born by midwife here, and my father died here."

His sister Briney, equally beefy, perspiring in the noontime heat, stood nearby.

"I just run the place," she said. She nodded toward her brother. "This one is the champ at picking chickens."

Then the chicken feathers began to fly. "The trick to the whole thing," David Yankelove said, grinning delightedly, "is medium hot water. Not too hot."

He announced this as though passing vital information to generations not yet born. But it was an art form about to become extinct in a neighborhood in decline. Farewell to chicken-plucking as performance art. I walked out of Yankelove's place and looked up and down the block. The old street stalls and the pushcarts and the curbstone businesses were long gone, but Lombard Street's storefront delis and bakeries still had some zest.

Across from Yankelove's was Stone's Bakery, started after Nathan and Zelda Stone arrived from Kiev in 1918. They worked twenty-hour days and slept on sacks of flour on the bakery floor to keep the business alive. Nearby was Pastore's Italian Grocery, started by Vincent Garafalo in 1911 and kept alive with the same kind of exhausting workday by Vince Pastore and his family. I walked to Jack's Delicatessen, the biggest place left on the block. The owner, Jack Goldenson, had arrived from Israel in the 1960s, penniless, sleeping on New York subways for a while. He was a newcomer but understood what gave Lombard Street its staying power. There he was, in the midst of a noontime lunch crowd, with his arm around a young woman.

"This girl wants to get married," he announced in the grand manner. The young lady rolled her eyes, but she wasn't quite walking away. "You already married?" Goldenson asked a man with saliva dripping from one end of a long cigar. He looked about seventy.

"Yes, married," the man sighed.

"That's okay," said Goldenson, "she ain't particular."

Halfway down the block from Goldenson's place was the sign for Tulkoff's horseradish. Harry Tulkoff, out of Russia, arrived in Baltimore in 1924. On Lombard Street one day he took a little walk. He saw a sign reading "For Sale." A woman inside said she was leaving town.

"What do you want for it?" Tulkoff asked.

"Seventy-five dollars," the woman said.

Tulkoff wanted three witnesses. The woman's name was Cohen, and into the room she called her three brothers, Mendel, Pincus, and Philip. From his pocket, Tulkoff pulled a clean handkerchief: an old-world ritual, said Tulkoff, in which each man would hold a corner of the handkerchief. Tulkoff held the fourth. And, into the handkerchief, in the autumn of 1924, Tulkoff dropped his downpayment for what became one of the largest horseradish supply businesses in America.

By the spring of 2000 Tulkoff was long gone, and Yankelove the chicken killer was gone, and so was much of that world. When the postwar suburbs opened, and the Jews moved northwest, they left behind two synagogues, this B'nai Israel Congregation and the Lloyd Street Synagogue, each in operation since the nineteenth century. But both had the slight sense of edginess about them, places that had to be locked down for the night, with metal gates around them and police cruisers routinely checking the premises. There was talk of urban renewal, but such talk had been around for years.

On Lombard Street, just behind the old storefronts, were the housing projects that shadowed everything. They were a half-century disaster borne out of semi-honorable intentions. The city of Baltimore had attempted to move black people from ramshackle slums to high-rise filing cabinets. But the buildings had an isolating effect, and drugs and family breakdowns had made everything worse. Now the projects were to be destroyed, and there were plans to build pricey new condominiums in the neighborhood, symbols of a lifestyle unrecognizable to both the current residents of the projects and the bathhouse denizens of long ago.

On this drizzly Saturday morning, I sat in the B'nai Israel Synagogue near a ninety-seven-year-old man who leaned on a wooden desk built into the row in front of him. He never lifted his head from his prayerbook. An eighty-nine-year-old man whose father had been president of this congregation—eighty years earlier—sat a few rows from him. This was their emotional sustenance, their connection not only with thousands of years of faith, but with a century on this street, in this very building. Each might have been part of the synagogue's original cast—except the building was 127 years old, the city's oldest continuously operational synagogue and the second oldest in the state.

There was a timeless quality to the sanctuary. The original architecture had been preserved and its wooden interior restored. A cantor sang a blessing thousands of years old. But there were also glimpses into an unanticipated future. A little girl in a lime dress skipped blithely up one aisle and planted herself next to me. She was Chinese—a visitor, perhaps, from one of the Asian groceries remaining on Lombard Street.

"What's your name?" I whispered. The cantor sang in a high tenor about fifteen feet from us.

"Jade," she whispered back.

"That's a pretty name," I said. It sounded ornamental and carried a sense of delicacy and grace across centuries of Chinese history.

"What's your last name?" I asked.

"Shapiro," she said.

All right, then: Shapiro, first name Jade. We are here too long for such things not to happen. Around the synagogue, I saw more unexpected faces: a Moroccan man, an Asian man, a couple of African Americans, each a member of the congregation.

"The little girl is our mascot," a man whispered to me. "She was adopted by one of our families."

Jumping from my side, Jade Shapiro skipped up the aisle now, singing in precise, delighted chorus with those around her: *Baruch atau adonai* . . .

And so, in the tiny figure of a five-year-old Chinese girl chanting praises of God in ancient Hebrew could we find America as it melted and blended and mutually embraced.

Or, glancing outside the same synagogue windows, we might have found a similar part of the process nearly a century earlier. Then, an eight-year-old boy stumbled onto this block and discovered hints of his own personality. He was Thomas D'Alesandro Jr., the son of a diminutive laborer from Italy. Tommy Jr. would become a U.S. congressman and then mayor of Baltimore; and his son would become mayor of Baltimore, and a daughter would become a U.S. congresswoman from California.

The first American D'Alesandro came out of the mountains of Abruzzo, Italy. In Baltimore, he found work digging a railroad tunnel, married a girl named Marie Antoinette Foppiano, and they opened a little grocery store on President Street in the city's Little Italy. The store went bust in a hurry. Too many customers, broke and jobless, were buying "on the book," getting personal credit but failing to pay later.

In the apartment above the store Thomas D'Alesandro Jr. was born. The father worked for the city during the day, and at night he worked in a munitions plant because eventually there was not only Tommy Jr. but twelve additional children to feed. In Little Italy as elsewhere, the neighborhood bond was the old world background, the language they spoke, the church they attended, the people they married within their own group. And sometimes the bond was a political leader who became their link to the outside world, and to jobs.

Early in the game D'Alesandro Jr. found flexible edges. He was an eight-year-old altar boy at St. Leo's Catholic Church when he became what the Orthodox Jews call a Shabbos goy—a Sabbath gentile—around Lombard Street, a few blocks from Little Italy, in the shadow of the B'nai Israel Congregation, among the religious owners of the little delicatessens, the makers of horseradish, the slayers of fresh chickens.

D'Alesandro found the Jews in his youthful wanderings. From sundown Friday to sundown Saturday, the seventh day of the week, the devout rested. To rest meant to avoid all exertion, including the lighting of stoves and candles. For this, a gentile was hired. It was D'Alesandro's introduction into the world beyond Little Italy, and into an extended urbanity. One Jewish man had a shoe store, another a tailor shop. D'Alesandro liked to dress. Some were schoolteachers and others were lawyers. Later, they helped support the early D'Alesandro political campaigns. Now they were paying him a few cents here, a few there.

He attended St. Leo's Parochial School for eight years, minus two weeks. For four years he sat in the same classroom with the same teacher, Sister Pauline. In his last year D'Alesandro won a spelling bee. Sister Pauline, beaming, pinned a large medal of the Blessed Virgin on him.

"You can wear it for a week," she said.

On the playground a classmate called D'Alesandro a sissy for wearing the medal. D'Alesandro picked up a rock and threw it at the boy. The rock split the boy's head. Now came Sister Pauline, hollering in exasperation.

"Bring your father to school tomorrow," she ordered.

D'Alesandro, too frightened to tell his parents the bad news, showed up alone the next day. Where is your father? He couldn't come, said Tommy. He has pleurisy. Sister Pauline said nothing. Pleurisy was a terrible thing, for which she would offer prayers. But the next morning, she saw Tommy's mother, Marie, at early morning mass, which the mother attended every day.

"I'm praying for your husband's recovery," said Sister Pauline.

"My husband is just fine," said Marie D'Alesandro. "I saw him off to work just before coming to church."

"But how can he go to work with pleurisy?"

"My husband," said Marie, "is in very good health. He doesn't have pleurisy or anything else."

Two weeks before graduation D'Alesandro was removed from St. Leo's School, his academic career now completely behind him. At thirteen, he lied about his age and went to work for a sawmill making ammunition boxes for wartime England and France. The pay was $6.60 a week. This was already a decade past Max Strull in his sweatshop in New York, and the pay was only three dollars a week more. Not yet fourteen, and still lying about his age, D'Alesandro then worked for the Harry T. Poor Insurance Agency. They offered him six dollars a week as an office boy; D'Alesandro held out for seven. After all, he was working a six-day week. He worked in the office for several years, until sent outside to sell insurance. It was 1925.

"That was the start of it all," his son, Tommy D'Alesandro III, was saying one morning seventy-five years later. He was seventy-one years old now, with a wave of white marmalade hair and a history of politics and the law behind him—but he was forever Young Tommy, his father's son. "The insurance business took my father out of the neighborhood," he said.

But the ethnic journey had changed dramatically since his father's time. The neighborhoods were different. If you were white, and spoke English, many of the old walls had come down.

"Today," D'Alesandro said, "you get Italian Americans who are CEOs, and they don't understand how much tougher it used to be. They didn't want Italians around back in my father's time. That's why the Democratic organizations didn't take him, because he was Italian. Hell, everybody was brought up that way. Stick with your own.

"When my father started out, Sheriff Degan took him over to the old Leonard Hotel to meet a couple of the big political bosses. He said they were

Thomas D'Alesandro III on his wedding day in 1952, standing with his proud father, Mayor Thomas D'Alesandro Jr. To make the reception as memorable as possible, the mayor invited five thousand guests, including much of the city's fire and police departments. The groom and his bride stood in a receiving line for four hours. *Courtesy of the D'Alesandro family*

playing cards and wouldn't even look up at him. Degan says, 'This is Tommy D'Alesandro, the young man I've told you about.' They said, 'If he's such a popular young man, go out and get 500 signatures and we'll support you.' Well, for my father, 500 signatures was nothing, because he was out there all the time. So he brought back the signatures, and they said, 'If you got those, you don't need us.'"

He chuckled ruefully over memories from another era. His father could have brought back 5,000 signatures, and it wouldn't have mattered to these entrenched politicos. There were walls. They were invisible, but they were stronger than Jericho's.

"When I was a teenager, I'd go to dances," D'Alesandro remembered. "And all these groups stood in different corners. Like Keith's Roof, over on Lexington Street. Or the Casino in Patterson Park, or the Alcazar. Crowded, noisy places, and the Italians are standing on one side and the Poles are on the other. You couldn't walk across the floor and ask a Polish girl to dance. So you danced with those that you brought, or else you might have fights break out."

Some of these were remembered over the years, and passed down not only as evidence of family toughness but of patriotism. At Keith's Roof one night during World War II someone at a dance uttered an ethnic slur. Another was tossed back. Then came a flurry of fists, bodies struggling all over the floor, voices shrieking.

One thing stopped it: the band struck up "The Star Spangled Banner," and everyone came to attention. "*You gonna show me who's American?*" "*We'll show you who's American.*"

"Sounds like 'West Side Story,'" I said. "The dance at the gym."

"A lot like that," D'Alesandro said. "I'll tell you a story, one time I was at Luge's Confectionery Store, where Sabatino's Restaurant is located now. I'm a kid getting a Coke, and I'm looking out the window. Somebody says, 'Isn't that awful? Isn't that awful?' Really worked up. Says a guy up on Albemarle Street got engaged to a Polish girl. 'Isn't that awful?' I said, 'What's wrong with that? What's wrong with that?' He says, 'You're supposed to marry an Italian girl. It's heresy.'

"In the forties, it was heresy," D'Alesandro said. "Today, my son's married to an Asian girl. My other son, a Spanish girl. Look, as long as they're in love, that's all that counts." He nodded his head for emphasis. "But me," he laughed, "I'm still looking for Italians in the box scores."

"The Jews do the same thing," I said. Baseball box scores and movie marquees and songs on the radio. "*One of ours,*" my father would say when Irving Berlin's "White Christmas" came over the air. *One of ours,* he said when Eddie Cantor appeared on the *Colgate Comedy Hour* or Phil Silvers conned some rube as Sergeant Bilko.

"We all take pride in one of our own," I said.

"Exactly," D'Alesandro said.

We ate breakfast in a hotel restaurant where people still knew him by sight and still called him by his first name. It was thirty years since he had walked away from a near-certain second-term election as mayor. He'd been in office barely five months when rioting and burning swept the city in the aftermath of Martin Luther King's assassination. Some said D'Alesandro was never the same after that and had retired with his political heart taken from him. He'd been primed for a career in politics since his adolescence but seemed relieved to walk away from it all.

"Your father must have been stunned when you told him you were leaving," I said.

"He couldn't believe it. He thought I was crazy. But, see, with him, the politics really started with the insurance business. He covered all the first district."

That was the city's southeast corner, the neighborhoods of transplanted Eastern Europeans, many of whom had gotten off the boat at Locust Point, then ferried to Fells Point, before migrating all the way—maybe thirty blocks, but it seemed like another world—to Highlandtown.

The Germans were the first to reach the neighborhood, in the late 1800s, arriving in Baltimore each week on one of the North German Lloyd Line's steamships. At one point, an estimated one-quarter of Baltimore's population was of German descent. They started their own newspapers. They built breweries and meat-packing houses that offered jobs for skilled Eastern European laborers. In Highlandtown they found lush Patterson Park, and Eastern Avenue's commercial district. There were narrow little neighborhood rowhouses where housewives scrubbed white marble steps, and ethnic taverns on each corner where men gathered and found a tribal atmosphere. And in the mornings all along Eastern Avenue, thousands of working men paid ten cents apiece and caught the Number 26 streetcar to Dundalk Avenue and Sparrows Point's steel mills.

In Southeast Baltimore D'Alesandro saw variations of his own insulated world. Little Italy had its own restaurants and church and civic organizations, and so did Highlandtown. The Poles had their own savings and loans, the Greeks their own church, the Germans their own schools. And each nursed its own insecurities.

"My father was outside the Italian community early," D'Alesandro said. "He broadened his horizon. He went to Highlandtown and met all the Polish people and the Czechs and the Lithuanians. He was one of the first ambassadors. He went door to door with the insurance and picked up a nickel here, a penny there. That's how they paid in those days. And that's how he built up his political base."

There are photographs of Tommy the elder as a young man on the move. Always, every hair was in place, the mustache trim, the outfit impeccable. His son, retired now from the law practice he had entered when he left City Hall, wore a tan sports coat with an open-collared shirt, far more relaxed than the father's outfits. The father had dressed in formal old-world fashion, dark three-piece suits and hats, reaching for a sense of dignity for himself and for Italians trying to escape derogatory stereotypes.

"A Dapper Dan of the first order," his son said. "And his parents were poor as church mice. My grandfather worked for the city at the pumping station for twelve bucks a week, something like that. They had nothing. We used to call my grandmother Grandma Buckwheat, 'cause every time we went to her house, that's all we ate, breakfast, dinner, didn't matter. Buckwheat pancakes. And they idolized my father and made sure he was decked out. He was like a movie star."

Thirteen children, but they found money to dress the son like a movie star. I thought of Max and Zlotte Strull with six children, with strangers sleeping on the kitchen floor to help pay the rent. I thought of Max in his undershirt in the sweatshop, and Tommy the elder, the son of those people in my great-grandparents' generation, getting himself all dressed up for something better.

And I thought about Felix Guevara, in his sweatshirt in the courtroom hallway, and the letters on the sweatshirt said, "United States of America." And the questions were flung at him in a language he did not understand, and he wanted to go home, and the look on his face came back to me again from somewhere long ago.

"Well," said Tommy the younger, "that's how it started, with my father selling insurance over in Highlandtown and meeting all the Polish people and all."

In Highlandtown they shared D'Alesandro's broadest political instincts. They were outsiders looking for a piece of the action. On Eastern Avenue was a bakery owned by the grandparents of Barbara Mikulski. Down the street was a grocery store run by Mikulski's father and a bakery run by her mother.

They moved there from Fells Point, the neighborhood where Mikulski's grandparents had settled when they arrived in America. It was also where Mikulski the public fighter first touched the municipal consciousness. In the 1970s she'd led an emotional struggle against the State Roads Commission planners who wanted to level large parts of the neighborhood and pave it over with a highway. Now, three decades later, instead of asphalt for speeding automobiles, Fells Point bustled with humanity.

One day I met Mikulski at Jimmy's Restaurant in Fells Point, owned by Nick Filipides. Nick's family arrived in America from Andros, Greece. His kitchen help were mostly Latin Americans who had moved into upper Fells Point over the previous decade. They had jobs like Felix Guevara's. The customers ranged from neighborhood working-class people to politicians who dropped in because the restaurant was a pretty good cross-section of the city. To eat at Jimmy's was to partake of *Bawlamer.*

"I'm meeting Mikulski here," I told Filipides. Mikulski was a regular. "We're gonna talk about people like you and me."

"Low-lifes?" he laughed.

"Ethnics."

"Ethnics. That's a good thing, right?" Nick said. Behind him, a stack of dishes tumbled in a big plastic bin. He seemed not to notice. A kind of rhythmic chaos prevailed. A Korean delivery man in an Orioles cap walked in the front door. "Hey, hon," Nick shouted to a waitress. "Take care of our man here."

"Is ethnic good?" I asked. "Sometimes it's been hard to tell."

"Ethnic? Oh, yeah," he said. He was born in Fells Point, and his parents moved out to northeast Baltimore, not far from the old Memorial Stadium, in the mid-1950s. For years, they owned the Acropolis nightclub, featuring Greek belly dancers, and simultaneously turned Jimmy's into a neighborhood mainstay.

"One time," Filipides remembered, "I dated an Italian girl. I brought her in here. My father was sitting on the stool over there by the counter, reading a newspaper. I introduced her to him. I said, 'This is Linda.' My father said, 'Are you Greek?' I told him, 'No, she's not Greek.' He turned back to his newspaper, wouldn't look at her. I said to the girl, 'He's got a lot on his mind.' It was embarrassing."

"A generational thing," I suggested.

"My mother told me, 'You gotta understand, she's not Greek. You know your father.' And that's all she said."

"Why was it so important?" I said. "Do we think, deep down, that anybody who isn't part of our tribe, we can't fully trust?"

"That they wouldn't understand us," Filipides said. "My father wanted me to go to Greece and find a wife. We talked about it a couple of times. He said, 'We got some people over there, some nice girls.' I remembered one, when we were over there with relatives one summer when we were kids. I asked a cousin about her, and he said, 'Yeah, she's built like a van and she's got red hair coming out of everywhere.'"

Instead, he married a Greek girl from the neighborhood—and got divorced. Married another Greek girl, and they'd been married twenty-six years. "You have things in common," Nick said. "There's a sense of tradition. You know, thank God, my son Jimmy goes to church, he goes to the Greek church, and we didn't have to force him."

"We'd go to synagogue," I said, "and slip outside to talk about ballgames."

"Oh, of course," Nick said. "We'd sneak out of church like we were going up to the balcony. We'd cut out the door and go play the pinball machines up the street. But you feel something comforting as you get older."

He put his hand on his chest for emphasis. A young woman approached our table, and Nick beamed at the sight of her.

"Here she is," he exclaimed, "the sweetest-smelling girl in the world. Don't she smell sweet?" He gestured toward me. "Tell him what you do, hon."

She muttered the name of her company. Nick Filipides of Fells Point might have been Jack Goldenson of Lombard Street thirty years earlier, kibitzing with the young ladies, embracing little pieces of the room.

"The sweetest-smelling girl in the world," he said again. "She works for the ones that do deodorizing for the bathrooms." He pointed gallantly to the lavatories and turned around as another stack of plates clattered behind him. The two of us looked around, waiting for Mikulski.

"I feel very, very fortunate to be raised ethnic," he said. "You have a sense of tradition."

"You never felt different from the other kids?"

"Oh, sure," he said. "You learn that very early in the game. But we all have to figure out that it's not a bad difference. That's the thing we don't always tell ourselves until we're older."

When Mikulski arrived a few minutes later, there were friendly cries from nearby tables. She was, as always, the prodigal daughter returned home.

"Hey, Barb," an elderly man said.

"Hi, how are you?" Mikulski replied, smiling appreciatively.

"Hi, hon," came another voice.

Mikulski understood the friendly instinct behind the "hon," but cringed a little at the absence of dignity. "Barbara" was okay, but maybe not "hon." She was a populist, but she was also a U.S. senator. She wanted the same kind of respect given to the men who went to Capitol Hill.

Years earlier, when she helped save this neighborhood, it got her started in politics. She'd gone around to the places like the Broadway Market, where John Prevas was helping out in his family's luncheonette. Their roots were in Greece. Prevas had just finished law school. Later, he became a judge. He'd heard Mikulski give a speech about the highway that the State Roads Commission wanted to run through Fells Point. Then one night, at Miss Irene's Pub around the corner, he saw Mikulski. She was shooting pool.

"I saw you on TV," he said. "I liked what you said. If you decide to run for office, come around the market and let's talk."

They met again six months later. A buddy of Mikulski's, a college sociology instructor named Toni Keane, was there. It was an American political crossroads: the Greek Prevas, the Polish Mikulski, the German-Czechoslovakian Keane. Prevas worried a little that Mikulski, the college-educated social worker, might seem a little out of step with the district's working-class neighborhoods.

"The image we have to convey to the public," he said, "is that you're not better than this community. You're the best of this community." Then he did two things. He complimented Mikulski on her pool shooting, and he took Toni Keane home. Thirty years later they were still together.

Thus, also, began Mikulski's political career—and an outlet for a point of view. She wrote a piece that the *New York Times* ran on its op-ed page, in which she said, "The ethnic American is forgotten and forlorn." It was about those she knew most intimately, and how they had been made to feel like fools. You could feel the resentment seep through Mikulski's pores.

"You came from an East Baltimore where people willingly divided up neighborhoods by nationality," I said. We found a table where the noise in Jimmy's was a little subdued. "Did that kind of thing lead to comfort, or to a bunch of people automatically putting other people down because they never got to know each other?"

"Well, you have to know how that sort of thing started," she said. "It was a way of preserving a heritage. Think of the melancholia of leaving a country and your family. This is hard to imagine, at sixteen years old, getting on a boat and saying goodbye, no matter how desperate or dangerous the situation."

Most of the arriving Poles did not speak English. Many of the women worked in canneries. Many of the men found work in the shipping industry. The best jobs at the port went to Germans and Irish, while the Poles and the blacks settled for unskilled jobs. The Poles lived in cheap housing and saved what money they could. Over the years, many pooled their savings and took over whole blocks of Highlandtown and Canton. They went to Patterson Park and formed athletic clubs that would last over decades. A generation worked overtime to pay mortgages that were often written for five-year terms. By 1914 there were twenty Polish building and loan associations, most of them located on Eastern Avenue.

"There was," said Mikulski, "a great grief and melancholy in leaving the old country. So they created these urban villages, and in those villages they could preserve a culture that was part of their heart and soul. But they also came to those neighborhoods because that was one of the ways they could get jobs. They could say, 'Well, the Masons control the steel and the Catholics control the waterfront.' Now, whether that was true or not, it was what people said. Did I know this kind of talk? Absolutely. Oral tradition. It wasn't written up in the *Baltimore Sun*. You weren't ever written up in the *Baltimore Sun*."

In that time, the *Sun* geared itself to the professional classes. Blue-collar people, European ethnics, African Americans, remained on the other side of its consciousness. The *Baltimore News-Post* found its audience among the city's working class, and the *Afro-American* lured black readers who were unable to find a word about their community in either daily paper. Thus was a sense of isolation reinforced, and the sense of a municipal collection of disparate peoples hearing different voices.

"Did it also lead to self-consciousness? Or ethnic pride?"

"Neither," Mikulski said. "We were just aware of it." But, all these years later, she was beginning to seethe at the memory. "What was clear," she said, "was that there was prejudice against us. We Poles were the ones who were stereotyped. There was the dumb Polack, the despicable Polack jokes. No joke about another group or sexual orientation would be acceptable."

An exaggeration based on the anger of the moment, certainly. The Polish joke had been around for decades, and was tedious and offensive—but it mirrored, in tone and insensitivity, the jokes about other minorities. It was the American way. We blew off steam, we unleashed our crankiness. We laughed at others' expense to build ourselves up and chafed when the punchline diminished our own people.

That Mikulski felt it so intensely was a measure of both her sensitivities and the country's. We believe others are out to get us. Which others? Sometimes we think we know, and sometimes we're not so sure. But it prods our self-consciousness.

"This is why we had to organize ourselves and form our own institutions," Mikulski said. It wasn't just the jokes. "We knew we were discriminated against by the downtown banks. So we created our own savings and loans. We knew there was discrimination against us even in terms of getting life insurance. Because we worked in coalmines and factories. So that's why the Knights of Columbus had an insurance policy. That's why the Polish Women's Alliance could buy insurance, because they weren't gonna give factory girls and sweatshop girls insurance.

"We created our own alternative economic system. And the church and the heritage groups were our social organizations. That was our way of empowering ourselves, of having a life, buying a home, and not depending on those who discriminated against us. Be able to start a business. We had some of the original merchant class pool their money. That's why they had all those savings and loans. That's why they called Eastern Avenue the Polish Wall Street."

And yet, despite this—despite walls that kept strangers isolated from each other, despite generations of suspiciousness of the Other, despite the politics of sheer chauvinism—there was the inevitability of America: of Tommy D'Alesandro finding a world beyond Little Italy; of Barbara Mikulski's family finding America but holding onto Polish traditions; and of a little Chinese girl named Jade Shapiro singing ancient Hebrew prayers to God, and nobody thinking it was such a big deal when it happened.

FOUR

TIMES SQUARE

On Findlay Avenue in the Bronx, my father peered through falling snow and first laid eyes on my mother in all her apparent vulnerability. My father was thirteen years old and walked with his friend Bernie Mayer. My mother was eleven and walked alone. My father was a ferocious schoolyard athlete and Bernie Mayer was the future shotput champion of the world. My mother was a tomboy player of stickball and a daredevil on the Grand Concourse who hooked her hands onto the rear bumpers of transit buses to hitch roller-skate rides in traffic.

Love at first sight, this would not be. Tenderness of the heart, not even. My father sent a snowball through scattery afternoon flurries and hit my mother in the middle of her expression.

"Liney, you shouldn't have done that," Bernie Mayer said to him.

My father, reaching down for snowball reinforcements, looked up and up. In this February of 1936, he resembled an undernourished peacock, all wavy hair and angular face atop a body comprised mainly of wires and bones. Bernie Mayer towered over him, at twelve years old already considerably on his way to six-feet-five inches in height. He was also on his way, nearly six years from the day of the snowball, to shooting a little eight-ball with my father in a pool hall near Times Square when the news arrived on the radio that the Japanese had bombed a distant place called Pearl Harbor.

"Pearl Harbor," my mother said wistfully, when everyone we knew was forty years separated from the Bronx and the war. "Who knew from Pearl Harbor? A Pearl Schwartz, sure. She lived in the building, remember?"

"Right, Pearl Schwartz, didn't she date . . . ?"

My father, now 200 miles south of Findlay Avenue, and from the pool hall off Times Square, and from Bernie Mayer who threw the shotput instead of the snowball, pushed aside Pearl Harbor for a moment and searched for a name misplaced in the thickets of memory.

"Was it Booboo who dated Pearl Schwartz?" He meant Booboo Blaustein from the neighborhood, who was killed in the war.

"No, not Booboo," my mother said, waving a dismissive hand. "Etsie from the grocery store, maybe. Don't you remember, we used to sing, 'Pearlie's the girlie for Etsie'?"

"You're right, it wasn't Etsie," my father said. "Was it Siggy Siegel?"

"What are you talking, Siggy Siegel?" my mother said.

Never mind, then. The names tumbled away in my parents' condominium in the suburbs of Baltimore County. They were American by birth and by instinct but children of those who weren't always so sure. Their English evolved by combining the vocabulary of the classroom and the streets with the vernacular of the home. Their elders took strands of Polish and Russian, and German and Yiddish, and evolved them into English, and nouns were sometimes lost from verbs, and the adverb went one way and the adjective another, and shrugs and inflections were added until it passed to the next generation. My parents spoke South Bronx with wisps of Eastern Europe.

"I sound like my grandmother's generation," my mother said once when she heard her voice on a tape recording.

My parents seemed to lapse into the bent speech patterns mostly when they talked about the old days. Sometimes they knew they were doing it, and found it both comforting and comic. They were performing riffs on departed elders. They were remembering authentic voices, the last remnants of chicken fat hanging from extended fingers, the echoes of the Lower East Side, of pickled herring, of the ghosts of lost European *shtetls*, each shrug of the shoulder a poignant image of long ago. When they conversed in the full Yiddish, it was their language of love and hiding. They expressed great affection, or comic insults, or said the things I was not supposed to hear.

As a boy I found all of this talk a little distracting, as it sounded nothing like my friends' jargon, or mine. My generation merely wanted to sound like America. What did America sound like? It sounded like television, where there hadn't been an ethnic, and certainly not a Jewish ethnic, since Molly Goldberg had been sent back out into the diaspora. And who was Molly Goldberg but the benign version of Ethel Rosenberg, some Jewish network vice-president's bid to show the world, Look, we don't all send secrets of the bomb to the Russians.

As I grew older, I recognized that the rhythms of my parents' speech connected me with an authentic past, and with kids from their treasured Bronx youth named Booboo and Pearlie, and Siggy and Bunzy, who were just crawling onto dry American land, sometimes single pieces of a family at a time.

"Like my friend Libby," my mother said. As a little child, Libby from Findlay Avenue came to America with her mother. Her father left Poland a few years earlier, working hard, putting together enough money for the journey for the rest of his family. Libby was six years old and had no memory of what her father looked like. When she and her mother reached America, Libby took one look at him and whispered to her mother, in Yiddish, "You couldn't find yourself a better-looking guy?"

So my parents' generation reached for the full America while carrying memories of old Europe: language and fashion, and the strange food that was eaten, and oddball marriages arranged on one side of an ocean and re-arranged here.

I would press my parents to tell me about their introductory snowball fight not only because it was about people I knew. It also seemed to have a roughhouse American sound to it. They hadn't had their families make relationships for them in Europe. They introduced themselves by the flying snowball. It was Tom Sawyer and Becky Thatcher exchanging a Bronx greeting.

So there in the winter of 1936, my father's snowball hit the face of this stunned new girl on the block, Selma Loebman, who would years later become my mother.

"Liney, you shouldn't have done that," Bernie Mayer said that day, surveying the damage and giving vent to a random, inexplicable prescience. "That's the girl you're gonna marry."

Fifty years after my father's snowball hit her in the face, I asked my mother, "What did you do?"

"What do you think I did?" she said. "I made my own snowball, and I threw it back at him."

"And you hit him?"

"No, but I wasn't going to stand there and do nothing."

She was never anyone's shrinking violet. The granddaughter of Russian immigrants, the daughter of a widowed mother, in the Bronx she played stickball in the street with the neighborhood boys and threw punches when provoked, including a roundhouse right that blackened the eye of Etsie from the grocery store, a year older than my mother, but a *shlemiel* who tried to break into her jump-rope game and wouldn't go away. The message was: He had it coming.

My father, by all reports, was a pretty good schoolboy athlete. In his sixty-fifth year, as he reclined on a living room couch with a newspaper in his lap and the television news playing, there were still visible traces of the boy he had been. The once muscular head of hair had given ground to genetics, but he continued to play handball and tennis. His middle had thickened, and his knees were shot, but he still needed the sports to burn off excess energy. This was not a man designed to slip placidly through his declining days. The handy newspaper and the television were his backups when the conversation slowed or got a little too emotionally sticky. He could reach for either in the middle of somebody's sentence.

"You ran the mile, right?" I said one day.

"Right," my father said. "And Bernie threw the shot."

"I know. What about the mile? What was your best time?"

"Who can remember?" my father said. "You know, Bernie held the record in the shot."

"Do I know?" I answered.

It was our little dance. *Do* I *know?* I said this in the same tone you would say, "You're telling me? Like I haven't seen the papers to prove it?"

I have them still, newspapers passed down like heirlooms not exactly my own. Great-grandmother Zlotte's Franklin Rosenfeld was in the White House, like a distant relative. The newspapers reported the Great Depression, and then the war. The boys on Findlay Avenue went off to fight, and the girls stayed behind and worried. They read *Life* and *Collier's.* They listened to the radio where they heard Jack Benny and George Burns, who were Jewish but not so anybody should particularly notice. They heard Father Charles E. Coughlin, who ranted about Jewish bankers so that everybody should notice. They bought egg-cream sodas at corner candy stores that would stay in their memories for the rest of their lives. The girls went to USO dances and felt like patriots. Everybody bought the *Daily News* for two cents and turned to the back page for the sports, where they learned that the great Jewish fighter, Max Baer, lost to the great Negro champion, Joe Louis, who would beat the great Irish fighter named Billy Conn. And they saw that the New York Yankees, playing baseball in their stadium a few blocks from Findlay Avenue with the Italians DiMaggio and Crocetti and Lazerri in their starting lineup, were winning and winning —to the eternal delight of those in faraway Italian neighborhoods such as Tommy D'Alesandro of Baltimore. And one morning they saw Bernie Mayer on that same page, throwing the shotput.

I still have the newspaper pictures of my father's friend Bernie when he came home from the war. He threw the shotput for New York University. On the yellowing back pages of the *New York Daily News,* there are four monster shots of Bernie, grimacing heroically as he comes out of his crouch, as he hurls his massive frame, as he lets fly with the shotput and follows its flight across fifty-six feet, ten inches of landscape.

"Never mind that," my father said. "What about Boston?"

Each name validated our family's tiny walk-on role in the national experience. Tiny, but not to be diminished any further. They never put it into words, but there was something beyond family, something about the country itself, in the retelling of these stories of the Bronx and Boston and Pearl Harbor, about the children of immigrants signing up for the big fight, and the kids like poor Booboo Blaustein never coming home from the war.

They were walk-on parts, every one, but not to be minimized. Like my father and Bernie shooting pool near Times Square when the news arrived of Pearl Harbor, and the two of them lining up at the frenzied military recruiting center the next morning. And my father going off to fly bombing runs in Europe, and Bernie shipping out with the Marines to the South Pacific. And my mother back in the Bronx with a baby on the way while she sweated out all those missions.

But my father wanted to talk about Boston and Bernie. He wanted this because he was a surrogate braggart. Of himself, he would never in his lifetime be guilty of a boast. In those he admired, he took ostentatious and proprietary delight.

"Bernie was stationed in Boston," my father said, "before they shipped out for the war. Some big indoor track meet, I think they had it at the Garden. Bernie wanted to throw the shot. They told him, everybody's restricted to the base. But he sneaks off, and the next morning, he's caught."

"How did they catch him?"

"The jerk," my father exclaimed proudly. "He made one mistake. He won. He made the headlines in all the Boston papers."

He puffed on an aromatic cigar and waved it like a baton. I imagined a massive shotput soaring like a cannon ball across the horizon.

"I guess that's the first time he got into trouble in the service," my father said, turning to my mother. She lifted a finger from her knitting and tried not to lose her count.

"What do you mean, the first time?" I asked.

"Well, he got into some fights. About Jewish stuff a couple of those Marines were saying."

But then the story was brushed away. There were occasional religious antagonisms in their lives, but the stories arose only by accident. My parents never dwelt on them, never told stories of anti-Semitism as warning lessons in persecution. If they sensed bias against them, they brushed it off as the sentiments of idiots. They saw themselves as cosmopolitan mixers. My parents didn't perceive themselves as anybody's victims.

My father sat beneath an old watercolor painting of a streetcorner in New York with an elevated stretch of the subway running overhead. Through the years, he and my mother moved from the Bronx to Atlantic City to Jersey City to five different places in Baltimore, and this reminder of their youth,

They were just boys, four months before the bombing of Pearl Harbor. *From left,* Liney Olesker (the author's father), Siggy Siegel, Bernie Mayer, and Richard Loebman (the author's uncle) on the Grand Concourse in the Bronx.

of the Bronx, of the El and egg-cream sodas and mothers leaning their heads out of windows to summon kids named Booboo and Etsie home from stick-ball games, this watercolor moved with them as a touchstone.

There is also a photograph of my father in August of 1941. He is weeks away from entering his freshman year at New York University. He is standing in front of the Joseph Arms Apartments on the Grand Concourse in the Bronx, maybe eight blocks from Yankee Stadium, with Bernie Mayer, and with Siggy Siegel who never dated Pearl Schwartz, and with my Uncle Dick whose bar mitzvah was the very morning of the photograph.

The country was beginning to come out of the awful Depression by then. My grandmother had closed Moe Loebman's last shoe store, in Canarsie, and moved my mother and my uncle first to Brooklyn and then to the Bronx, where they found a two-room apartment on Findlay Avenue for thirty-two dollars a month and lived on relief. The humiliation of that era stayed with everyone for a long time. Too ashamed to shop with food coupons herself, my grandmother would send one of the children.

"I'd go to Mr. Cohen on a Hundred Sixty-fifth Street," my Uncle Dick remembered. "He had a grocery store in the middle of the block. My mother would tell me, 'Get a half of a quarter-pound of cream cheese.' Those were the instructions, a half of a quarter-pound. If the check hadn't come yet, Mr. Cohen would put a mark in his little black book: 'Loebman, six cents.' When the check came I was permitted to go back to Mr. Cohen and get a pound of Malomar cookies with the nut in the middle. For twenty cents a pound."

My mother and my uncle remember the price of things, and the smells: chicken cooking on Friday nights at Zlotte and Max Strull's apartment, and homemade baked goods.

"They made today's cakes taste like dehydrated sawdust," my uncle said.

Absent a father, my mother found an aunt: Moe Loebman's sister, Ann, a decade older, who watched over my mother, and took her on dates with boys. They were the boys intimidated by Ann's father, Willie Loebman, who gave them the third degree about financial prospects when they arrived at the house and, as a last resort, tried to sell them insurance.

Finally, a young Bernard Kimerling proposed to Ann and passed Willie Loebman's inspection. Bernard was a promising young man with a sales job for a rubber factory. A wedding ceremony was planned for the Loebmans' narrow apartment, accompanied by only two problems. The rabbi, a pious man accustomed to a certain respect, required that a car pick him up and deliver him to the service.

"But Rabbi," my mother's Aunt Ann said, "you only live three doors away from us."

"Respect," the rabbi declared. Surely the holy men of the gentiles would expect no less.

The other problem arrived when the rabbi commenced the wedding vows. Bernard's friends, including the best man, were discovered not in attendance. They were in the bathroom shooting dice.

I grew up listening to such tales of Findlay Avenue and the Bronx. Located a few blocks from the Grand Concourse, it was a largely Jewish enclave brimming with kids who came sprawling out of apartment buildings each morning. A block away was College Avenue, where the Italians lived. Between the two streets was an empty lot, on occasion the site of rock battles between the two groups for reasons either long-since forgotten or never entirely clear.

"They would attack or we would attack," my uncle remembered. "I caught one on the nose one time and went home bleeding like crazy. And Morris Avenue by the Fleetwood Theatre, there was a building with black families. But we didn't see much of black kids. You were still taught to stay with your own."

In August 1941 my uncle had his bar mitzvah. Today, the bar mitzvah party can take on the size and scope of Roman orgies. On this occasion, my grandmother simply picked up sandwiches at a corner deli and brought them back to the apartment. "Pastrami, corned beef, salami," my uncle said. His face took on a beatific countenance, as though imagining the aromas of grand historic sandwiches. "And she filled up the bathtub," he said, "with sodas. And the grandmothers made cakes, and some of the kids came in."

And that afternoon a photograph was taken: my father and my uncle, and Bernie Mayer and Siggy Siegel, on the Grand Concourse. All seem delighted with this moment. They might be Jewish versions of the Bowery Boys, kibitzing their way through the endless American Depression. They seem playful and carefree and terminally young, and oblivious to the thing that would happen in December, when the war changed everything.

"I'm going," my father told his mother when he and Bernie Mayer returned from the Times Square pool hall on the day the radio announced Pearl Harbor.

"Where are you going now?" his mother asked.

"Tomorrow," he said, "Bernie and I are gonna sign up for the war."

"They could win the war without you," said Esther Olesker. "Don't be in such a rush."

She was an immigrant from Poland but spent her life claiming to be German. That she had Polish relations one day heading for the German concentration camps, most of whom would not survive, was still unimaginable. Never mind Nazis, it was the Poles she couldn't stand. She considered them thick, and would not risk guilt by association. That her husband, my grandfather Max Olesker, was also a Polish immigrant, was of little concern. He could make up his own lies if he chose to have a problem with the Poles.

Max Olesker was a sickly man who survived childhood rheumatic fever but lived with a damaged heart. In his twenties, he collapsed on a New York streetcorner with heart failure and never worked again. The family survived on a disability policy Max had had the foresight to buy, and some extra money from a boardinghouse on St. Charles Place in Atlantic City which Esther ran in muggy summers while Max rested on their front porch recliner half a block from the boardwalk. Esther was a disciplined woman with a compulsion for neatness and a desire that her only child finish his college education, and never mind this business about the war, which would take care of itself.

"Of course, we saw it coming for a long time," my father told me years later, when I was considerably grown.

"You mean, about Hitler and the Jews?" I asked.

"I can still remember," my father said, "sitting in our apartment in the Bronx one night, and the newsboys were running down Findlay Avenue and screaming. You could hear them from the open window in the living room. 'Extra, Extra! Hitler Persecuting the Jews!' I still remember the chill, in the dead of a spring night, ten o'clock. It was the *New York Mirror,* which sold for two cents, and they were charging ten cents on Findlay Avenue. 'Hitler Persecuting the Jews!' I had such a chill run through me."

My father did not talk of such things as chills. Of Findlay Avenue, he talked of Bernie Mayer and stickball games and snowballs flung by way of romantic introduction. Of emotions, he talked not at all. They were a foreign language, and my father emotionally illiterate, or pretending to be. He was an upbeat, confident man who found life easier if he kept his emotions at a distance, even from himself.

"You know, there were cousins on my father's side," he said one day.

We were sitting in my parents' living room in northwest Baltimore County, in the safety of 1988. He had mentioned these cousins before, in passing moments, but always let the narrative slide away, or ducked behind his newspaper.

"Some of them got out of Europe in the thirties, when it was still possible," he said. "I guess I was thirteen or fourteen, I was still in school in the Bronx. My father and I would take the ferry out to Ellis Island, and we'd bring them back and they'd stay with my Aunt Bertha, who had a small apartment building on Findlay Avenue and took in everybody."

He remembered a cousin called Abraham No Last Name.

"What do you mean, no last name?"

"Who remembers?" my father chuckled softly. "He had a last name, and it went away. That's how things were. In our family, we had a standing joke: 'How did you get your name?' Some of them had names they couldn't pronounce for the customs inspectors. Or they couldn't translate them. It became easier just to change the name."

Such as Abraham, whose last name is now vanished down some dimly lit tunnel of lost identities. Or the cousin from Czechoslovakia, who arrived at Ellis Island just before the war and spotted a *Daily News* on a bench. In New York were two clothing chains, the Howard chain and the Crawford chain. The cousin from Czechoslovakia saw advertisements in the *Daily News* for this Howard company and this Crawford company, and reached for his little piece of America.

"Name?" the Customs inspector asked.

"Howard Crawford," replied the cousin, inventing a brand-new American self, as Great-grandfather Max Strewl had become Strull and Abraham No Last Name had become someone else.

My father and his father took the ferry to Ellis Island. My father remembered huge crowds, bedlam, and people shrieking, "Look how he looks," as they embraced relatives left behind some years earlier.

"They kept touching them," my father said. "As though to make sure they really were there."

Among them was Abraham No Last Name, who arrived from Germany with no facility in English and no ability to hear in any language. Deaf, completely. But he knew all about America. His father, Chaim No Last Name, was chef on a German ship that docked in New York several times, and when he went back to his seaport home of Altona, near Hamburg, he told his son of the wonders of this place. Abraham decided to come, just as the last doors of Europe were closing before Hitler's war. Aunt Bertha on Findlay Avenue gave assurances to the immigration authorities: He won't be a welfare case, he will stay here with me.

"My father and I found Abraham at Ellis Island," my father remembered. His voice was soft, and the color in his eyes seemed to fade in the late afternoon. "A sweet little man in his twenties, and delighted to be here. And we brought him back to Findlay Avenue, and the next morning we get up, and Aunt Bertha tells us he's gone."

The family was frantic. In the vast city of New York, where do you cry out for a man who cannot hear? How does a stranger find his way back to an apartment in America who communicates only in German and Yiddish?

All day they looked for him. My father was dispatched to search the neighborhood but lost himself in a stickball game. My grandfather Max contacted the police, who stifled a collective yawn. My grandmother Esther wrung her hands and declared that Abraham never should have left Germany, and never mind this business about Hitler and the Jews who were still there.

To great declarations of relief, Abraham reappeared that night. At dinner came a knock on Aunt Bertha's door, and there he was, smiling delightedly. In the morning he had taken the New York subway and gone from the Bronx into Manhattan in search of—who knew what? And he'd found it, and he'd taken the subway back.

And now, half a century later, my father remembered how they questioned Abraham that night, until there came this:

"Where were you, Abraham?"

"Timsk Var."

It sounded Eastern European, most likely a reference to a small *shtetl*. Was there perhaps someone from this Timsk Var village who was now living in New York, whom Abraham had gone off to find?

"Where?" he was asked again.

"Timsk Var, Timsk Var."

Finally, somewhere in the linguistic forest of his mispronunciation, came a clearing.

Timsk Var: Times Square.

In Europe, Abraham's father Chaim had told him of this fabulous place—

Timsk Var, he had pronounced it—and Abraham had gone off to find this glittery centerpiece of American wonder.

"And the rest of Abraham's family?" I asked.

"Never got out of Europe," my father said, meaning the death camps. "Letters would come from Poland, saying, 'Please get me out.' And you feel helpless, because what can you do? Finally, my mother managed to get papers for her sister Anna. But Anna wouldn't come. Because her brother Leo had been taken to the camp at Bergen-Belsen, and she wouldn't leave until she heard something."

Anna, waiting for her brother, was snatched up and died in a camp whose name has now been lost to time and confusion. There were variations of such stories all over Europe. In November 1938 the Nazis unleashed Kristallnacht, the torching of synagogues, the looting of Jewish shops, the arrest of thousands of Jews. In America Franklin Roosevelt said he would not increase immigration quotas, no matter the clear desperation in the face of Hitler. He had other pressures. That year there were 220,000 applications for visas to America at consulates throughout Germany. But America's annual quota for German immigration was only 27,000. And, in 1938, America did not fill even this pathetic quota. Instead of 27,000, only 18,000 Germans were allowed in.

My great-grandmother Jenny imagined a president named Franklin Rosenfeld. But Franklin Roosevelt and the balking congressional reactionaries still saw her as someone named Zlotte.

Six months after Pearl Harbor, and the frantic morning-after at the military recruiting office, my father still awaited word from the Army Air Corps. Chafing through his freshman year at NYU, he contacted military recruiting officers who told him to be patient.

The streets in the old neighborhood in the Bronx were beginning to empty out. No more stickball games, no more snowballs thrown at passing girls. The boys in their ripe teenage years were getting their marching orders. The Air Force declared it would get to my father, but there were millions of boys on waiting lists, and everyone would have to wait to join the killing.

"Leave the Air Force alone," said my grandmother Esther. "They have enough on their mind without you mixing in."

"I want to go," my father said.

"The war will still be there," said my grandmother Esther, who knew.

The war kept my mother awake each night. She and my father survived their introductory snowball and became sweethearts in their high school years. When my father's orders finally arrived, he was sent to Baton Rouge, Louisiana. In the summer of 1943 he telephoned my mother from an airbase in Alexandria, near New Orleans, and asked her to come to him to get married.

The train ride from the Bronx took the better part of two days. My mother wanted a Jewish wedding, but there were no Jewish weddings to be had in Alexandria. A weekend pass, a flight to Baton Rouge, and a rabbi was found at a synagogue and two strangers pulled from the sidewalk as witnesses.

My father shipped overseas in the winter of 1944, leaving from a base somewhere in Texas where he and my mother lived for several months. My mother returned to the East Coast and discovered she was pregnant. My father, stationed in North Africa, and then in Italy, began flying bombing missions over German and Romanian oilfields and occupied Polish cities and places where flak burst all around him.

"What was that like?" I asked him for the next forty years.

"Who can remember?" he answered.

This much my mother remembers: Four days before Germany surrendered, in my grandmother Ruth's apartment in the Bronx, my mother went into labor and walked gingerly into the living room. She was twenty years old, and petrified. Her water had broken. My grandmother, having lost her late husband Moe's shoe stores at the dawning of the Depression, had since gone into the practice of electrolysis and was now working on an unfortunate woman named Mrs. Bluestone, who had a mustache.

"Ma, I'm ready," said my mother.

"Your brother will take you," said my grandmother, remembering the worst of the Depression and unable to conceive of losing a paying customer.

My Uncle Dick, sixteen years old, stood in the shadows of the foyer, so terrified he could barely stand.

"I'll be right behind you," said my grandmother.

The two of them, my mother and my uncle, headed into a late Friday afternoon in the Bronx to look for a taxi. The next morning, my mother sent a telegram to my father: "Baby Michael born May 4. Looks just like you."

Into the hospital, in the next week, came GIs from the neighborhood already home from various places of the war, each of them gaining rights to see my mother by claiming to be my father. Among them was Bernie Mayer, injured in the South Pacific, hospitalized for weeks, about to be sent back since the war in Europe would end this very week but the fighting with Japan continued. He strode into a long dormitory room of ten beds, eight of them empty. He was fully stretched to his six-feet-five now, but the war had left him gaunt and shaky.

"Selma," he called out.

"How many fathers?" cried the woman in the next bed, having lost count.

The war went on until the final bombs were dropped, but millions of boys couldn't come home all at once. My father waited on a base in Foggia, Italy. My mother and I were now in Atlantic City, in the autumn of 1945, staying with my father's parents. Max Olesker's rheumatic heart was failing. Another telegram was sent to my father, which he showed to his base commanding officer.

"Your father?" the commanding officer said.

"His heart," said my father.

"If you can find a way home, take it."

For many years, my father's trip home was the only story I heard about his war experience: how he hitchhiked home aboard military transports until finally landing at an airbase in Miami in the midst of a terrible heat wave; how he caught a train all the way up the East Coast to Atlantic City; and how none of this was known to the family, sitting in the boarding house my grandmother Esther ran on St. Charles Place.

And then my grandfather Max suddenly declared: "Liney's home."

"We thought he was crazy," my mother said, remembering the moment years later. "We thought Daddy was still in Europe."

But she went to the back window, which overlooked New Jersey Avenue, and coming up the street on an overcast, misty afternoon, in an Army Air Force uniform, was this skinny fellow who was my father, home from the war.

FIVE
THE HOME MOVIE

One overcast morning in the winter of his seventy-sixth year, John Pica Sr. watched himself celebrate the end of World War II more than half a century earlier in a scrap of half-forgotten home movie.

He watched with the eye of some grand orchestrator anticipating one treasured philharmonic moment. This was not the massive V-J Day celebration of Times Square in New York, where a sailor famously kissed a girl in a white nurse's dress and symbolized a nation's unbounded joy. But it was pretty good.

This was V-J Day in Baltimore's Little Italy fifty-five years earlier, with flags flying from lampposts and window sills, and the streets clogged with joyous revelers celebrating the end of the organized killing. In the heart of it, there was Pica, twenty years old and newly home from the fighting. In a war that had once involved fighting on Italian soil, the boys from the neighborhood had distinguished themselves as fully American.

And to mark the end of the war quite properly, Pica had sneaked into the Della Noce Funeral Home, in the heart of Little Italy, where he quietly pilfered a coffin.

"That's it, that's the one I told you about," Pica declared now, pointing to the coffin on the screen.

He was lean and white-haired and his voice rumbled across a living room in northeast Baltimore County. August 14, 1945, in America: Was there ever a better moment to be alive? He sat in his daughter Maria's home, seeing faces from another world ago at the height of their giddiness. Maria Pica had discovered this old, misplaced home movie a few days earlier, unseen over decades, and had it converted to videotape.

There was the D'Alesandro family on Fawn Street, beaming for the camera on that distant summer day. Look at Tommy, said John Pica. His voice was barely above a whisper now. Look at Nancy, he said, and Nicky and Roosie. Then there appeared the forgotten neighborhood fellow who dressed up as Uncle Sam that day, and the other fellow dressed as the Japanese General Tojo. A crowd of kids gathered around Tojo and mock-pummeled him for the benefit of the home-movie camera, sensing that all this unleashed exuberance should somehow be preserved.

And now on the screen the youthful Pica, dark-haired and skinny, smiled delightedly and leaned across the Della Noce coffin he had stolen with his customary insouciance. Always, he seemed to live a life of minimal editing. Seize the moment, take the chance, worry about the consequences later.

"Where did this instinct come from?" I asked Pica one time. "You march to your own drummer."

"I marched to my own drummer in the Army," he said. "I was a machine gunner. They told me, 'Don't fire until we say so.' Hell, if a leaf moved, I shot it. I wasn't gonna listen to them."

After Pearl Harbor, young men headed off to recruiting centers from every neighborhood in the country. The stories have been passed down through the generations: America called, and they were there, boy. Many were stirred by patriotism, or its shifty second cousin, peer pressure. Others, worn down by the relentless and dispiriting Depression, saw the military as a fresh start.

Between the signing up and the coming home, though, the heart did not find more stirring tales. They were passed down by parents to children, and reinforced by the postwar combat movies, and they stirred the baby boom generation that sent imaginary G.I. Joe hand grenades across suburban back-yards to the sound of explosions rumbling out of their schoolboy throats. And they resonated emotionally, and bonded Americans across all disparate backgrounds, until the very moment the country discovered itself lost in Vietnam.

It was different in '41; it must have been. My generation heard a store-house of wondrous, heart-wrenching, hilarious stories of the good war, and the selfless generation that fought it. But when our war arrived we lingered by the millions on protective college campuses, huddled nervously around our draft deferments. We found compliant doctors to furnish notes that would satisfy skeptical Army physicians. We burned draft cards, bombed ROTC buildings, dodged tear gas, got drunk, got high, packed luggage for Canadian eventualities. We learned all the lyrics to folksongs that seemed to imply we were doing the noble thing, even if we weren't so sure we were. And the confused elders who had lived through World War II chose up sides be-tween those kids who desecrated the flag and those who wore it draped over their caskets.

It was different in the shadow of Pearl Harbor, we told ourselves.

In our time, we watched boys our age getting blown to bits on the televi-sion news every night. In our fathers' time, the adrenaline rush wasn't com-promised by such awful sights. In our time, the safety of the nation did not seem to be at stake. In their time, the country had been blind-sided. In our time, we learned to assume our politicians were lying. In their time, cyni-cism had not come into full flower. In our time, no one quite understood the purpose of the fighting. In their time, the purpose was sheer survival.

In December of '41, newsboys stood on raw streetcorners, shouting head-lines and slapping newspapers into hands reaching toward them. In Mary-land thousands of kids went to military recruiting offices—and, in thou-sands of households, there was the element, often unspoken, of boys' backgrounds. America's military was segregated by race. The country was at war not only with the attacking Japanese, but with Germany and Italy. Dis-tinctions had to be drawn, loyalties made clear. Their people may have come here years earlier from these warring nations, but they were American now. And, in going off to war, their sons and grandsons were offering implicit

John Pica Sr. in his Army days. Though a certified war hero, Pica modestly explained, "Every time I ran for my life, they gave me another medal." He arrived home in time for a raucous V-J Day celebration in Baltimore's Little Italy. *Courtesy of the Pica family*

declarations of citizenship on behalf of families who wished to be seen as patriotic.

"There was a bunch of us from the neighborhood who signed up together," John Pica remembered. He thought about it over a morning cup of coffee. "Russo, Culotta, the Abatto boy, myself. And the Georgilli boys. Hell, old man Georgilli was pulled out of his house and questioned by the police because he wasn't a citizen yet. And he had five boys in the service."

I knew that story. Gus Georgilli was a friend of mine for the last twenty years of his life. He was part of a group that met every week at Sabatino's Restaurant, in Little Italy. Joe Pizza would be there. Joe landed at Normandy on D-day, so terrified that he crawled onto the beach before realizing he had left his rifle behind on the landing craft—so he grabbed a weapon from someone who no longer needed it and moved on. John Vicchio would be there. John was a high school kid watching the old Pathé News at the Parkway Theatre at North Avenue and Charles Street one day during the war. On the movie screen, American infantrymen were charging along hedgerows. It was a full, dead-on camera shot into their faces—and one of the faces was Nick Balzano's, from Twenty-third Street, Vicchio's neighborhood. Then came a scream from the theater balcony. Fifty years later, Vicchio's voice still trembled as he remembered it. It was Nick's teenage sister Annie, screaming at the sight of her brother heading into hell. Vicchio was sixteen then; months later, when he turned seventeen, he dropped out of high school, lied about his age, and joined the war.

"And Gus Georgilli," John Pica said again. "Him and four of his brothers were all serving overseas, and the authorities are still questioning their old man's loyalty." The anger held in Pica's voice, and then it broke, and then he remembered the day they all left Little Italy for the war.

"We met on the corner," he said. "And my mother comes down the steps, and she's dressed all in black. I said, 'Ma, you're dressed for a funeral.' She always wore black, to keep my brother's memory alive." The brother had died nearly twenty years earlier. "I said, 'Ma, you dress all in black, I ain't coming home, there's no way.'

"And I'm standing there with my old man now. We're getting ready to go. I said, 'Daddy, I'm fine.'" He was a boy leaving for war, and still addressing his father the way a child might. "And somebody says to me, 'What are you gonna do if they send you to Italy?'" Pica remembered. "And my father says, 'Shoot 'em.' Just like that. 'Shoot 'em,' he hollers. Hell, we were Americans, what the hell did they think we were gonna do?"

That is the kind of moment that thrilled the generation that followed: the image of worried parents and cocky kids, the laugh in the face of terror, the image of every group joining up for the common cause. And, in the grand telling and retelling, we knew how the story would turn out: parades in the street, sailors kissing pretty girls and winding up in *Life* magazine photographs, and everyone vowing not to forget the poor heroic guys who never made it back.

And no one thinking about the thing that would begin to happen twenty years down the road in the jungles of Vietnam.

When World War II began Tommy D'Alesandro Jr. was in Congress. In California and elsewhere, there were roundups of Japanese Americans, who would spend the war in holding camps. In Baltimore D'Alesandro knew it was important to send clear, repeated, high-profile signals of Italian American loyalty. Once, through the Office of War Information, he broadcast a shortwave radio message to Italy, which he made certain was carried the next day in the *Baltimore News-Post*.

"Mussolini is just one individual," D'Alesandro declared. "Fascism has brought nothing but destruction to the Italian nation. You are fighting for a lost cause. For the honor of Italy and yourselves, I call upon you to quit in a war you cannot win. I warned you before that the United States is a mighty nation. They do not wish to destroy Italy, but you will make it possible unless you quit now for the honor of yourselves and Italy."

The message was made as clear as possible as often as possible: We are Americans. Our families' roots are somewhere else, but our hearts are here now. In that spirit, all families watched their sons go off to war, the great democratizing process for those who managed not to get killed.

Nick Filipides' father, James, was one of them. He arrived in the United States in the late 1930s, when he was seventeen. He was a merchant marine in Greece who jumped ship when it reached New York because he wanted to become American.

"He had a cousin in Yonkers and hid out there," Nick recalled one day while handling the lunchtime crowd at Jimmy's Restaurant in Fells Point. "The cousin had a diner, and my father washed dishes. Anybody that came over, it was considered a privilege to be an American, an honor. So he jumped ship, so then the war breaks out, so he enlisted in the Army. He was sent to Fort Riley, Kansas, where he got stomach ulcers. They operated on him, and he was out in a year. Boom. But he was proud of what he did. He signed up, see? It was his way of becoming an American."

Tommy D'Alesandro Jr. led cheers in Baltimore's Little Italy in September 1943 after Italy surrendered to the Allied forces in World War II. The *Baltimore News-Post* reported "wide-spread jubilation" in the neighborhood. D'Alesandro was a U.S. congressman on his way to becoming mayor of Baltimore.

The words were swallowed in the noise of the restaurant. Nick Filipides was born in 1947, two years after me. These notions of our fathers signing up for war resonated deeply in both of us.

"My father signed up the day after Pearl Harbor," I said.

"Did he see much action?"

I asked that question for forty years.

"*What was it like flying those missions?*"

"*Who can remember?*" *my father said, ducking his head protectively behind the sports pages of the newspaper.*

"*What places did you bomb?*"

"*Didja see,*" *my father said,* "*Brooksie got three hits last night.*"

"He flew eighteen combat missions," I told Filipides. I never knew much about them until the end, and so I imagined the romance of that time. "He wasn't one to talk much about it."

"Then, of course, Vietnam," Nick said. "It was, like, something's missing." A thought occurred to him. "How many Jewish guys were in Vietnam?" he asked.

"As few as possible," I said. "We were in school, dodging the draft."

"Like the Greeks," said Filipides. "Hell, like a lot of guys."

"A whole generation."

We said these things without self-consciousness. Just as we understood our father's impulses, we understood enough to speak in generational shorthand about our own. We knew what we knew: It was a different enemy, a different war. If there was guilt, we knew there were millions of us who shared it across all denominational lines.

In the Bronx, my father, the only child of Polish parents, joined the Army Air Force. On one mission, he said many years later, he bombed the town where his father had grown up. He sent a letter home, offering regrets.

"Never mind regrets," Max Olesker wrote back. "I never liked the place."

He was also telling his son that the new place, America, is better; never forget what we are now.

And my father was telling me, his older son: This is how some of us had to pay our dues to America. We obliterated our own parents' past.

That generation had to draw clear lines of loyalty. In September 1943, when Italy surrendered, the *Baltimore News-Post* carried a six-column photo beneath a headline, "City's Little Italy Jubilant at Surrender." The picture showed Tommy D'Alesandro Jr. with a few dozen neighbors carefully posed in a group, hands extended in V-for-victory salutes, with a big American flag in front of them.

"Baltimore's Italian colony received the news with high jubilation, mingled with tears of joy," the newspaper reported. "In private homes, restaurants, taverns and stores of all description, it seemed that serious work for the day was at an end."

D'Alesandro declared, "Thank God. I always knew the Italian people had no enmity against the United States." Behind the sigh of relief was an implicit message: Do not judge Italian Americans by this unfortunate business in fascist Italy, which is no reflection of our own loyalties.

On June 7, 1944, the day after the D-day invasion, a Combined United States Press story filed from the combat transport USS *Barnett* ran beneath a front-page headline in the *News-Post* reading, "Baltimorean First to Invade Europe."

The story said: "Lieut. Abe Candiotti, U.S.N.R., a twenty-three-year-old Spanish-Jewish American boy from Brooklyn, today commanded the first wave of small assault boats which set troops ashore in this section of Adolf Hitler's Europe. The boat carried members of an infantry company commanded by Capt. Leonard T. Schroeder, Jr., twenty-five, who comes from Baltimore, Md., and is of old German-American stock."

The Spanish-Jewish guy from Brooklyn; the German guy from Baltimore.

The paper ran the story big, just below a six-column photograph of Allied troops hitting the beach at Normandy.

Barbara Mikulski was a schoolgirl during the war years. Her Polish family had moved to a largely German neighborhood, where Mikulski was enrolled at the predominantly German Sacred Heart of Jesus School.

"Well, World War II, that's when a lot of the ethnic stuff here changed forever," Mikulski recalled in the spring of 2000. She was sixty-four now, and remembered vividly when that world changed.

"The war was the turning point," she said. "Back before the war, when we had all those people coming over from Europe, the Catholic Church was really the settlement house. That's what all those ethnic parishes were. Because it was there that you learned the language of your faith. The institutions had a definite identity, and they were bilingual, and you learned all the regular American stuff, plus Polish or Italian or German or whatever. And this was a bridge back to your family. And this bilingual nature continued all the way up to World War II.

"And then," said Mikulski, "all that stopped. It just stopped. Because the Germans and the Italians didn't want to speak German and Italian. Particularly the Germans. Not because they were ashamed of their language or their heritage, but what was going on had been overtaken by fascism, and they didn't want there to be any misunderstanding. I mean, there used to be singing clubs, very much a part of the German tradition, and they'd meet at Haussner's Restaurant. All that stopped. There was a great self-consciousness. You didn't want to be misunderstood, you wanted everybody to know you were an American."

There was an annual event in Baltimore, called the I Am an American Day Parade, a standard civic feel-good exercise, a chance to include one's own group in a few hours of mainstream America. It started before the war, but picked up steam during the fighting.

"And people marched with the Sons of Italy, with the Polish Women's Alliance, the Marching Order of Hibernians, all these heritage groups," Mikulski said. "They were saying, my people come from these countries, but we're all American now. It was very important to say that during the war."

Several months before it was over, John Pica came home. He had left Baltimore's Little Italy to join the combat in Italy. He was a certified hero, the winner of the Silver Star for "heroic gallantry in action" and the Bronze Star for "bravery and valor." The War Department records say Pica served with the 34th Infantry Division near Mount Paniano, and volunteered for a hazardous mission scouting German defense positions, crossing flat terrain under enemy fire with no trees or rocks to hide behind. He was twenty when he won the Silver Star.

"It was nothing," he said years later. "Every time I ran for my life, they gave me another medal."

In the radio and newspaper reports of that time, he said, "I zigged and zagged to dodge the fire. I remembered the zigzag dances we used to do back home after a football game."

He combined self-deprecating humor with a schoolboy incorrigibility. But the Army records tell a story of remarkable bravery. After scouting enemy positions, Pica made his way back to his own lines and heard a man moaning. It was an American officer who had wandered into a minefield, set off an explosion, and lost his eyesight and one of his legs. Pica made his way across the field by setting off mines with his bayonet. Then, through bursting shells, an exhausted Pica carried the officer for six hours until they reached safety.

Twice during the war, he was taken prisoner. Once, he and a Jewish kid from Brooklyn named Bobby Polansky were captured by the Germans in the Italian town of Cassino.

"They'll kill me," Polansky whispered to Pica, "just for being Jewish."

"Not anymore you ain't," said Pica, thinking fast. "Throw them dogtags away."

Then Pica took off his own dogtags and slipped them around Polansky's neck.

"You're Catholic now," said Pica. "Only . . ."

"Only what?"

"Only, you better learn to say the 'Our Father.'"

It's all there in the war records. That, plus the time Pica was hit in the knee and hand by shell fragments. Blown thirty feet by the concussion of a German shell, he spent thirty-five days in a hospital, then was sent back into action, where he spent days and nights in a driving rain, crouched in a foot of water barely a hundred yards from the German lines.

He was shipped home a few months before the end of the war in Europe. He found his mother at St. Leo's Church, deep in prayer, still dressed in black. He put his arm around her. His mother looked at him, shrieked, and fainted dead away.

"I shouldn't have done that," Pica said half a century later. "She could have had a heart attack."

Stationed at Fort Meade for the next few months, he would sneak down to his parents' home, 244 South Exeter Street in Little Italy, for Sunday evening dinners. Military police were sent to bring him back. When they arrived, Pica told his mother, who spoke no English, "Don't worry, Mom, they just came to invite me back."

The mother, delighted, invited the MPs to stay for dinner. On all subsequent Sundays when he felt unscheduled urges to go home, there were MPs at Fort Meade vying for what became known as Pica duty.

Late that winter he came home to stay. With his military days behind him, Pica could now march to any available drummer. One night he found himself in a high-level dice game. Nancy D'Alesandro, wife of the congressman, approached him on the streetcorner. Pica told me this story several times over the years, and so did Tommy D'Alesandro Jr. before he died.

"Tommy's bringing in Truman," Nancy D'Alesandro said. "Pick them up at the train station."

There were two problems, neither of which Pica passed on to Mrs. D'Alesandro. He had no idea who Harry Truman, the new vice-president of the United States, was. And he had no car.

"Well, I had George Durago's car," Pica remembered. Durago was one of the characters from the neighborhood. He never had a job, but he could play cards, and he had a car. With the car, he would drive ladies from the neighborhood to work and make enough money to play cards.

"Only problem was, his car had got burnt out the night before," Pica said. "It caught fire, I don't know how. And it's got no seats in it. So we put in fruit crates for seats, and Durago and me pick up Tommy and this guy Truman at Camden Station. We got the fruit crates from Benny Sudano, who worked in the produce business. So we get Tommy at the train station now, and we walk right past the car. And I say, 'Tommy, here's the car.' He looks at this burned-out wreck and says, 'Are you crazy? This is the vice-president of the United States.' I says, 'This is all I could get.' They both had on white suits and white hats.'"

From Camden Station, where the Baltimore Orioles would play baseball fifty years later, it was only a five-minute drive to Little Italy. Everybody braved it, including Truman, who, in those long-ago days, remarkably felt no need for Secret Service protection.

"So we bring him to Little Italy on this fruit crate," Pica said, "and he had a nice plate of spaghetti and walked around the neighborhood. George Durago goes off to play cards, and D'Alesandro says to me, 'Go get something nicer to take him back.' I went down to the Della Noce Funeral Home. Jerry the owner says, 'You got Truman? He's the vice-president.'

"Meanwhile, Truman's walking around the neighborhood. No Secret Service, none of that. And Truman says to Tommy, 'Where's George?' He thought the fruit crates were funny, and he wants to thank George for driving him. Well, George is playing cards. And he's losing. We know he's losing, because his leg is twitching like crazy. His back was towards us.

"We slip in and say, 'George.' 'What?' he says. I says, 'Truman wants to say hello.' He thinks we're kidding. He says, 'Fuck him.' So Truman says, 'Hey, George.' George almost fainted. And here comes Jerry from the Della Noce. He's decked out in a tuxedo and he's got a funeral limo to take Truman back to the train. Truman didn't want to get in. He thought it was too much. I think he was more comfortable in the burnt-out car."

Now, fifty-five years later, in his daughter Maria's suburban living room, Pica watched the movie of the day the war ended. He saw a thrilling, ghostly procession across the screen.

"Tommy," he said, spotting the elder D'Alesandro. His voice rumbled and caught. Then, spotting some of the D'Alesandro children, he said, "There's Tommy the younger. There's Nicky." They were boys then. Around them were flags flying from light poles and bunting hanging from window sills—and a coffin in the middle of the street, with Pica leaning over it and grinning with the grandest assurance.

"Like I told you," Pica said, turning to his daughter Maria.

When he came back from the war, he had reunited with D'Alesandro, his old political friend. One evening D'Alesandro's wife, Nancy, approached Pica, who was standing on a neighborhood corner with George Durago, owner of the burned-out car.

"Decorate the neighborhood," said Nancy D'Alesandro. "Put some flags up."

When she walked away, Durago said, "You know what it is, don't you? The war's about to be over. They're gonna announce it."

Pica went over to Lombard Street, to a place called Blank's Fabrics. Now, half a century later, Pica remembered, "I told him, 'The war's gonna be over,' and Mr. Blank says, 'Vhat, you crazy? Vhat you saying?'"

Pica delivered Blank's lines in a German-Jewish accent. "He says, 'Are you sure?' I says, 'I'm sure, Mr. Blank, the war's over, and we gotta get the neighborhood decorated.' He calls his daughter out, and some other Jewish kid, and all of us, Mr. Blank and these kids, we all rush over and decorate the neighborhood, and we're waiting for the official word.

"And the announcement came that evening, and everybody's kissing, and everybody's happy. And the church bells are ringing, and everybody went to St. Leo's Church. The whole neighborhood was there. Even some of the Jews from Lombard Street were there, I'm telling you, it was packed and jammed."

"Could we recreate that kind of a scene today?" Maria Pica wondered aloud.

"Not without somebody getting shot," her father said. His voice softened now. "But it was emotional, too. Oh, yeah, everybody started to cry. Some of the mothers had sons who died in the war. They stood there in their doorways by themselves, and we brought 'em out of the house, and we all went to church together." His voice caught for a moment. He remembered vanished boys, and the tears of their grieving mothers. "There were fourteen kids in the neighborhood who died," he said. "And the line from the church came out on the street, and small tables were set out on the sidewalk, and people put tablecloths over them and sat on their front steps and everybody drank wine. Aw, it was beautiful that night."

And the night was only beginning.

Pica grabbed a buddy, Anthony Peretti, who lived two doors away and knew where to rent a white horse for twenty-five cents an hour. They tied the white horse to the back of a car and put somebody in an Uncle Sam outfit on top of it. Then they went to the Della Noce Funeral Home, where John Pica stole the famous coffin.

Into the open coffin went Peretti, dressed as Hitler. Then they paraded the coffin through the streets. It was there when the home movie was shot, and there was Pica, in the sunlight at the end of the war, leaning across it for somebody's movie camera, awash in the sheer delight of being himself.

"Christ, I was a good-looking guy, wasn't I?" he said now. "Christ, didn't we have fun that time? We never had so much fun in our lives."

A few days later, somebody bumped into Nicky D'Alesandro in Little Italy, not far from his parents' old house at Albemarle and Fawn Streets, and told him about Pica, and the old movie, and how Pica said it had all been so much fun when the war ended.

"He's a liar," D'Alesandro said. "Johnny Pica spent the whole day crying. He cried for all those kids who never came home."

SIX "AMERICAN WAS WHAT YOU SAW AT THE MOVIES"

One raw winter morning off Falls Road, in northern Baltimore County, I went to see Ted Venetoulis, the man of sweet ebullience who grew up in working-class East Baltimore and nearly became governor of Maryland. He was better off without the job, but maybe Maryland was not.

We stood by a picture window overlooking a backyard the size of the Ponderosa, a fabulous wooded vista that seemed utterly diminished by little photographs sitting on a nearby table. The photos showed Venetoulis's people. They posed on a bent and stony little street on the Greek island of Rhodes, before their journey.

They could have booked passage with the ghost of Max Strull of czarist Russia, or the first Tommy D'Alesandro. These were small, rugged, iron-willed people who would first deal with America on their own terms and then, in generational installments, on America's terms. Venetoulis's backyard stretched before us in full Technicolor. The old photos were shot in the glorious black and white of their era. The little photos dominated everything, backyard, rolling hills, and the vast woods behind them. Venetoulis held onto the pictures as a lifeline to another world from which he had once sought the full emotional distance. Max Strull might have understood, as he had children of his own.

A generation after my great-grandfather found the Lower East Side of New York, these people, Venetoulis's parents, found the east side of the city of Baltimore. They settled in the little Greek section of Highlandtown, separated psychologically from nearby Poles and Germans and Lithuanians and Slovaks. But the geographical boundaries began to blur in the years when the young men from the neighborhood crossed the ocean to go to war, and their younger brothers and sisters learned to navigate their own oceans— street-corner intersections—to discover the country beyond their doorsteps.

The Venetoulis family ran a little restaurant called Nick's that catered to Highlandtown's working-class ethnics. Then they moved the operation to Lombard Street and called it Gustav's Sandwich Shop. They clung to the ways of the old country and produced the son Ted, who became Baltimore County executive and ran for governor of Maryland, and another son who moved to California and changed his name because he imagined it would help him assimilate. Nicholas Venet, he called himself. Then he launched the music careers of Linda Ronstadt and the Beach Boys and the Kingston Trio.

"How much more American can you get than the Kingston Trio and the Beach Boys?" I said.

"Exactly," Venetoulis said. "And, of course, he changed his name to Venet to get away from the long ethnic name. We were all angry with him. And then he decided he'd made a mistake, and he made his first name as Greek as he could, making it Nicholas to overcompensate—Nicholas Venet. He regretted it in the long run. But that's the way it went."

The Venetoulis parents spoke Greek at home, and a little English, but the children wanted to be American. The first sizable numbers of Greeks had not arrived in Baltimore until the final years of the nineteenth century. Then they settled near city markets and became confectioners and bootblacks and fruit dealers. But it wasn't until 1907, when the Reverend Constantine Douropoulos and his young family arrived from Greece, and lived on Fairmount Avenue near Patterson Park, that the Greek community had its own

At their wedding celebration in June 1931 Flora Baouris and Kostantinos "Gus" Venetoulis gather with family and friends on East Baltimore's Ponca Street. The wedding lasted three days, with much of the immediate neighborhood in attendance. The parents of Baltimore County executive Ted Venetoulis left Greece and struggled with mixed success to pass on the ways of the old country to their children. *Courtesy of the Venetoulis family*

full-time priest. Five years later, they had their first Greek-language school. A year later, the first Greek American savings and loan. By the 1920s, enough Greeks had settled in East Baltimore that St. Nicholas Greek Orthodox Church was built, at Ponca and Fleet Streets.

The Venetoulis family lived at Ponca and Oldham, surrounded by other Greek families. But a few blocks away were other versions of America. Half a century later, Venetoulis sat in his big living room off Falls Road and rattled off the names of boyhood chums from those narrow rowhouses. They sounded Polish and Italian and German. He mentioned the little stores of the neighborhood: Karpouzie's Grocery, and Nardone's Food Store with the pinball machines. And the crowded little coffeeshop where Venetoulis's father and the other immigrant men played cards, conversed in Greek, drank coffee with ouzo, and stationed somebody by the door to look out for the cops.

"They always had somebody standing by the door," Venetoulis said. "If it was police they knew, that was all right. But any new guys on the block, watch out."

The ouzo and the card games were comforting reminders of the old days. But the Venetoulis boys wanted no part of those days, neither the rituals nor the language. They lived in the new world. The parents saw this as an act of rebellion to be squashed, but good. They hired a tutor for home lessons in Greek.

"This was a conscious rebellion?" I asked.

"Damn right," Venetoulis laughed heartily.

"Why?"

"Because we wanted to be American, we didn't want to be Greek."

He glanced a little wistfully in the direction of the old family photos from Greece. He'd grown up in Highlandtown during the war years, a bundle of restless, upbeat energy, and hung around neighborhood kids who seemed unburdened by so much unassimilated baggage. He went to the movies where the face of America looked like John Wayne and Spencer Tracy. There were also swarthy ethnic faces in some of the movies, lummoxes whose accents murdered the king's English. They were bit players who showed up for a few minutes of comic relief and seemed to know when to get themselves killed off. But, when the movies let out and the neighborhood war games commenced around Patterson Park, all boys had starring American roles.

"You didn't hold it against any of the kids in the neighborhood," Venetoulis remembered, "but you knew some of the countries were hooked up with Mussolini and Hitler, and you let it go at that."

His memory, and his heart, were kinder than some of the actual history. Though there was much public trumpeting of the country pulling together, some incidents tore at the surface fabric. There were confrontations in the streets and the schools. There were tensions in some of the workplaces. The weekly *East Baltimore Guide* newspaper, a drum-beater for patriotism, cited a series of "situations rearing [their] ugly head more often than not."

At Patterson High School a teacher named Mary Morgan put together an Americanization class. Every student in the room was a European ethnic. Morgan was reaching for a sense of conciliation among edgy kids. The *Guide* called the class "almost . . . fatal. All the groups disliked the one and only German girl, although she was American-born. The Poles and the Czechs disturbed the Russians, and one Romanian girl expressed pure hatred when she said upon the entrance into the class of its one Greek student, 'I hate the Greeks.'" But Venetoulis was right: everyone knew there was a larger American cause that pulled disparate people together.

When the war ended and the soldiers from the neighborhood started coming home, the country began to change in unanticipated ways. The war had taught everybody lessons in getting along—but the peace that followed was the ticket for many to go their separate directions.

On the outer edges of the city, housing developments popped up everywhere, each with its own little patch of lawn instead of cement, each part of a new vision of the country, each with young families lining up to buy homes.

In the postwar years, as Americans of different backgrounds were feeling a little more comfortable with each other, they were simultaneously saying goodbye to each other, and to the crowded city neighborhoods where the Depression and then the war had frozen not only families but entire ethnic tribes into place for so many years.

The Venetoulis family moved out of Highlandtown as Ted was entering junior high school. They went to Charles Street and Bellona Avenue. At midcentury, this was considered suburbia; by century's end, it was a northeast Baltimore neighborhood with its charms but also its vulnerability to many of the city's anxieties. Venetoulis was a bright kid who needed accelerated schooling. He went to School 59, in the northwest corner of town, on Reisterstown Road, where the kids had names like Caplan and Hettleman and Shimmel.

"It was all Jewish kids and then a handful of other kids," Venetoulis remembered. "We did three years in two. For me, this was a big part of assimilating. I mean, just going through the Jewish holidays, when all these kids showed up with matzoh in their lunch bags. What was this? They didn't want it, so I'd take it. It was great food." He laughed delightedly. "But the whole thing, you see, it was this great learning process. There was something that we understood about each other, without even saying it. We understood feeling outside the mainstream, and that became something we had in common."

The city's postwar mayor was Tommy D'Alesandro Jr. In the war years Baltimore had taken in all sorts of newcomers, many from the South, drawn to the big steel mills at Sparrows Point and the ship-building operations at Locust Point.

By war's end they had put down roots. At midcentury the city's population topped 900,000. By the end of the century it had fallen by a third. Most of those who fled in those fifty years were white; many of those who arrived, and expanded their families, were black.

D'Alesandro spent twelve years at City Hall. He understood ethnic tensions, and also their political implications. These were confusing years, remembered now as a mix of postwar optimism and the first blossoming of the suburbs. But they were also a time when a great seething was coming of age. The cold war gave us McCarthyism, which made us suspect not only large communist nations but each other. The Supreme Court handed everyone marching orders on school desegregation, but no one issued instructions about the treacherous terrain of real estate offices. At midcentury Baltimore was three-quarters white; by century's end, the city was nearly two-thirds black.

For all his generous goodwill, and his sensitivity about ethnic differences, D'Alesandro was an untutored man pushed and pulled by the same emotional tides as his constituents. He was dealing with a city council comprised of various white ethnics. Here, he was comfortable. But the city's blacks were increasingly restless. How could he mollify them without sending the wrong signals to whites?

"My father was a liberal who would be considered a conservative today," Tommy D'Alesandro III said years later. "He would see to it that blacks got city jobs, the fire department, that kind of thing. He thought housing projects were a good thing because they got blacks out of the slums. On integration, the school board people get credit for keeping things calm, but my father was fine. When the word came, he said, 'Let's go.' Even though a lot of people were trying to tell him he shouldn't."

He was trying to make sense of a larger world than he'd been prepared for by an eighth-grade education and a life spent in an Italian American community of rigid, changeless truths.

D'Alesandro the elder reached City Hall after two terms in the state legislature and two congressional terms. Along the way, he married and he received an honorary high school diploma. The marriage came before the diploma. For years, the D'Alesandro family lived at 235 Albemarle Street. Annunciata "Nancy" Lombardi's family lived at 205 Albemarle. Nancy was two years old when her family moved from Italy. For the next sixteen years, living fifteen rowhouse doors from each other, Tommy never knew Nancy existed, and she knew nothing of him or his political life.

"She was Sicilian-cloistered," her son Tommy recalled years later. "My mother was eighteen, my father was twenty-four. In her old pictures, she looks like a movie starlet. My mother went to the Institute of Notre Dame, on Aisquith Street, and left there and got a job at Billig Auction. In those days, for a girl to have a job—well, her family thought she was crazy. But she'd been kept cloistered all those years.

"My father spotted her in church. He asked her out on a date, and she didn't even know who he was. She didn't know he was in the House of Delegates, didn't know anything about him. And living right up the block from each other all those years! That was how cloistered it was for those girls. Of course, later, she was the political power. Oh, yeah. They weren't afraid of my father, but they were terrified of my mother."

D'Alesandro was in Congress when he received his full academic honors. The nuns at St. Leo's, now quite proud of him and recognizing his achievements in the outside world, set up a special graduation ceremony in the same schoolyard where he had gotten into so much trouble years earlier.

D'Alesandro told the story of his diploma for years and years. It wasn't only the graduation. He understood the charm of the story and the sweet simplicity of the nuns, whose standards were so high that only after he had achieved some of the nation's highest honors would they see fit to honor one of their own sons.

It was a throwback story to which he could cling when so much else had changed, and would change more when his own son would become mayor, and was still changing when Ted Venetoulis, out of the city's east side ethnic pockets, became his generation's leader of the new, homogenized suburbia, which seemed emotional light years removed from the young Venetoulis and his Greek tutor.

"Oh, the tutor, the tutor," he said years later, blushing a little. His parents smiled from their black-and-white photos on the table across the room. The son had belatedly come to appreciate the wisdom of their thinking.

They wanted to be Americans (*front row, left to right*): Ted Venetoulis with brothers Steve and Nik. Behind them is their Aunt Mary. They met their parents' efforts to bring the old country to East Baltimore with the best rebelliousness they could muster. *Courtesy of the Venetoulis family*

"You know," said Venetoulis, "we wanted to assimilate very quickly, and if we spoke Greek, we weren't assimilating. If we went to the Greek church and spoke the Greek language, we weren't American. That's how kids think. So my parents tried to rein us in. We had a Greek teacher at our home once a week."

His eyes danced around the big living room. In his early years in that little Highlandtown rowhouse, he could not have imagined such a place as this. These grounds were manicured, the pool in the backyard huge, and the built-in bookshelves in the library stretched to a high ceiling with a skylight. He'd made money in publishing after leaving politics. His parents never had much, but found enough for the tutor, because they wanted to hold on to something they thought worth keeping.

"And we were awful," Venetoulis said. He shook his head and laughed wistfully. "She would come after school once a week. And, you know, we didn't have a lot of money. I remember we had cans of fruit salad. And that was one of our delights, you open up this can of fruit salad for dessert. And my parents would open it up for her. And we were really ticked off. She was eating our fruit salad. Never mind that we had to take Greek, she was eating our luxury, our one luxury. Her name was Thea Maria. *Thea* is aunt. *Gidyda Maria,* Miss Maria. She was elderly, and then there was another one, not as strict. And we rebelled."

"What do you mean? You wouldn't show up?"

"Oh, no," Venetoulis said with comic earnestness. "I remember once, it was snowing, it was slippery, and we poured water on the front steps to create ice. To make her slip on the steps. Oh, we were terrible. We fought, we would hide the fruit salad, we would find ways to sabotage her efforts. Because we wanted to be Americans."

"What made an American?"

"Who knew? But she was Greek. American was what you saw in the movies, in the community. You'd get on a ballclub, you didn't want to be called a Greek guy, you wanted to be part of that bigger thing. Kids can be nasty, you know. Greaseball, Polack, whatever, it can get very nasty. You didn't want that. So you played to that larger community."

This is what happens all over the country. The first generation arrives, and clings to the familiar. But their children reach for the full America. The public schools and the playgrounds and the parks become the meeting ground. As a kid, Venetoulis played ball for the Red Shield Boys Club and captained all the teams.

"And my father," he sighed, "would come to all the games. And I had mixed feelings. We didn't like to bring kids over to the house because we were afraid our folks would talk Greek or something to 'em."

The thought struck a chord. I said to Venetoulis, "I remember thinking, if my parents spoke in Yiddish, I didn't want any gentile kids to hear it. It would mark me as being strange, and maybe even subversive."

"The irony is," said Venetoulis, "as you grew up and maybe hit your late teens or twenties, you began to assemble that old ethnic stuff and make sure you extended it to your own kids, and you began to brag about it. When I ran for office one of the great thrills was the Greek community, how they responded to me. But, as a kid, the threat that somebody might overhear them speaking Greek . . ."

"As you get a little older, that's the difference," I said. "By my twenties, if I heard a friend drop an '*oy vey*' or a '*gevalt*,' I'd think, 'Hey, that's me.' By then, it was all right for my generation to say these words, the way our parents did. Each one felt like a friendly password sent from one generation to another."

"But it's different when you're still a kid," Venetoulis said, "because of the self-consciousness. So I'm playing ball for Red Shield, and my dad would come to the games. I played shortstop and caught. We had a great catcher we stole from one of the other neighborhoods, and a foul ball smashed his mask and rammed his eye and broke his cheekbone or something. The kid was hurting bad. And I had to go in and catch.

"My dad went out and, I want to tell you, we didn't have five bucks to spend, and he bought a mask for the team. He knew his son was gonna use it, but it was for the team. And I could tell the behavior of the team to my dad, how it changed. Not that it had been negative, but I was still embarrassed by having him there. They weren't feeling anything, but I was. But then my whole attitude changed. I needed that confirmation from them so I could have better respect for my parents than I previously had."

The athletic teams helped him fit in, but the process only went so far. It was one thing for a Greek kid and a Polish kid to toss a ball around Patterson Park. America thus becomes the ballgame. But black people were in some other country. The public schools were still segregated, and so were plenty of restaurants and movie theaters and swimming pools. In the public parks, there were separate pools and separate tennis courts. Downtown Baltimore department stores allowed blacks to buy clothing, but they couldn't try anything on for size before buying. Pale skin would not touch material first touched by dark skin.

In such an atmosphere, ballgames played by kids became important. They were expeditionary ventures. Venetoulis remembered Red Shield basketball games in a little bandbox of a gymnasium on Clinton Street, between Eastern and Fleet, where the edge of the court met the interior walls of the building.

"You'd ram somebody, and they'd hit the wall," he said. "That's it, you splattered 'em. And we had this Red Shield team, we hustled and we roughed people up. We won championships all over the place, mainly because we hustled. And we played a black team from Dunbar or somewhere. Our first real experience, and we were all afraid. It was ridiculous, but we had fear, okay? On the other hand, we knew we were gonna beat 'em. We just knew we were gonna win, we were cocky as hell going in."

"Maybe," I suggested, "there was something psychological going in. Your side knew you were first-class citizens. Their side, maybe they were intimidated at the thought of playing white guys."

"That may be it," Venetoulis said. "But there was one kid, we met again the next year, and we hung around, we kibitzed. I can't remember his name, but we'd see each other at games and make a point to talk. The thing is, I never heard any of our guys slam the blacks. Maybe we understood we were only one step above them in somebody else's imagination."

"It's funny to hear you say that," I said. "It's what the Jews always said. 'The blacks are the last line of defense before they come for us.'"

"Right, who did the blacks have? Hispanics? Puerto Ricans?"

Venetoulis finished his schooling and served a few years in the Army, including some time on Capitol Hill in Washington. He wore civilian clothes. The Army wanted to keep an eye on the Senate labor rackets committee looking at Teamsters boss Jimmy Hoffa. One of Venetoulis's friends there was a Greek fellow named John Konstanty, who knew Bobby Kennedy and introduced them. Venetoulis started thinking about politics. He did some advance work for the Democrats when John Kennedy ran for president and stayed friends with staffers in the Kennedy White House.

"The Kennedys were just the masters of ethnic politics," he said. "In the Greek community, Jack Kennedy was God. They didn't need any training. They understood. We were all outsiders who wanted to get in. And then, you remember, the Kennedys went to Greece, and Greek dancing was the rage. And *Zorba the Greek* came out later. And I became a hero to some of these guys who worked at the White House because I could show them the Greek dances. So now, what do you know, it's kind of cool to be Greek."

Venetoulis was living just outside Washington by then, studying for his doctorate and living with his brother Nik. They rented a split-level house. Venetoulis remembered carpeting in all of the rooms. He'd never seen such a thing. Nik Venet was pals with big-league entertainers by this time. Sammy

Davis Jr. came to the house, and the guys in the Kingston Trio hung out there. Bobby Darin slept over.

"That was the life," he said wistfully. He worked in a couple of congressional campaigns in Maryland, and then he ran William Donald Schaefer's first campaign for mayor of Baltimore. It was 1970, two years after the Martin Luther King riots, and the city was still suffering after-burn. Black people were trying to break into the middle-class job market, and white people were fleeing faster than ever to the suburbs. Schaefer, the city council president, seemed uncomfortable in public.

"Don, Don," the old-timers would cry out happily when they saw him. They knew him from his years in the council.

"Hi. How are ya?" Schaefer replied, deadpan, keeping his distance, his lips barely moving. "Good to see ya." He seemed a schoolboy whose mom had insisted he attend the church dance, and he would struggle to endure his way through it, but he wasn't going to like it.

His opponent that year was George Russell, who was smart and sophisticated and looked like the future to a lot of people. Russell had been the first African American city solicitor, and the first black judge on the city's Supreme Bench. No black person had ever seriously run for mayor of Baltimore. Many thought Russell towered over the uptight Schaefer. Shaky Schaefer, the wags called him. This was a time when Kennedys were still political role models, when John Lindsay walked the New York streets to keep them calm. The trendy political word was *charisma*.

"Schaefer," I said to Venetoulis, the first time I met him in that campaign, "doesn't have any charisma." At twenty-five, I thought charisma was something a politician could spread confidently over the city, like pixie dust, to keep everyone from fighting. Venetoulis snapped at me that day, the amiable angel suddenly turning into a Highlandtown streetfighter.

"The hell with charisma," he said. "This guy knows every brick in the city."

Schaefer won easily, the first of four mayoral terms. A few years later Venetoulis ran for Baltimore County executive, a position that had launched Spiro Agnew toward the White House. On his own route, Venetoulis heard voices.

"We don't need another Greek in Baltimore County," they said.

The words chilled him. Venetoulis seemed temperamentally blessed by the gods of all nations. He had the aura of someone perpetually on the edge of delight. He had imagined, by the time he ran for office, that he was seen as an authentic American.

"And you hear something like that," he said now, sitting in his big house a quarter-century later, "and it takes you back to who you are, and everything your parents went through along the way."

The two of us glanced through the window leading to his enormous backyard. A few arthritic old trees swayed in a wind husky enough to make itself heard. On the table by the picture window, on a bent and stony street in Greece, Venetoulis's parents smiled inside a picture frame, when their journey was just beginning.

SEVEN

SINATRA AND DiMAG

A kind of reverence washed over Tommy D'Alesandro III. As he recalled the postwar years in Little Italy, he began to talk *sotto voce,* as though the events of fifty years ago were too precious to share with passing strangers. He remembered the smell of sauces from open windows. He remembered Christmas services where everyone filed out of church long past midnight. His voice sounded like a man at confession. He remembered dances and ballgames, and the great Yankee Clipper DiMaggio arriving one Saturday night in the neighborhood, and the sidewalks every evening so filled with people that they spilled into the streets, and then the streets themselves were filled. And he also remembered, eventually it was time to move on.

As the old ethnic insularities began to break down after the war, his father, Tommy D'Alesandro Jr., became Little Italy's ambassador to the city of Baltimore. He was mayor from 1947 to 1959, when the city had swollen to nearly a million people, many of whom had arrived during the war and then stayed. Then other people began to leave. Among those citizens staying were blacks just beginning to discover the strength of their own voices. Among those leaving were whites discovering the suburbs. And those in government positions of alleged power discovered they had almost no influence over the pace of arrivals or departures.

"You have to understand what we were coming out of," Tommy the Younger said one day over lunch. "In the thirties and forties, it was a fight for survival. Everybody was speaking a different language, everybody was hustling for the buck, and it wasn't there. It was survival. The luxury was to go to church on Sunday with your best clothes, and then eat a good meal. That was the high point of the week."

He said this with no sense of martyrdom in his voice; he was not that kind of a man. His tone was that of the awed youngster, still grateful that the grownups in his life had pulled everybody through. The Depression was behind them, but it lingered in everyone's sense of dread. The war was done, but a cold war took its place. Now the old walls, dividing communities by race and religion, and by nationality, were coming down. And the racial mix would change everything.

As his father's oldest son, D'Alesandro had always had a life a little different from his friends'. "I would go to the Polish home, the Knights of Columbus in Highlandtown, just go in there," he said. He sounded as if he had been an emissary to foreign countries, allowed in because he had proper authorized papers from men in high places. "But my crowd was back in the neighborhood," he said.

"And you were out there finding America," I suggested.

"I wasn't aware of it, not then," D'Alesandro said. "But that's what it was. All that experience was telling me, you gotta get out. I mean, everybody wanted to be American, but everybody wanted the protection of their own people. And I would go down to the Broadway Market, and there's people there speaking Polish, and they're speaking German, and they're speaking Italian. I'm telling you, it was tough finding English. But that was the Americanizing process, see?"

It was also the accordion effect felt by all those on the fringes, the rhythmic push and pull creating the great cosmopolitan music. There were rich, textured, unnamed possibilities out past the previous neighborhood borders, a world beyond the old, changeless truths and the ancient, numbing rituals and the moral choices that seemed to offer no sense of nuance or ambiguity to those who were coming of age. On the other hand, in his retirement, D'Alesandro's eyes still glowed at the mention of the Little Italy of his younger years.

"The greatest," he said. "The greatest, that's all I can tell you. The greatest times, the dances with all the kids from the neighborhood on Friday nights, the CYO dances at St. Leo's hall. And Sundays, you could walk on any street and smell the sauce coming out of the kitchens and you were welcome in any house, any house. Midnight mass on Christmas. Two masses, one in English and one in Italian. And the one-thirty mass right after that, and everybody walking home afterwards.

"After the war, you could not see macadam," D'Alesandro said, so full of delight that even the memory of the tar and asphalt streets stirred him. "In the evenings, people would come, people would come, people would come. You couldn't see the street beneath you, it was so crowded. And then all the homes were open, and there was food, there was sausage and eggs . . .

"And once a year," he said, "a baseball game." He let out a yelp like a happy child in a highchair. "The married men versus the single men, down at the pumping station. There was a playing field across from the water. And the corners, the corners." He was rhapsodic now, remembering nothing more than jammed street-corners and faces, and the faces become names, and each was attached to a story.

"The barbershop on Gough Street," he laughed. "Every Saturday night, the place is packed with guys getting shaves. And Dooty was there. Dooty from the neighborhood, who was Joe DiMaggio's biggest fan. And DiMaggio's in town, eating at Maria's, and my father sends me down to get him. I say, 'Dooty, DiMaggio's at Maria's and wants to meet you.' The guy turned to stone. I said, 'Come on, you gotta do it, come as you are.' Here's a guy, talks a mile a minute, and I take him down and introduce him, and he can't talk. It was like he was meeting a god, see? DiMaggio was a god to us."

In the neighborhood canon, there were two nonsectarian gods. There was DiMaggio. And there was Frank Sinatra.

"Oh, Sinatra," said Vince Culotta.

Culotta owned Sabatino's Restaurant, located in the geographical heart of Little Italy at Fawn and Exeter Streets, a few doors from the D'Alesandro home. Culotta was a former kid from the neighborhood who figured he got lucky. He and two other fellows bought the restaurant from Vince's uncle in the 1970s, and the place became home to all known characters. Major league ballplayers ate at Sabatino's. So did governors and judges and bookmakers. There was even a dish called the bookmaker salad, which was invented by the bookmaker Al Isella and favored by federal prosecutors feeling a little frisky. Ted Kennedy ate there when he ran for president, and Marvin Mandel ate there when he was governor of Maryland. Mandel would schmooze with Isella. Politics and the law mixed with the culture of the street here. Spiro Agnew was not only a Sabatino's regular, but dined there the very evening he pleaded *nolo contendere* and ceased being vice-president. Frank Sinatra went there when he came to Baltimore. He and Isella had both had relationships with Ava Gardner. Sinatra's was somewhat more public. Once, Sinatra slipped in with an entourage and took a private room on the restaurant's second floor. Word of his arrival spread through the neighborhood like a shot of adrenaline.

Across the street from Sabatino's was a bar, and a few guys drinking there dragged a jukebox outside and ran an extension cord to a plug. They turned up the volume. In the street below Sinatra's room could be heard the sound of one distinctive voice.

"*Come fly with me*
Come fly, let's fly away
If you can use some exotic booze
There's a bar in far Bombay . . ."

"What's that?" Sinatra asked.

"Some fans out there," Vince Culotta told him. "They're playing your music."

Sinatra rose from his chair and walked to a window with a fire escape outside. He gazed at the crowd beneath him and smiled broadly. People looked back, thrilled to their bone marrow.

"It was like the pope," Vince declared. "Everybody just looked up at him."

Sinatra was like these people in the street, only he was not. He had come from a neighborhood like theirs, and then made the whole world his neighborhood. He was the dream they had dreamed of becoming, or falling in love with, and his people and their people had come from the same place, long ago, on the other side of an ocean. It was the tribal instinct at its most prideful.

Sinatra had nearly fifty people with him that night. His pal Jilly Rizzo was there, and the comic Pat Cooper. Vince Culotta said to Jilly, "Look, Mr. Rizzo, I know a lot of people downstairs, and they wonder if they could get some autographs."

"Let him eat, Vince, he's in a good mood," said Rizzo. "Afterward, when he's relaxed, he'll sign some."

After dinner, nearly a hundred people waited downstairs. They wanted autographs, or just wanted to meet Sinatra so they could tell everyone for the rest of their lives that they had met him. Now Jilly Rizzo turned to Vince Culotta and leaned his face close.

"Listen, kid," he said. "You know how to spell 'Sinatra'?"

"Yeah."

"Well, I know you can spell 'Frank.' Just sign the fuckin' papers, they won't know."

"So then," Vince remembered, "we got Ralph Marsilli, who's Sinatra's biggest fan in the world, right? Ralph would go to Atlantic City to see him all the time. And he's been waiting all night." Vince decided to ask Sinatra for a favor.

"Look, Mr. Sinatra," he said, "I got a very good friend down there. I haven't brought anybody else up here. I mean, my wife is down there, and I won't even bring her up. But this guy's been a fan of yours all his life, and all he wants to do is meet you."

"Yeah, bring him up," Sinatra said.

Culotta introduced the two men. They started talking. Ralph Marsilli, in his mid-forties, was about to marry for the first time. The two men had one drink, and then another. Marsilli began to feel a little brave.

"I'm getting married next week," he said.

"You are?" Sinatra said.

"Yeah, you know what?" Marsilli said. "You gotta sing at my wedding."

Frank Sinatra turned to Vince Culotta. "What is it with this fuckin' guy?" he said. "First he was dying to meet me, and now I gotta sing at his wedding."

We sat at a small table on the second floor of Sabatino's now, only a few steps from Sinatra's room the night of the jukebox. Vince Culotta's posture is the shrug of the shoulders: Live and let live. He is delighted by the characters who ad lib their way through his restaurant each day.

"You know," he said now, "Sinatra was the kind of guy, every once in a while he had problems with the press. And with people. But he came here, and he was really terrific."

It sounded like an apology made on behalf of a member of the family. Sinatra's life was an endless test of his fans' loyalty. He was the Catholic who divorced his Italian wife for another woman in a time when such things weren't done. He was the embracer of Roosevelt and Kennedy who later fawned over Nixon and Reagan, and stood by Spiro Agnew in his hour of disgrace. Years earlier, though, Sinatra had opened a door for me, and over time it connected to a place where the outsider Felix Guevara of El Salvador looked so frightened in a Baltimore courthouse hallway. Sinatra had granted a kind of citizenship. Thus, he had gone miles past the need for anyone's ethnic defensiveness.

In the modern era, Little Italy seemed like something out of old family albums: its rowhomes and front-stoop gatherings and bocci-ball players on soft summer evening were a throwback to the old ethnic strongholds. But, for all the comfort such neighborhoods had given, they also reinforced cultural isolation.

Years earlier, when it was an island of first- and second-generation Italians, it was so removed from the rest of the city that the future war hero John Pica, sent out of the neighborhood to attend Loyola High School, went to lunch on his first day and heard a voice say, "What's that?"

"What do you think it is?" said Pica. "It's a veal-cutlet sandwich."

He looked at the other kid's lunch. Whatever it was, it was packed between two slices of white bread, which was referred to in Little Italy as American bread.

"What the hell's that?" Pica asked.

"Peanut butter and jelly," the kid said.

"I never saw it before," said Pica.

Vince Culotta came up in the generation after Pica's. His father, Vincent Rosario Culotta, came from Sicily; his mother, Anita Canzane, from northern Italy. They spoke differing dialects of Italian, and though they did not discourage their son from speaking the language, they did not encourage it.

"They didn't specifically say, 'Don't speak Italian,'" he remembered. "But they didn't go out of their way to teach it. My father wanted me to go into the mainstream of America without an accent."

"Even an accent?" I asked.

"Oh, yeah," he said. "See, this neighborhood, when my father was born, it was like taking a village in Italy and transporting it here. Everybody spoke Italian. Nobody spoke English."

"Nobody?"

"Well, your parents didn't know how to speak English, so you spoke Italian to them. With your friends, you spoke English. But you had a little bit of an accent, and so did they. So you were ostracized." He paused a moment, as though considering what he was saying, and then said it again. "You were, you were ostracized. I don't want to say...Yeah, you could say they were discriminated against, because they were different. And when you're different, you're discriminated against. So both my parents, they wanted us to go full run into the mainstream of America. It's a good country, and they realized it."

They were different; there it was. The country encouraged a great mixing, in which differences could be tolerated as a public posture, but the differences were looked upon quizzically at close range. *What was that accent? What's that strange sandwich your mother made you take to school?* And so, for millions, the goal was assimilation, the sense of belonging to a bigger group—but there was the risk of losing the nuances that defined their uniqueness.

In Little Italy there are still traces of a variety of groups. The neighborhood went through the same kind of history Barbara Mikulski had described in Highlandtown: each new group of immigrants, ill at ease and unable to speak English, settling in with those who shared their culture.

In the mid-nineteenth century, the neighborhood had been Irish, who left behind a storefront on a corner, Kelly & Poggi. The Jews followed the Irish and left behind a synagogue's Hebrew lettering on the side of what became a parking lot. As Italians moved in the Jews shifted a few blocks north to Lombard Street.

"And then the Italians stayed," said Culotta, "because we had the restaurants. And also because there weren't any more great influxes of immigrants. They closed it up."

When Vince Culotta was about five years old, his family moved out of Little Italy to northeast Baltimore. The neighborhood—around Milton and Luzerne—was a mix of Poles, Germans, Irish. It was the 1950s. By the next decade, blacks were added. But the family always came back to Little Italy. Relatives were there. His mother had a brother Joe, who bought a restaurant from a man named Sabatino Luperini. Sabatino's flourished. Years later, he took his sister's son, Vince, into the business. In 1974 Vince, along with Ricky and Renato Rotundo, bought the restaurant from Canzane.

On the upstairs walls at Sabatino's, there are photographs of young men in the neighborhood from years and years ago. They were people struggling with a strange language, with wisps of a formal education, and with almost no connections outside of their own community. Vince Culotta's father had a sixth-grade education. He did odd jobs for food hawkers, men hustling produce on the street. Then, in 1928, the family purchased a car and turned it into a taxi. Two Culotta brothers each drove twelve-hour shifts. At the end of the week, they took all the money and gave it to their father. He gave them each five dollars a week and money for gas. Then Vince Senior sold produce from a truck. He took it to places he had never seen, to swell North Baltimore neighborhoods such as Homeland and Guilford. He sold to people who had money to spend. The banking class lived there, the old-line business and professional people. Few had vowels at the end of their names. It was still the city, but it had some distance from its noise and traffic and immigrant classes. And there was money there. Apples that sold for a nickel in East Baltimore went for fifteen cents in North Baltimore.

But life was the constant hustle. The kids would have to learn discipline to survive. This came not only from parents but from the nuns at school. Vince Culotta went to St. Catherine's until high school. Two older sisters preceded him there. The nuns were surrogate parents. They specialized in tough love. There were fifteen-minute recess periods. On snowy days there were orders not to throw snowballs.

"So they wouldn't let you take your gloves outside," Vince remembered. At the end of recess, everyone's hands were checked. If they were red, it meant you had been playing in the snow.

"They had these yardsticks, thick and heavy," he said. He smiled ruefully. "They'd hit you on the palm of your hands. The penalty for throwing snow-

Joanne, Rosa, and Vince Culotta (*left to right*), at play on the sidewalks of the city. Behind them are Bell, Marie, and Anita Culotta. Vince Culotta was part owner of Sabatino's Restaurant in Little Italy, when it became home to "all known characters." *Courtesy of the Culotta family*

balls was six hits, and after the second hit you'd instinctively draw your hand back, because it hurt. Well, if you drew back your hand, you got doubles. Then you'd close your eyes so you couldn't see it coming. They used to say, 'No. You gotta watch.'"

He shrugged his shoulders. Sometimes the nuns called his father to school. The old man had no patience for this. His son was becoming an embarrassment when he wanted him to be a good citizen. When he'd gotten one call too many, Vince Culotta's father arrived at school with a broomstick.

"Hit him with this," he told the nuns. "Don't hit him with your hand, you'll hurt yourself."

He wanted his son to fit in, to obey the rules. American boys played by rules; that was what school was all about, learning to fit in, learning to adapt. He wanted his son to be an American.

"They were Italians first, but they wanted to be Americans," Vince said. He remembered a question from his youth that became a refrain: What are you?

"People asked me, and I asked people," he said. "'What are you?' Like, a Jewish name or an Italian name, you knew. But if it was an 'American' name, you couldn't tell who the Americans were. You couldn't tell if they were Irish, English, whatever. Jones or Franklin or Wills. You'd say, 'What are you?' They'd say, 'We're Irish.' After a while, I lived around the Irish long enough, I knew Irish names. Nobody said, 'American.' Everybody said, 'Italian,' or whatever. Don't get me wrong, I don't mean more proud. I mean, you were automatically an American. By that time, your people were here, you were American. We were asking: What are you, besides that?"

Culotta's father grew up with Tommy D'Alesandro Jr., the first mayor. D'Alesandro's brother, John, later killed in the war, was the best man at the elder Culotta's wedding. One city election day, Vince and I walked through Little Italy, past Muggsy Muggavero's corner luncheonette, to St. Leo's Church. This was the neighborhood polling place every election day. Tommy D'Alesandro always made it a point to cast the first ballot. Consecrated ground, he called it.

"What I remember most about the D'Alesandro family," Vince said, "was the pride. They were ours, they were showing everybody what we were made of. And not just Tommy, you know? Miss Nancy, too."

He was fifty-seven years old, but it was still "Miss Nancy." Annunciata "Nancy" D'Alesandro, cloistered as a girl, became a political force in her own right when she took the hand of Tommy D'Alesandro Jr.

"Oh, are you kidding?" Tommy D'Alesandro III said one morning, remembering his mother. "When she met my father, she didn't know anything about politics, but she wound up knowing more than him. They weren't afraid of my father, but they were terrified of my mother. Oh, she was vicious." He laughed out loud. Once, an opposing precinct worker at Eden and Gough streets tore up some of D'Alesandro's election day ballots. Nancy hit the guy so hard the police had to be called.

Also, she had an army of ladies from the neighborhood who worked the phones and sent out letters, who organized rallies and cooked spaghetti and ravioli for fundraising dinners. It was a time before politics was played on television, when the campaigns routinely went into the neighborhoods, where there were parades and bull roasts, and then everybody would go back to Albemarle Street, to the D'Alesandro home on the corner, and figure out what to do the next day, and the day after that.

"They'd all get together down in the cellar," D'Alesandro laughed. "That's where the power was, down in that cellar, all those sweet women, about a hundred of 'em who turned into the most vicious people you'd ever see in your life in a political campaign. I mean, they would go out and tear wild dogs apart. It wasn't a ladies group, it was like a pack of wild animals. They controlled precincts. They worked year 'round. They went out with vengeance from that cellar."

John Pica had been one of D'Alesandro's closest confidants, and held his own city council seat for a term. He knew about Nancy D'Alesandro's armies, and about loyalties. He had a son, John Pica Jr., who was elected to Maryland's House of Delegates. In his first race, the son discovered there were people he had counted on who were instead backing his opponent.

"Don't hold it against them," Pica's mother, Antoinette, counseled. They sat in the family living room, and for a moment there was no sound.

"Your mother's right, don't hold it against them," John Pica Sr. finally said to his son. He spoke each word slowly. "But write down their names."

The game was played differently then. Pica remembered driving D'Alesandro through Little Italy one election day when the bells of St. Leo's began to toll, indicating someone was being buried. A member of the electorate, surely. D'Alesandro shot an alarmed look at Pica. Pica sent back a look of calm.

"Don't worry," he said. "He'll vote."

Elections were battlegrounds. In 1983 William Donald Schaefer ran for a fourth term as mayor of Baltimore. His opponent was William "Billy" Murphy, a high-profile defense attorney who was elected to a judgeship but found it confining. D'Alesandro backed Schaefer. In these retirement years, it was D'Alesandro's job to count the election day ballots in Little Italy.

On the night of the election I saw D'Alesandro at Schaefer's campaign headquarters. I was now writing a column for the *Baltimore Sun*.

"How did the vote go in Little Italy?" I asked.

"Schaefer won, 487 to 1," D'Alesandro said. One vote for Murphy in the entire community?

"Yeah," D'Alesandro said. "And we're gonna find that guy."

I ran D'Alesandro's line in my column the next morning. Murphy had suffered an overwhelming defeat. The next day, there was a knock on the door of Sabatino's Restaurant. Vince Culotta shouted through the door, "We're not open yet."

"That's all right, I'm not here to eat," said the voice on the other side. "This is Billy Murphy. I'm just looking for that guy who voted for me."

"Yeah," John Pica remembered years later, "but Nancy, she was the one. She took care of her house and her family, plus the political work. She told Big Tommy how to run the precincts, who the workers should be. And that huge ladies group, which was like the CIA. They'd hear all the gossip, and they'd bring the messages. Nancy would tell Tommy, 'You can't trust this one, we had bad dealings. This one's okay, you can trust him.' The ladies would work the phones and send out the letters and put together the rallies. In fifteen minutes, she could put twenty or thirty of them together. One time, she had so many women working for her, they had to put 'em all at St. Leo's."

Then Pica remembered years ago, when he had gone with Big Tommy to the U.S. Congress. He remembered Lyndon Johnson's casual slurs and D'Alesandro's anger.

D'Alesandro learned to swallow that anger. His wife did not. Years later, when Johnson ran for president, the Democrats held a rally for him at Baltimore's Fifth Regiment armory. Nancy D'Alesandro was introduced to Johnson.

She said, "My husband's name is Thomas John D'Alesandro. It is not Tony."

"I was standing right there," John Pica said. "Johnson's ears started flapping. His eyeglasses got bent out of shape. They had to take him into a lounge and get his composure back. When it came to her family, Nancy didn't pull no punches."

Her husband was mayor of Baltimore for three terms, ending in 1959, and eight years later her son Tommy became mayor. But it was a changed city by then. The racial balance turned dramatically, and so did the emotions attached to it.

EIGHT

THE MAN IN THE CLOSET

My father came home with dreams of making up for the lost war years, and quickly went to work for the Brown & Langer Company in Harlem. He stuffed sour pickles into glass jars. Then he ran a six-lane bowling alley in Manhattan, calling on my Uncle Dick to break away from his schoolwork to help out whenever one of the establishment's pinboys failed to show up. This didn't work out, either. Mob guys kept coming into the place to gamble, and my father found it unacceptable that such activity might take place in his presence without his own enthusiastic participation. My mother insisted he find another line of work. So we moved to Jersey City, New Jersey, and they ran a mail-order business for cigarettes and nylons, a natural since Jersey had no cigarette tax. The business went nowhere.

"You couldn't get jobs after the war," my mother remembered years later. "You couldn't get housing, and you couldn't get jobs. It was that way all over the country. And they weren't trained for anything."

"The pickle works," my Uncle Dick said, sitting across from my mother at a little kitchen table and chuckling at the memory. He worked at the factory with my father. "I think we were the only two white guys there."

"You used to stand in water all the time," said my mother, "with the wet feet."

"Pickle brine," my uncle corrected her. "Oy, what a dirty business. I vowed I'd never eat another pickle."

One afternoon in the Bronx in the summer of 1949, somewhere between the pickle factory job and the bowling alley job and the mail-order cigarettes and nylons, my father and my uncle played handball against a schoolyard wall. My uncle's back twisted and went into unrelievable spasms. A few days later, someone mentioned a chiropractor.

"What's that?" my uncle asked.

"They work on your muscles," he was told. "This guy's name is William Weisberg, and he's making a fortune."

My uncle went to him three times, at two dollars a visit. The chiropractic adjustments worked. My uncle attended New York University at this time, but my father, still looking for his ship to come in, heard about a school in Baltimore, the august-sounding Columbia College of Chiropractic, where he could learn this healing method and make a fabulous living at two dollars a visit like the famous Dr. Weisberg. So we moved to Baltimore while he tried that for a while.

For the next four years, we lived in the government-subsidized Latrobe Housing Projects in East Baltimore. There were 700 apartment units. The projects were hilly, crowded, busy, and trash-laden. The trash seemed to collect like some endemic fungus, on streets, on sidewalks, in bushes, and in the development's cement courtyards. The projects consisted of a series of these courtyards with a line of red-brick box-like apartments around each court. Residents tended to be families trying to find themselves after the war, or those whose history seemed lost and floundering at least since the Depression.

It was a place and an era where men in trucks still made daily house calls. They poured coal into furnaces. They delivered ice for all those with no refrigerators, splitting the air each morning with operatic cries: "Ice maaaaan!" Men in snappy white uniforms delivered Cloverland Milk to people's homes and others delivered Bond Bread. Women hung their family's apparel on outdoor clotheslines without fearing it would vanish. A little corner grocery store at Stirling and Ensor Streets had pungent onions and pickles floating in a barrel and sold crabcakes for twenty cents apiece and summertime snowballs, chopped ice with flavoring, for a nickel. Running boards on cars were beginning to disappear, but boys still scuttled through the streets on homemade scooters that were nothing more than pieces of wood hammered atop rollerskate wheels. Johnny Ray was the raciest thing on the radio, which was not yet monopolized by rock and roll, and television was beginning to take over people's evenings. "Say, kids, what time is it?" asked a man called Buffalo Bob at 5:30 each day, summoning millions of children to the new national campfire. We had no television when we arrived in the projects, but we had a few neighbors with TV sets, and their closeness added to the allure of this new medium, just out of reach but for occasional tantalizing glimpses.

Where we lived, on Abbott Court, residents walked to one end of a concrete courtyard to drop their trash into large community dumpsters, and went to the other end to pray at the altar of the Church of St. James, located on hilly Aisquith Street immediately above the Institute of Notre Dame, the school once attended by the future Nancy D'Alesandro, the same school where young Barbara Mikulski's parents now sent her every day from Highlandtown.

My family lived on the GI Bill, which gave millions of men a shot at an education or a little money to put down on a house in newly created suburban neighborhoods. Every month a government check for $120 arrived in the mail, enough to survive with occasional lettuce and tomato sandwiches for school lunch, and a slight amount of nerve. One month the check was late. We were completely out of food, and thirty cents was all that separated us from empty pockets.

"The hell with it," my mother declared. She took the thirty cents and walked across the courtyard to the tiny grocery store on Stirling Street and purchased a pack of Camel Cigarettes for eighteen cents. If she was going to go to the poorhouse, she would do it with a cigarette dangling from her lips like a gutsy movie dame. The next morning a small survival check from the government arrived.

The projects were a mess, but it was the only world I knew so I thought it was fine. We played games of tag and kick-the-can, and cowboys and In-

The author's parents, Selma and Sgt. Lionel Olesker, on their wedding day, having survived an introductory snowball in the face. The bride rode a train from the Bronx to Baton Rouge, Louisiana, for the ceremony; the groom was soon on his way to the fighting in Europe.

dians. Or we played war. This consisted of aiming imaginary rifles and hand grenades at the German army, or the Koreans, or whomever America was now fighting, to keep them from establishing a strategic military foothold in the 1100 block of Abbott Court.

"Your father fought in the war," my mother told me on occasion.

"You did?" I asked my father.

He nodded, and suggested I finish my breakfast.

"He was in the Air Force," my mother said.

My father said little about it. But simply knowing he had served represented a kind of citizenship. I saw war movies on Saturday afternoons at the Apollo movie theater. They connected me to something, even though the movie wars seemed heroic and glamorous, and my father was now living in poverty in government-subsidized Baltimore. Was this where the war planes landed after they had flown off into the sunset? My mother showed me a few medals he had won, but my father never discussed them. They seemed part of a history that belonged to some other fellow.

Compared to others in the projects, our lives seemed pretty secure. I had friends poor enough that they shared chewing gum with each other. A boy named Jerry would chew for a few minutes and then hand it over to his sister Davona to finish it off. Sometimes there were angry words: "Hey, save me some flavor." Then they might smack one another, each certain they were being cheated. The most consistent and hurtful insult hurled by one child at another in the projects: "Trash picker." It hit close to the bone. Sometimes children walked a few blocks up Aisquith Street, to the Bond Bread bakery where its ovens gave off a heavenly aroma, to search barrels for stale buns that had been thrown away. Others casually picked through neighborhood dumpsters for items they might carry to the junk dealer a few blocks below the projects. Mainly, though, the "trash picker" characterization referred to winos who sometimes staggered by and sifted through trashcans, oblivious to all eyes watching them.

One summer evening a hopeless, grizzled fellow stumbled along Aisquith Street until he reached the front steps of the church, where he silently emptied his pockets of all his money. Hair matted, teeth gone, he dropped everything in the gutter, where it lay only a few seconds before a mad scramble of kids from our courtyard fought for the coins while the poor fellow walked a few steps off and then collided with the sidewalk. I ducked into the melee reaching for the old man's money, and then ducked back out. There was a ferocity inside the scramble that jolted me; I had no money in my own pockets, but these kids were ravenous for it, and I would not get in their way.

There was one other use for trashcans in the neighborhood. At Abbott Court, before the changeover to the big dumpsters, there were rectangular metal cans, about four feet high, which some of the bigger kids, beginning to approach adolescence and desiring some privacy, would turn onto their sides. Then they created exotic domestic areas inside, complete with pillows and blankets and no parental figures to monitor their behavior. They were simply playing house, and it did not feel out of place to them to keep house inside an available trashcan.

When my father saw me near these makeshift domiciles, he ordered me away. He did this while rushing to go to class or to the YMCA where he played handball. I waited until he faded from sight and then went back to the trashcans with the other neighborhood kids, though the older ones tended to eye me warily and make me feel unwelcome. Something private was going on in the trashcan forts, something out of my depth, something to do with bodies in heat.

Many of these children had no known fathers to issue stay-away orders the way my father did. Tommy and Johnny across the court had no father, and Harold a few doors away had none, nor did Melva who played with Jimmy and Martha, who also had none. My friend Jerry had a known father, but he was known mainly for drinking whiskey and turning mean, thereupon smacking hell out of his children in front of all those sitting on their front stoops on humid summer evenings, after which the children ran off somewhere to hide their humiliation.

All of the residents of the projects were white. Their rent was twenty-nine dollars a month. The projects were ringed by mournful, decaying, ramshackle rowhouse apartments whose tenants were black. Their rent was too much, whatever it was.

I walked past these homes each morning on my way to P.S. 20 with a boy named Billy McKnight, who had a pale, freckled face and lived next door to our apartment at 1103 Abbott Court with his sister, Evelyn, and his mother and a man they called Gross. Billy was a year older than I, and passed on much useful information, such as the business that went on inside the Maryland Penitentiary, which hovered over the west side of the projects, facing the Church of St. James on Aisquith Street on the east side.

"Swear to Christ," he said one day.

From Christ, I knew from nothing. He was a word I heard, a name inscribed on the big church where many of the gentile families in the neighborhood went to pray on Sunday mornings. Or he was the middle syllable my father employed when ticked off: "Fuhchrissake," he would bark, seeming, even in some burst of anger, to appreciate the very clang the word made. Or he was the one, this Christ, whose name was invoked by Billy as an apparent gesture of authority whenever there was a difference of opinion.

"Up there," he said, pointing toward a spot high above the penitentiary.

"No," I said.

"Swear to Christ."

Or else Christ was part of a name: Young Men's Christian Association, where my Uncle Dick worked part-time and my father played handball several times a week, each a token Jew amid a flotilla of hearty, good-humored gentiles. My uncle, after finishing college at New York University, moved in with us in the projects while he attended Columbia College of Chiropractic. On Saturdays the two of them took me along to the YMCA, where my uncle worked in the Y's Health Club, giving deep massage mixed with chiropractic subtleties to men's aching muscles while my father play handball and I watched from a ledge high over the court's rear wall.

On many Saturday afternoons my father's doubles partner was a man who wore sneakers and a jock strap with nothing over it. His name was the Reverend John Hetteman. He was given to much expectorating into a spittoon kept for such occasions, placed discreetly in a little doorway separating the Y's two handball courts.

"Baptizing the spittoon," Father Hetteman called out merrily, whenever he let loose with a wet one.

The good father was said to be a man of Christ, though I had no idea what this meant. I wondered if he was the same Christ mentioned by Billy McKnight on the day he told me the story about the penitentiary.

"Up there," Billy said.

We sat on the front stoop of our adjoining apartments one grey autumn afternoon. From Billy's apartment, you could hear his sister Evelyn singing along with the radio, where rock and roll was beginning to enter our little corner of East Baltimore:

"*Sh-boom, sh-boom*
Yadadadada dadadadada,
Sh-boom, Sh-boom . . ."

"No," I said.

Between the music washing over our stoop, and the unnerving revelation passed on by Billy, I seemed to be suffering a kind of sensory overload.

"Swear to Christ," he said.

He pointed to the nearby penitentiary, a fortress of blackened stone whose guard tower high above the large complex of prison buildings seemed to cast a symbolic shadow over the neighborhood, matched only by the church shadow from the other side, each a reminder that we were being watched, and each a muscular symbol of the battle for our very souls.

"That's where they keep the witch," Billy said, gesturing toward the prison watchtower.

"No."

"Swear to Christ," he said. "If they catch you doing something bad, they take you up there and you have to see the witch."

I imagined a gnarled one-woman branch of the Maryland penal system who offered no last-minute plea bargains to those sent to her, a heartless Disney cartoon shrew brought to life who condemned her victims to spend eternity with those dangerous men behind the prison's walls.

"No," I said again, though I wasn't sure.

"Wanna bet?" Billy extended a bent pinkie to make the wager official. I mulled this over, looking toward the courtyard from the front stoop we shared. I felt I knew a little bit about the penitentiary because my father and my uncle and I sometimes strolled outside the old cobblestone walls of the prison and the adjacent Baltimore City Jail on Sunday mornings.

On occasion, my father and uncle went inside the prison. On the Jewish high holidays, they helped form a *minyan* because there weren't enough Jewish inmates for a full ten-man service without outside help. They sang the *Adon Olom* with a Jewish murderer. They read the *Shemah* with some Jewish swindlers, and with a Jewish gambler they recited the Kaddish. About witches, they had failed to utter a syllable in my presence.

Nevertheless, Billy stood confidently by his story. He was a fellow of experience, and I was just a little guy. Maybe he knew something. Maybe my father and my uncle had been introduced to the witch during a special Rosh Hashanah holiday tour of the prison and tried to protect me by keeping it a secret. They did such things. Whenever my parents or my uncle wanted me not to know something, they spoke to each other in Yiddish.

"What does it mean?" I asked.

"If we wanted you to know, we would tell you," they replied, invoking the ancient gesture of love and secrecy of all ethnic persuasions.

I wondered if they had kept the witch from me by speaking about her in Yiddish. From the front stoop, I looked across the cement courtyard that sat between rows of apartments and saw some of the Decker kids. There were six of them, each with a nickname—Chappy, Bubby, Doll, each name cuter and more cloying than the next—and a father who worked as a guard at the penitentiary but had never mentioned any witch-in-residence.

"Why don't we ask them?"

"They don't know nothing," Billy said.

I felt hemmed in. To my left, the image of the witch. To my right, the shadow of the church. Inside the church was a huge congregation hall and an imposing visage of a bearded man that took up most of one wall. I saw it one summer evening when the church's front doors were wide open. A wedding was being conducted, and an organ played loudly. I walked a few feet inside with a couple of kids from the neighborhood. I had never seen a man's image so enormous, and turned away with a sense of intimidation so deep that I could not ask anyone what I had seen. But these friends of mine, elementary school children like me, visited the church regularly, on Sundays and on holidays not linked to my own life, and sat beneath the overpowering image of this man and were not intimidated. They seemed to be made of braver stuff than I. And I was intimidated by that, too.

"Why don't we go to a church?" I asked once.

"We're Jewish," my mother answered pleasantly. "Jews don't go to church."

The answer offered relief—I wouldn't have to sit beneath that frightening image; I could play Sunday morning war games in my room, bravely standing watch over the neighborhood from a corner window in case enemy soldiers invaded via Stirling Street, while my gentile friends gathered in prayer. But it also brought a sense of isolation. What was a Jew? Sometimes my Uncle Dick made up comic stories about "the great Jewish cowboy, Tex Goldenfarb." Cowboys, I knew—but, Jewish? One spring morning, my father read a story to me from a book with strange colorful pictures. The story was about a man named Moses leading the Jews to their freedom. We were Jews; thus, it turned out, I was a part of something, even though this story occurred many years ago, a time before cars and television, and didn't seem to connect with anything identifiable in the projects or with anyone I knew at school.

One night I slept at a friend's apartment. At bedtime the friend's mother told us it was time for prayers. I was comfortable enough with that. Each evening, I said the familiar children's prayer, "Now I lay me down to sleep," as my mother looked on. But I was going for the full performance in front of my friend's mother, and knelt by the side of the bed with my hands clasped in front of my face.

"We don't pray that way," the friend's mother said.

Neither did I. But I'd seen that image of the kneeling child in countless books and magazines and Christmas advertisements. I had assumed I was the only child who did not pray that way—the American, brand-name products, commercial way—and so I was acting out that image to show my friend's mother that I knew the procedure, that I'd been tutored properly, that I was like any other child.

"Swear to Christ," Billy McKnight always said.

I was just trying to do the next best thing.

Billy and I walked to school each morning while my mother stood in the doorway and tried to hide her anxiety. We trudged up Aisquith Street past dark and crumbling rowhouses rented to colored people. The little one-story buildings seemed to be standing only by some act of whimsy. In mild weather their doors were opened to allow any random gasps of air to enter. This allowed peeks into living rooms tiny and unpainted and shabbily furnished. The sun never seemed to shine on this street; it existed in perpetual shadow, even on the brightest of days. At least, that is my recollection.

"Mawnin'," the women of these homes said as we walked past.

It wasn't "morning," but "mawnin'," an accent previously unheard, which added to the foreign effect of their dark skin. But they were so unfailingly pleasant that, on the rare occasion when one woman neglected to say "mawnin'," I wondered if I should feel offended. I had no idea they were greeting me out of not only friendliness but also a sense of cautionary manners passed down through generations of the American caste system.

Sometimes some of their children ventured tentatively down into the projects for games of war or tag. We gathered in a circle and extended one foot toward the center and somebody, invariably one of the bigger white kids because they seemed to have authority in these matters, would chant:

"Eeenie, meenie, miney, moe
Catch a nigger by his toe . . ."

I could feel myself cringe at the word—I had heard it used contemptuously by adults in the neighborhood—though I understood its meaning about as well as I understood the word "Christ." But the colored boys' and girls' faces were deadpan. *Nigger* was still just a word to them, not necessarily attached yet to the full range of official cruelties that would order their lives. They ignored it, or accepted it as a small price to pay for inclusion in the white children's games of tag, or stored it in some memory bank.

But I never saw any of these colored children at school, where all but one of my classmates was a white gentile American.

"Why is that?" I asked Billy one day.

"Boy, are you dumb," he said dismissively. "Niggers don't go to white schools."

The message was simple. We may lunge for a few coins dumped by a forlorn wino in front of a church; we may turn our trashcans into hovels of domesticity; we may call each other "trash picker." But no one will deny us our skin color and call us by some other name.

Walking to school each morning Billy and I trudged past the colored homes until Aisquith Street blended into Harford Avenue. We passed the Bond Bread bakery with the thrown-out buns in trashcans, and the Apollo Theatre where we went to war movies on Saturday afternoons.

Then, turning right on Federal Street just past the Apollo, we came to P.S. 20. Boys played buck-buck against a wall, or chased girls across a cement playground and held them behind the swinging gate of a fence at recess. A classmate in leg braces named Robert Harriss guarded them there. Then we raced out to capture more girls, careful not to alert any members of the school's Safety Patrol. Cotton Belts, Billy McKnight called them derisively. One of the captured girls was named Marie White.

At day's end, Billy and I left school together. We ran the rooftops home, schoolbooks in our arms, atop a line of second-hand shops and battered rowhouses that began just below the Apollo Theatre. As we raced across these rooftops, I imagined prison breaks out of the movies. I imagined myself heroically rescuing Marie White from the gated fence, with husky Safety Patrol officers pursuing us.

From the roof, I could see the penitentiary, and the jail, and the watch-tower with Billy McKnight's witch. I could see rooftops and treetops and tall buildings in the distance. From up here, I saw what appeared to be all of known America.

We descended by shinnying down a narrow gap between two buildings, the last available area where no one could spot us and arrest us for rooftop running, and send us off to see the penitentiary witch. There was a slender ledge to plant one foot, and a tiny patch of ground beneath that. And there was an exposed electrical wire, which I did not see. The wire hit my body, and sent a jolt that lifted me across the space and into a wall. A minute earlier, on the roof, I thought I had been gazing happily at America in her fulsomeness. Now I was shocked back into my own existence.

"Billy, I'm gonna die," I said.

"No, you ain't," he said, spotting the wire. "It's just an electric shock. See?"

I didn't want to look. A white light flooded my head. All of my nerve endings seemed to be standing at attention. Maybe I was already dead. I seemed removed from the moment, and my own words seemed to arrive from some other place. I wanted to lie down and sleep in this space, instead of going home to tell my mother the bad news. In a world of witches in prison towers, of winos and trash pickers, her son Michael was about to leave this earth.

I stopped crying when Billy threatened to slug me. The world would go on, after all. I picked up my schoolbooks from the ground, and the two of us walked down Harford Avenue and crossed Chase, where Harford became Aisquith, and we passed the row of homes where the colored families had their front doors open, waiting for a stray breeze. And we entered the white projects a block below that.

I had seen other colored people. There were some on Gay Street, where my mother and I walked to buy groceries. And, toward the end of our stay in the projects, when my father was beginning to make a slight living in real estate and leaving the notion of a chiropractic practice behind, my parents hired a Negro cleaning woman once a week named Leah Freeman. She was sweet and toothless, and was paid six dollars a day.

And there was a colored man. His name was Shorty, and he sat in a closet at the YMCA, with a shoeshine stand. I saw him there on Saturdays when I went into the basement area called the Health Club where my uncle gave deep-muscle massages. On one side of the room were two rubbing tables. My uncle stood over one, and an older man named Lee Halfpenny, who ran the place and coached amateur boxers in his spare time, stood over the other and did thirty seconds of shadowboxing every time a bell went off, telling men who were lying under sunlamps for tanning that it was time to take the plastic cups from their eyes and turn over. Also, there were two steam boxes in the room, square white structures with heat lamps inside where men squatted to sweat off excess poundage.

And there was Shorty's closet.

Shorty was a diminutive black man who sat in his closet and never seemed to come out. Sometimes I stood by the nearby rubbing tables and looked in at him, sitting under his dim closet light, and wondered if he was ever allowed out. The closet was dark enough that I couldn't see everything in it. Sometimes I sensed nothing but Shorty's eyes. Did he have food in there? Was there a back door, through which he might leave and meet other dark-skinned people?

Shorty seemed to be a kind of trapped animal. When I arrived, he was sitting silently at his shoeshine stand, and when I came back from watching my father play handball or swimming in the YMCA pool, he was still there, silent but for the rare moments when Lee Halfpenny would call to him in a voice that mixed good nature and veiled bullying.

"Shorty, make yourself a quarter," Halfpenny would say, implying Shorty should work a little harder, even if it was just for twenty-five cents, the going price on a shoeshine.

"I already got a quarter, Mr. Lee," Shorty replied from the darkness, implying he wasn't asking much out of life, and also playing along with the joke: I'm not much, I'm only a colored guy, I'm satisfied with what I have.

I saw Shorty outside his closet only one time, in a small sitting area near the Health Club, leafing quickly through the pages of a magazine on a table between two couches. He was standing. I wondered if he would get into trouble if anyone spotted him outside his closet. How could he get back into the closet without Halfpenny and the other men seeing that he had escaped? These weren't intentionally bad men at the YMCA, who would take pleasure in demeaning another man. They were products of a time and a mindset and an entrenched system whose rules were written long before their own time. Shorty was black, and therefore he was different. The YMCA was for white Christian men, and a few token Jews, but certainly no place for blacks. This was an established fact, reinforced by common practices of the time.

In the local newspapers classified ads for apartments stipulated race. The employment ads did the same. The papers' crime stories routinely carried headlines that said: "Negro Arrested." Even the government-subsidized housing projects were segregated.

Distinctions were made; that was all. That was how second-class citizenship for black people was justified by civilized, first-class citizens who were white: they have their world, and we have ours. And those who disagreed were just beginning to find their voice, or the courage behind their voice.

In such an atmosphere Billy McKnight's remark made a certain awkward sense; the colored had their schools—though I had no idea where these might be—and we had ours. I was part of that "we," though I seemed to have gotten in on a pass. I was not part of it on Sunday mornings when my neighbors went to church, nor on the American holidays of Christmas and Easter, but I was a kind of part-time honorary American, subject to review at any time.

But then a door opened. One afternoon at School 20, several classes were ushered into a large room to sit cross-legged on a bare floor and watch a twenty-minute movie short. It was called *The House I Live In,* and starred Frank Sinatra. The movie had been made in 1944. It opened with a boy running down an alley, pursued by a gang of about ten kids.

In the winter of 1999 I watched this movie again. The boy had a small cap on his head that could have been a yarmulke. As he reached a wall, hemmed in by these angry kids, his cap fell off and was not seen again. The point had been made but was not belabored. In 1999 I began to connect faces. I knew that kid, I'd seen him somewhere else.

In *The House I Live In,* Frank Sinatra emerges from a recording studio, taking a cigarette break between songs, just as the gang gets ready to beat hell out of this boy.

"Somebody in for a licking?" he asks, positioning himself between the young thugs and the outsider.

"You bet," says one particularly obnoxious boy. "We're gonna smear him."

"Yeah, but ten against one, it's not very fair," Sinatra says. He says this so gently, with such consummate good grace, that the kids are becalmed.

"We don't like him," a second boy sneers, gesturing toward the outsider, who's plastered against the wall behind Sinatra. I knew that face, I'd seen him somewhere not long ago.

"We don't want him in our neighborhood or going to our school," another kid says.

"What's he got, smallpox or something?" Sinatra asks.

"We don't like his religion," he is told.

"His religion?" Sinatra seems utterly stunned, and says the words slowly, as though finding them impossible to digest in a place such as America.

"Look, mister," another kid says, "he's a dirty . . ."

"Now, hold on," Sinatra says. "I see what some of you mean. You must be some of those Nazi werewolves I've been hearing about."

It was 1953 when I saw this for the first time. I was eight years old and had only heard this term, "Nazi," hollered in our neighborhood war games, without understanding exactly what it meant. But I knew what Sinatra was getting at, and found it thrilling.

"Not me," says another boy. "My father's a sergeant in the Army. He's been wounded, even."

"Say, I bet he got some of that blood plasma," Sinatra says.

"Three times."

Sinatra turns to the outsider, still pressed against the wall behind him. In the winter of 1999 I knew that face, it was someone searching for a friend in a strange place. "Son," Sinatra asks, "anybody in your family ever go to the blood bank?"

"Sure, my mother and my father."

"You know what?" Sinatra says, turning back to the obnoxious punk, who seems to be softening slightly. "I betcha his pop's blood helped save your dad's life. That's bad."

"What's bad about it?"

"Well, don't you see? Your father doesn't go to the same church his father does. That's awful. Do you think, if he'd have known, he would rather have died than take blood from a man of another religion? Would you have wanted him to die? Would your mom have wanted him to die?"

The kid gulps, "No."

"Look, kids, religion makes no difference except to a Nazi or somebody that's stupid," Sinatra says. "People all over the world worship God in different ways."

Sitting in that schoolroom as a boy, listening to this civics lesson, a light went on in my head. Sinatra hadn't mentioned Jews by name, but he seemed to be handing over a passport to a kind of fuller citizenship than I had felt. Maybe I could slip into the country's heartland on a technicality.

But, half a century later, that boy behind him reminded me of another frightened face.

"This country's made up of hundreds of different kinds of people," Sinatra says. "And a hundred different ways of talking. And a hundred different ways of going to church. But they're all American ways."

He mentions Pearl Harbor to the boys, and how "the Japs really socked us so we could never do anything about it. But, a couple of days later, something very important happened."

He tells them about a Japanese battleship. Sitting in that schoolroom fifty years earlier, I saw a ship on the movie screen, and an American airplane heading toward it with flak bursting all around. My father flew in such a plane in the Army Air Force.

They sank that ship, Sinatra says, "and every American felt much better. The pilot of that plane was named Colin Kelly, an American and a Presbyterian. And you know who dropped the bomb? Meyer Levin—an American and a Jew. You think maybe they should have called the bombing off because they had different religions? Think of that, fellas. Use your good American brains."

And then, this being Frank Sinatra, he began to sing.

"*What is America to me?*"

His face was a mass of knobs stuck atop an Adam's apple, but his voice seemed to belong to the handsomest man on earth. He sang of the house he lived in. He sang of the grocer and the butcher, of children in the playground, of

"*all races and religions*
that's America to me."

And, in the winter of 1999, I now knew the face of that boy in the alley behind Sinatra. It was Felix Guevara's in the courthouse hallway, hemmed in by strangers shouting at him in a language he did not understand. He seemed to be thinking: What do they want from me? He was that kid in the alley in the Sinatra movie, wondering what he has done to deserve this, wondering how to find safety in a strange place, wondering why this is not the America he had heard about in El Salvador.

"I want to go home," Guevara said in the crush of bodies in that hallway.

But where is home? The America we hear about—the country of myth and song, of those who find the bright lights of Times Square and can pronounce it properly, and of movie heroes who save the day in the last reel and don't live out their lives in a housing project when the war is over—this is a place that seemed just out of reach in the Latrobe Housing Projects, and just out of reach to Felix Guevara so many years later.

NINE

MICHELE AND JAKE

One morning in the spring of 1954 John Jacob "Jake" Oliver Jr. heard the historic news about school integration and did not know what to make of it. He was nine years old. The news was delivered to him as he sat in Miss Johnson's classroom at P.S. 112, Calhoun and Laurens Streets, in West Baltimore. Shirley Johnson, in her first year of teaching, was a graduate of segregated public schools and the all-black Coppin State Teachers College. She was, as they say, an educated woman. And she did not know what to make of the news either.

The U.S. Supreme Court, in a decision known as *Brown vs. the Board of Education of Topeka, Kansas,* declared that America's public schools could no longer be separated by race. Thus, in thousands of places such as the Latrobe housing projects, where white children left their homes each day and walked through black neighborhoods to public schools that did not allow black children to enter the building, this would change. Now all children who lived near the same public school would attend that school together, no matter the color of their skin. Or they would move to distant suburban neighborhoods, in their parents' belief that they could outrun the American future.

On that May morning in 1954, Shirley Johnson had not yet figured out the impact of such a legal landmark. It was too early. Much later, at the opening of a new century, having had nearly fifty years to ponder it, both she and the rest of the country were still trying to figure it out. But that morning, as Johnson stood before her young students, she felt she had to say something.

"Does everyone know about Washington?" she asked. "It's our nation's capital." She stared into blank faces.

"Do you know what that means?" she asked. "It's the place where they make the laws that we live by."

The blank faces did not change. The schools would be integrated now, she said. Their lives would be changing. Next fall, she told the children, some of you will go to school with little white boys and girls, and some little white children will be coming to this school to be your classmates here.

At his desk, Jake Oliver listened to his teacher talk about this for a few minutes, and he began to think about images across the color line.

"We had experienced white folks," he remembered years later.

There was a reason for this. For generations in Baltimore, blacks moved into rundown neighborhoods as whites discarded them to move elsewhere. In West Baltimore, in an area bounded by North Avenue on the north, Franklin Street on the south, and Madison and Fulton on the east and west, blacks moved into homes previously owned by German Catholics and German Jews. Schools that had been English-German in the mid-nineteenth century became African American schools by the turn of the century. Like the homes, the schools tended to be run down by the time black children moved in.

Many of these blacks had moved there late in the nineteenth century from South Baltimore, from neighborhoods terribly overcrowded, and filthy. The rate of epidemic disease was frighteningly high in homes around the harbor. Then, in the early years of the new century, more South Baltimore blacks moved to the west side, having been displaced when their homes were torn down to expand the Camden Railroad Station.

When they reached West Baltimore, the poor moved into dilapidated apartments. Many had no running water and no indoor bathrooms. They had leaky roofs and cracked walls that let in the wind and rain. In the early part of the twentieth century, those with any money—professional people such as preachers, teachers, and undertakers—moved into homes on Druid Hill Avenue that still contained hints of a vanishing gentility.

But most blacks were poor, and powerless to change it. The largest black labor union was the stevedores' and the best-paid laborers were the hod carriers who worked with white bricklayers and plasterers. The building crafts kept blacks out. There were black wagon owners who moved furniture, coal, and ice, rags and bottles and junk. They were driving these wagons when whites were driving trucks. Black women were servants, unless they were lucky enough to get factory work, where they were paid less than white workers and often entered through separate doors and worked on separate floors.

Many black people simply snatched part-time jobs when they became available. A Depression-era Urban League study estimated perhaps 700 black-owned businesses in the entire city—but they were small operations, barbers or hairdressers or pool-hall operators. Only a handful of businesses had more than six employees. The *Afro-American* was one. Not until World War II could blacks find work as busdrivers or police or firefighters. Even at the height of the war, when Bethlehem Steel tried to hire fifteen black riveters, thousands of white employees responded by walking out. There were more than 200 black churches—but many were tiny congregations of people who huddled together, praising the Lord but also seeking mutual sustenance when there seemed nowhere else to turn. Even some Baltimore hospitals had separate accommodations, while others simply did not accept black patients.

Then, between the two world wars, came changes. There were more teachers, more doctors, more real-estate owners. They pushed for new housing—and, as they did, whites tended to move further away, leaving behind their old, decaying schools—which were resegregated for black children. From World War II to the brink of the 1954 *Brown* decision, the number of Baltimore children increased by 50 percent. Classrooms were badly overcrowded. In the early 1920s a special commission had recommended demolition of nearly sixty dilapidated public schools. Three decades later, more than half were still in use—as colored schools.

The Olivers lived at 1835 Madison Avenue, which felt to Jake Oliver like the heart of a village. In his mind, his family knew everyone, and everyone seemed to know his family. When he or his sister Marilyn walked out of their house, they sensed protective eyes watching them everywhere in the neighborhood. Also, he felt vaguely special. Oliver's mother, Marye, was descended from the founder of the *Afro-American,* and his father was president of the company and ran the production side of the twice-weekly newspaper. Their lives were confidently fixed at Madison Avenue near Eutaw Street, and also within the confines of a newspaper devoted to the lives of black people such as themselves.

But Eutaw Street cut into Linden Avenue, and on Linden Avenue there were white people. Hillbillies, his people called these whites. They were poor, and some of them had arrived in Baltimore in the war years when jobs were plentiful. Then they had stayed around. These white people seemed, to Oliver, out of their minds.

"As you went toward North Avenue, toward the old Nate's and Leon's Restaurant and Read's Drug Store, you saw a lot of white folks," he recalled one night. "We had to walk a two-block course on North Avenue. Invariably, you'd see violence. They'd get in fights, and blood would be flowing everywhere. It was white on white, somebody saying something about a guy's wife or something. But it was real fighting, and you'd see real blood. Walking up to Read's Drug Store one day with a couple of kids from the block, and some guy came out of the house on the corner and he was coated with blood. He'd been in a fight. We just stood there and looked. We said, 'Wow, *they do this.*' And then, of course, there was Emmett Till." Till was a black man hanged from a Mississippi tree for talking to a white woman. "We said, 'My God.' So when they actually started moving us into white schools, you know, we weren't sure this was a good thing."

More than four decades later, he laughed for a moment at the memory of his anxiety. He was a skinny little boy then, and now he was grey-haired and well tailored. He had been through a few difficult surgical procedures for collapsed lungs. Only a few years earlier, he had moved out of the old family home on Madison Avenue into a large house with land in a stately section of suburban Baltimore County.

We sat at a table in Baltimore's plush Center Club, where Oliver was a member. It was a chilly March night, and our table overlooked some of the

John Jacob "Jake" Oliver (*back row, far left*) in his West Baltimore Little League days. The future publisher of the *Afro-American* newspaper hit a baseball only slightly better than he hit a punchball at Garrison Junior High School. Courtesy of Jake Oliver

city's modern pleasures: the Inner Harbor tourist area, the ballparks, the waterfront neighborhoods where young professionals were moving into pricey renovated rowhouses once rented to working-class immigrant families fresh off the boat. At our elbows a uniformed white waiter offered a choice of salmon or crabcakes as a dinner appetizer. The people who preceded Jake Oliver at the *Afro-American* could not have conceived of such a world inviting their attendance.

At fifty-five Oliver was now publisher of the newspaper. It was an impressive title with a rickety foundation. He was also president of the Black Media Alliance, the coalition of African American newspaper and broadcast types from around the country. This was another vulnerable enterprise. He was an attorney by profession, educated at Columbia University School of Law, who had worked in major legal firms and eyed the prospects of considerable money—and had walked away from it to try to keep a history alive.

All around the country, black-owned media were paying the price for assimilation. The country was integrated, or professed to be. Daily newspapers that once ignored black readers now catered to them enough that publications such as the *Afro-American* had lost considerable numbers of readers and advertisers. Talented young reporters once drawn to black newspapers now found more lucrative work on mainstream dailies. Oliver had grown up in a time when the country's leaders talked of integration. He had come of age when such notions were challenged by ideas of black nationalism. Now he attempted to offer a tricky balance to readers who were divided over which view to take: the melting pot, or two parallel worlds that sometimes touched convivially and sometimes kept a wary and suspicious distance.

In the spring of 2000 the *Afro-American* was 108 years old. It was founded by the Reverend William Alexander, pastor of Sharon Baptist Church, as a one-page weekly bulletin of community news. A few months after its birth, it was purchased at public auction by a man named John H. Murphy. He was fifty-two years old, a former slave set free by the Maryland Emancipation Act of 1863 who had enlisted in the Thirtieth Regiment Infantry, U.S. Colored Troops, Maryland Volunteers, and rose to the rank of first sergeant.

By 1892 Murphy was the Sunday School superintendent of the Hagerstown District of the African Methodist Episcopal Church, and published a newsletter of his own, the *Sunday School Helper,* from the basement of his home. With $200 borrowed from his wife, he bought the *Afro-American.*

Murphy ran the paper for thirty years and found an audience ravenous for a publication in which African Americans were perceived as citizens. The mainstream papers tended to ignore the black community, or described it in demeaning stereotypes, such as an article from August 12, 1906, in the Sunday *Sun,* in a column headlined, "Here in Baltimore."

"The race of colored washerwoman is dying out in Baltimore," the article declares. "According to authorities, cocaine and the steam laundries are to blame. A dozen years ago the spectacle of an ample-looking negress wobbling down the street with a basket of 'wash' on her head was a familiar one, but today it is rather rare. . . . Half a dozen years ago the colored washerwoman began to degenerate. . . . Idleness led her into rushing the beer can, and from the malt she passed on to 5-cent whiskey. Then the cocaine habit began to spread among the Africans of Baltimore. . . . It makes them dream fine dreams—and it engenders in them a growing distaste and incapacity for labor. . . . All of the steam laundries now make special rates for family 'wash.' They take it at so much a pound, and there is never any doubt that they will return it on schedule time. Of course, they don't wash half so well as the old-time darkey, but compared to that of the modern wash-lady, their work is very satisfactory. A steam laundry, at worst, never steals and never rubs cocaine on its gums."

Compared to this, the *Afro-American*'s reporting looked like the work of Joseph Pulitzer. When John Murphy died in 1922, the *Afro* was a twelve-page spread with the highest circulation of any black newspaper in the country, and a history that included a legendary deathbed imprecation by Murphy that the paper should always stay in the family's hands. His son, Carl, paying close attention, ran it as editor and publisher for the next forty-five years. When John Oliver Sr. died three decades later, having served as president of the company, his son Jake delivered the eulogy at the Madison Avenue Presbyterian Church. He remembered, "Daddy always said, 'As long as we have the paper, we have jobs for the family.'" The *Afro* was a sanctuary in many ways.

By midcentury, the company produced editions in eight cities with a circulation of more than 200,000. For many readers the *Afro* was a beacon in the wilderness. In the 1940s the paper lobbied for integration of both the armed services and major league baseball. Week after week it attacked Jim Crow practices. Its sports editor, Sam Lacy, accompanied baseball's Jackie Robinson on his odyssey, and was with him the morning Robinson awoke to find a cross burning outside his window. (Long past retirement age Lacy was still writing his sports column, and still focusing on social issues instead of simple athletic skills; when he finished writing his column, he would play nine holes of golf. He was approaching ninety-five years of age.)

In the 1950s the paper discovered Dr. Martin Luther King long before mainstream white publications. When King delivered his "I have a dream" speech in 1963, the paper ran several pages of coverage. Returning from the march, *Afro* reporter George W. Collins wrote, "It was as if voices from the graves of generations of an oppressed people joined in word and song with voice of the living and those yet unborn, and pleaded with God and man to right the wrong that has gone unchecked in America for centuries."

When Emmett Till was lynched in Mississippi, the *Afro* ran his story and his photograph on page one. Jake Oliver saw it when he came home from school.

"That's when everything awoke in me," he said that night at the Center Club. It was an odd juxtaposition, sitting high atop the city's glitter and talking about a man swinging from a Mississippi tree limb nearly fifty years earlier. But, even now, the memory moved him.

"In fact," he said, "Emmett Till is probably the thing that woke up all the black male recognition of race in my generation. You didn't hear about it, you saw it on the front page of the *Afro,* you saw what they did to him." His voice swelled and broke, and he looked away. "My father brought the paper home and put it on the coffeetable," he said. "I don't think I looked at anything else for two days. I asked everybody, 'Why?' And that's when they began to tell me about the power of racism and the role of the paper. And the paper's mission to stop such things."

He heard most of it from his mother, an elementary school teacher who was the great-granddaughter of the founder, John Murphy. Oliver's father ran the paper's production operation, which absorbed most of his time when Jake was growing up. John Sr. was constantly focused on deadlines. When he came home, he grunted hello, changed his clothes, and went back to the paper for meetings, for production problems, for crises involving printing presses or the supply of paper rolls or some editor trying to squeeze in a late-breaking story when the clock in the battered, turn-of-the-century news-room on Eutaw Street said it was too late to remake the front page.

When the announcement came, in May of 1954, that the nation's schools were now to be racially integrated, the city of Baltimore braced itself. The school board quickly ordered "desegregation in compliance with the law." In the public schools of that time, there were 87,000 white children and 57,000 black children. Of these, only about 1,800 black children—about 2 percent—immediately transferred into white schools.

Two years later, when he was a fifth-grader, Jake Oliver learned he would be transferred to a new elementary school, at North and Linden. This school was integrated. His own feelings were mixed, but his mother's were not. She understood there was a world beyond their little village at Madison and Eutaw.

For many black families, this would have seemed a revelation. There was their West Baltimore, and somewhere beyond it was the rest of America. In that America there were clean and productive schools. In Baltimore the notion of comparable schools could not have been mentioned without muffled laughter from whites. In the pre–World War II years the colored schools taught vocational skills—but no construction skills were taught, except carpentry, and no new crafts such as radio or automotive work. The only subjects for girls were trade cookery and cafeteria service. A 1934 school-board report explained, "A public school must be careful not to train pupils for such skills as to upset a usually neurotic labor market."

There was one more tell-tale discrimination. Though the public schools were funded by the state, the funding formula was rigged. School taxes paid by whites went to white schools, and school taxes paid by blacks went to black schools. Since blacks had far less money, so did their schools. "Separate but equal" this would be called by white people arguing for continued segregation.

"It was strange, come to think of it," Jake remembered of his first year at an integrated elementary school. "Everybody was sort of friendly. The kids all lived in the area, and you got to know some of them, and some you didn't. There were maybe seven black kids in my class. And Miss Shields, a matronly old white lady, was the teacher. She worked real hard with every kid in the class, and I didn't sense any prejudice at all with her. It was fine. I wasn't intimidated at all."

For several years, city officials congratulated themselves on the lack of any violence over integration. But white people responded in other ways. From 1954 to 1970 white children withdrew from Baltimore public schools at the rate of 10,000 a year. Then the rate slowed—because most of them were gone.

Jake's mother, Marye Oliver, had familiarity with white Baltimore. At midcentury, blacks could not yet try on clothing in department stores or eat in certain restaurants. But his mother and her sisters were sufficiently light-skinned to pass. They went to department stores and tried on outfits to their hearts' content. They sat in restaurants and movies, just like citizens. Sometimes Oliver's mother took him shopping at the integrated Lexington Market. White women would approach his mother.

"What are you doing with that little black boy?" one asked. Jake was dark, like his father.

"He's mine," his mother said, "and I am just as dark as he is."

"They'd look at her," Oliver remembered, "like she was crazy. But that's how light she was. My father, there was no doubt." He toyed with his food for a moment. "You know, there was a whole thing with skin tone. And I was, my family was, was not . . ." He paused to pick his words carefully. "We were sort of exempt from it, but then again we weren't because we were part of the Murphys."

Among the Murphys were well-known executives at the *Afro-American*, as well as Oliver's uncle, William Murphy Sr., who became a District Court judge; a cousin, Arthur Murphy, who became a high-profile political analyst; and another cousin, William "Billy" Murphy Jr., who ran unsuccessfully for mayor of Baltimore.

Now, on this winter night years later, Jake Oliver sat at the Center Club and remembered when racial divisions meant not only black and white, but shades of black.

"I was darker than a lot of my cousins," he said, "and sometimes I felt I wasn't treated fairly. Because of that, yeah. The skin-tone thing. But that was the nature of the entire society."

He remembered wanting to see *Forbidden Planet* sometime in the 1950s. The *Star Wars* of its day, he called it. The movie played at the Town Theatre. But the Town had segregated seating. His cousins could pass, but Jake could only be admitted if he sat in the balcony. The indignity stayed with him: not just the segregation, but the value of skin tone within the black community.

"Hell," he said, "when we were in high school, there was a rumor you couldn't get into Howard University unless you were light. Like they would automatically turn you down, like there was some kind of weeding-out process of dark-skinned blacks, in order to improve the race. 'To improve the race.' That's what we were hearing, and we were really hung up on it."

Only a few blocks from Oliver's home, also on Madison Avenue, a girl named Michele Winder lived with her older brother, Michael, and her mother and grandmother. The mother worked for the telephone company, a rarity for a black woman in that time. The father, divorced, was somewhere else. The father's mother was a white German woman.

Michele Winder was Jake Oliver's age, and she would become his future classmate—and mine. In the mid-1950s she had her own experience at the movies. She and her brother were light-skinned like their father. One day her mother said, "Let's go to the Rialto Theatre." West Baltimore's Rialto allowed no blacks.

Mrs. Winder said, "I'm gonna scrub you guys and take you to that movie theater." The scrubbing seemed, even then, a subconscious act of attempting to lighten her children's skin beyond any questioning by the white people who ran the Rialto.

"Don't say anything to anybody," she told the children.

They sat in a corner of the theater, bracing themselves through the afternoon. The movie itself was later blocked from all memory. What lingered in Michele Winder's mind, for the rest of her life, was the sense of fear and discomfort, of waiting for an authority figure to arrive and humiliate her in front of everyone, of trying to be something she was not. And of the thing she would come to call cultural loneliness.

"Mom, I never want to do that again," she told her mother.

She was fifty-five when she related the story. She was a tall, slender, strikingly attractive woman who had gone to college, married twice, divorced twice, raised two children, and had returned to school again for a religious pastorate.

"You mentioned cultural loneliness," I said.

We sat in a corner of a large, nearly empty bookstore in Baltimore one overcast winter afternoon, not far from Michele's apartment. She was Michele Lee now.

"Yes," she said. She was dressed in greys and tans, with scarves hung loosely around her neck and her long hair tousled. "I don't know, I was always out of step. I just never felt I was in the mainstream of wherever I was. It seems like it's always been that way with me. Being poor, the single-parent family. Then, my father's mother being German, and all that mix thing going on in his family. They had their share of issues."

"With you?" I asked.

"Oh, sure."

"Did you spend a lot of time with his mother?"

"I've been in her company," she said carefully, "a few times." This was her grandmother she was talking about. "My father had sisters that decided to live as whites, there was that kind of stuff. I wasn't going to do that. I was never close to his family, and I wasn't going to do what they did."

"Today," I said, "there's all kind of mixes going on."

"Yeah," she said warily. "But then, who are you? And who are your children?"

The contact with her father's side of the family was minimal, and there was no other serious contact with white people during Michele Winder's formative years in West Baltimore. When the Supreme Court issued its *Brown* decision on schools, there was no reaction that she could recall. But, two years later, when her brother, Michael, was ready for junior high school, he was enrolled in the accelerated program at School Number Fifty-nine, on Reisterstown Road, the same one Ted Venetoulis had attended a decade earlier. Michael Winder was one of a small number of black students there.

"My brother was real smart," Michele said, "and everyone was investing their hopes in him."

"You were also smart, right?" I said.

"Yeah, but he had been identified as smart. Going to that school made it official: You were smart. He was on, like, a genius path. My mother and my grandmother just wrapped their hopes in him. And he went to this school, which was just about all white, and I don't remember him ever expressing trouble."

And then, in the summer of 1957, Michele had to make her own decision. She was a good student, but not an accelerated type. She had a choice. Continue attending all-black public schools with her friends in the neighborhood, or take the bus each day to northwest Baltimore, to Garrison Junior High School, which was taking in the city's first racially mixed generation of students.

"Oh, there were big discussions in my family that summer," she remembered. "My grandmother would say something, and then my aunt would say something else, and then my mother would have her say. They had all kinds of misgivings, and they were kind of challenging her. But my mother was a very progressive personality."

The Winders were moving a lot in those days. By the summer of 1957, they lived on Reisterstown Road, below Park Circle, just above Fulton Avenue. In that time, black migration in Baltimore reached as far as Park Circle, but not yet much farther. North of Park Circle, on Reisterstown Road and on Park Heights Avenue and all the residential side streets, the Jews had migrated from East Baltimore, carved out a middle-class lifestyle, or better, and later jokingly referred to their corner of northwest Baltimore as the ghetto— the Golden Ghetto.

In the other great corridor of the city's northwest corner, Liberty Heights Avenue, gentiles had arrived first, but the Jews had moved in and mixed without serious incident. The public schools were calm and productive, the big Gwynn Oak Amusement Park a mixing ground for whites, and so were the Little Leagues and the Cub Scouts and Brownie troops. It looked like America in all her grandest midcentury white face.

"We were on our own by this time," Michele Lee remembered. "We weren't actually living with my mother's mother anymore, but we were living very close. We always stayed within walking distance of my grandmother. Because that's where our main meals came from." She laughed, and then seemed to laugh at her own reaction. In those years, she was seen by many as beautiful, poised, well mannered, well dressed, a pioneer middle-class Negro in the historic integration of the schools—but a grandmother stood between her family and hunger.

"So we stayed in that Reisterstown Road corridor, down below Park Circle," she said, "and all that summer there were conversations in my neighborhood. 'Where are you gonna go next year?' 'Where are you gonna go?' And a lot of my friends decided to go to the neighborhood school, which was all black. Booker T. Washington Junior High, I guess. And they seemed very happy, so I thought, 'What am I doing? I'm going into uncharted waters, leaving my friends.' And I think they made me feel that way, too."

When she arrived at Garrison Junior High, she found a school roughly three-quarters white. The majority were Jewish. Among the blacks was a classmate named John Jacob Oliver Jr. But there were other black youngsters who looked at Michele Winder, with her light skin, and her refined ways, and thought her distant and aloof.

It was one more element to add to the thing she called her cultural isolation.

TEN

"YOU DO NOT HAVE TO MELT TO BE AN AMERICAN"

For a while, as she made her way through school, Barbara Mikulski thought about doing God's work. Maybe she could become a nun and spend her life changing people's hearts. Then, examining her own heart, she realized this would never work. She was too rebellious to accept the discipline of a religious order, and maybe too emotionally bare-knuckled to traipse sweetly among a gentle flock. So she went for the next best thing and became a social worker, imagining she would help change the direction of people's lives. This, too, she quickly realized, had its problems. She could not change the simplest kinds of institutionalized cruelty embedded over generations.

After high school at the Institute of Notre Dame, she went to Mount St. Agnes College in Baltimore and then earned a master's degree at the University of Maryland. She worked first for the Associated Catholic Charities and then for the Baltimore Department of Social Services. On one of her first days with the city she had to appear in Juvenile Court.

"I was," she said years later, pausing for just the right professional jargon to recall that dreadful morning, "a little klutzy."

There is philosophy, and there is practice. The nuns taught philosophy, and the court system took a baseball bat for practice and swung it at your kneecaps. As Mikulski reached for her composure, another colleague came to her rescue. It was a black woman, who had just gotten her master's degree but also knew the idiosyncrasies of the courthouse.

"Let me help you," the woman said. Mikulski remembered feeling awash in gratitude. Here is where you find this, and here is where you find that, the woman explained. And here is what to avoid, and here is what to hold onto, and this is how you deal with the various bumpkins and self-important swell-heads. In a short time, a system began to crystalize in Mikulski's mind.

"Thank you for all the help you gave me," Mikulski said appreciatively, when she saw the woman at the end of the day. "Can I take you somewhere and buy you a drink?"

The woman looked at her as though realizing, for the first time, that she beheld someone who was perhaps ten minutes off the last boat from Slobovia.

"We can't go anywhere," she said. "They won't serve me."

"They won't?"

"Maybe at Woolworth's," the woman said.

"Woolworth's," Mikulski repeated, forty years later. "Here we are inside a courthouse, and they've segregated every place around it. I said to her, 'Woolworth's?' Because I'm thinking, you know, whiskey sours, which was the thing. And we're chums, and I want to show my appreciation, and I just could not believe it."

The shock of that moment lingered. One of Mikulski's colleagues was a woman named Irene Schmoke, the mother of Kurt L. Schmoke, who would become the first black person elected mayor of Baltimore. This was a fact having no meaning whatsoever to all those business people who could not see the future arriving on their doorsteps. The world had always operated within certain proscribed boundaries, and they imagined it always would. Perhaps one day, long after they were gone, the world would change; but, until then, they would cash in on the system as it had been presented to them when they were inheriting it.

"So we'd socialize on Friday nights in people's homes," said Mikulski. "Because the bars, the restaurants, everything was segregated. So that was part of my politicization into the civil rights movement. Here, I'm working with people. I'm in Protective Services Child Abuse, and Irene's in Foster Care. There were other people with master's degrees, who were better than I was at what they were doing, and they were helping me. And they're black, so they can't go somewhere for a simple drink.

"And when this woman first said this to me, I just could not believe it. You know that it happens, you know it dimly, but coming out of the enclave, and not knowing downtown much myself, I couldn't believe a sister college graduate, someone who's trying to help the poor, trying to rescue the battered children, trying to look out for them, foster care workers, people I work with all day long, and there's this enforced segregation that stops everybody the minute we walk out the door."

Thus arrived the great crossroads. For Irene Schmoke there were stories out of a lifetime to pass on to her son, who would carry them into a political career that seemed full of grandest promise but stopped dead at Baltimore's City Hall. And, for Mikulski, sheltered by the ethnic enclaves of East Baltimore, sheltered by sixteen years of cloistered nuns preaching philosophical values, sheltered in her parents' home until she was twenty-seven, it was the first adult test of philosophy meeting real life.

"But, again," she said one winter afternoon, "it comes back to the things I learned in school. It was that mix." Her mix was limited: white, Catholic, female. Still, she was saying, there was a healthy conglomerate within that framework. She was classmates with the daughters of judges, and with Ukrainian immigrants whose mothers were charwomen so they could go to Notre Dame.

"We came from different backgrounds," Mikulski said. "But, when you're all in uniform, all at basketball, or debating, or trying to struggle through geometry or, like me, failing sewing . . ."

"Wait a minute," I said. "You failed sewing?"

"I failed sewing and geometry in one year," she said. Her expression paused somewhere between a prideful smile and a wince.

"Geometry," I repeated.

"Yes."

"I always assumed you were a straight-A kid," I said.

"No, I was a very mischievous student. When I graduated high school, I was eightieth out of a hundred twenty. By the time I graduated college, I was dean's list. But, no, in high school, I was rockin' and rollin', I was mouthy. I was always . . ."

"Mouthy?" I said. "It's so hard to imagine."

She slipped past the sarcasm without breaking stride. Mikulski does not suffer foolishness. She is sharp and funny when the mood strikes or the audience is right. But, to reach for the empty laugh, the gesture that detracts from her vision of herself as a serious person doing work for which judgment will one day be made, is to risk the chilling glare, the sudden, diminishing putdown.

In school she excelled in drama and debating. When she failed geometry, she and her mother met with Notre Dame's principal. To remain in drama and debate, her academics would have to improve. For Mikulski these weren't simple after-school activities. She was finding an identity through them.

"But where did the political passion come from?" I asked. "You had it before the Juvenile Court incident, didn't you?"

"Oh, sure, when you grow up in the kind of family I have, and the values of my church, the Judeo-Christian ethic, they really give you values. And you had to put those into action." Now Mikulski's voice softened considerably, and slowed, and seemed to caress each word she uttered. "The nuns told us, 'You know, when Jesus said, "Love your neighbor," he really meant it.'" She smiled quite tenderly. "Love your neighbor. And the way you loved your neighbor was feed the hungry, heal the sick."

In the family's East Baltimore grocery store, when laborers at Bethlehem Steel went on strike, Mikulski's father put people on credit. If somebody went through financial trouble, he carried them on the book. When Mikulski was elected to the city council, strangers approached her to say how her father had helped them, and how Mikulski's grandmother had helped them in the bakery during the Depression.

"My grandmother always said, 'Just come by,'" Mikulski said. "And then there was Joe Staszak."

Staszak would become a state senator, but when he left Depression-era

Michigan and arrived in Baltimore, he was broke. Mikulski's grandmother let him sleep on the floor of her bakery while he looked for a job. Stay here a few nights, she told him, my boys get up early and they'll wake you.

"The way I grew up," Mikulski said, "your neighbor really was your neighbor. And the wonderful sisters of Notre Dame, and the Sisters of Mercy— well, we were gonna be the generation that was not only pious but intellectual. And in college, we had to minor in philosophy. So we knew, it was taking that message and putting it into action. You know, light one candle."

"But so many people have heard the same message," I said. "If we're all given the same message to be nice to each other, what's held us back for so long?"

"Well, these patterns were established long before the European ethnics came," she said quickly. Don't blame my people for the troubles, she was saying. She had an instinctive defensiveness, a quick finger for the pre-emptive strike if she saw accusations coming that her people had created anyone else's problems.

"Because we had our own communities, I think we presumed everybody else had their own communities," she said. "That's the way it was. And there was a larger culture that was bigoted to a lot of people."

Thirty years earlier she had written an op-ed piece for the *New York Times*, in which she thrashed out that argument.

"The Ethnic American is forgotten and forlorn," she had written. "He is infuriated at being used and abused by the media, government and business. . . . The Ethnic Americans are forty million working class Americans who live primarily in fifty-eight major industrial cities like Baltimore and Chicago. Our roots are in Central and Southern Europe. We have been in this country for one, two or three generations. We have made a maximum contribution to the U.S.A., yet received minimal recognition. . . . We called ourselves Americans. We were called 'wop,' 'polack,' and 'hunky'. . .

"The one place where the ethnic worker felt the master of his fate and had status was in his own neighborhood. Now even that security is being threatened. He wants new schools for his children. . . . He finds that the only things being planned for his areas are housing projects [and] expressways. When he goes to City Hall to make his problems known, he is either put off, put down, or put out.

"Liberals scapegoat us as racists. Yet there was no racial prejudice in our hearts when we came. There were very few black people in Poland or Lithuania. The elitists who now smugly call us racists are the ones who taught us the meaning of the word: their bigotry extended to those of a different class or national origin."

Now, thirty years later, there were new ethnic minorities coming to Baltimore: the considerable Latino population, the new arrivals from Southeast Asia, from Jamaica. "Go up Park Heights Avenue," she said. She meant the area from Baltimore's Park Circle to Northern Parkway and the Jewish Community Center, a kind of unofficial dividing line. Above the Jewish Community Center was still heavily Jewish; below it, where the Jews had lived in their post–World War II migration, African Americans were now joined by Jamaicans.

"The Jewish community isn't homogenized," Mikulski said. "In your grandfather's day, it was the difference between the Russian and the German. Now it's the orthodox and the Russian Jews, the way they've established their own apartment buildings and so forth."

She was right about that. Like those who had preceded them, the new Russian emigrants were perceived as insular and sometimes arrogant. Who perceived this? Sometimes Jews whose American roots went deeper and had forgotten their own grandparents' insecurities and inhibitions and language problems when they first arrived here.

"My point," said Mikulski, "is that we are a mosaic, we are not a melting pot. And you do not have to melt to be American. You come with your history, your identity, your culture that's part of your family heritage. But you have to come with part of a bigger picture called America. You can assimilate, and yet have tremendous pride in your own identity, because it is not separatist, it is who we are. This is our clan."

The tricky balance is to embrace the clan, but not denigrate the other clans in the process of building up your own.

"I used to wonder," I said. "We heard people holler, 'Christ killer.' I'd wonder, 'Is that what the preachers are saying on Sundays?' Is that where that came from?"

"Central Europe," Mikulski answered, not answering the question. "There was a whole legacy of anti-Semitism. In my family, there was a lot of contact with Jews, because there were so many wholesalers in East Baltimore. The retailers were Catholic, but the wholesalers were Jewish. You know, you have this concept of *tzedakah*"—the Hebrew word for righteousness, for helping others, for acts of charity—"and I was a high school girl when I saw this in action, and it'll be with me forever."

Her father's grocery store was destroyed by fire. It burned through the night, killing a man who lived above the store. Early the next morning, the fire was out and Mikulski's family began sifting through the ashes and wondering how they would rebuild.

"And there were two men who came by," Mikulski said. "One was Duffy, the city councilman. He put his arm around my father and said, 'Willie, I'm gonna get the trucks down here, 'cause there'll be junk all over the street.' My father said, 'I can't pay, I don't have the money.' He was in shock, we all were, we lived directly across the street and everything we had worked for and created was just gone.

"So Duffy says, 'I'll take care of it.' A couple of hours later, city trucks came by and cleaned up. So that's when I knew what a city councilman did. And then there was Mr. Dopkin and the Joffe brothers, these Jewish men who did business with my parents. I was there. It was 1954, I'm eighteen years old, and Dopkin says, 'What are you gonna do?' And my father said, 'I don't know. I don't have money for this.' And Dopkin said, 'Just don't worry.' Can you imagine that? He says, 'Just don't worry. We'll give you credit. You'll pay when you can.'"

Mikulski wept. As she told the story, she took off her glasses and dabbed a paper napkin against her eyes, and forty-six years ago lingered in her mind's eye.

"Those two men just shook hands on it, that's all it took. Two *mensches*." Two honorable, decent people. "What did we know? Those things counted." Now more tears came down Mikulski's face. "We were forever grateful. They were wholesale grocers, and they showed us they were friends."

She dabbed at her eyes some more, and composed herself "So you say, what politicized me? I'll tell you. One was the sisters, and the values they instilled in us. But this, these men who came to my family's aid," Mikulski said. "And you ask about Christ killers? Well, there are many ways you can kill Christ, one of which is being a bigot."

Perched on one of Highlandtown's famous white marble steps, beneath all that wintry bundling, is toddler and future U.S. senator Barbara Mikulski, who already had begun to understand that all politics is local. Courtesy of Barbara Mikulski

Many years later, her old neighborhood had changed significantly. There were working-class whites still there, but now there were black families, too. In the postwar years, as the old ethnic enclaves of Mikulski's East Baltimore loosened, young people who left home often went to suburbia instead of merely around the corner. But her old Highlandtown area had stayed almost exclusively white until the Martin Luther King assassination riots of 1968, when the damage set loose the beginnings of a bitter exodus.

Meanwhile, East Baltimore's Jews had long since moved out. Before World War II, they were leaving for the city's west side, and then for its northwest corridors after the war, leaving behind Lombard Street's Corned Beef Row and a couple of synagogues as lingering artifacts of a vanished migrant tribe.

As they left, there were political repercussions. In one, a young Marvin

Mandel became a political accident. In the postwar years the future governor of Maryland was a struggling lawyer who rode the bus from his parents' home to Lexington Street every morning, and scuffled around the city's district courts, and got nowhere in particular.

One day Mandel's Uncle Dave called. Uncle Dave's closest friend was Sam Friedel, an East Baltimore city councilman trying to get re-elected as his Jewish constituents were moving away.

"Can you help him?" said Uncle Dave. "This election's gonna be tough."

"What do you need?" the young Mandel asked.

"Nothing," said the uncle. "Just drive people back and forth on election day. Make sure they vote. He'll appreciate it."

Friedel appreciated, but he also lost. A smattering of votes the other way, and he would have held on for another four years at City Hall. But the game of ethnic politics was shifting, and Friedel knew where to go next. He followed the Jews to Northwest Baltimore, where a new congressional district was created. He aligned himself with a fellow named Irv Kovens. And he spent the next twenty years in the U.S. Congress, until the Jews moved again and left him vulnerable to Parren J. Mitchell and a new wave of Northwest Baltimore black voters. In the meantime, though, Friedel remembered Mandel. The year after his council defeat, he telephoned him.

"They need a young Jewish veteran to run for the state central committee," Friedel said.

"What's that?" said Mandel, who had not yet conceived of a life in politics.

"It guides the party," said Friedel, "but you don't have to know, so don't worry about it. They just need a name. They just want to put you on the ticket."

And he won.

"Just like that," Mandel said years later. "That's how it started."

He leaned back in a big office chair with a look of contentment on his pink face. It was late on a March afternoon, just weeks shy of Mandel's eightieth birthday. He had been governor of Maryland, and he had been a federal prison inmate. He had been married once, and famously divorced, and married again. His first wife, Jewish, nicknamed Bootsie, refused to move out of the governor's mansion when he left her. On the day a Mandel aide, Frank DeFilippo, slipped a hastily written notice to reporters that Mandel had sep-

Speaker of the House Marvin Mandel, the self-described "accidental politician," circa 1970, on his way to becoming governor of Maryland when Spiro Agnew departed the State House in Annapolis for the White House. *Courtesy of Marvin Mandel*

arated from her, Mrs. Mandel declared, "I don't know what everybody's talking about, the governor left my bed this morning." Then she simply hunkered down in the mansion's living quarters for weeks while the business of the state of Maryland went on around her. Now, a quarter-century later, Mandel's second wife lay immobilized with amyotrophic lateral sclerosis, Lou Gehrig's disease.

"She understands everything," Mandel said. "But she can't talk, and she can't move."

A few days earlier, he had been told the end was near. Then his wife had unexpectedly rallied. Mandel went on with his life, lobbying state legislators, meeting with political pals, finding a twilight acceptance as a man who had been a smart, savvy governor—except for that dreary criminal trial business, whose particulars, and whose overturn on appeal were now, two decades later, a blur in the collective consciousness.

The detritus of his life hovered around him. He worked in a building a few miles from the State House, and his office walls were covered with photographs of Mandel in sunny times. Even the dreadful years turned out well on these walls. Newspaper headlines trumpeted the overturning of his guilty verdict. Photos of his second wife, the former Jeanne Dorsey, were everywhere.

And Mandel, long after he had left the governor's office in disgrace, long after he had been banished to prison and written off, was still remarkably here. He was a player, and wished to be seen as one. He sat behind a big desk, in a chair so large that it resembled a throne. His thinning wiry hair was white now, and he wore boots to give his diminutive frame a little more height when he stood. His chest and stomach had thickened over the years, and filled his dress shirt and suit. He looked prosperous, and pleased that he was.

Three-quarters of a century earlier, Mandel preceded the Jews to Northwest Baltimore. He was born in East Baltimore but moved to the Pimlico Racetrack neighborhood when he was two years old. It was 1922. His family lived on Oakmont Avenue, five blocks from the racetrack. His father was a clothing cutter who took him to the track on Sunday mornings to watch the horses work out. A few years later Mandel was there every afternoon selling newspapers to the sporting set.

"They'd let us in after the fourth race," he remembered. "We'd sell the *Evening Sun* and the *News and Post*. They went for two cents each. If a guy was a big winner, he'd give us a quarter for a paper."

He learned his first lessons in hustling, and in fighting. There weren't many Jews in Northwest Baltimore in the 1920s. Mandel remembered getting into fistfights every week as he walked to school.

"They'd call us dirty Jews," he said, shrugging it off. It was just part of the era, name-calling based on suspiciousness of another clan. Mandel went to

Pimlico Elementary, and then Garrison Junior High School. He was starting to learn how to defend himself. He became friendly with another Jewish kid, whose name was Irv Kovens. In high school Mandel went to Baltimore City College, which had a sizable Jewish student body.

One night he and some friends went to the Greenspring Inn, on wooded Greenspring Avenue in Baltimore County. Mandel was seventeen. He remembered the manager approaching his table and bluntly asking, "Are you Jews?"

"Yeah," Mandel said.

"You'll have to leave."

"And that," Mandel recalled sixty-three years later, "started the fight. A fistfight, yeah. The whole place got into it, and we snuck out under the tables, and they were still fighting." He opened his mouth and smiled slyly. "And then, of course, you had Gwynn Oak Park, which didn't want Jews or blacks. And then they let Jews in, but not the blacks. And the swimming place, where they had the sign."

The sign was legendary—"No Jews, Blacks or Dogs." Every Jewish kid heard about it, and carried the message in his head: Somewhere out there people do not like us, and they put us in the same category as Negroes. The blacks heard about it, too, but it was merely part of a much larger message. And the message had a double edge for both groups: not only the sense of ostracism, but some notion of understanding, and maybe even emotional alliance.

Mandel went to the University of Maryland. When the war arrived, he was sent to Texarkana, Texas, where the Army readied for its invasion of Africa. Mandel found it dispiriting. In these early days of the fighting, the only available rifles were relics from the Spanish American War.

"Was there any ethnic stuff going on?" I asked.

"Nah," he said. "Some of those guys from the mountain areas, but they didn't even know what a Jew was. And I was boxing in the Army. If you boxed, you didn't have to do all that other stuff."

Home from the war, struggling with his legal practice, he took the telephone call from his Uncle Dave that hooked him up with Sam Friedel and the Democratic State Central Committee. From there, he moved to the

House of Delegates when a seat opened unexpectedly. The job paid $1,200. Another accidental job, Mandel called it.

He arrived in Annapolis in 1952, with his boyhood friend Irv Kovens whispering in his ear. Kovens was tall, lean, wavy-haired, raspy-voiced, and smoked big cigars. He'd grown up with money, inheriting his father's furniture store, and married into more money.

In this time, before TV news sound bites, and before federal prosecutors sniffing out conspiracies, Baltimore was still a town of machine politics. Tommy D'Alesandro Jr. was still mayor, and in the city's ethnic neighborhoods votes were traded for favors. If a son needed a job, if a street needed repairing, people went to the party organization. All that was asked was loyalty: a promised vote, a little campaign money, some help getting out the support on election day. It was, as it had always been, the outsider's way of trying to break into the game.

The Jews had a couple of these political godfathers: James H. "Jack" Pollack, the ex-boxer who became an insurance agent, quoted Shakespeare to give himself some class, and put together a machine—the Trenton Democratic Club—on the city's Jewish west side whose members backed Pollack out of a sense of practicality. He could get them city jobs. He could fix courthouse problems, or make people think that he had.

Among the old Pollack group was Sam Greenberg, a deputy sheriff who later owned businesses on Baltimore's X-rated zone called The Block. He found out how Pollack pulled strings. Guys would show up at Pollack's clubhouse meetings just to have him fix their traffic tickets.

One man complained to Greenberg, "I ain't coming back. I went to court and got beat. If Pollack ain't taking care of me, the hell with him."

Greenberg went to Pollack and relayed the complaint. "You're naïve," Pollack told him. "I don't fix those tickets. Most of those guys will beat those tickets on their own if they just show up in court. I just tell them I'm putting in the fix. And when they win, they think it's because of me."

Pollack played the angles—but he also helped put a series of smart and sensitive men into city council seats and judgeships. They were Jewish. And they held onto their political seats until the ethnic numbers changed.

Behind Pollack came Kovens. Jews who had first moved to West Baltimore after the war moved further northwest as increasing numbers of blacks moved into their neighborhoods. Some of them left Pollack's political tent for Kovens'. He helped Sam Friedel get elected to congress. He helped Theodore McKeldin become governor. In 1968, when Hubert Humphrey needed money in his run for president, Kovens bragged that he raised $100,000 for him in one morning.

Kovens liked a variety of action, betting a hundred dollars or more on horseraces, shooting craps at European sporting clubs when he went on vacation, and routinely tapping into big money political backers, Jewish and otherwise, when he picked up his telephone on the second floor of the family store on West Baltimore Street. In the old political smoke-filled rooms, Kovens provided most of the smoke.

"He got into politics because he liked to play with it," Mandel said. "It meant nothing financially. He liked to have the prestige of being someone who could pull the strings. He understood the base was Jewish, but he worked outward. If people needed something, he helped out. For instance, he was in business with Little Willie."

William L. "Little Willie" Adams had parlayed a numbers business into enough money that he became, in Mandel's estimation, "one of the wealthiest black men in the United States." He made enough money, in fact, to sink his resources into legitimate businesses. In the 1950s, though, the U.S. Senate investigated racketeering and invited Adams to testify before the Kefauver Committee, which was touring big cities around the country.

"When Kefauver came to Maryland," Mandel said, "all the other guys had taken a powder. I mean, they were in Florida, they were in the Bahamas, they were all ducking subpoenas. Not Willie. He testified. He told them how he'd been in it, how he ran the business, and how he got out. And, also, he made the case that there was no other way for blacks in America to make this kind of money."

Mandel, the early arriving Jew in Pimlico, the boy who had fistfights on the way to school, the teenager tossed out of the Greenspring Inn for being Jewish, felt good that he and Kovens had been friends with Adams. Implicit in the story were two things: He was sophisticated enough to understand Adams's reasons for breaking the law, and he understood what it meant to be a minority.

"Let me tell you something," Mandel said. "Down here, in this area, people don't realize. I came here in 1952, and I became Speaker of the House in 1963. Two years later, Irma Dixon's elected to the legislature. Her husband's Bill Dixon. They're black, right? The first day we're sworn in, Murray Abramson comes running into my office, the Speaker's office, and he says, we got a terrible problem." Abramson was a state delegate from Northwest Baltimore.

"What's the matter?" Mandel asked.

"Dixon's being sworn in," Abramson said, "and I called the Maryland Inn to make a reservation. They said, 'We don't serve blacks.'"

Mandel, finishing the story thirty-five years later, said, "I told him, 'Let me handle it.' Murray said, 'Well, do something.' And I told my secretary, 'Call over there and tell them the Speaker wants reservations for ten people.' She did. I said, 'Murray, get a few people.' We walked in and sat down. They looked at me, they looked at Dixon, they never said a word. What could they do? From that day on, the Maryland Inn was desegregated."

It was a nice story, and Mandel saw himself as its figure of nobility. And maybe he was; nobody else with his power had ever done such a thing. But the year was 1965. Mandel was a liberal Jew, fine-tuned to the pain of discrimination, friends with the influential Willie Adams—and he had been coming to Annapolis for thirteen years, the last two as one of the most powerful men in state government. Surely he had noticed, before this, that there were insulting conditions for black citizens in the state capital. Surely Irv Kovens had noticed. They had, indeed. But they also wondered, what will the others think: the gentiles, the ones who still controlled the votes, some of whom weren't too crazy about having Jews around, much less blacks. It was one outsider's empathy with another, balanced against the fear that the old-line entrenched would be angry and take it out on both groups.

Blacks had been furious about these exclusionary practices forever. But they had no political power and few overt friends in high places. They still lived in different worlds. Their white allies tended to move warily. Philosophically, these whites understood the cruelty of segregation; practically, though, they knew where the votes were. And no one had yet been directly moved by the threat of riots, which were merely waiting for an appropriate moment.

Mandel and Kovens saw themselves as common-sense men. By the time

Mandel became governor, they were each approaching fifty, each settled, married men with grown children. Mandel became governor when Richard Nixon reached into the ranks of political unknowns and picked Maryland Governor Spiro Agnew to be his vice-president. Mandel succeeded Agnew on a vote of the legislature. Kovens later admitted that he might have made "a few" telephone calls to political allies to ensure Mandel's vote.

It was simply the way they played the game. Where the game got tricky was the intersection of politics and money, and sex. As governor, Mandel was paid $23,000 a year. As a man going through a divorce, his finances, already stretched thin, were ready to break.

It was Kovens's habit to help him financially, and it was Mandel's habit to let him. Other friends also helped out. Kovens bought suits for Mandel. A governor has to dress well, he explained later, and who could dress well on such an embarrassing salary? Then Kovens's generosity got bigger. He put up $155,000 in bonds for the first Mrs. Mandel to guarantee a peaceful divorce settlement.

Such money was nothing to a man of Kovens's wealth, and Mandel accepted it in the spirit in which Kovens said it was intended: one friend helping out another. But federal prosecutors considered it bribery, and they said Kovens's check for $200,000 to another Mandel friend, Harry Rodgers, for the purchase of the Marlboro racetrack was another. And they based their criminal case on such transactions.

Mandel denied all impropriety, and Kovens denied it. Among Baltimore's Jews, some of the old defensiveness reared its head. There was talk that the *Baltimore Sun,* editorializing steadily against Mandel, was showing too much glee in the governor's discomfort; some Jews said they sensed anti-Semitism. But the uneasiness came from more than that. The case was about a Jew and his money; and it was about a Jew who had pursued a *shiksa* instead of staying with his first wife, the mother of his children, the member of his tribe. He had tried to be someone he wasn't, had reached too far into the American mainstream, and the price that was being extracted was public embarrassment reflecting on all the Jews.

The trial, the retrial, and the appeals took years. Mandel was a beaten man but never showed it. If he understood the Jewish sensitivities, he never admitted it in any public way. To do so would only have stoked the fires. He always behaved as if someone else had committed some terrible mistake that would be understood at some later date.

He plugged on; it is what a man on the ropes does. The boxer knows how to stick and move, throw the jab, duck the counterpunch and not stay in one place. For Mandel, the early ring lessons transferred to his whole life. And now, in retrospect, he was laughing openly at his worst time.

"When I was in prison," he said, remembering from a distance of more than two decades, "I learned that you worked with whatever you had. You were entitled to practice your religion. So I went to see the warden one day. This was the old Eglin Air Force Base, in Florida. There were only about ten Jews in the whole place. And we wound up with a kosher kitchen, and one Jewish guy who made the best food you ever tasted. They flew it up to us from Miami.

"Then we said, 'We want religious services on Friday night.' They took us into town by bus. After that, a big *shabbat*. Bagels and cream cheese and lox, and we get to see our wives there, and we stay till ten-thirty, eleven o'clock. I tell the warden, 'This is all part of our religious practices.'"

Mandel had no sense of shame in telling the story, no concept of having used previously untapped religious fervor to get a break—and no sense of the rich irony of having famously married out of the faith on his way to prison religious practices. He was simply using the system wisely, the way any smart politician would use it. He told the story the way a great raconteur would, full of swagger and delight.

"And one day, at Yom Kippur"—the Jewish high holy day of repentance before God, of seeking forgiveness for all of the previous year's sins and humbly requesting inclusion in the Book of Life for the coming year—"the warden decides he's gonna be a nice guy. He says, 'Anybody wants to go to Jewish services, sign up.' He didn't say 'any Jew,' he said, 'anybody.' So we had fifty guys at services.

"Then he finds out, and he's screaming about all these guys. He wants to punish. I went in, I said, 'Wait a minute, you didn't say any Jews, you said anybody. How can you punish?' So he didn't."

He leaned back in his chair with a look of satisfaction. While he was away, there was sneering talk back in Maryland: The governor and his friends had gotten a break, prison was a country club. Now, years later, Mandel seemed to be saying as much.

"It was easy?" I asked.

"No," he said. "No, it was terrible, it was horrible. So I had to give it back to them the best I could." He spoke evenly, and all traces of the bon vivant inmate vanished from his tone.

"I wrote all the letters and appeals for guys," he said. "I taught the Spanish guys stuff. You work the system, because you know they're trying to work you. There was one nasty captain, a big strapping guy. He was trying to give me trouble. I said, 'Let me tell you something, captain. No matter how it goes, in four months, I'm outa here, and you're still here. And then your ass is gonna belong to me.' And from then on, I didn't have a moment's trouble from him.

"And then my case was overturned," Mandel said. "Man, I was the only inmate that they were so glad to see me out of there, they wouldn't even let me pack. The president signed my special commutation, and they pushed me out of there and sent my clothes home Special Delivery."

He smiled delightedly. The boxer ducks and weaves, and tries to fight another day; the tough, hard-nosed Jew adapts to the bigger world, and fights for his place in it.

ELEVEN
CROSSING PARK CIRCLE

My father kept God at a discreet distance. He was respectful, but he felt a little space benefited them both. Each autumn, he reserved tickets for the Jewish high holidays as far from the action as he could get. Far behind our synagogue's polished wood congregational benches, rows of metal folding chairs were lined up for the overflow holiday crowds. My father always insisted on seats in the last row. This was his privilege as a citizen but a curiosity for a man who was president of the synagogue brotherhood.

From our seats in the building's remotest location, religious services seemed a series of vagrant dispatches from some distant Israeli outpost. We could take part in the ancient Hebrew prayers but see only traces of those who were leading the holy rituals. They seemed to belong to a faith similar to ours, but they appeared to observe it in a more devout fashion. In our section, all the way back by the synagogue doors and the traffic on Liberty

Heights Avenue just beyond them, religious fervor did not seem constant even on these most reverent days of the year.

"Why do we always have to sit in the last row?" I asked my father.

"In case," he explained in his succinct way, anticipating no further inquisition.

"In case what?" I asked.

"In case we have to leave," my father said. "It'll be easier."

No one was supposed to leave, not during services for Rosh Hashanah and Yom Kippur, those solemn days commemorating the birth of the world and the hour of supreme human penitence. But my father was a great one for leaving places. He was a restless, impatient man. Sometimes, in the midst of high holiday services, he would look my way and say, "Jake's doing pretty good today," a reference to Rabbi Jacob A. Max, the spiritual leader of the Liberty Jewish Center, Anshe Emunah Congregation, located on Liberty Heights and Marmon Avenues.

By "doing pretty good," my father meant Rabbi Max was moving the holy services along at a robust, peppy clip. He checked his watch as he said this, like a railroad official proudly anticipating the arrival of the Silver Streak from Aberdeen on track number 3. If the service moved too slowly, my father would gesture in the rabbi's direction and mutter with some annoyance, "He's not trying." Cantors were judged not merely on the purity of their singing, but their speed. One year a record was set for quickest time, and men walked out of the synagogue with warm, satisfied smiles on their faces and told each other, "Now *that* was a beautiful service."

In the Bronx of his youth, my father had been raised in an Orthodox synagogue and attended a Hebrew school on weekday afternoons. In the Baltimore of his adulthood, he made certain that his two sons did the same. My father had a strong sense of propriety, of respect for his religious roots, and he was not an impious man. But in his restlessness, he seemed to need something additional, something more immediate than a language 5,000 years old. Whenever a Jewish holiday coincided with a Sunday afternoon, this arrived in a whisper.

"Unitas," a hushed voice would say.

The reference was to John Unitas, the football quarterback. The whisperer was a synagogue usher with discreet radio connections to the outside world, like a French Resistance operative.

"*Shema, Yisroel,*" came the prayerful cry of Rabbi Max. "Hear, O Israel."

"To Berry," said the whisperer, intending to be heard by my father, if not all of Israel.

In Northwest Baltimore on the edge of the city, where the Jews settled into their 1950s neighborhoods, the football Colts were the great secular religion. They were the Colts of John Unitas throwing to Raymond Berry, and Lenny Moore stutter-stepping around tacklers, and Artie Donovan and Gino Marchetti smothering opposing ball carriers before delirious crowds at the city's Memorial Stadium. Donovan had even come to a synagogue brotherhood breakfast one Sunday morning. He said he grew up in the Bronx. As it happened, it was not far from my parents' old block, in a neighborhood of Irish such as Donovan's family, and Italians and Jews. So the men in the synagogue called him Art Davenin'. In Yiddish, *davening* is praying. Art Donovan laughed heartily at the nickname, and everyone at the Liberty Jewish Center felt warmly embraced by this goodwill ambassador from the gentile world.

The Colts seemed a collective role model for the universe outside the synagogue doors at a time when many Americans were reaching cautiously across racial and religious lines. Nobody stood on a soapbox to talk about it, but it was there. It was barely a decade since Jackie Robinson had broken baseball's color line, and only a heartbeat since the Supreme Court outlawed segregated public schools. By their very makeup the Colts seemed to imply: This is how it could work. If these tough, brawny men could get along, maybe the rest of us could. They were victorious with white players and black players and, never to be minimized among outsiders seeking even a sliver of community identity, a team owner who was a Jew.

"Carroll Rosenbloom," my father informed me, when my football consciousness was first dawning. "One of ours."

"A woman?" I asked.

"Better," my father said. "A *landsman.*"

In the Yiddish pronunciation, *lahntsmon.* In translation, a countryman. In the idiomatic, a fellow Jew. And, in the glory days of the Colts, a generous team owner who helped his ballplayers establish outside business ventures.

Who said the Jews were tight with their money? The Lithuanian Unitas had a bowling alley. The Italians Marchetti and Alan "The Horse" Ameche had hamburger joints. Rosenbloom the Jew helped set them up, and then humbly issued press releases making certain everyone in Baltimore knew about his grand gesture.

"And the *shvartzer*," my father said. He meant Lenny Moore, the spectacular halfback whom Rosenbloom financed in a lounge operation on Gwynn Oak Avenue after the neighborhood began changing. Moore was nicknamed "Sputnik" for the out-of-this-world speed of the first Russian satellite. He was nicknamed "Spats" for wrapping white tape around the outside of his shoes to support his ankles. But, to my father, who found Moore utterly thrilling, he was nevertheless the *shvartzer*, Yiddish for black, insider lingo for something a little more nuanced and discomforting.

One Yom Kippur Sunday afternoon, as congregants at the Liberty Jewish Center recited the centuries-old Hebrew prayers, my father shifted on his back-row metal chair. The service was moving too slowly. "He's just not trying," my father said, motioning toward Rabbi Max. Then he glanced over his shoulder at the whisperer standing behind him. He wanted more spiritual uplift.

"Gimme a score," said my father.

"Colts up by ten," said the whisperer.

"What period?"

"Second."

"How much time left?"

"What am I, Chuck Thompson?"

My father shrugged and passed the whisperer's bulletin to my Uncle Dick, who sat next to him and in turn relayed the information to the man sitting beside him. The news made its way down our row, heads turning left to right like the tide coming in. The Colts were ahead; God was good. The gentiles were having their day on the athletic field, and the Jews were taking a little second-hand pleasure. At our distance in the back row, we had the best of both worlds, where God might note our attendance but Rabbi Max would remain oblivious to our minor transgressions.

The whisperer stood between our row and the synagogue doors that separated us from the outside world. Out there, men followed football games without guilt and toasted touchdowns in their ballpark upper-deck seats with hearty swallows of National Bohemian Beer. In the synagogue, we fasted for twenty-four hours and sought forgiveness from God for all of our sins, including the most trivial misdemeanors. Out there they talked of Hail Mary passes, marrying the gentlest of their religious images to the most hairy-chested of games and finding no irony. In here, men bent over books of Scripture, chanting in a strange language while wearing tiny caps on their skulls and prayer shawls wrapped around their bony shoulders.

This image alone separated us from all popular culture images of America. I imagined the gentiles finding our religious services not only foreign but vaguely subversive had they but known about them. I had no notion that gentile kids with ethnic-minority backgrounds might be going through the same uneasiness. I found comfort in my religion, because it was practiced by my family and by many of my new friends, but I had no idea how I might explain these rituals and this strange language to mockers gathered on my public school playground located several blocks from the synagogue. Their religion was everywhere, like part of the air we breathed. It was on television and radio, and validated their way of life; ours seemed to sit in a corner, unnoticed, and not unhappily so.

We were now living in a new land that millions of midcentury Americans were discovering, called suburbia. It was still the city, but it was nothing like the old city. We left the projects and moved to Northwest Baltimore in 1953, when I was eight years old and my brother Mitchell was a baby, and we stayed there for the next decade.

I thought we had stumbled onto a Hollywood set. It was a neighborhood without trash dumpsters in the streets. In my youth and my cultural isolation, it had not particularly occurred to me that such a place existed. Instead of the projects' cement courtyards where we played war games, ducking for cover between clotheslines heavy with neighbors' underwear, there were enormous trees above our heads and plots of grass outside of little brick homes. There was no longer the casually racist version of "eenie, meenie, miney, moe," but a polite version in which a tiger was caught by his toe. Instead of trashcan forts, there was a vast, undeveloped wooded area leading to a pond. Instead of running rooftops home from school, we could ride bicycles. Traffic was sparse enough that streets were free for games of stickball, in which second base was a manhole cover, or touch football games in which three completed passes were a first down and parked cars defined passing routes unlike those run by Raymond Berry or Lenny Moore. And, after a few years, when most of us were entering adolescence and the Colts had become our athletic gods, there was a new schoolyard around the corner to take our ballgames off of the streets.

The neighborhood was set between two of Northwest Baltimore's main thoroughfares, Liberty Heights Avenue and Reisterstown Road, and in the decade we lived there it became our world, and other neighborhoods seemed like distant cultures. What we knew about them, we knew by shorthand. Teenagers appeared on the popular television show *Pinbusters,* where they announced the schools they attended and the places where they bowled: Southway Lanes, Patterson Lanes. Where in the world were these places? We discovered Toots Barger's bowling alley at Gwynn Oak Junction, where grown men called pinboys smoked cigarettes while they crouched behind duckpins and felt themselves fortunate to receive ten-cent tips tossed to them at the end of thirty-cent bowling games. Television commercials informed us there was a neighborhood called Hampden, famous because it had a rug cleaners ("Belmont five-oh-six-oh-oh," in the familiar basso profundo announcer's voice), and a downtown savings and loan called Baltimore Federal ("where Fayette Street and St. Paul meet," the TV commercials informed us). There was a beer called National Bohemian, made in a place called The Land of Pleasant Living, which included a Chesapeake Bay. But all of these places could have been on the moon for all we knew. When the television broadcast shows for little children, such as my brother, a woman named Miss Nancy encouraged them to be a good Do-Bee, and don't be a Don't-Bee. For a long time, all of the children on all of the television shows were white, as were all of the broadcasters and all of the actors and all of the *Pinbusters* bowlers. The bowling alley pinboys were black. The only other black people in our consciousness were ballplayers, and the neighborhood mailman, and the cleaning women who showed up to give our mothers a break with the housework. When we left our neighborhood, it was strictly for school, or ballgames at Memorial Stadium, or occasionally to take our lives into our hands on the roller-coaster ride at Gwynn Oak Amusement Park.

Children were taught not only to do good things, but to believe in good things. The schools still held paper drives, the way they had during the war.

The boys of Crawford Avenue (*front, left to right*): Stan Nusenko, Jake Rubinstein, Joel Kruh, Ron Sallow; (*back, left to right*) Phil Rubinstein, Michael Olesker, Harvey Hyatt. In midcentury America their generation discovered the suburban mosaic.

The scout troops were packed, and so were the Little Leagues. When we heard about people called beatniks, we thought they were kidding around. If they weren't, they were certainly about to get themselves into big trouble with the authorities.

It was still a time before air-conditioning or cable television, and so the streetcorners and school yards were natural habitats. When transistor radios arrived, stickball games were played against a backdrop of Chuck Thompson describing the Orioles' Bob Boyd hitting "frozen rope" line drives, or Hoyt Wilhelm tilting his head to one side as he delivered his knuckleball. Every street ballplayer developed a style that was banned not only on his own instincts but the theater created in his imagination by the radio.

Over the years everybody in my neighborhood became a little good at something. Joel Kruh could run forever without coming up for breath. Harvey Hyatt, caught necking with a girl, was quick enough to explain he was actually giving her lessons in underwater swimming. Rob Meyer could play ball like nobody else (at five-feet-four, he starred in football and baseball for Forest Park High School) and Phil Rubinstein was the neighborhood genius; he graduated Johns Hopkins University while barely out of his teens. Ron Sallow knew all the best places to cut school (the back of Toots Barger's bowling alley wasn't bad), and Stanley Nusenko could hit a punchball a mile. Barry Director could keep everybody laughing—even on the night the police grabbed us and a desk sergeant told the arresting officer, "Good, I see you picked up some Jews."

We lived in a little brick two-bedroom bungalow with an unfinished basement and attic, and a kitchen where my mother stood at her sink and gazed through a window at a long, leafy backyard that blended into a series of neighbors' yards. These had no fences, and seemed to stretch as far as the imagination. In summers the yards became a sea of chlorophyll; in winter's snow, blinding white; in autumn, the blaze of leaves changing color made my mother feel sentimental and poetic. Those yards, and the tall trees, and the streets where her two sons could play safely near the house, were heaven to her. The houses sold for just under $12,000, with monthly mortgage payments of about $100. She had never in her life known such security.

On the day we moved in a girl named Nancy knocked on our front door, and I answered. She was ten years old and said she lived across the street. Then she asked, rather shyly, "Are you Jewish or gentile?"

In the four years we lived in the projects, nobody had ever asked me such a question. I had learned I was Jewish, and that most people in the world were not, but I had never felt a need to hide it.

"Jewish," I said.

"Oh," she said, visibly disappointed. And then there seemed nothing else to talk about. In a moment or two, she walked back across the street, and I closed the door wondering if I had done something to hurt her feelings, and might I make it up to her in some way?

A little later, another girl arrived. She had blonde hair in a pixie cut and said she lived next door to us. Her name was Geri Tilles.

"It's not a boy's name," she explained. "It's short for Geraldine. Did you meet Nancy from across the street yet?"

"Yes."

"Did she ask if you were Jewish?"

"How did you know?"

"She asks everybody when they move into the neighborhood. She asked me when we moved in. She was disappointed when we said we're Jewish. But she's nice."

That chilly afternoon I stood on the front porch as two boys from the neighborhood slowly walked past the house and glared menacingly in my direction. One had dark, curly hair and seemed a little older than I.

"Dirty Jew," he called out. The two of them kept walking. I had never heard the phrase before, but there was no mistaking the boys' glower.

It turned out there were discreet differences within the neighborhood. After that first day, the differences were almost never expressed with outward antagonism. There was simply a polite social distance among some of the adults, and a slight geographical distance. There were the newly built homes, such as our stretch of bungalows and semidetached houses around Crawford Avenue, and there were the older, larger stucco homes on Groveland Avenue toward Rogers Avenue. These had been built years earlier. Gentiles lived in these older homes and watched as a wave of young Jewish families moved in during the 1950s. Then these Jewish newcomers moved into the public schools. By coincidence or otherwise, virtually every gentile youngster in the neighborhood—at least a dozen of them who were my age—went off each morning to parochial schools. They came from families without noticeable money, and without particularly noticeable religious fervor. Though some of the schools were reasonably close, such as All Saints School on Liberty Heights Avenue, some were quite far away, such as Calvert Hall and St. Paul's School. The nearest public schools, however, were within walking distance.

Only in distant retrospect did I become aware of this. At the time, it was simply the natural order of things. We all played together after school, and this was what counted to us. But, by parental decision, the Jews and gentiles of my neighborhood did not attend the same schools.

I went to Howard Park Elementary School, Number 218, on Liberty Heights Avenue just below Gwynn Oak Junction. In the three years I attended, which immediately followed the Supreme Court ruling outlawing school segregation, Howard Park remained religiously mixed but all white, a reflection of the surrounding, middle-class, contented neighborhoods.

But there were already hints of changes to come. One afternoon my father brought home a copy of the *Saturday Evening Post* magazine, with a story about a Northwest Baltimore neighborhood near Lake Ashburton that mentioned the man my father worked for in the real-estate business. The story was headlined, "When a Negro Moves Next Door." It was a feel-good piece about people learning to accept each other's differences in a changing America.

"What does that say?" my father said, holding up the story as he walked into the living room. He wanted me to notice his boss's name, but I focused on the headline, and read it aloud.

"When a Negro Moves Next Door," I said.

My father exploded. "What did you say?" he roared.

I read it again; he calmed himself. He thought I had said "nigger," when I had merely pronounced it, in the local drawl, as "nigro."

"But you say '*shvartzer*,'" I said.

"What?" my father asked, somewhat incredulously.

"Lenny Moore," I said.

If my father saw the connection, he dismissed it. The lesson was: Our people did not use such hurtful language as "nigger." We were not that kind of people. We were people who used *shvartzer*, a kind of Judeo tribal reference, but did not intend it as slander. Our people thought it was fine when magazines published stories about Negroes moving next door. We were not intolerant; distinctions had to be made.

In any case, my new public school had nothing but white students. About one-third of the students were Jewish. The two-story brick schoolhouse was originally constructed in 1907, and later charmingly refurbished. It still had its original wooden floors and stairways and desks with inkwells. A girl named Dorothy Majors sat in front of me. I knew that, in another era, I would have been expected to dunk her pigtails into my inkwell, like Andy Hardy. The school looked the way America was supposed to look, like an MGM stage set. Boys who rode bicycles to school left them in a bike rack, unlocked, in a leafy area of the schoolyard just across Woodbine Avenue from a Dodge dealership with patriotic bunting outside.

Each morning, on a crowded hardtop strip of the playground, boys played games of throwball and punchball and scattered those girls who gathered in foul territory for their games of hopscotch. Neither gender outwardly acknowledged the other, and such behavior was tacitly encouraged by school elders. It was simply deemed safer that way in the 1950s.

Sometimes during the day, without warning, bells went off and everyone was herded out of classrooms and told to crouch silently in the halls for air-raid drills. No one explained who might want to drop bombs on an innocent elementary school in Northwest Baltimore; the only war talked about in the schoolyard was the one in which my father had flown missions. But he had long since come home.

One day on the playground, a high-level discussion broke out concerning hand grenades: how to pull the pins, and how to throw the grenades properly. We had all seen John Wayne's movie technique, but troubling questions of Hollywood veracity had now arisen among our little group of cognoscenti. A crewcut boy named Jay Pugh clasped an imaginary grenade in his fist, put it to his mouth, and pulled an imaginary pin out with his teeth.

"You don't know nothin," said a boy named Jimmy Lambert. He talked out of the side of his mouth. "You don't pull the pin with your teeth. You'd yank 'em out. That's stuff's just for the movies."

"Oh, yeah?"

Then a boy named Jeff Remmel pretended to toss a grenade and let out a growl indicating he had just blown up the back end of the school. Remmel was nicknamed "Rommel," after the German "Desert Fox" general, and was given to comic outbursts in which he gazed across the dusty school playground and cried out, "Sand . . . nothing but sand."

Now he tossed another imaginary grenade. But the throwing motion was like an outfielder trying to catch a base runner going from first to third.

"You can't throw a grenade like that," said a blond, skinny boy named Billy Cunningham. "I know a guy who did that and broke his arm. Grenades are heavy. You gotta throw it like this."

He lobbed his own imaginary grenade with a stiffened elbow. Did Cunningham really know a guy with hand-grenade experience? The claim seemed to give him new credibility. How do you challenge a fellow with a first-hand source? I stood along the edge of the argument, in no way certain who was right but believing I had my own insider knowledge of American military procedures.

"My father was in the Air Force," I said.

"There you go," said Jay Pugh. "Tell 'em, Olesker."

I sensed that my father's credentials gave me a momentary status I had never previously felt, and managed to fake my way through the moment. It was the first time I felt any sort of equal footing with my new classmates, and I resolved to ask my father more questions about the war when he got home that night so I could score a few more playground combat points.

In the 1950s, in a time when the battles were routinely staged at the Saturday afternoon movies, World War II still resonated. It was part of the homogenizing American mythology of the era; to absorb it, to believe in its fighting men and their noble cause, was to belong to something. The night of the hand-grenade debate, I sat in front of the television set with my father to watch the Phil Silvers comedy show about peacetime Army life. It was about as close as my father and I would get to discussing the military. Silvers played the con man Sergeant Ernest Bilko, whose gambling exploits made my father laugh out loud.

"One of ours," said my father. He meant Silvers. Silvers was Jewish. But my father relished Bilko's entire platoon, a conglomerate of men with clear ethnic diversity: Barbella and Henshaw, Fender and Paparelli, Kadowski and Ritzik, Mullin and Doberman. There was even a black fellow in the platoon. Bilko called him, without irony, the Genius. The Genius understood wires and gizmos. That all of these men took such clear delight in each other sent another lesson, without belaboring the point: Mixing people together was fun, it was American.

"Was there really anybody in the Army like Bilko?" I asked.

"Are you kidding?" my father said. "Everybody was like Bilko."

I digested this stunning news for a moment and then, during a commercial break, set it aside to ask about the great hand-grenade debate. What, exactly, was the proper throwing technique?

"Hand grenades?" he said. "Who knew from hand grenades?"

"Some of the kids at school were talking."

"We were 20,000 feet up in the air," my father said.

Then the commercials ended and Bilko came back on, signaling the end of that conversation but giving me a sliver of military information on which to build: a number, 20,000. It suggested insider status. My father's experiences had given me a tiny sense of belonging with these new kids, who cared about soldiering, and whose fathers had been in the same war as mine.

But what was the business behind these school air-raid drills, and the possibility of some new conflict? It seemed to have no connection at all to my father's war. At recess one afternoon on the school's large dirt playground, there was a new arrival. Her name was Martha. She had wispy blonde hair and skin that appeared never to have seen sunlight. She spoke English, but with a strange European accent. Weren't we ducking our heads in those hallway air raids because of some disagreements in Europe? There seemed to be schoolyard suspicions of a connection to Martha.

On the playground someone called her a name. I heard it when the name became a chant. I looked up from my outfield position in a lunchtime ballgame and wandered over to a small crowd that had gathered around Martha.

"Commie, commie," some classmates were chanting.

Martha, standing inside this chorus, glanced about in apparent bewilderment. I didn't know if there was a language problem or simply a breakdown in idiomatic expression. The chant grew louder, and had a clear taunting edge, though some on the outskirts of the crowd grinned goofily and seemed to be having a fine time. So I joined the chant, the way one joins a football cheer, simply to take part in a rollicking moment.

"Commie, commie," I called, without the vaguest idea what a commie might be. I had never heard of Joe McCarthy's hearings in Washington, or of Roy Cohn or Hollywood celebrities naming names. Joseph Stalin was among the newly dead, and Ho Chi Minh was a name still waiting to be born in the collective consciousness. The word "commie" was just a sound in the air, something that had found its way to an elementary school playground from confusing activities down the highway in Washington.

After a few moments, as the crowd lost interest and dispersed, I returned to my baseball game. Baseball was American, and included no known commies, whatever in the world commies might be. Sometimes, on spring evenings, my friend Joel Kruh and I would walk from our block all the way to the Howard Park schoolyard, carrying our baseball gloves and a ball, just to throw grounders and pop flies to each other. It felt like more than a catch; we were conducting some small American ceremony. On this baseball diamond, in this yard where we went to public school, we were signaling a commitment to the great American game.

Many of the boys from Howard Park Elementary joined the community's Little League and paraded in full uniform through the area's leafy streets one Saturday each spring. The parades seemed like Norman Rockwell paintings sprung to life, with parents waving from front porches and sidewalk perches; I was aware of taking full part in a ritual that gave not only good cheer but civic comfort to all who watched. The center was holding.

Some of us also joined the community's Cub Scout troop, whose meetings were held at the Howard Park Methodist Church, on broad Gwynn Oak Avenue, around the corner from the elementary school. The church seemed transplanted from another MGM back lot. June Allyson could have married Jimmy Stewart in such a setting. A deep expanse of lawn led to the church's gray stone exterior, and inside was a long hallway with a portrait on a wall of a man with long hair. I was about ten years old, lined up for a scout meeting, the first time I noticed it.

"Who is that?" I asked Jay Pugh, standing behind me, who had seemed a little shaky on hand-grenade technique in the schoolyard but went to church and thus had religious insights I lacked.

He studied me for a long moment and then answered, "God."

I found this confusing, as all the Hebrew teachers at the Liberty Jewish Center had described God as invisible. Moses had gotten a peek, it was explained. But God had shown himself then as a burning bush. Here was an actual man, the real goods.

"It's Jesus Christ," said Billy Cunningham, the blond, skinny, hyperactive kid who had differed with Pugh on the hand grenades and now, as near as I could tell, was differing with him once again.

I walked into the Cub Scout meeting in embarrassment and confusion, hoping no one in authority had overheard the conversation. I was a visitor in the home of their God, and had come up lacking. There seemed many religious distinctions about which I was unaware, not only about Christ but about all of the numberless Christian denominations.

I understood no distinctions. A Lutheran was no different from a Catholic or a Seventh Day Adventist in my vocabulary. They all believed in Christ, who was himself little more than a name to me since the first time Billy

McKnight had brought him up in the projects. Then I remembered Christ's huge, intimidating image there, on the wall of the Church of St. James. We were now gathering in a Methodist church. But the word "Methodist" seemed to belong to the English language in a way no different than the term "Howard Park." It was just part of a familiar name, woven into the everyday chatter of a community, inextricably connected to a Little League and a Cub Scout troop and an elementary school. Merely to say the word "Methodist," and to connect it to "Howard Park," was to construct not a religious identification but a fully American one.

At one father-and-son Cub Scout troop meeting at the church, we opened the evening by singing the national anthem. I heard a voice directly behind me soaring dramatically above all others and turned to see a blond, square-jawed, handsome man. He was making the song an operatic call to arms. I thought: Here is the American ideal, a man unashamed to show his devotion to his country.

One night, there was a dance in the same basement recreation room at the church. Fifth- and sixth-graders from Howard Park Elementary School were invited, and adult supervisors gathered on a stage at one end of the big room and played phonograph records. I stood along the edge of the dance floor with a couple of classmates.

"I can slow dance," I said, "but I've never jitterbugged."

"You got it made if you can slow dance," said a boy named Bobby Lueckert, the best athlete in the school.

"Yeah," said Jay Pugh. "The jitterbug, you just throw your body around. That's the easy one."

It was my first organized dance, and I noticed Jewish boys and girls pairing off, and gentile couples doing the same. It wasn't like Tommy D'Alesandro's youthful dances, with their rigid ethnic antagonisms. The culture had stumbled past that as we broke out of our little national enclaves, and some of us found ourselves coexisting in the new neighborhoods and their public schools. We mingled without much self-consciousness. But, without anybody issuing instructions, we stuck to our own kind on the dance floor.

"No," I said to my two classmates, "I think the slow stuff is easier."

I had sneaked in a couple of lessons with a girl named Alice Buchdahl, who lived on Marmon Avenue near the Liberty Jewish Center. We had admitted, one spring afternoon, that we liked each other. The relationship had never gone beyond those few words, but I thought it counted enough that I could ask her for a dance lesson.

In her club basement one afternoon, Alice taught me something called the box step. No one else was home. The box step involved one of my hands holding one of Alice's hands, and my other hand touching her waist. But there was no hint of sexuality in the room, so strong was my fear, and so firm were Alice's instructions about keeping a certain decorum. It was, truly, the box step. I felt boxed in both by its steps and by Alice's sweet but vaguely distant demeanor. How could a boy so joyously athletic feel so clumsy doing such a simple step?

After a while, we sat at a piano in the basement, and she taught me how to play half of "Chopsticks" while she played the other half. Conversation was awkward, but then she offered up bits of gossip: a female classmate, she said, had kissed a boy, and shamed her mother. Yes, yes, I quickly agreed, that was a terrible thing for a girl to do to her mom. I was ready to agree to anything. I had visions of Alice's mother throwing herself in front of traffic on Liberty Heights Avenue because her daughter had kissed an eleven-year-old boy not yet her husband. When we got back up to practice the box step again, I kept even more distance than I had from Alice, not wishing the ruination of such a sweet young lady or her mother's fragile sense of shame.

On the night of the dance at the Howard Park Methodist Church, I asked Alice to dance the first box step, and Jay Pugh and Bobby Lueckert took their own nervous chances. But the evening picked up steam when the beat did. It was a song about a hound dog. Somebody said, "That's Elvis Presley." I had heard his name but not his music.

This moment changed everything. It was not just music, but the opening of a door into a culture, and emotions, about which we had previously only heard rumors from some of the bigger kids. It was the spring of 1956. The adults in charge of the recordplayer put on "Heartbreak Hotel" and "Hound Dog" and "Don't Be Cruel." The tinkling of "Chopsticks" never entered the room, or our consciousness. The box step took its place next to the colonial minuet. At eleven years old, I felt the release of emotions previously untapped and unanticipated, the debut of sexual glands suddenly given a rhythm and a language. Presley sang:

"I *want you*

I *need you*

I-I-I *love you*..."

I could feel myself shudder. All dancing inhibitions gave way that night, all previous social strictures seemed to leave the room, and something thrilling and dangerous entered. A piece of me wanted to pull Alice closer to me, and never mind the shame that her poor mother might feel. But another wanted to find a quiet place and sort things out, to put some familiar borders around these new emotions, some language that I could understand, something that related to previous instructions handed out by responsible authority figures.

As the evening grew late, an adult on the stage called out, "Last dance." It was another Elvis number. The crowd hollered, "No, we want more." I was astonished. Who were we, to talk back to adults? They might tell our parents, and then God alone knew the penalties to be paid. But there were no parents in sight.

"We want more," the crowd chanted.

I looked toward the other end of the room, toward the church doorway, certain that my father had arrived early and would snatch me away from everyone else. He left his own house of worship early; would a church be any different? I feared he would yank me away for talking back to adults. I sneaked in one guilty, "We want more," and looked again toward the door. My father was not there yet. The men at the recordplayer agreed to give us another song.

It was, in retrospect, our first tiny act of generational rebelliousness.

Until then the merest gesture of public disagreement seemed unthinkable. Each piece of our daily behavior seemed closely monitored. Once a week my mother gave me thirty cents to eat lunch at a narrow luncheonette half a block from school. I went with a couple of other boys from my class. The place consisted of a lunch counter with a few stools, several small tables, and one big table in the back of the place, where the Howard Park principal, Miss Bennett, gathered with a few teachers. Near their table was a jukebox. One week, finding an extra nickel in my pocket, I headed for the jukebox and selected a record. Miss Bennett looked up at me.

"Michael Olesker," she said, "what would your mother say if she knew you were wasting money on jukeboxes?"

I looked down at my shoes and muttered something inaudible, hoping that she wouldn't place emergency phone calls to my parents as I made my way back to my table. In midcentury America, the box step wasn't the only manner of boxing us in.

The luncheonette was located at Gwynn Oak Junction. In 1950s Baltimore, the heart of the junction was the Ambassador Theatre, next to the Ellsworth Armacost Funeral Home, around which an enormous line of young people wound on the Saturday that Elvis Presley's first movie, *Love Me Tender,* opened. Across from the Ambassador was a Read's Drug Store with dark, wood-paneled rooms over it. For a year, as congregants raised money for a new synagogue, those rooms were the home of the Liberty Jewish Center. When the new building was ready for occupancy, half a mile further out Liberty Heights Avenue, the rooms above Read's were converted from a Hebrew school to a pool hall, which seemed closer to their best usage.

Two afternoons a week, when Howard Park Elementary let out at three o'clock, I walked down Liberty Heights Avenue, past a couple of gas stations and a used-car lot and a small cluster of houses, past a pharmacy and a firehouse, to the new synagogue. There, from four until six in the evening, I sat with about twenty classmates—almost all of them boys—and studied Hebrew.

We sat in small, airless classrooms while I imagined gentile public school classmates romping through carefree hours of outdoor bliss, kicking footballs and throwing imaginary hand grenades. Through a row of windows on one side of the Hebrew classroom, I could see the back yard of a gentile family who lived next door. Their children played ball while we practiced reading prayers in Hebrew. Their children wore football helmets while we tried to keep our tiny yarmulkes from slipping off our heads as we bobbed them in gentle prayer.

At the front of one classroom sat Mr. Aaron, who sold insurance most of the day and supplemented this income with a little teaching. He had a friendly but weary countenance and five o'clock shadow like Richard Nixon. He might have been discussing term-life policies for all the attention I paid as the evening sky darkened each winter and I yearned to race home before the last traces of daylight vanished and I might yet play a few minutes of ball in the street.

I stared at a clock on the wall behind Mr. Aaron and watched the seconds drag by. I imagined the Baltimore Colts, and John Unitas leaning over center with time running out. He was the master of the so-called two-minute drill, moving the team to one inconceivable victory after another with final-second heroics. In Hebrew school, in my head, was the voice of the broadcaster Chuck Thompson.

"Unitas calling signals," I heard him say. "He's glancing over the defense." I glanced at the clock above Mr. Aaron. "Less than a minute on the clock."

With seconds to go, Unitas would throw the bomb to Lenny Moore, racing down the sidelines and leaping over some hapless defender for a miracle touchdown catch.

"Go, you *shvartzer choleria*," I heard the echo of my father's voice cry out deliriously to Moore. "Go, you crazy black man."

One day on the playground at Howard Park Elementary, I heard a classmate say a word. It was the son of the man at the Cub Scout meeting who had sung the national anthem more proudly than anyone else. At first, I couldn't make out what his son was saying, but he took clear delight in repeatedly calling out this word that no one else understood.

"Fatzah," it sounded like.

And then it dawned on me: He was trying to say *shvartzer,* but was mispronouncing it.

"Where did you hear that?" I asked him.

"It's Jewish, don't you know that?" he said. He was gentile. "I learned it from my father. He heard it from a Jewish guy."

"Do you know what it means?" I said.

"Yeah," he said. "It means nigger."

I turned and walked away. As my father's son, I felt embarrassed. As someone who knew how the language connected to the old world, and the old ways, and to people who had passed such a word down to my father, I felt more embarrassment. The gentile kid and I had stumbled onto a connection in the traditional, unifying American way: the putting down of some other people.

I wanted to explain that my father would never use such a word. *Shvartzer* only meant black, and black was merely a color. Yes, there were nuances in the translation. Yes, polite people didn't refer to Negroes as black. But we weren't the kind of people to discriminate the way this boy intended—because we had our own fears of discrimination. But I couldn't explain this. And my father hadn't quite explained the distinction when he cheered another spectacular run by Lenny Moore.

One afternoon I left school and crossed Liberty Heights Avenue to a little barbershop. There were three middle-aged barbers named Lee, Al, and John. They were there for years, and seemed to know the landscape. Lee, with steely gray hair and glasses, looked like the scold in a Frank Capra movie and stood by his big window looking onto Liberty Heights Avenue to get a read on the neighborhood. He issued troublesome pronouncements to his partners, who held their tongues.

"They've crossed Park Circle," Lee said. He did not specify who "they" were, but his tone was ominous.

"You want a haircut like John's?" Al asked, pointing to the third partner in an attempt to break the tension.

No, of course not. Who would want a haircut like John's? Everyone in the barbershop laughed heartily every time the question was posed. John was bald, and the barbershop's customers were mostly children sent here after class. Sometimes the kids' mothers accompanied them. The three barbers seemed amiable cusses who wouldn't harm a hair on their children's heads.

"They're up past the junior college already," Lee said. "Some of 'em, they're starting to move around Forest Park."

Then, if there were no mothers in the shop, the word "nigger" would be muttered.

Lee was right. By now black people had begun moving into homes further down Liberty Heights Avenue. Those Little League parades, and the sea of white faces reassuring neighbors each spring that life was unchanging, would vanish within a few years. So would the faces at the neighborhood schools. Black families had moved around Garrison Boulevard, and Forest Park High School, and the streets around Lake Ashburton featured in the *Saturday Evening Post*, and they were clearly headed our way.

One of those people moving in was Lenny Moore, the *shvartzer* of my father's vocabulary.

TWELVE
LENNY AND ARTIE

Lee the barber was right. Black people were moving into Northwest Baltimore, and it meant nothing at all that one of them was named Lenny Moore. As Moore moved onto Yosemite Avenue, a couple of miles below the Howard Park barbershop, the neighborhood's white people had already begun to move out. It did not matter that they cheered Moore on Sundays in a ballpark, or that Moore's teammates, white men named Unitas and Donovan and Ameche, whom they also cheered, seemed to accept Moore as teammate and friend.

A fear had begun to take hold across the city. In some neighborhoods, this was expressed with outward antagonism—"Why can't they stay with their own?"—and in other, more liberal places, with genteel code words. Property values, some said. Real-estate values, they declared, as though this eliminated the connection to color. If someone mentioned race, denials filled the room. They said they needed more space for the kids, found only in the new suburban tract developments. They said the schools were better out there. And maybe they mentioned how the colored girl who cleaned for them twice a week was like a member of the family. They hotly denied that race had anything to do with it. It did, of course—even among those who were not racists. It was the fear of being the last white people to leave the neighborhood, the sense that a drawbridge would be going up soon, trapping all behind it who did not make haste. Something bigger than belief, something bigger than ideals, had arrived in their lives, and to stay too long was to risk everything.

Moore bought his house on Yosemite Avenue from a man who owned a furniture store on Baltimore Street. The man was Jewish, as were most of those living on Yosemite and wondering about the neighborhood's future. When Moore spotted one of his new neighbors with a moving van in front of his house, he asked, "Hey, man, why are you moving out?"

"It's nothing, it's just that the neighborhood's breaking up," the man said.

"Oh," Moore said as diplomatically as he could, knowing it was too late for debate. "I know what you're saying."

It was 1958. The Colts were on their way to professional football's championship, and Moore was playing his third spectacular season in a career that would take him to the game's Hall of Fame. That year he averaged more than seven yards every time he carried the ball from scrimmage, a breathtaking number. He caught fifty passes, averaging a remarkable nineteen yards a catch. Late in the fourth quarter of the game that clinched the conference title, with Baltimore trailing the San Francisco Forty-niners, he zigged and zagged a heart-thumping seventy-three yards for the winning touchdown in a return-from-the-dead triumph. He felt the cheers of adoring fans caress him like velvet. Then, in the televised championship game against the New York Giants, he and the Colts electrified the country in the so-called Sudden Death overtime contest that would be called "the greatest game ever played."

But when he moved into a neighborhood that year—home to the great liberals, the Jews, who understood prejudice and marched in picket lines against legalized segregation—he was simply another Negro in a tidal wave, watching For Sale signs appear, and moving vans arrive, and a whole neighborhood changing color in less than a year, the way it did in white neighborhoods across the city, across every religious and ethnic line.

"Yeah, that was how he put it," Moore remembered four decades later. "'The neighborhood's breaking up.' Years later I saw the guy. He said, 'I wish we'd have stayed.' I said, 'Yeah, I wish you had, too. We could have learned a lot from each other.'"

"Were you aware," I asked Moore, "that every time the Colts took the field, you were role models for a community trying to figure out how to act on race?"

"It wasn't a thing that was popularized at the time," he said. "It became popularized later, the role-model thing."

"But, up in the stands," I said, "we were watching black guys and white guys together. This was new for Baltimore. Nobody had seen it."

"Vitally important," Moore said. He nodded his head emphatically. "That started to build something, and horizons opened up that had never opened up before."

But he was right—it was only later, in retrospect, when older fans had reached a certain aesthetic distance from that era and decided which memories to toast, and which ones to discard as politically inconvenient, that the Colts were recalled not only for their triumphs, and the pride they had given a self-conscious city, but for the symbol of brotherhood it was recollected that they had been.

As these men reached middle age, the city honored them as war heroes, and held them even closer because their former team no longer existed. They were the caretakers of memory. Carroll Rosenbloom had dealt the Baltimore Colts to a drunk from Illinois named Robert Irsay, and Irsay sneaked the team to Indianapolis one snowy night in 1984. The city bled for a long time.

Some of the old legends—including Unitas and Moore, Donovan and the great blocker Jim Parker, all of them Hall of Fame members—stayed in Baltimore when their playing careers were done. As the city struggled for a decade to bring back professional football, these old Colts became symbols of all that was held dear, and all that the community longed once more to become.

And they sensed, perhaps even more than they had realized in their playing days, the abiding affection in which they were held. Unitas, the most laconic of men, called the city's football fans the best in America. Donovan, the rambunctious one, became a raconteur spinning endless tales of glad times with the old team. Former Colts of that era, such as Jim Mutscheller and Sisto Averno, and Tom Matte and Ordell Braase, basked in the glow.

But I sensed something different in Moore. Whenever the old Colts gathered, there seemed a wistfulness about him. There was something that he wasn't saying. It wasn't that he denied the good times, or that he didn't remember the cheers pouring out of the stands. Those memories warmed him. He never showed a hint of bitterness. But he was keeping certain things inside—and, compared with the hearty Donovan, the gatekeeper to all laughter, he seemed to have inhabited a different psychological terrain while playing in the same era in the same town.

One evening, forty years after the legendary Sudden Death championship contest, I asked Art Donovan what he remembered about the night before the game. I wondered about the enormous pregame nervousness.

"We stayed at the Concourse Plaza," he said.

"What did you do that night?"

"Brought in pizza. Spinney and me." The lineman Art Spinney was his roommate. "I brought it over from my old neighborhood."

"Could you sleep that night?" I asked.

"Me? Sure, I could sleep after twenty-three hot dogs," Donovan said.

"No," I said, "I mean from feeling nervous about . . ." Suddenly, it dawned on me. I was talking about emotions, and he was talking about hot dogs. "You could eat twenty-three hot dogs in one sitting?"

"Oh, sure," Donovan said. "Hell, more than that. Kosher dogs, I could eat fifteen of 'em."

"The kosher dogs had more meat in them?"

"Oh, yeah. The other dogs, it was like eatin' peanuts."

That was Donovan's memory of the historic game: the eating and the laughs were uninterrupted by the drama. Lenny Moore's memory of the great game included the meaningless contest that followed. It was an exhibition game the next summer, when Moore and the other blacks on the Baltimore Colts were humiliated, and almost no one seemed to notice.

It was, in retrospect, what separated the memories of one man from the other. Moore, coming from impoverished Reading, Pennsylvania, and wanting to cross racial lines, could not. Donovan, the gregarious and embracing man from an ethnically mixed white neighborhood in the Bronx, watched from a racial chasm that neither he nor anyone else knew how to cross.

Moore, born in 1933, went to Reading's public schools. Then, signed by the Colts as their top draft choice after an All-America career at Penn State University, he arrived in Baltimore and went downtown one day with his new wife. They stood in line for movie tickets to the New Theatre, on Lexington Street. When he reached the box office, the white woman inside said, "You can't go in."

"What?" Moore said.

"Sir, you can't go in." Then she pointed to Moore's wife, who was light-skinned. "She can go in, but you can't."

He turned and looked at the people behind him in line. All were white. He thought, where can I go now?

When he told me the story, I said, "Nobody in line reacted to this?"

"No," Moore said, "they didn't know who I was."

That nuance came with a history: Moore learned, over the course of his life, that there were places he could not go as an African American; and there were places he could go strictly because he was Lenny Moore the football star. Now, by either measurement, he had been turned away.

He grew up in a family of twelve brothers and sisters, in the Depression, with a mother who cleaned houses and a father who eventually landed work at a steel mill. Over time, the family lived in a couple of houses with neither electricity nor indoor plumbing. Each backed directly onto railroad tracks.

Moore's father was a big, muscular fellow with no education, whose wife taught him to read and write. This opened up a world for him, and for the family. He wired the house for electricity. Later, he learned how to fix televisions for extra money. He would half-sole the kids' shoes with leather scraps from the steel mill.

"I never saw one hungry day," Moore said. "Saw a lot of one-pot meals, but no, never hungry."

He looked around the club basement of his home. To describe the layout as cozy diminishes the word. It is womb-like and welcoming, with couches and reclining chairs all around, and a few pictures of Moore in his playing days.

The future "Sputnik" of Baltimore, Lenny Moore, a big man on certain parts of the Penn State campus. One of twelve children, he imagined joining the military after high school to ease the family burden at home. Then college football coaches came to call. *Courtesy of the Moore family*

Lenny and his wife, Edith, moved to this street of ranch homes tucked behind Liberty Road in Northwest Baltimore County after his playing days. When black people in Baltimore began moving out of the city, Liberty Road was the primary destination. In the last fifteen years of the twentieth century, as more blacks moved into the area, many whites moved even farther out. It wasn't the kind of frenzied exodus of years earlier, but there was a steady, plodding attrition. Middle-class whites had not exactly stopped fleeing middle-class black people, but they were moving a little slower.

Moore's Hall of Fame bust rested on a shelf just inside his front door, but it was easy to walk past without noticing. At sixty-six, he worked for the state's Juvenile Services Administration, dealing directly with youngsters whose lives had fallen apart.

"You know, I've got an alarm system here," Moore said. He swept a hand around the room. "Got every area covered, even got a sensor. When I was a kid growing up, we'd leave the door open. Nobody stole from each other."

He grew up where neighborhoods were divided by race and by nationality, but the kids discovered each other in school. Moore remembered white boys coming to his house, but no return invitations. It was unwritten social custom, but it hurt. The slight stayed with him his whole life, because it recurred his whole life.

In his last year at Reading High School he broke all existing football records. In class, he coasted. He'd always imagined he would leave school when he reached eighteen and join the military, the way two of his older brothers had.

"One less mouth to feed, okay?" Moore said. "So I figured, I'll do the same. I couldn't have cared less about the school work. But then came the scholarship thing at Penn State. Oh, man, that was a rude awakening." He sighed as he said it. "There was only like a little more than a hundred of us out of all those thousands of white kids. And I'm including those that came from other countries, like the Africans."

I said it sounded lonely. Moore didn't seem comfortable with the characterization. He joined a black fraternity and socialized at the fraternity house. Blacks were not only segregated from white fraternities, they were not allowed inside white fraternity houses.

"But you were a big man on campus," I said. "You didn't get invited to fraternity parties?"

"You couldn't go in the white fraternity houses," he said. "That was taboo. No, that was cut. The only time we could go in was once a year, open house. Other than that, no, no blacks."

College fraternity parties are, of course, a frivolous measure of the American racial divide. Who cares about exclusionary parties for young people half a century ago when the era had so many methods of institutionalized isolation? But they gave Moore a heightened sense of the divide, and they made him notice things: the silence when he entered a room, the snide reference to minstrel shows, to Aunt Jemima. And he was always outnumbered, and always self-conscious about how others perceived him.

"I didn't know anything about my own culture," he said. "If you said 'Africa' to me, I'd say, 'Hey, man, the only thing I know about Africa is the Tarzan movies.' I'm serious, I knew nothing. We used to sit in the movies and we'd watch the natives, man, with the bones in their ears and the spears and stuff. So, when you said 'Africa,' I'm looking at it the same way Caucasians are looking at it. The only experience I have is the Caucasian point of view. Because this is all I was taught."

He was talking about an education ten years before my time, but it lingered into my own school years and slightly beyond, until the great militant upheavals of the late sixties. He remembered Tarzan movies; I remembered blacks lightening their skin and conking their hair. He remembered minstrel references; I remembered black kids inserting knives in hearts simply by calling each other black.

"Coming up through schools, I was only taught this movie stuff," Moore said. "So when it came to the breakdown of cultures, we were always taught about Europeans with sharp features and straight hair, or whatever, and they'd talk about the Africans and say, 'Nappy hair, thick lips, flat nose.'" His voice went lower as he said this. "It was degrading. But then, to support that, if you went to the movies, you would always see the thing backed up."

He remembered feeling outcast at a junior high school music assembly. Everyone sang "Swanee River," with its darkeys at play. Or they sang "Dixie." He felt all white kids' eyes on him. He remembered old movies with black people showing lots of teeth. Years later, when he went to sports banquets, white men would approach Moore and say, "Show me some teeth, Lenny."

"To this day," Moore said wearily. "To this day."

When Moore was growing up in Reading, Art Donovan was coming of age in the Bronx. Moore's father toiled in obscure poverty, while Donovan's father was the third man in the ring in some of professional boxing's most fabled fights. Arthur Donovan Sr. officiated at so many of Joe Louis's heavyweight championship bouts that some called him Louis's personal referee. Once the New York sportswriter Jimmy Cannon wrote, "Joe Louis is a credit to his race—the human race." The twist on the old, patronizing racial cliché lent a nobility to Louis. He was a Negro who could be embraced by whites,

Arthur Donovan, the famous boxing referee, and his son, Art Donovan, the famous football player and bon vivant, with Art's daughter Debbie. A U.S. Marine veteran and football Hall of Famer, the younger Donovan thought his father found him "too soft." *Courtesy of the Donovan family*

especially after he decimated the German Max Schmeling in one round at New York's Yankee Stadium as Adolf Hitler, declaring Aryan supremacy, readied for war in Europe. Donovan Sr. was in the ring that night.

His son reveled in his father's fame, and has since spent a lifetime reveling in his own. He is the grand time had by all, recalling the tales that remind his listeners of shared histories. Moore calls Donovan "a great man." Donovan uses similar words about Moore and calls him "the greatest football player I ever saw."

Donovan plays the buffoon to cover a sharp intelligence. Also, he reaches instinctively for ethnic identification as comic relief: We all know who we are, and let's have a laugh at our own expense. It is the Arthurian embrace in the face of any hint of self-consciousness.

He and his wife, Dottie, own the Valley Country Club, in Baltimore County's Towson area. They married as the Colts were entering their glory years of the 1950s, and then they bought the club. Nearly fifty years later, they still lived in a handsome brick house on the grounds.

When I went to see him one cold and drizzly April morning, we sat at the club's bar, with blown-up photographs of Donovan in his playing days covering all the walls.

"You know these weren't my idea," he said right away.

"You look at them much?" I asked.

"Never," he said. "You were never out here before?"

"You never invited me," I said.

"Well, we don't let Jews in the place," he guffawed. It was untrue. It was Donovan reaching instinctively for the ethnic give-and-take, and it also echoed a familiar theme between us. Whenever he saw me, he would declare, "There's my Jew-boy from the Bronx."

"What do you want to talk about?" he said now. "Bullshit like the Ravens?"

"Hell, no," I said. "The Bronx."

His face beamed. This was territory of his heart.

"The Bronx," he said. "We used to walk on the Grand Concourse." It was territory of my own heart, as well: where my father and my uncle posed for a picture in the last burst of youth before the war, where my mother and I lived with my grandmother in the Joseph Arms Apartments until my father came home from the fighting. *That* Grand Concourse.

"Oh, it was great," Donovan said. "We'd walk along the Concourse to the movies. The RKO Fordham or the Loew's Paradise. And people would stop my father to get his autograph. I thought that was the greatest thing."

Nearly half a century after his arrival in Baltimore, he held onto his thick Bronx accent. His father was a public man, and a little preoccupied. Between fights he taught boxing to rich men's sons at the New York Athletic Club.

"My mother really raised us," Donovan said. "My father never knew I played football till I was a junior in high school."

"No," I said.

"Yeah," he said, shrugging. "Then somebody told him I was on the team and he showed up. I never told him. Well, he was busy." Donovan lived in the Bronx until he went off to the war. The neighborhood was a mix: lots of Irish like Donovan, and lots of Italians and Jews and Germans.

"But you see," Donovan said, "in Baltimore, everybody lived in rowhouses. In the Bronx, we lived in apartment houses. So really, the people alongside you could have been Italian or German or Jewish, and it meant nothing. Everybody the same, a great, great melting pot. That's what it was.

My two closest friends were Abie Goldberg and Lefty Weisberg. And Lefty got shot down over Europe, and spent a year in a stalag, and he came home and married an Italian girl named Agnes Pasarelli. So, you know, it was a mixture."

"Goldberg," I said. "Was that the Goldberg from the candy store?"

Donovan laughed at the name. A different Goldberg, he said. He loved telling a story about hanging out at Goldberg's candy store for years, and then returning there triumphantly on the morning after the Colts defeated the New York Giants to win the football championship.

Donovan, the All-Pro from the neighborhood, was on top of the world. He felt like the most famous man in America. Goldberg the candy-store owner hadn't seen him since Donovan moved to Baltimore. Now he took one look at him.

"Donovan, you big bum," said Goldberg, "you out of work again?"

Donovan's stories were all like that, full of laughter and unself-conscious mixing: the Irish kidding the Jews, and the Italians needling the Germans, and laughter as the great common denominator.

"You have to understand," he said, "if you're Catholic, Protestant, or Jewish, if you come from the Bronx and they say, 'Where you from?' you say, 'I'm from St. Philip's Parish,' or wherever. You knew that. Christ the King was where you lived, on the corner. We used to walk over across the park where Lefty Weisberg went to Hebrew school on Wednesdays and wait for him to play stickball."

Donovan played football on a cinder field. He was 225 pounds, much bigger than his father, but he still looked up to the old man. The morning after Donovan Senior refereed matches, he went off to work teaching rich boys how to box. The mother worked in the kitchen. Donovan looked at the shirt his father had worn in the ring. It was covered with blood.

"Man, that's Joe Louis's blood," he thought.

He had a sister, and there were twelve cousins living within two blocks. All, including Donovan, were born in the same house at 252 East 202nd Street.

"My parents were both born here," Donovan said. In America, he meant. "My grandmother, Mrs. Wall, was like the matriarch of the neighborhood. I used to pass her house on the way to play ball, and I'd walk on the other side so she wouldn't see me. I wanted to play. She'd call me over and I had to play cards with her. She was going blind, and I used to cheat at war. She'd say, 'How come you're doing so good?' All my uncles had to play bridge with her. And she had to win, or she didn't talk to you."

As Donovan tells stories, the sense of joy comes through his pores. His laughter is high-pitched, and usually starts with self-deprecation. He is a tough, brawny guy. Implicit in each story: If I can laugh at myself, and my own continuous foolishness, how serious should any of us take life?

"Your father," I said, "lived in a world that was a real mix of race and religion." I wanted to know how that extended to Donovan's later life on the Colts.

"Yeah," Donovan said, "but he never hung around any of the people in the fight game. He worked at the New York Athletic Club, teaching those rich boys. I used to go down to the club with him. He'd be teaching the sons of these rich members, and he wanted me to box them. And he'd say to me, 'But you gotta lose.' And I'd say, 'But, Pop, by the time I'm fifteen, I'm gonna be punch drunk.' I'd get in the ring with these kids, and they'd hit me in the head and everything else, and I had to try to stay there and take it."

He laughed at the memory of such preposterousness. When the war came, he signed up for the U.S. Marines. Donovan's father, distraught, hollered to his wife, "Mary, kiss him goodbye, he's gonna get killed."

He spent two years in the South Pacific. He served on a Marine aircraft carrier, and then he went to Okinawa and Guam. Donovan minimized those war years. The Colts' game against the Bears in 1960, he would say. *That* was rougher than World War II. Or he remembered laughter in the middle of the grinding Marine boot camp.

"In the Marines, I was always hungry," he said. It was early one evening, and we had been talking about his father's fame. "So I stole a case of Spam, thirty packs in a case. And I got caught. They took me to the commandant, a guy named McFadden. I figure, he's gonna look out for me. McFadden, right? It's the great ethnic game. He says, 'Where are you from?' I tell him, 'The Bronx.' He says he's from New York. He says, 'Are you related to the famous fight referee?' I said, 'Yeah, he's my father.' He says, 'Okay, I'm gonna give you a break. You've got one week to eat the whole case of Spam. All thirty packs.'" Donovan paused for a beat. "Fortunately, I love the stuff."

"You're telling me that was the worst part of the Marines?" I said.

"Well," he said, "there were times on the aircraft carrier, the kamikazes coming in, it was pretty unbelievable. The ships are getting hit. All kinds of planes are coming down on us. But we were lucky."

Then he dismissed the memory. He was happier remembering the glad homecoming, the ride from Bainbridge Naval Base into Baltimore, and then the train to New York's Penn Station. He rode the subway home, still in uniform, lugging his duffel bag.

"And there's a kid from my neighborhood named Tommy Lionelli," he said. "His job was delivering false teeth for a company. And he's sitting on the subway. I says, 'Hey, Tommy.' He says, 'Hey, Artie, where you been?' He never even missed me. So I got home, I went up to the 203rd Street exit of the subway, and my cousin's there waiting. He knew I was coming, I'd called."

As Donovan told the story, I thought of my father's Atlantic City homecoming from the war, and John Pica's in Baltimore. The homecoming scene was the great common denominator for those lucky enough to make it back from the war.

"So we walked across the street to the apartment," Donovan said, delighted at the memory, "and my mother was in the kitchen cooking a ham. I said, 'Ma, I'm home. You know, I helped win the war, Ma.'" Donovan laughed at his own line, and then his voice softened a little. "And, naturally, she started crying and everything else. It was very heartwarming. 'Cause, you know," he muttered, "some of these guys never came back."

He went to Boston College after the war and played football. Then, in the summer of 1950, the Baltimore Colts drafted him. Professional football was different then. Baseball was still the national pasttime, and the most glamorous football was played in the colleges. The pros were still seen as a backward, little-known bunch of tough guys who hadn't been able to find legitimate jobs. Donovan figured he'd give it a shot.

"And my father said, 'Where are you going?'" he remembered. "'I'm outside the apartment in the Bronx, packing the car. I said, 'I'm going to Baltimore.' He said, 'What are you gonna do there?' I said, 'I'm gonna try out for the Baltimore Colts.' He says, 'There he goes again. Maaary!' And my mother sticks her head out the window of the second-floor apartment we had. He says, 'Mary, do you know what he's doing?' She says, 'Yeah, he's going down to Baltimore to try out for the football team.' He says, 'Those big guys will kill him down there.'

"See," Donovan said now, "I really believe my father thought I was sort of a sissy."

"But you'd been in the Marines," I said. "You fought in a war, and you played college football."

"I was Little Arthur," Donovan replied.

The Colts trained at Western Maryland College, in Westminster, using a men's dormitory to bunk the players. In that summer of 1950 pro football was so ragged that the ballclub didn't even have enough equipment to outfit all the players trying to make the team.

"So I go out there on a Monday morning," Donovan remembered, "and there's a hundred fifty guys trying out. Clem Crowe was the coach. I'm standing there with Sisto Averno and Don Colo. And Sisto says, 'Don't take any equipment, and they won't know if we're good or bad.' So we stayed out there, we didn't have any shoulder pads and we didn't have any helmets for a week. Guys are coming and going, and they still don't know if we're good enough to play. We hid out long enough that we made the team."

It was the training camp that launched a generation of good cheer. When practices ended, Donovan and his teammates would slip off to Westminster's taverns and restaurants and backyard barbecues thrown by local fans, where the mutual adoration began that would sustain itself for the next three decades.

"You had that appealing mix on the Colts," I said. "The melting pot."

"We sure were," said Donovan. "We came from all over the country. Polish, Irish, German."

"How about racially?" I asked. "Was there much mixing?"

"I don't know," Donovan said. He shifted uneasily. This was emotional home turf to him, the great American mix. Donovan was the enduring symbol of the Colts as happy band of brothers. But the moment was awkward.

"They had their own thing," he said. "I think they had a better time than we did. When we went on exhibition games in the South, they wouldn't let the African American guys stay in the hotels. Carroll Rosenbloom didn't like that. And the black guys, they got mad."

He seemed more uncomfortable now, and I felt uncomfortable for asking. It was long ago, couldn't we let it rest? But I wanted to know what it was like when the country was making that transition, and hungered for role models, and the high-profile Colts had seemed like something worth emulating.

"I don't know," Donovan said. "The black guys, they stayed with black families, I think. But they had no bed check." He guffawed. "We had bed check, and they didn't. When they put 'em in with us, Jim Parker says, 'What are they doin' to us, they're ruining our lives.' 'Cause they had bed check now and couldn't stay out all night. And that's the God's honest truth."

Then Donovan seemed more reflective. It was forty years after the fact, and we mustn't judge yesterday's values by today's. "I never gave it a thought," he said softly. "It was just the times. But I never gave it much thought. Period."

When Lenny Moore arrived at his first training camp, six years after Donovan's rookie season, he found Westminster a shock. Color was everything. In the summer of 1956, as Moore entered professional football, Claude "Buddy" Young was leaving. He had been the Colts' most exciting performer in their early years, and he was black.

"This area is very, very segregated," he told Moore on the first day they met.

He pointed out a little confectionery store down the hill from the college. You can go there, Young said. And there was a Twin Kiss nearby, where Negroes were allowed to buy ice cream, because it was strictly carry-out. The Colts, like most National Football League teams, had never had more than a handful of black players, so the club considered segregation more an annoyance than a serious social problem they needed to challenge, no matter how much the team's presence meant to Westminster.

So Buddy Young, knowing how much was riding on his image, adapted. He was there as a role model for cheering crowds, and as a willing foil when players wanted to joke around. Donovan was one. Teammates knew his aversion to animals, and Donovan knew Young's.

One summer in Westminster, Donovan's roommate, Art Spinney, shot a groundhog and slipped the poor animal under Donovan's covers. Donovan, the city boy, thought it was a fish.

"Who would do that to a poor fish?" he bellowed. "Where's Buddy Young? I'd like to see his eyes when I show him this."

Donovan called Young and Buddy arrived from his dormitory room moments later. "Here, Young, have fun," Donovan said. Young bolted from the building and didn't return until the animal had been dispatched elsewhere. It was raw, sophomoric jock humor—but it had included Young. In the early days, that was a statement.

By the time Moore arrived for training camp it was not. Young sat him down and explained the rules of life in Westminster. Just about every place was off limits to him. He was twenty-two years old, away from home, and isolated. He found a spot about a mile from campus, across the main highway, Route 140: a little duck pond and a few picnic benches. He went there regularly to blow off the pressures of the day. When teammates went to the local taverns for beers and easy laughs, Moore went to the duck pond and imagined, incorrectly, that it would be much different when the club broke training camp and moved down to Baltimore.

It was different, but marginally. He was turned away at downtown's New Theatre. He moved into a West Baltimore neighborhood, on Brighton Street off Poplar Grove, which was all black. When white teammates went off to party, Moore and the huge defensive tackle Eugene "Big Daddy" Lipscomb went strictly to black West Baltimore. Integration ended on the playing field.

"Separation was a total gulf," Moore said. Years afterwards, he said it flatly, without rancor or sadness. It was simply a fact. "We did nothing socially together. In fact, over twelve years, we did almost nothing off the field unless it was a team function. But getting on the phone or being invited to one of the guys' houses, we did nothing socially, ever, not during those years." It was an echo of Reading. But he had expected something better among consenting adults.

He and Lipscomb went to clubs around the city's Pennsylvania Avenue: the Alhambra, the Club Tijuana, the Casino, the Comedy Club. Pennsylvania Avenue was still a hurricane of night life. It was the closing era of music and booze, about to be destroyed by the vast heroin trade coming within the decade that would take Lipscomb's life and thousands more anonymous victims.

Lipscomb, an enormous six-foot-six, 290 pounds, a folk hero on the ballfield, was a mass of emotional scars and insecurity. When he was eleven his mother was stabbed to death on a streetcorner. He never knew his father. He had gone directly from high school into the Marines and, almost exclusively among the pros, he had never attended college.

"He'd say, 'Oh, man, why you guys always talking about that bullshit college?'" Moore remembered. "So we cut it. That was no problem. Daddy was big and strong, but he had a lot of complexes. We'd be in a cab—this was before we got our cars—and he'd start crying. I'd say, 'Hey, man, what's wrong with you?' He'd say, 'The Daddy don't feel too cool, man.' I'd say, 'What's wrong? You hurting somewhere?' He'd say, 'No, I'm all right, Sputnik. Don't worry about it, Sput.' And these episodes would happen all of a sudden. He'd just break down and cry. His protective covering was to drink. That was his shield."

The two men were cheered on the ballfield, and isolated elsewhere. In 1958, when Moore had already established himself as one of football's most dynamic stars, his mother died and was buried in York, Pennsylvania. Buddy Young, Jesse Thomas, and Lipscomb were there. Nobody else from the Colts came to the funeral. Nobody cried harder than Lipscomb.

"We came out of the church," Moore said, "and I grabbed his hand and Buddy's and Jesse's. 'Thanks for coming, man, I appreciate the support.' Big Daddy looked at me and said, 'Hey, Sput,' and the tears, man. He grabbed me. I said, 'Don't worry, we're together.' He just cried and cried. I stood by her casket as folks were coming by. He was just—well, reliving his life."

On a wall in Moore's cozy club basement, there are two large portraits, side by side. One is Moore. The other is Lipscomb, found dead of a heroin overdose in the spring of 1963.

In 1958 the Colts drove to their first football championship, still the most heartfelt event in Baltimore sports history. It lifted an entire community accustomed to self-consciousness. Late in the regular season, though, Baltimore needed a victory over San Francisco to clinch a division title. At halftime, the Colts trailed, 27 to 7.

Then, in the fourth quarter, having rallied for two scores, they trailed by six points. The day was bitterly cold. Moore took a handoff from John Unitas and swept left end. Then he changed direction. He twisted away from one tackler, and then another. Breathlessly, he outran several more, and then cut back to the left. And then he was gone, seventy-three yards to a touchdown, and the Colts were on the way to their first conference title.

"All I thought," Moore remembered years later, "was that we had the lead."

He said nothing about the roar of the crowd, which bathed him in cheers and must have made him feel like the most beloved man on the planet—until he went home that evening, and noticed all the For Sale signs still in people's front yards.

On December 28, 1958, the Colts defeated the New York Giants for the championship of professional football. Baltimoreans remember that moment as the centerpiece of all sports history; football fans know it as the Sudden Death overtime game so exciting that it changed a nation's sports-watching habits. All recall John Unitas rallying the Colts in the final two minutes to set up a tying field goal seven seconds before the end of regulation time; how Unitas found receiver Raymond Berry with twelve passes that day; and how Alan "The Horse" Ameche, head down, behind a crucial block thrown by Lenny Moore, charged into the end zone for the winning touchdown.

Moore recalled all of this, too. But the memory that haunted him was the following summer.

In an exhibition contest billed as a replay of the championship game, the Colts played the New York Giants in Dallas, Texas. They arrived the night before the game, and their plane landed and did not approach the airport terminal. Two buses pulled alongside the plane. The white players on the club were told to get onto the buses.

"This is the first time we knew," Moore said. "The white players were staying one place, and we had to stay at another place." It was the incident Donovan had mentioned.

"Didn't you say, 'Wait a minute, I'm part of this team?'" I asked.

"Kellett took us aside," Moore went on. He meant Don Kellett, the Colts general manager. "He told us, 'We'll get your bags, we'll get you a cab,' stuff like that. And these two buses pulled off with all our teammates."

Left behind were Moore and Lipscomb, Jim Parker, Sherman Plunkett, Milt Davis, Johnny Sample, Luke Owens. They were the only blacks on the team. Moore remembered five taxicabs passing them by as they stood outside the airport terminal. Finally Kellett went inside and arranged for a couple of cabs, and the players were driven to a place called the Peter Lane Motel.

"We're looking at each other, ready to get into a rage," Moore remembered. "I said, 'Wait a minute, be cool. Let's see what the deal is.' Kellett was with us. He said, 'Mr. Lane, the boys are here.' Lane says, 'Don't worry about it, I got everything squared away.' Kellett says, 'Anything else I need to do?' He's going to the Sheraton Dallas, with the team. And he leaves, and Lane takes us to our rooms."

Moore shook his head at the memory. "It was a room with a bed in it," he said. "That's it. Not a radio, not a TV, nothing. Just a room with a bed."

Then came a telephone call. It was Mel Triplett, the New York fullback. Giants' management had done the same thing to their black players. They were staying in a dump around the corner: Triplett and Emlen Tunnell, Roosevelt Grier and Roosevelt Brown. Triplett mentioned a nearby restaurant where they could all meet that night.

"So we get there," Moore recalled, "and we say, 'What are we gonna do?' Say, 'We ain't playing.' Giants say, 'Okay, we're not playing either.' We order our food. We're talking. 'How were you handled? How did you get here? Did you know beforehand? No. Neither did we.' All that stuff. Saying, 'Owners talk. They make policy. They all knew what would happen.' So we're not going. Not gonna play. We'll go to the locker room but we won't take the field. We're saying, 'Nobody told us ahead of time, and we wouldn't have come if they had.'"

Then came a quiet voice of dissent: Emlen Tunnell's. The Giants' veteran defensive back reminded everybody of those black players who had come before them. He mentioned Marion Motley of Cleveland. Went through hell, Tunnel said. Some men had gotten death threats, he said. They made it easier for those who followed. What about the guys behind us, if we don't take the field? And there's gonna be some of *our folks* in the stands.

"None of those players could stay with the team in the early days," Tunnel said. "At least sometimes we're staying together. But let's tell management how we feel."

"You know," Moore told the little gathering, "I'm thinking about Jackie Robinson. He was the only one on the team. Jackie didn't have anybody to bounce it off of. Who's he got? But the cat was out there every day. The heck with it. Folks want to see us, so they'll see us."

But the ballplayers decided for one symbolic gesture of anger: They would show up late. They arrived, as a group, barely in time for dressing and brief pregame warmups.

"Guys were milling around, getting taped, bantering like always," Moore said. "Soon as we hit the door, everything stopped. So we went to our lockers. Nobody said anything. Start taking our clothes off. Nothing."

Then Moore noticed Raymond Berry move toward Big Daddy Lipscomb. Berry was not only the team's superb receiver, but a native Texan. He muttered a few words to Lipscomb. Then he moved to Jim Parker and to Milt Davis, talking for a moment to each of them.

"Then he came to me," Moore said. "I don't remember the exact words, but he said he was sorry this happened, and the way it happened, but, 'I'm with you.' And it was just the idea that he would get up. And he was the only one, see? Nobody said anything. Got taped, went on the field for warmups. And I'm standing there, and Alan Ameche comes over. 'Ah, Lenny.' That's just the way he went. 'Ah, Lenny.'" Moore shrugged his shoulders helplessly, remembering how Ameche had gestured. "I'll never forget it. His expression said everything. I said, 'Hey, man, thank you. You don't need to say a word, my man. Thank you. Appreciate it.'"

But the humiliation stayed inside Moore, where it festered silently, until it spilled out of him one night a quarter of a century later.

THIRTEEN

TWENTY-THREE NATIONS

Several floors above Southeast Baltimore's Boston Street, Toni Keane stood on her back balcony one evening at century's turn and swept a hand across the city's harbor. The face of things was changing all along the old waterfront neighborhoods and Keane, a professor of sociology, wondered how much memory would be lost along the way.

In Locust Point, where anxious and exhausted immigrants first ventured onto land from their ocean voyages, the neighborhood's old factory spaces were being converted into high-tech offices, and refurbished little nineteenth-century rowhouses were fetching six figures apiece because pleasure boats in the harbor could now be glimpsed from rooftop decks. Federal Hill, where newcomers had labored for a few dollars a week around the Cross Street Market, was now the weekend destination of yuppies seeking sushi and companionship. Just north was the Inner Harbor, once a muscular shipping port and now a waterfront shopping mall for tourists in running shorts.

And nearby was Fells Point, the cobblestone Eastern European neighborhood where modern college vulgarians arrived for weekend beer romps.

So the past retreats from view. Keane grew up in a Baltimore where entire neighborhoods identified themselves by their churches. It was Artie Donovan's Bronx demarcation transported 200 miles south.

"*Where do you live?*"

"*St. Ambrose Parish. You?*"

"*Our Lady of Pompeii.*"

Such was the standard colloquy of generations. Keane's family had roots in Czechoslovakia and in Germany. With her Czech relatives, she worshipped at St. Wenceslaus Church; with the Germans, at St. Michael's. At sixty, she went to Twenty-three Nations Church, originally founded by Germans but now, at the end of a long half-century's suburban exodus, with a congregation about half Spanish.

This was the nature of things. One generation bequeaths whole neighborhoods to the next, including its houses of worship. In nearby Fells Point, there was St. Stanislaus Church, originally founded by immigrant Poles in the decade after the Civil War. Once, the church had its own school, and hundreds of children filled its halls and paraded ceremoniously each spring through streets where housewives stood on the marble front steps of rowhouses to cheer them on. It was part of the neighborhood's legacy. But in the last few decades of the twentieth century so many of the Poles had moved away that the church closed its doors after Easter services in the spring of 2000. To many, it felt not only like the end of the church's history but the closing of a collective memory.

"Believe me," Toni Keane said now, "if it wasn't for the Latinos coming to Twenty-three Nations, we might be St. Stanislaus."

She glanced through her back window, toward the harbor, where the sky was turning inky. I came to see her because of Barbara Mikulski. "You're gonna write about ethnics, you gotta talk to Toni Keane and John Prevas," she had said.

I'd known Prevas since high school. He'd started his career as a prosecuting attorney and was now a city judge. For many years, his family owned one of the stalls at the Broadway Market. I knew Keane mostly by nice reputation. For fourteen years, she had appeared on a televised current events program in Baltimore, called *Square-Off*, where she butted heads over the era's most contentious issues but managed to keep both her composure and her wit. She taught sociology at Loyola College, in North Baltimore, where many of her students' families had moved after World War II when the old ethnic strongholds were starting to break up. Keane was slightly breathless when she talked, and affectionate and funny and fast.

"I was like a sociologist as a kid," she said. "I've always loved different kinds of cultures, it's the spice of life. We used to spend Friday nights at WASP friends. It was like ethnic withdrawal." She laughed at her own joke, then upped it. "Like stimulus deprivation," she said. "So now I go to Twenty-three Nations, which is half Spanish, and I find myself so touched to watch these immigrants off the boat, and to experience what they're experiencing vicariously."

I thought about Felix Guevara and wondered if he went to a Spanish church. I remembered him standing in that courthouse hallway, with the rogue policeman Dorian Martin lurking nearby. For Guevara the courthouse had become his church of secular worship, where God might make his presence known in some righteous criminal verdict against the bully Martin. Toni Keane knew Guevara's case. But she went to church on Sundays and saw rows of Felix Guevaras, each of them trying to find a sense of home.

"I go to Holy Communion," Keane said. She sat across a couch from Prevas, with whom she had shared a life since they found each other during Barbara Mikulski's first city council campaign. Prevas's eyes danced behind his glasses.

"And these Spanish parents," she said, "are obviously very, very poor, and the kid is in the best outfit. And the older brothers are all hanging on the car outside. Men don't go into church at that age. But the parents are there beaming. And you know it's cost them a fortune."

She smiled happily as she told the story. Keane is naturally upbeat but now, as she remembered these Latino families, her voice was the sound of a high-pitched lute on a musical romp.

"And you have this nun," she said, "Sister Sonya. She's taught them how to read the Bible, which is hard reading for anybody, much less a seven-year-old kid who hears Spanish all the time at home. And the kid has practiced

Baltimore Circuit Court Judge John Prevas and Loyola College's Toni Keane. Their love blossomed out of the mixing bowl of Fells Point and the first political campaign of Barbara Mikulski. *Courtesy of Toni Keane and John Prevas*

and practiced, and he's so proud of himself. And then you watch the bishop come to the church, and he's from Los Angeles. It's a beautiful church, but it's old and poor. And when the guy gets up with the flamenco guitar, the bishop has these tears coming down his cheeks because he's homesick.

"And you realize," Keane said, "that you're watching something so special. I can't go to a fast-food church. I have to feel that connection. But the thing is, I'm getting something I didn't bargain for. I mean, I feel my ghost when I go there. But I'm also reliving this experience that I never lived, that I never had to cope with, this immigrant thing." She stopped for a beat. "And that's been a gift," she said. "A gift."

Outside Keane's back window, the lights of downtown were twinkling on. You could see them reflected in her eyes, or just imagine it. "And I sit there thinking," she said, "that that's the Catholic experience. It goes back all those years, and you can still live it today, and it binds us. But the thing is, you've got some people in East Baltimore saying, 'Who are these people that are coming in?' You know? 'Who are *these people* that are coming in?' It's the eternal question, isn't it? And I wind up sort of the peanut butter in the middle of the sandwich. Because, at Twenty-three Nations, we'd be singing the same sad tune as St. Stanislaus if it wasn't for the Spanish."

She glanced across the living-room couch at Prevas, who nodded back. He had thick curly hair and a Pancho Villa mustache.

"You know," Keane said, "they bring somebody in for a week every year to see what's gonna happen. 'What should we do with the church?' So I brought John that week. I said, 'Wear a suit and look like a Mexican.' It was a Memorial Day service, and half the crowd is Hispanic, and half what we call Anglos. And they're telling us, 'Well, we don't want to have to close the church, but . . .'

"And this one Hispanic woman said, 'I came here in 1958, I had no money, and the church was here for me. My husband says we should go to this air-conditioned church. I say no.' And then another lady says, 'I came from Guatemala. My child was hit by a car and spent all night dying, but the priest stayed with me and held my hand. I'm not gonna let you close this church.' And so on and on like that. They were saying, 'This is our church, and we won't let you hurt it.'"

"That loyalty," Prevas said.

"That loyalty," Keane agreed.

Today we move around. When the old ethnic enclaves began to come apart after the war, it was sometimes a gift. It helped us get past ancient suspicions of each other that were based mainly on distance and self-imposed ignorance. In the second half of the twentieth century, the old white ethnic antagonisms often seemed as distant and irrelevant as the Middle Ages. Partly, this was because whites united over a common outsider: nonwhites. But sometimes it was simply because whites overlapped, lived next door, took each other's kids to school, shopped at the mall, watched their children marry, and sometimes mixed religions. By the end of the century the inter-marriage rate among America's Italians topped 70 percent, and it was 65 percent among the Irish. The Polish intermarriage rate topped 80 percent, and among Japanese-Americans, it was 50 percent. Things got a little blurry. It was harder to stereotype an entire category of strangers once they had married into your family.

And then came the new concern: Were we losing our sense of heritage in the process, willfully cutting ourselves off from our uniqueness in a desire to fit in, to make things smoother all around, and forgetting the ingredients that make us who we are?

At Loyola College Keane taught a course about the nature of families: those we embrace for a few years and imagine we will hold together for the length of our lives, and those that disappear, first from sight and then from all memory.

"I teach kids who are pretty assimilated," she said. "They're upper-middle-class suburban kids who haven't bothered to ask where they came from. When you talk to them about ethnicity, they kind of draw a blank."

One day she told her class, "A lot of stories are getting lost. I want you to do a thing on family folklore that you can give to your children. I want you to write a paper by talking to your own families."

Some of those families left Europe and first settled in these waterfront neighborhoods that were visible from Keane's back window. But the children never knew any of this, or never seemed to have cared when somebody tried to tell them about it. It was ancient history, and history was boring.

"But it was amazing," she said. "You know, I hate to say this, but college professors do not necessarily like to read papers. Especially sixty papers, Christmas time, you have to be a crazy person to do this. And I couldn't stop reading them. They were exquisite. The Italian kids all wrote about holidays and food, and relatives, and World War II love stories. And the Irish kids, it was tales of poverty, it was *Angela's Ashes*. Then I had one girl whose family had been in the Greek civil war. She only knew snippets before this. We sat here reading them, and we cried."

She looked at Prevas, who nodded. The papers echoed pieces of their own lives: Prevas, the Greek kid whose mother and father had differing outlooks on the importance of their own heritage; and Keane, half Slovakian and half German, who worshipped at the church now embraced by Spanish parishioners caught between their old and new worlds.

"And all the mixed messages that the parents send out to their kids," said Prevas. His father pulled him one way, his mother another. The father had a deep sense of his Greek roots; the mother wanted assimilation. Where they lived, in Northeast Baltimore's Hamilton neighborhood, there weren't many other Greek families.

"My mother was much more assimilative than my father," Prevas said. "She was much more self-conscious about ethnicity. With her, it was, like, 'Don't speak Greek.' As they began to raise my brother Bill and me, she made sure we spoke English. Greek was for hiding things. But then my father made sure we went to Greek school starting in the sixth grade. We learned the language there and met other Greek kids. That they were Greek was just a fact, it didn't particularly translate to camaraderie. But they were there."

He had a sense that his mother was holding him back from such things, that she wanted the full America for her two sons, and this involved shedding some of the old ways like an unnecessary skin.

"She would indicate, 'Your grandmother and her friends are too Greeky,'" said Prevas. "She didn't want to be in a crowd where they spoke Greek, and she didn't like some of the customs that she thought were too primitive. Like, my grandmother and my great-grandmother didn't drive. Neither one of them. They were always getting people to drive them down to Dundalk so they could go out into the fields and pick greens. Just like they did in their village in Greece.

"That was the regular thing. I was in fifth or sixth grade, and my mother drove them one time and I was sitting on the fender of the station wagon listening to the Orioles–Kansas City game, waiting for these old ladies to pick their greens out of a field so we could go back to Hamilton, where it was good. This was on a farm in Dundalk. My father said the farmer thought they were up to no good the first time and came out with a shotgun. Then he saw what they were doing and said, 'Oh, you can pick those weeds all you want, you're doing me a favor.' They'd boil 'em and eat 'em. Dandelions were a delicacy. They'd mix those weeds with olive oil, and the kitchen smelled of it."

Prevas and I met in high school, Baltimore City College. We both wrote for the weekly school newspaper, *The Collegian,* whose faculty advisor was an English teacher named Charlie Cherubin. Prevas and I would both quake at the thought of him. Cherubin would call groups of staff members into his office to berate us in a voice like sandpaper. He would light a cigarette and then glance toward the door to make certain no one from the principal's office caught him puffing. He could be as incorrigible as his students. Then he would let us have it: The paper wasn't good enough, he rasped. We weren't working hard enough. We sat around him with hearts beating, hoping he wouldn't get personal. He took a drag on his cigarette, and then went for the big number. Cherubin knew we all had visions of going to college.

"I have letters of recommendation in my desk," he declared, insinuation dripping from every syllable, "that could get Hitler into the Hadassah."

The line was not only a hoot, but a revelation. Hadassah was a Jewish women's service organization; Hitler was the Jewish devil. And here was a joke combining the two. I looked around this little high school newspaper office, wondering if I should be offended. But Cherubin was Jewish, I was pretty sure, and so were many of the boys in the room. So I guessed it was all right, and there was no need to rush off and alert the authorities.

Never before, in the entire history of public schooling, had a teacher ever offered an awareness of ethnic distinctions in my presence, joking or otherwise. Rarely was there an assigned literary reference to things not wholesomely American, or anciently British. We read *Tom Sawyer* and *Treasure Island*. The only Jew identified by birthright in a public school classroom was Shakespeare's Shylock, whose stereotyped profession everyone was supposed to overlook. This being the Eisenhower-Kennedy era of much talk of the melting pot, and then of racial inclusiveness, and of blindness to each other's differences, we weren't supposed to be aware of such distinctions, or to admit to them if we were aware. Ethnicity was still considered tricky ground, a dangerous reminder that we were not all necessarily alike and that, therefore, to mention differences might seem to imply that one group was better—or worse.

Cherubin, unable to resist the joke in the middle of his little tirade, was opening a door a tiny crack. Behind the door was the land of caustic adult sensibility, a place beyond the well-intended but bland melting-pot generalities we had always been served.

"Me, I never ate a piece of white bread till I got to Eastern," Toni Keane said.

She meant Eastern High, the all-female school across the street from the all-male City College. Keane graduated high school in 1958. Eastern shut its doors in the 1970s, around the time City was welcoming its first female students.

"I wouldn't say Eastern was a melting pot," Keane said. "The schools had only been integrated a couple of years, so there weren't many black girls. There might have been a few Jewish girls, but not many. The Jewish girls went to Forest Park out in Northwest Baltimore. But I hung out with Leon Uris's niece and read books like *Marjorie Morningstar*. It was an intellectual world that intrigued me. The other stuff kind of threw me."

"What other stuff?"

"Well," Keane said, "I don't know if it was ethnicity, or just Protestants that threw me."

"See, with us, it was just gentiles," I said. "We didn't make distinctions between Protestants and Catholics." I had no idea there were distinctions. I heard names, but I didn't know what they stood for. "To us," I said, "you believed in Christ, or you didn't. That was the only distinction, and we figured it was you guys who were making that distinction."

"The Jews weren't even on our radar," Prevas said—not in Northeast Baltimore's Hamilton section. "They didn't even register in our consciousness."

He began to understand the American agglomeration when he went to Fells Point, to the family-owned lunch area in the Broadway Market. The grandmother had the lunch counter, and her brother-in-law the soda fountain. When John was twelve, he started helping out. In high school he worked there each summer. The market opened his eyes.

"The mix," he said. "You still had merchants hollering across the aisles in their different European languages. I mean, Hamilton was German Catholic, and it was Protestant. But there was a strong dichotomy. You didn't associate with kids who went to Catholic schools. You played Little League with them, but you didn't see them the rest of the school year. After school, we stayed in cliques. The public school kids stayed together, and the St. Domenick's kids were together."

"When you're a kid," Keane added, "the world is divided in two, Catholic and public. And all this ethnic stereotyping goes on. *They eat meat on Friday, and they'll try to make you eat meat.*' And the Protestant girls knew more about sex than you did because, of course, you knew nothing about sex. They used to send me to the old Number Thirteen branch of the library to look up sex words. It was stereotyping. You were led to believe their level of morality wasn't the same as yours."

My mind backflipped more than forty years at the mention of morality. There was a knock on the door one autumn morning. Joel Kruh, my Howard Park baseball-practice pal who lived across the street, stood there with his eyes popping. We were supposed to go to synagogue that day. It was a minor Jewish holiday, noteworthy mainly for the chance for Jewish kids to claim the depth of our devotion and kiss off public-school drudgery for a day. Joel muttered the name of a woman who lived on our block. He sounded awed by the sound of his own voice saying her name, as though he had never fully considered it before.

"She's dead," he said.

"That's not funny."

"I'm not kidding. I just saw them take her body away. She was inside a bag."

He gestured across Crawford Avenue to a narrow front porch. The woman's young son and daughter, friends of ours, sobbing convulsively, sought comfort from a neighborhood woman. Their father, who worked out of town all week, was apparently still unaware of the bad news. Joel and I walked across the street to try to offer consolation.

"What happened?" we asked.

They shrugged their shoulders and turned away to cry some more. There were no words for the thing they were going through. Their mother was alive when they went to sleep and dead when they awoke. She was only in her thirties, and God had considered this an appropriate time for dying.

We learned later that she had had an abortion. They were illegal then, and so she had gone to someone who panicked, and botched the job, and she bled to death, a fact that began to be whispered by adults in the neighborhood over the coming weeks.

But, as we stood there on this Jewish holiday, we only knew that something inconceivable had happened: Our friends had been robbed of their mother. They were Catholic. The death of somebody's young mother had never happened to any Jewish families, at least none we ever heard about. This must be something endemic to the gentiles, who apparently were not protected by the same God who protected the Jews.

Toni Keane's words echoed: "*You were led to believe their level of morality wasn't the same as yours.*" Whose morality did she mean? Anybody who was different than you. Religions divided themselves in such a manner, and comforted themselves in their separate camps, and made deals with their notions of God: We'll abide by your rules, Lord, if you'll just be nice to us. We'll show up to pray, and we'll sing your praises. We Jews made our most fervent appeals at Yom Kippur services. Only the need for the latest details on the Baltimore Colts occasionally got in the way.

My friends went to St. Ambrose School, on Liberty Heights Avenue. Maybe the nuns could help them find comfort in the loss of their mother.

Many of us in the neighborhood went to public schools, in whose classrooms and playgrounds the great mix was removing some of the old sense of separation.

The year my friends lost their mother my sixth-grade class at Howard Park Elementary put on a Christmas play for the school's younger students. Our teacher was Mrs. Dennis. It was a small play, with roles for about ten actors. Mrs. Dennis, who was Catholic, selected students for each part. The play was about the true Christmas spirit, the sense of looking out for others. "Christmas with a heart in it," a classmate named Linda Saltz declared in the play's closing line. As it happened, Linda Saltz was Jewish. As it also happened, Mrs. Dennis had picked Jewish boys and girls for almost every role in the play.

A cynic might have taken this for insensitivity. Would she have cast as many gentiles in a play about Chanukah? (Had it ever dawned on the public schools to stage a play about a Jewish holiday?) I was in the cast. If there were any misgivings—and I remember none, by Jews or gentiles—they went unspoken. Christmas was something bigger than a gentile holiday, it was a festival of Americana marked on all the big television shows and watched in all living rooms. Ozzie and Harriet did their half-hour televised Christmas, and so did that nice Anderson family on *Father Knows Best*. Christmas gave all of us a ten-day winter vacation. It made our elders inflate the minor Chanukah holiday into a big deal so that their children could have presents like the gentile kids. Merely to breathe the winter air was to be touched in some manner by Christmas.

By acting in a Christmas play, we weren't turning our backs on our own religion. This wasn't about religion at all. We understood, even in our youth, that it was a simple acknowledgment of the majority culture in which we lived. Christmas was American; to take part in a Christmas play was to take part in a piece of America, and to show yourself good-natured enough not to make a big deal out of it. It was a small, painless, ecumenical step toward the center.

"We were all taking those little steps," John Prevas said.

On Boston Street now, overlooking the Baltimore harbor, he remembered the ambivalence he felt about his background.

"The Greek stuff was a pain in the neck for a while," he said. "But then, at Greek school, I got some pride. When I got to high school, there were three

Greeks in my homeroom. So we were now an identifiable group." He chuckled at the thought. "So we banded together. We started going to dances from the Greek church. We were wallflowers, but we were there, and we're meeting some Greek girls. That helped.

"In the tenth grade, I dated maybe four times. The next year, I asked a girl for a date to the City-Poly game. She stood me up. She wasn't Greek. I said, 'That's it, I'm sticking with Greek girls.' But it was a narrow, isolated dating community, too small a pool. I ran out the string of all the girls in a short period. My parents didn't care who I dated. They just wanted me home on time. I'd been reclusive, sitting my room having fantasy baseball games with the Orioles, long before rotisserie baseball."

"That's every guy," I said. It was not coincidental that Prevas and I both wrote about sports for the school newspaper. We loved the games, but we also knew they were a piece of the cultural mainstream.

"Milt Pappas," he said. "Gus Triandos."

They were two Greek ballplayers with the Orioles. Pappas was the early ace of the ballclub's pitching staff, Triandos the first legitimate home-run slugger in the modern franchise's history. I remembered talking to Ted Venetoulis about them. He had the same pride; they were his guys. It was no different than Tommy D'Alesandro rooting for Joe DiMaggio. But I also remembered something about my father. When Triandos homered my father hollered exuberantly, "Go, you Greek." I was about ten years old. The word *Greek* meant nothing to me; he might as well have said, "Go, you Chevrolet."

But I understood now that it was a cheer for him the way it had been a cheer for Lenny Moore, who my father called the *shvartzer* only at triumphant moments: cheers for Triandos and Moore came from the same instinct as cheers for Irving Berlin and Phil Silvers. They were all "one of ours." It did not have to be a Jew; it was any kind of outsider, who understood what we understood about the desire to belong. To see the home-run-hitting Triandos as a fellow outsider was to intensify the experience; to refer to Moore, as he broke a long run, as the *shvartzer,* was to speak in our version of the secret language of any outsider. In that anxious era's desire to mix everyone as gently as possible, the country was willfully setting aside our differences; my father was instead trumpeting each one's victories.

One of ours, indeed.

"The thing is," John Prevas said now, "when you go to a school with such a great mix, there's a liberating effect. You're not the only outsider. I had two black guys in my homeroom, Johnson and Joiner, and I made a point of meeting them right away. Like, right in the beginning, I felt like I shared outsider-ness with them."

"That's a definite connection," I said.

"Yeah," Prevas said. "In the early days, we watched each other's backs while we were getting used to the turf. Them, and the Jewish guys, who were my best friends at City. The school was such a melting pot, who could feel like an outsider? Different was valid instead of different."

At Syracuse University, Prevas joined the Tau Kappa Epsilon fraternity.

"That was the animal house when I was at Maryland," I said.

"The nerd house at Syracuse," he said. "But they got rid of all the nerds and brought in jocks and guys from a bunch of different backgrounds. My whole dorm floor pledged. Blacks, Jews, Christians, everybody. A very cosmopolitan mix. But then some of the black guys got into this separatist thing. There was a lot of fighting over what Stokely Carmichael was saying. You know, 'You all want to help, but you want to come in and run our affairs. Leave us alone, go to your own communities and change their consciousness.'"

It was the same thing that was beginning to move Jake Oliver, and Michele Winder, too. Not only was that brief episode of genuine integration already falling apart in the public schools, but the basic philosophical assumption underlying it—that we could live together harmoniously and ignore color—was falling apart.

After Syracuse Prevas went to the University of Maryland Law School and worked part-time at his family's place at the Broadway Market. He remembered those black fraternity brothers, and Stokely Carmichael. He was also living in a city that had erupted in riots after the Martin Luther King assassination.

One day Barbara Mikulski walked through the market. Prevas had seen her once before, shooting pool at Miss Irene's Bar in Fells Point. Not too bad a player, he thought. Then he saw her on television, where she was arguing against plans to build a highway through Fells Point. The next time he saw her, he said, "I saw you on TV. I liked what you had to say. I haven't met many intelligent people, but if you run for office, I'll support you."

Six months later, as Mikulski walked through the market, she told Prevas she had decided to run for the Baltimore City Council.

"You want to help?" she asked.

At the first strategy meeting Prevas attended, Toni Keane was there. He drove her home that night, and they began their life together. Keane lived across the hall from Mikulski.

"The day Barbara moved in," Keane said now, "I went over and asked if she needed anything. It turned out that my department chair had been her teacher. So we started talking about the ethnic thing. And then the riots came, and we're sitting there watching it on TV, and our hearts are breaking. This was the city we loved. And we kept saying, 'What do we do when this thing is over? How do we rebuild this city?'"

We sat there on Boston Street now, the three of us still awed by the memory of that time three decades earlier, and the generations of cruelty and stupidity that had fueled such rage, and the price everyone continued to pay for it over the coming years.

"And there we were," Keane said, "thinking, 'What do we do to rebuild society?' You know, we were heavily influenced by World War II. We were very idealistic, we came from people who fought in the war. So we have very cornball values, very mainstream values, that was our model. You always watched the war movies, and here it was in Baltimore. 'What about an urban Marshall Plan?' But how do you get past all that fear? We were so frightened of each other."

And yet it was less than a decade earlier that we had seemed headed for something so much better.

FOURTEEN

RAY CHARLES IN
THE CAFETERIA

By the end of the 1950s families whose wanderings had previously not extended beyond the Greenmount Avenue trolley-car line were now speaking earnestly of the joys of pulling crabgrass in Timonium. Or they raved about that convenient Woodmoor Shopping Center on Liberty Road on the way to Randallstown, or the splendid junior high school in Towson. They talked about bungalows in Parkville. They mentioned ranchers in Cockeysville. They searched out the proper suburban houses of worship. They became first-name pals with real-estate agents. They went for Sunday afternoon drives to take a look at the new split-level homes advertised in the morning newspaper. Sometimes they didn't come back. Entire city neighborhoods fell overnight — if not literally, then psychologically. When Lenny Moore moved onto Yosemite Avenue with its For Sale signs pounded into the dirt of nearly every front yard, my friend Gary Levin was living on Fernhill Avenue about half a mile north. Moore was twenty-five years old, at the top of his professional game but still on the shakiest social rung. Levin was fifteen, a student at the old Baltimore Polytechnic Institute, on North Avenue, and living in a neighborhood that was almost entirely Jewish and wondering about its own social level.

"Every day, you heard stories about black people moving in somewhere nearby," Gary remembered years later. We sat on a deck behind his townhouse in suburban Hunt Valley, where he suspected his might be the only Jewish family in the community. This seemed to matter to no one. We had been friends for forty years now and had roomed together one year in college. He was always smart, level-headed, and verbal. Now he was newly retired after more than thirty years of teaching English in the public high schools, whose upheaval had reflected exactly what went on in their surrounding neighborhoods.

"Around 1960 when we were back in high school," he said, "we had two black families move onto Fernhill Avenue. Very middle-class people, good people. And we had a rabbi who lived on the block, a good, reasonable man, and he came around and talked to all the neighbors. He said, 'These are wonderful people, I've met them, let's stay firm and not be like other people in all these other neighborhoods who are running.'

"It was a wonderful message," Gary said. "But, while the rabbi was telling us this, he was secretly working with the real-estate people to sell his house and move. After those first two black families moved in, he was the first one out. The neighborhood was stable, and he was already negotiating. It sent a message to everybody, and the hypocrisy of it stayed with us forever."

Such things would happen in every part of town. In Northwest Baltimore, though, you could chart the movement with pins on a map as black families moved out of West Baltimore and made their way north along the three main thoroughfares: Reisterstown Road, Park Heights Avenue, and Liberty Heights Avenue.

By the time I reached Garrison Junior High in 1957, the school was drawing youngsters from the white neighborhoods north of Garrison Boulevard and the racial mix from below. Michele Winder and Jake Oliver took buses up from West Baltimore, while the white kids from my neighborhood walked along Belle Avenue, cut through the Forest Park High School grounds and onto Barrington Road, until we reached the big three-story junior high.

Thus began, for thousands of us in that crowded little era, participation in the first racial integration of the Baltimore public schools. The integration lasted little more than a decade, and it was going away even as it came in. Adults wrestled with their sense of morality: Segregation was unfair, but wasn't it also unfair to expose your family to unknown dangers? Children sometimes took their cues from parents, but also from the things that they saw around them. On Crawford Avenue, where I lived, most of the Jewish families had moved into the neighborhood around 1953. My friend Joel Kruh, skinny, funny, an epic in kilowatt energy, moved to Baltimore from Queens, New York. His father drove down first, to scout about for a house. Not knowing the area, he drove through Dulaney Valley, in northeast Baltimore County, with a realtor.

"These are nice," said David Kruh.

"They aren't gonna sell to you here," said the realtor. "Jews aren't wanted."

When David Kruh packed up his family in Queens and drove them to Baltimore, they stopped on Reisterstown Road for a quick lunch at one of the area's old Harley Sandwich Shops. Harley Brinsfield, owner of the string of eateries, had a nightly jazz show on the radio. Also, he befriended Negro jazz musicians who came to town. Turned away from decent hotel accommodations, unable to eat in many restaurants, those such as Louis Armstrong and Billie Holiday slept at the magnanimous Harley's home and ate their meals there.

When Joel Kruh went to the men's room at the Harley's sub shop on Reisterstown Road, though, he noticed a sign: "Whites Only." Conscience had its place, but business was business.

"What does 'whites only' mean?" Joel asked his father.

"Things are different down South," said David Kruh. "It's not like New York."

Until the Supreme Court ruling on school desegregation, Baltimoreans still lived in a world with inflexible borders. If the old, rigid, ethnic enclaves were coming undone, some of the religious barriers were falling a little slower. A few neighborhoods in the city still quietly maintained housing restrictions, and some outlying areas weren't so quiet about it.

"I remember driving with my parents one day," Gary Levin said. "We were somewhere around Riviera Beach, in Anne Arundel County. A sign said, 'Restricted.' I said, 'Mom, what does that mean?'"

"It means they don't allow Jews," his father, Louis Levin, answered.

"Why?" Gary asked.

"They just don't want Jews there," his father said. "Some people don't like Jews, they don't want 'em around."

"And he just shrugged," Levin remembered years later. "As though, 'We've got our own places.' I remember when they let Jews into Meadowbrook Swim Club. We knew it had been all gentile, and then a new guy bought it and opened it up. We started going and never thought twice about it. It wasn't a big deal to us. My world had been a Jewish world, and that was all I knew, so it was okay. And now it was just something else."

But, if religious coexistence was becoming more comfortable, race was not so easy. In my neighborhood, the gentile kids were still heading off each morning to their parochial schools, and the Jewish kids to the public schools. Then we came back to the same neighborhood every afternoon and played ball together. But late in the summer of 1957, as we approached the first day of junior high school and racial integration, there were nervous overtones.

Dire words were passed down from some of the older boys. They said the colored guys at Garrison all carried knives. They made it sound like an exotic sort of genetic strain: "the knife-carrying colored." The news passed among my friends like a storm warning.

There were additional worries. Garrison was said to have a "spit pit," a stairway leading to a basement area into which younger students were sometimes lured. Avoid this area, wiser heads advised. Those wandering into it were cornered and showered by expectorating mobs. There were so-called zip guns, as well, weapons surreptitiously constructed in one of the school's mechanical shops. Zip guns were said to be capable of firing pieces of metal that could put out a person's eye.

These dangers were not connected with Negroes, but with "drapes." These were white boys who greased back their hair and wore black-leather jackets with the collars turned up. Later, such boys would be softened into John Travolta starring in *Grease,* but at the time they seemed far more intimidating. Some of them stood on the front sidewalk outside Garrison each morning and afternoon, defiantly smoking cigarettes and imagining themselves to be James Dean instead of merely working-class kids beginning to realize the American class system was stacked against them. Other drapes met at Gwynn

Oak Junction. They met at the pool room that had been the temporary Liberty Jewish Center a few years earlier. Or they worked on second-hand cars at one of the gas stations along Liberty Heights Avenue where they had visiting privileges because one of their buddies had a job in the grease pit. In the 1950s now seen as quite placid, these were the people beginning to understand they would be left behind as other white families fled to the suburbs.

The talk of colored guys and knives concerned me, but didn't quite hit a nerve. For one thing, the message always came from people who were suspect. One was the guy in my neighborhood who had called me a dirty Jew the day I moved in. He also used the familiar epithets about Negroes. If he said the colored guys were carrying knives, what did he tell people the Jews were carrying? Cases of anthrax?

My boyish concept of black people was a mix of pop culture and victimization. I remembered the man in the closet at the YMCA. I remembered the kids who lived around the Latrobe Housing Projects who heard "catch a nigger by his toe" and shrugged it off just so they could hang out with the white kids. I heard the Colts crowds cheering Lenny Moore when he ran with a football and had no idea what his life was like when he left the ballpark. And I heard music on the radio.

The music was a constant. In my neighborhood, in this era before air conditioning, you could walk through the streets and hear the beginnings of rock and roll coming out of open windows, along with the voices of parents hollering at their kids to turn it down. You could hear it on the new transistor radios my friends carried everywhere and sang along. Barry Director knew the lyrics to all of the Platters' songs and sang them like a bar mitzvah *maftir*. "*Heavenly shades of night are falling—it's twilight time.*" Stanley Nusenko sang "Alley-Oop-oop-oop-oop" with the radio next to his ear while he spat the words out of a corner of his mouth. Spontaneous doo-wop sessions tended to break out whenever no adults were around. We weren't Negroes, certainly, but we were beginning to discover attractive elements of being one.

The most affecting songs we knew were sung by black singers, and it did not particularly matter that they were black. Chuck Berry sang cheerful lyrics about riding in a car after school. Little Richard sang "Tutti Frutti." Some parents found this threatening. We found it hilarious. The Coasters sang

> *"Walks in the classroom*
> *Cool and slow*
> *Who calls the English teacher*
> *'Daddy-o?'*
> *Charlie Brown."*

In the face of all this, lectures about the brotherhood of man might have seemed heartfelt but slightly superfluous. Nor, in any case, did my parents offer any. My father occasionally tossed the term *shvartzer* about, but saved it for his odd, celebratory moments: Lenny Moore breaking off a marvelous run, or the sound of Nat "King" Cole's voice on the record player haunting a moment. "That *shvartzer* could sing the phone book and make you cry," my father would say.

But my parents thought of themselves as open-minded, cosmopolitan people. They were still only a few years separated from their New York lives. The house was filled not only with the music of Nat Cole and Frank Sinatra, but *Guys and Dolls* and *My Fair Lady* and *West Side Story*. When my parents invoked the names of Rodgers and Hammerstein, they made them sound like friends from the old neighborhood. My father read all of the learned political columnists in all of the great boring newspapers and headed the synagogue brotherhood; my mother acted in sisterhood plays there, and studied heavy books about art and religion. Within their economic constraints they lived in a big world.

On humid summer nights, long before anyone we knew lived in air conditioning, my parents sat on our little front porch and chatted with neighbors. Sometimes they would prop a radio on the front windowsill and listen to snatches of the Orioles game. The humid Baltimore air hung like a shroud.

"Sshh," my father would say at odd moments. "A breeze."

He wanted to enjoy it in its fullness. Then, as it faded, he would add, admiringly, "Too good for the *goyim.*" That was how good it was: too good for the gentiles. It was a comic line, which my father would toss about through the years. If food was particularly good, if a splash in the Atlantic Ocean was particularly refreshing—"too good for the *goyim.*"

It set us apart, but only comically. It acknowledged what everyone acknowledged: there were differences. It was my father's gentle way of making fun of them, of scoring points that only minorities can score.

Michele Winder in her high school years. In the first generation of integrated public schools, she left her West Baltimore neighborhood for Garrison Junior High School. She seemed to have disappeared until the Barry Levinson movie *Liberty Heights* and a stranger's telephone call. *Courtesy of Michele Winder Boyd*

But I never heard either of my parents utter a disparaging word about anyone's race or religion in any sort of seriousness—and this alone seemed a kind of unofficial declaration of family policy. If there were judgments to be made, I would be allowed to make my own. And, at age twelve, as I entered my first racially integrated school as part of that first integrated generation in Baltimore, my heart was anxious but open.

In our adult years, when we were old enough to reminisce, Jake Oliver and I followed a light-hearted ritual. It went back to our last year at Garrison Junior High, and to the dreamy girl named Michele Winder who seemed to symbolize all possibilities.

"Remember how beautiful Michele was?" one of us would ask.

"Oh, my," the other would say, as though suffering an attack of puberty.

The three of us were in the same homeroom the year before we went to senior high school. Michele was a sweetie-pie. She was charming, willowy, heartbreakingly pretty, coffee-colored, and utterly unaware of all but the last. She thought of herself as skinny and awkward and a misfit. Perhaps she was looking elsewhere. I was the skinny one, a crewcut perched atop a mass of bones, and Jake was the awkward one whenever he tried to hit a punchball in the daily games on the boys' blacktop playground.

Punchball was simple. The ball was a so-called pinkie, a tennis ball without the hair. You tossed it in the air and, before it came down, you made a fist and hit it as hard as you could and ran the bases. But Jake could not hit the ball. He would toss it into the air and catch only a piece of it on the edge of his knuckles on the way down, so that the ball dribbled away disappointingly. I made certain he and I talked about this, too, every time we met, right after we reminded ourselves how beautiful Michele Winder was the last time either of us had seen her. In my case, this was years earlier, when I would blot out the droning of all teachers and gaze with secret longing at Michele, who returned my hidden ardor with sheer obliviousness. I thought she was beautiful and sensitive and sunny. That she was a Negro mattered only peripherally. She was out of reach by sheer dint of beauty, never mind race.

Jake had seen her once or twice since we'd all graduated Garrison in the spring of 1960.

"And she was still beautiful?" I would ask.

"Oh, yeah," he said. "But it was years ago, so who knows?"

But the memory of Michele, and schoolboy reveries, went beyond her beauty. In that little opening between the mid-1950s and the late 1960s, as the public schools in Baltimore went through their brief flirtation with racial integration, America preached color-blindness, a notion well intended but subsequently discovered to be ludicrous. What was meant was: We could set aside color and judge each other first as human beings. After that, anything might be possible. In public school—in three years at Garrison Junior High, and three years of City College, and the years we each attended the University of Maryland in College Park—Jake Oliver and I were friendly, but not exactly pals. Distance prevailed. We lived in different neighborhoods, or different dormitories, or we sat in different classrooms.

"Plus, I couldn't hit the punchball," he would say with comic regret.

"That's right," I said. "And I tended to rate guys on how well they could play ball." The games had a youthful purity about them. In our desire to win, and to express our ruggedness in that crowded, chaotic schoolyard, the punchball games made skin color momentarily incidental. You could play, or you could not.

The first time I noticed Jake, he was leaping above me to take a pass out of my hands in a seventh-grade touch football game on the boys' schoolyard. Football, he could play. When we went to high school at City he tried out for varsity lacrosse. The first few days of practice, he seemed to score at will. On the third day he was creamed by a defenseman by the name of Charles A. "Dutch" Ruppersberger, the future Baltimore County executive. Jake remembered flying through the air. When he landed, he found another sport to occupy his time.

If these memories were sometimes painful, at least they were shared. Laughter could now echo across decades. Such a thing had never occurred between black and white students of the public schools—not in Baltimore, or in many other American cities.

Years after college, Jake and I stumbled back into each other through newspaper work and then, I think, by a kind of loyalty to good intentions. It was as if each telephone call, each lunch, each reminiscence based on some small scrap of memory was validation that the process had been worth it, that our elders had done the right thing when they threw us all together in the schools—and that our generation had at least made an honorable search for common ground. That was how we started when we began to reconnect: stories of punchball, of the homeroom teacher we could not abide—I remembered Jake furiously pumping the muscles of his clenched jaw as we sat through Mrs. Jacobson's awful algebra lessons—and of Michele Winder. And, if our memories were scattered, they did have some texture. We knew each other when we were young, when we hadn't yet learned how to hide.

Our adult concerns overlapped. Jake was publisher of the *Afro-American* newspaper, and I wrote a newspaper column. We had both started out as spiritual children of Martin Luther King and detoured somewhere else. But where? We tried to retrace some of the old steps.

We remembered the awkwardness of the old school years, when Americans tried pretending we did not notice our separate skin colors. There was too much danger in noticing. To notice was to compare, which could lead to choosing up sides. "*Do you know so-and-so?*" "*What's he look like?*" Etiquette did not permit using race as an identifier; you were not supposed to notice such things. "*Is he colored or white?*" "*Gosh,* I *didn't notice.*" Our self-consciousness took on silly proportions, as though merely to take note of human appearance was the characteristic of a racist. Before we could learn to celebrate our differences, we first had to ignore them, and to focus on things more compelling.

To fourteen-year-old boys, naturally, there were few things more compelling than a fourteen-year-old girl. Michele Winder was the delight of our ninth-grade homeroom—though she did not know it then and seemed stunned when we told her about it much later.

One night in the winter of 1999 my wife, Suzy, and I went to see the director Barry Levinson's newest ode to midcentury Baltimore, called *Liberty Heights*. Levinson attended Forest Park High School while Jake and Michele and I went to Garrison. The two schools were a block apart. When Lee the barber peered through his front window overlooking Liberty Heights Avenue and talked about blacks moving to Northwest Baltimore, this neighborhood was about to become the heart of it.

Liberty Heights was about crossing over. A teenage Jewish boy falls for a black girl in his class, making the exact schoolboy romantic move I had failed to make forty years earlier with Michele Winder. The morning after I saw the movie, I called Jake and told him I had seen a vision of Michele on the screen.

"No, you didn't," he said. "Because Michele's like us. She's fifty-four years old, and she lives in Virginia with two grown kids."

I told him about the Jewish boy in the movie romancing the black girl.

"I would have done that," I said, massively overstating my adolescent *savoir faire*, "but guys like you would have beaten me up."

"Guys like me?" he said. His voice rose incredulously. "Are you kidding? Guys like *you* would have beaten you up."

Probably we were both correct. In late 1950s Baltimore people of all races and religions would have united in pummeling me for going out with Michele. For all the talk of color-blindness, we were self-segregated whenever possible, like guests at a wedding who sit on opposite sides of the aisle and then put on pleasant faces during the sit-down dinner, showing off their social graces—and then go their separate ways.

Now, the day after my conversation with Jake, I wrote a newspaper column in the *Baltimore Sun* about the movie, and race relations in mid-century Baltimore, and memories of a girl named Michele Winder. The next day my telephone rang.

"Michele just moved back to Baltimore," a voice said.

"Excuse me?"

"I'm Michele Winder's mother," the voice said. "She's Michele Lee now."

A few nights after that, Michele and Jake and I sat together for the first time in forty years. She was still lovely—and still in denial about years ago.

"Skinny as a stick," she said. "I thought I was skinny, and uncomfortable, and didn't have any friends."

She laughed about it, but the laughter seemed wistful. She was divorced for a second time, and had a grown son and daughter still living in Virginia. She moved back to Baltimore to be closer to her aging mother and to pursue a new calling. She was studying to become an ordained minister. She had a student pastorate at Johns Hopkins Hospital, where she offered religious solace to the sick and the dying.

Our memories of school days came from different places. The three of us sat in the same classrooms for six hours each day but separated the moment the afternoon bell rang.

"You all went in your direction, and we went in ours," Jake said.

"I remember going to the cafeteria every day," Michele said, "and wondering if there would be another black girl I could sit with. It seemed like I was the only one around."

"What about Dara Woodley?" I asked. "You two were good friends."

"Yes," Michele said. "But I don't remember anybody else."

When I went home that night, I found our old ninth-grade homeroom photograph. There are thirty-six of us in the picture: seventeen white boys, five black boys, three white girls—and eleven black girls. I made a copy of the picture for Michele and gave it to her a few weeks later.

"And yet I remember feeling so isolated," she said.

"You had never had any contact with white kids before Garrison?" I asked.

"No," she said. "And then, when you think about it, we were friendly. I say 'white kids,' but it was really mostly Jews. I don't remember any antagonisms at all. We'd talk about last night's homework or something, because that's what we had in common. I just don't remember anybody reaching out."

"When I got to Garrison," Jake Oliver said when we talked again a few weeks later, "we just said, 'We're going to the new world.'"

"A lot of your friends had never been with white kids before, right?" I said.

"Right. But it wasn't such a big deal. It was a bigger deal to our parents than it was to us. We were there just to go to class and be kids. It didn't matter who sat next to me. He was a kid, just like me. It didn't bother me. And at lunchtime, you associated with some people and not with others, whatever their color was. Hell, I was fascinated by the range of *black* kids I'd never met before."

We both used the word "black" with mixed feelings. In our time at Garrison the word was a slur. We were shifting from "colored" to "Negro" then. I remembered a fight in a first-floor hallway one day. Two black kids were swinging wildly at each other, neither inflicting much hurt, until words began to fly.

"You're black," one of them cried.

"I am not," the second one said. He seemed stunned by the slur, and then enraged at such a thought, or at the unexpected reminder of every single thought he had tried to push aside.

The first one took another swing. "You're black," he hollered again. The second kid looked around, saw a mix of schoolmates watching. As he swung back, ducking his head to make everyone around him vanish, he began to cry in embarrassment and rage.

"I am not black."

"Black."

"I am not black. You're black."

"Am not. You are."

And on and on like that, the rage turning to tears of abject defeat. I saw variations of that a few more times at school, where the veil of self-delusion was stripped mercilessly away. They had dark skin, and nobody had quite assured them that this was all right. To be white was still the ideal; it said so in all the television shows and the movies. To say the word "black" seemed the last refuge of a fellow desperate to inflict the worst kind of emotional hurt. I mentioned this to Jake Oliver.

"Because," he said, "everybody was uptight about their color."

"I'm talking about guys reducing each other to tears," I said.

"Yeah, it was like calling you the worst possible thing in the world. Calling you black, and calling your mother black, I mean, you're gonna get into a serious fight. That's where we were at that time. It was the result of our parents' generation, in connection with their values. It's why we had to get to black pride and black power."

"Also," I said, "there was a whole history of white people making black people feel they should be ashamed of their color."

"Yeah, but it was black folks making ourselves feel that way," he said. "It wasn't white folks, it was ourselves. We thought the only way we could be accepted was to be white, or to be like white. So they were getting their hair straightened, and getting their skin bleached. All that stuff. It was part of the society. It was a self-hating ritual, but they thought it was hip."

Every summer his family went to Cape May, New Jersey, where they owned a house. His light-skinned mother drove the car. African American families arrived from many cities. Some of the older boys had straight hair. Others had rags around their heads. Jake had seen fellows like this in the neighborhood back home but from a distance.

"Up close," he remembered, "you saw how much pain they went through to get their hair like that. They burned the hell out of their head. My mother would have killed me, killed me. I couldn't have even thought about it."

"But, again, the white culture inflicted it."

"But we had permitted it."

"It's tough not to permit it when all power has been taken away from you."

"Yeah, but that power had been taken away from us before our generation even got here. So we rejected that. When you got to bombings and burnings and lynchings, those are the things. The older I got, the more aware I was of what the *Afro* was doing. And you look around and you say, Hey, there are no blacks on TV, there's none in the *Sunpapers*. There are black radio stations and we all listen to that. There's black music. But you don't hear it on white stations. You got disc jockeys like Fat Daddy and Hot Rod playing our music. But that was on black stations, which felt like another form of segregation.

"And then you drove through Baltimore," he said, "and it was so segregated. And you began to think, yeah, maybe I'd better not object too loudly, because then I'll be a victim. That was always in the back of my mind. And then Martin Luther King steps up. The white press portrays him as a trouble-maker, but not as a leader. For us, young black guys, we were waiting for someone to say, 'Well, Dr. King is right, nonviolence is wonderful, but don't piss me off too much.' Because at some point I'm not really gonna care too much about being a victim because I'm already a victim, so there isn't much else you can do to me. And I'm gonna start to lash out."

Most of this was lost on white people like me. Having gone to segregated elementary schools I knew that such an era had ended. So I assumed that all fair-minded people were happy now. There were Southerners who showed up on the television news with firehoses and angry dogs whenever black people tried to integrate the schools there. But in my world, I saw neither firehoses nor angry dogs. I saw punchball games in the schoolyard. I saw a Negro girl named Barbara Quarles elected president of our senior year at Garrison, and another Negro girl, Vivian Jones, elected secretary. These seemed like healthy gestures in a graduating class nearly two-thirds white, in a school whose population was still more than half white. I saw a black kid stand on a table in the center of the school cafeteria one day. His name was Claude Young, but everybody called him Henny.

"You remember Henny Young?" Jake asked.

He was a big kid whose father was Buddy Young, the Colts halfback who had counseled Lenny Moore on Lenny's first day at Westminster training camp. Jake used to go to Henny's house after school, and Buddy Young would be there, and Big Daddy Lipscomb, too. He rented an upstairs room at the Youngs' house. The house was on Hilton Street.

This was the time when the Colts were winning two straight world championships. Hilton Street was about as good as it got for blacks in that time. I remembered Henny Young standing atop a lunchtime table in the Garrison Junior High cafeteria in a moment when no teachers seemed to be lurking.

"Hey-e-ey," Henny sang out from his table top.

A chorus of voices, immediately catching the rhythm, called back, "Hey-e-ey."

For a moment, I didn't understand what was happening. I was too busy wondering if a teacher would burst into the room and break it up, and too busy enjoying Henny's sheer chutzpah. He was doing Ray Charles's "What'd I Say," and enlisting everyone in the cafeteria to join in.

"*Hey.*"

"*Hey.*"

"*Hey.*"

"*Hey.*"

"*Ooooh, baby, what'd I say?*"

"*Baby, what I say?*"

It was the integrated version of the Elvis night at the Howard Park Methodist Church a few years earlier, musical anarchy in the face of adults—and it was sublime fun, transcendent of all race, all religion, all self-consciousness. This time, we weren't asking the adults to play another record for us. We had taken over the place and were making our own music.

That moment, and the punchball games, were my simplistic sense of racial harmony. History lectures about World War II never mentioned the segregated armed forces—or the Holocaust, for that matter. That the Civil War was fought over slavery was a touchy issue approached with delicacy, or not at all. Civics lessons never addressed housing discrimination in our own city—or any kind of discrimination. We were a generation being asked to change the nation's public-school history—and everyone in the schools was either too nervous to talk about it or had specifically been ordered not to talk about it.

"I remember little things," Michele Winder said one blustery winter afternoon when we looked back. "Nothing major. I came to class late one day, and a teacher said, 'Are you people late for everything you do?'" She smiled wanly over the cliché.

"Then there was a history teacher, a gray-haired older woman. She was painting a picture that the slaves were not as bad off as we had heard, that they were being fed and clothed, so it wasn't so bad. I got very defensive. I was not one to be outspoken, but I responded to what she was saying."

Her voice sounded a little helpless, like someone who had felt like a pipsqueak at the very moment she wanted to roar.

"And she approached me later," Michele said softly. "Of course, I had the other issue that people did not always understand that I was black. So the next day before class, she said, 'I couldn't understand why you were so vocal. And somebody said you're a Negro. Is that true?'"

"I said, yes. She stared at me. I was so proud that I was getting good grades, you know. And the next grading period, I dropped two grades in her class. To this day, I'm convinced . . ."

Her voice trailed off. To lament junior high school grades forty years later seemed absurd, but it stayed with her because it seemed to set something off. When Michele reached Forest Park High School the following fall, her mother decided she had the aptitude of a future secretary. So Michele took business courses instead of the college prep program.

"The girl thing, too," she remembered. "My brother took the accelerated route, and I was the girl."

Then, almost overnight, her mother decided to move to Washington. Michele had finished high school and went with her. She found a secretarial job at Howard University and figured she would take college courses while she was there. Howard University said no. They looked at her high school transcript and saw she hadn't taken the required academic courses. Her mother, hoping to give her daughter the occupational security she had never known in her own life, had instead squeezed her daughter out of education possibilities for which she hungered.

"I realized how much I wanted it," Michele said, "and I found an all-black college in the south, North Carolina Central."

"Back to segregation," I said.

"Yeah. I was always sort of out of step. I just never felt I was in the mainstream of whatever I was a part of. Being poor, the single family, my father's German mother. So now I'm twenty-one and going to a school with curfews. And I'm really too old to live on campus. I majored in psychology and married a guy when I was in my third year. The next year, I got pregnant with my daughter. And I had grant money that was helping pay my way, but I lost it when I got pregnant. You're out of the program because you're not continuously enrolled. That really crushed me. So I became a mommy but not a college graduate."

In North Carolina she also refined her sense of race. Martin Luther King was preaching brotherhood, but Malcolm X was urging separateness. She bounced between the two, and envied those friends who had worked it out. In that summer after high school graduation, she went to Washington for King's powerful "I have a dream" speech and found it liberating. But, later, she heard Malcolm reflecting some of her own anger.

I worked as a delivery boy that summer, in a little office supply company on Paca Street, across from the city's bustling Lexington Market. There were black men in suits and bow ties outside the market, selling a newspaper called *Muhammad Speaks,* about so-called Black Muslims and a Nation of Islam, and of Malcolm X. I had never heard of any of these. I believed in Martin Luther King, but I wasn't too clear on the details. King was talking about brotherhood, and I embraced that. He talked of love, and I wondered how my own friends felt about that. He talked of ideals, and even then I knew the game was more calculating than that.

Muhammad Speaks said white people were blue-eyed devils. It said racial integration was a naïve dream and Martin Luther King a false prophet. Malcolm X was the cynic to King's lofty idealism, the warrior to King's pacifism, insisting that color was everything while King was telling us it didn't have to be.

In Baltimore that summer, there were still places where black people could not buy a meal. When they went for jobs, white employers held out their hands but winked when nobody was paying attention. The fix was still in. Meanwhile, white people drove to downtown jobs through black neighborhoods that were frustrated, demoralized, furious places they thought they could ignore and Malcolm X insisted they had better not. He was the one who brought white America the bad news: Things were going to get worse before they got better.

"It was pretty stunning," I told Michele. "I thought integration was everybody's goal, except for rednecks in the South. Which shows how naïve I was."

"I embraced it," she said softly. Not Islam exactly, but the notion that we did not necessarily have to integrate.

"But did that feel disloyal to what Dr. King said?"

"Yes," she said. "But I had been through the loneliness and the isolation of the so called integration thing. In North Carolina I started seeing things.

People had begun integrating certain neighborhoods, but not in Durham. There were railroad tracks separating the white neighborhoods from ours, but there were no slums. They didn't want us, but it was all right."

She remembered the segregated slums of Baltimore, and realized modest means did not have to mean decay. She remembered leaving teenage friends to attend mostly white schools where she searched for a friendly face in the cafeteria. She remembered her father's half-German sisters trying to pass as whites. She remembered her mother scrubbing her in the tub, as though trying to lighten her skin before taking her to the segregated Rialto Theatre in West Baltimore. And she remembered the history teacher at Garrison, and all of this turned something inside of her.

"The biggest building in Durham," she said now, "was black-owned, which was this huge symbol of pride. And one of the big banks was black-owned. And the neighborhoods were so pristine and great and so proud. And I'm thinking, you know, this is okay. Why do we have to integrate? And the thing Malcolm was saying about separateness fused in my head."

And there was one other thing: John Kennedy's assassination. The record on Kennedy is clearer now than it was then. He dragged his feet on race and had to be coaxed into action because he understood the political damage that would crush the Democratic Party. In his lifetime, though, there was the sense that he was young, he understood the changes that had to be made and, as the first Catholic president, he was sensitive to all manner of inclusion.

"The day of his assassination," Michele said, "that was just . . ." She shook her head. "It was the most devastating thing because it was like a prophecy of where everything was going. It just wiped me out. It was the beginning of a loss of hope."

Jake Oliver and I were freshman at the University of Maryland on that Friday afternoon, November 22, 1963, when Kennedy was killed in Dallas. We had been enrolled there barely two months. In two minutes anyone could see the racial makeup of the College Park campus.

"The moment I got to Maryland, the shit hit the fan," Jake said. "We had, what, 20,000 kids on campus? And maybe a hundred are black." He sounded like Lenny Moore talking about Penn State's campus a decade earlier.

"Every place I went, I was relegated to a small corner. There was nothing. We could go into this little community across the tracks behind Town Hall," one of the taverns along U.S. Route 1 where students gathered to drink beer. "You went into some of those bars, you were gonna get into a fight because somebody's calling you, 'Nigger this,' and you're not gonna have it."

"I remember only three black guys in my dorm," I said. "All from Baltimore. Earl Wynn, Ron Jones, and Melvin Potillo." Jake remembered them all; they had been a very small tribe.

"I was in Allegheny West Dormitory," he said, "in the back of the quadrangle. First day, my parents drop me off, and they've put three of us in a two-man room because, you know, nobody wanted to deal with a black guy rooming with a white guy. So I walk down the hall to the bathroom. I look up, and there's this football player. He took one look at me, said, 'Oh, God, the niggers are here.' Just like that. And now he runs a social program allegedly for underprivileged kids in Prince George's County."

"So," I said, "is he a hypocrite, or did he grow?"

"I don't know," Jake said. "But when he said that, I just turned around and walked out. He was big. A senior, drove around on a motorcycle. And I'm just saying, 'Welcome to the University of Maryland.' We were all unhappy. You try to create the promise of college life, and mix with people, and it doesn't happen. And then, the worst part, John Kennedy was killed. All that hope, all that stuff we imagined he was gonna do . . ."

He was sitting in a math class, with his sister Marilyn, when they heard the news. Marilyn, a year younger, had skipped a grade in high school.

"And they didn't know who did it, or what," Jake remembered. "And the first thing that hit my mind, if it was a black guy, we're dead. They will just come after us." You could hear the dread in his voice: It would be Emmett Till at the end of a rope all over again, only multiplied hundreds of times. "So I grab my sister, and I race her back to her dorm, which was all the way across campus, and then I had to race and hide."

"You went into hiding?"

"You had to hide. You had to close the door and wait to find out exactly what was going on, and make sure it wasn't some black guy who had killed the president."

The next summer, he stayed in College Park to catch up on a few courses.

He remembered a white supremacist parade, and people in green and white robes marching down Route 1. It was the summer of Martin Luther King's speech in Washington.

"Yeah, but you see that kind of stuff, people marching down Route 1," Jake said, "and that becomes stronger than a message about nonviolence and brotherly love."

It also meant that, in that narrow time since we had entered our first integrated public school six years earlier, full of simple illusions about integration, we were learning to choose up sides all over again.

FIFTEEN

CITY COLLEGE

Merely to arrive at the high school called Baltimore City College was to feel slightly overwhelmed. This wasn't Forest Park, which drew neighborhood sissies from Northwest Baltimore. It wasn't Patterson or Southern, whose students dropped out early to take jobs at Sparrows Point's steel mills or Locust Point's shipyards. And it wasn't Baltimore Polytechnic, either. The Poly boys called themselves "The Engineers"; we called them future meter readers for the gas and electric company. If we called everybody else enough names, it kept us from calling ourselves what we suspected we really were: awkward boys stumbling uncertainly toward manhood.

City College was a dark gray stone structure sitting atop a hill like some impregnable fortress, with an enormous tower from which ancient soldiers might have hurled bolts of molten lead at invading armies. It seemed like some incarnation out of ancient history books, and was gloriously nicknamed the Castle on the Hill. Next door to all-male City was Eastern High

School. It was gloriously all-female. And, across broad Thirty-third Street was Memorial Stadium, home of the Orioles and Colts. We had clearly entered major league territory.

We were aware that this was the nation's third oldest public high school, and it impressed us. We knew that its annual football contest against Poly was the oldest schoolboy rivalry in the country, and we wished to be a part of this, because it seemed rugged and muscular. And we quickly learned that the school had many famous alumni, including the novelist Leon Uris, the television star Garry Moore, and the actor Edward Everett Horton. We learned that Uris, the author of *Exodus,* had flunked English here; and that Moore, the star of quiz shows, had flunked history; and that Horton, comic foil for Hollywood's Fred Astaire, had never landed a part in the school's prestigious theatrical productions. This was not considered promising news. If these great men had struggled at City, what chance did the rest of us have?

We were clearly not in their league. From North Baltimore came Charles Ruppersberger, of German-English heritage, who was known as "Dutch," and from Northeast Baltimore the Greek John Prevas, and from West Baltimore the African American Jake Oliver: a future county executive, a future judge, a future newspaper publisher, each awkwardly feeling his way—and each aware of taking part in something that felt like the full American mix.

From my neighborhood, half a dozen of us attended City each day, most of us undistinguished by any previous evidence of academic inclination. But Joel Kruh, known mainly for his ability to run long distances without stopping for breath, would become a track and cross-country star here, and later forge a successful law career. Stanley Nusenko, who hit punchballs by tossing the ball into the air and kissing his knuckles before swatting it, as though announcing, "You can kiss this baby goodbye," would find his voice here and later work for the government. And Ron Sallow, who would first become a city policeman and later lead Maryland's insurance fraud division, was on his way to signing up for the military while still in high school, thereby setting off a face-to-face Fort Holabird confrontation between Molly Sallow—his mother—and the U.S. Marine Corps.

From my block, we defied most stereotypes of the bookish Jews. While still at Garrison Junior High the previous year, some of us had discovered the rising of our hormones and the simultaneous plummeting of our grades.

On the late autumn afternoon we received our quarterly report cards, we trudged home dreading the worst kind of parental wrath. One of my friends had just set a school record by flunking every course, and getting a red *U* for conduct—in every slot, in every subject.

"That's it," he vowed. "I'm gonna do better from now on."

It sounded like Scarlett O'Hara, vowing never to be hungry again. As we reached the corner of Belle and Rogers Avenues, only a few blocks from home, he strode suddenly toward a nearby pile of leaves and began kicking them.

"What are you doing?" I asked.

"Turning over a new leaf," he explained.

Geniuses, we were not. Though City College is often recalled as the home of Baltimore's most intellectual boys, that was only part of it. It opened its arms to a wide cross-section—intellectual, racial, and religious—and then held us to higher standards than most of us had previously imagined.

On our first morning we gathered in the school auditorium, where City's principal, an elderly, sweet-tempered man named Henry Yost, stood before us. I sat with Stanley Nusenko. Yost had coke-bottle glasses and wore what was surely the last high-collared shirt in all of America. When at last he quieted the crowd of about eight hundred of us, he announced in a rheumy voice, "Gentleman, you have passed your first intelligence test by choosing City College as your high school."

We imagined Yost was mistakenly addressing his remarks not only to the wrong audience, but to some different era altogether, when the high collars of shirts must have cut off circulation to their brains. We saw ourselves not only as skeptics, but as cynics. We did not yet understand that cynicism was a form of self-defense.

"The future mayor of Baltimore is sitting in this room right now," said Yost. "That is the City College tradition."

I turned to Stanley Nusenko, who laughed out of the side of his mouth. "He ain't talkin' about me," said Stanley. We took a certain pride in our disdain. We did not yet know that such political leaders as Marvin Mandel, William Donald Schaefer, and Benjamin Cardin had preceded us to this auditorium, or that Elijah Cummings and Kurt Schmoke were on their way, or that Dutch Ruppersberger sat among us and found Yost's words as difficult to imagine as everyone else.

As we shuffled along a crowded hallway one of those first days, an upper classman in a letter sweater looked at some of us and sniffed, "K-Ds." It was school shorthand. "K-D" stood for knuckle-dragger. He was comparing us, not without justification, to cavemen.

Instructors sometimes seemed to take the same approach. One day a gym teacher named Jerry Nathanson, who coached triumphant track and cross-country teams, gathered a big crowd of us in the school wrestling room to deliver a lecture on the importance of personal hygiene. He was tall and lean, with a fringe of gray hair and a high, scratchy voice.

"Men," he said, pacing in front of us in a white terry cloth bathrobe, "you gotta put that deodorant on. Now, you take World War II." We listened raptly, not yet perceiving the connection. "We lost more men in World War II from the stench of their buddies' body odor," said Nathanson, "than we did from enemy bullets."

I leaned over to a classmate sitting next to me, Jules "Sonny" Morstein, and whispered, "I didn't know that."

"If you paid any attention to your history books, you would," said Morstein.

A geometry teacher named Luther Dittman strode across the front of his classroom each afternoon, grade book in hand, and gave pop quizzes on material he drilled repeatedly into our heads, without apparent success. Many of us relied on a benevolent classmate named Gus Sitaris to slip the correct answers our way. Anxiety swept the room with each question. An incorrect answer meant a zero in the grade book. One afternoon, Dittman called on the class tough guy.

"Brooks," he said, pointing to the blackboard, "what about the opposite angles of a parallelogram?"

In a voice that seemed to come up from his sneakers, Brooks grunted, "Well, what about 'em?"

Such responses were the cry of the recalcitrant, declaring, "You will not break us." But it was also the fault line offered by City College. There were worlds from which to choose. Between the opening bell and the close of school, I never saw the guys from my neighborhood. We were simply thrown into this enormous collection of 4,000 boys from every part of the city and left to discover what felt comfortable, and what did not—or find some other school, one that was nearer to home, nearer to the last remaining comforts of childhood, nearer to people from backgrounds resembling your own. City was the school that felt like the full melting pot.

These were John Kennedy's White House years. After eight years of the grandfatherly Eisenhower, Kennedy seemed ideal for the new time: impossibly handsome, surrounded by speechwriters to turn the perfect phrases for him, sociologists to refine the national perspective, and poets and artists to burnish the new national image. When he said America would "pay any price, bear any burden" to assure the spread of liberty, we thought this sounded wonderful. It was brave, it was muscular. We didn't connect it to anything like Vietnam; we connected it to Kennedy standing coatless and unprotected on that freezing inauguration day, looking as handsome as we imagined we might look, if only our complexions would clear up. That he was Irish Catholic was a bonus. It seemed to symbolize great liberating possibilities for everyone who felt they still hadn't been admitted to the full America.

At City College, a lot of us felt that way. Gus Sitaris, the savior of souls in Mr. Dittman's geometry class, had always felt like the odd one in his northeast Baltimore neighborhood. He had been taunted. His parents came from Greece. He didn't want kids to come into the house for fear they would hear a strange language. At City his closest friend became a black classmate named Turhan Robinson, who was known as "Robby" by almost everyone. But Constantine "Gus" Sitaris always called him Turhan. There was something exotic about the name, something that reminded him of his own name's oddness, and of their mutual feelings of marginalization.

"This name," Gus thought, "is his identity. It is who he is. Whatever it means, it is who he is." It was the first step for Sitaris to relax with his own identity—and to head toward a life in the Greek Orthodox Church as the Reverend Father Constantine Sitaris.

For most of us who went to City, the road to self-discovery was traveled via municipal transportation. At the end of the school day, swarms of us raced down to Thirty-third Street, where a steady line of buses carried boys back to the far corners of town from which we had arrived that morning.

Riders had to push and shove to get on early enough for a seat, and then watch the aisles fill up, and hope there was enough space left to fit in some of the girls from Eastern High School waiting on the next block. Before the girls arrived, talk tended toward the usual biological tales. Everyone was a hero, puffed up with fables of weekend conquests, or future possibilities of some miraculous weekend just over the horizon.

The girls from Eastern tended to ignore the City boys, who pretended to ignore them back. When the girls appeared, all talk of conquests went away. The buses went silent. Some of the girls were headed to Television Hill, where they danced each afternoon on the *Buddy Deane Show*, the local version of Dick Clark's famous *American Bandstand* program. The girls wore makeup that seemed to have been cemented on in layers, and lacquered, immovable hair. We thought they were stunning. If you stared too long at them, they were likely to snap at you, "Why don't you take a picture, it lasts longer." Instead, many boys ran home to stare at these girls dancing the jitterbug on live television those same afternoons with lanky fellows who had peroxide blond hair and tight pants bought on layaway at Lee's of Broadway in Fells Point.

The bus rides home seemed to take bleak hours. From University Parkway, they wheezed past the Rotunda shopping area and over the Forty-first Street Bridge past Television Hill, where they discharged all of the Buddy Deane types, white teenagers dancing to soulful Negro artists—Sam Cooke, Jackie Wilson—and clean-teen white performers—Frankie Avalon, Fabian—whose talents often seemed limited to their haircuts. The show was segregated. It was one thing for parents to tolerate integrated public schools, but another to allow them on the same television dance floor. By the time enough pressure was brought to integrate the show, its producers and nervous advertisers first allowed black teens to appear on separate days, and then simply took the program off the air.

From Television Hill the afternoon buses drove past Druid Hill Park to Park Circle, where most of the Jewish boys transferred to buses going up Park Heights Avenue or Reisterstown Road. Some of us stayed on past Carlin's Amusement Park to Liberty Heights Avenue, where another pattern developed. Between the old Baltimore Junior College and Lake Ashburton, almost all those getting off the bus were Negroes. From Lake Ashburton to Garrison Boulevard, a mix of Jews and Negroes. From Garrison Boulevard to Gwynn Oak Junction, a mix of gentiles and Jews. You could watch the change of color, and religion, and the immediate future of the city, along the drive up one long boulevard.

At Gwynn Oak Junction, we disembarked in late afternoon haze near some of the leather-jacketed drapes hanging by the pool hall and the corner gas station, and we began the long walk home past Read's Drug Store and Toots Barger's Bowling Academy, past Howard Park Elementary and then the Liberty Jewish Center. I knew some of the guys on that Gwynn Oak Junction corner. One was the boy from several years earlier at Howard Park Elementary who had picked up *shvartzer* and transmogrified it into "fatzah." His father was the man who had sung the national anthem with such fervor at the Cub Scout meetings.

Another was the Jew-hater from my neighborhood. He was the angriest kid I knew. In our neighborhood football games, he did not tackle ball carriers so much as throw his fists at them. When he hit a home run in baseball, instead of running the bases as the ball traveled over the outfield fence, he would slam his bat to the ground, a warrior plunging in a sword, and walk away. He had proved his manhood; there was no need to circle the bases. Over the years, seeing himself outnumbered by Jewish boys in the neighborhood, he had changed his target.

"You want a gar?" he asked one day, when some of the boys had begun to take up smoking.

"A gar?" I asked. "A cigar?"

"No," he said, "a niggar." This became his trademark joke. He laughed nastily and headed across the neighborhood schoolyard to the home of a high school pal who had somehow come into possession of a Nazi military uniform and strutted around the house clicking his heels.

He lived in his world, and we had ours. But we began to hear strange talk about some of these boys. They would gather at Gwynn Oak Junction on weekend nights, and a small caravan of cars would head down Liberty Heights Avenue, where the neighborhoods were changing most dramatically.

The fellow with the Nazi uniform seemed ludicrous. We were patriotic fellows, still going to the movies to thrill over World War II, and still seeing ourselves as those guys on the screen. John Wayne and Randolph Scott had stopped fighting, but then came Audie Murphy whose baby face looked about our age, and then Lee Marvin and Steve McQueen. The ironies of *Catch 22* and *Dr. Strangelove* hadn't yet crossed our consciousness. It wasn't the fighting and killing that grabbed us so much as the notion of American boys joining together for a great cause, like a football game with distant fireworks.

One day Ron Sallow decided to prove his manhood and his devotion to country. Ron lived across the street from me on Crawford Avenue. He knew the best places to hide out any time we cut school. He had worn glasses since childhood and skipped a grade in elementary school. He was smart but restless. He rode the bus to City College every day. One morning, he didn't show up.

He had secretly met with a recruiter from the U.S. Marines and was told to report to Fort Holabird on this school morning. He told no one: not his father, Will, who worked for the city of Baltimore, or his mother, Molly, a determined woman whose mother, Jennie, took the telephone call from Ron that afternoon.

He had spent that winter morning going through physical and mental exams at Fort Holabird. By midday, he had signed enlistment papers. Then a sergeant announced the recruits would soon climb aboard a bus for Camp Lejeune, North Carolina.

Ron decided it was time to call home. Having signed his enlistment papers, it was now too late for his parents to stop him. He didn't want them to worry when he failed to show up for dinner that evening. He found a payphone, and his grandmother answered the call.

"Bubbie," he said, "I joined the Marines. I'm gonna be shipping out."

In her Polish accent Grandma Jennie replied, "Vait a minute." Then she called Ron's mother. "Molly, it's Ronnie."

"I joined the Marines," he repeated to his mother. "I'm leaving for Camp Lejeune in a little while."

"You did what?"

"Joined the Marines."

"No, you didn't," said Molly Sallow.

"Yeah. I'm in. Don't worry."

It was the language of his own father, signing up for the Army when World War II had come. Or it was my father's language after Pearl Harbor, when the Air Force took too long and his mother, Esther Olesker, told him, "Don't be in such a hurry." It was any boy wanting to be a man for his country, and every mother feeling horrified.

Only now, there was no war but the cold war.

"Where are you?" said Molly Sallow.

"Fort Holabird. I'm shipping out at any moment."

"Don't move," said Molly Sallow.

He hung up the phone and stood in a yard with the rest of the Marine recruits. From Crawford Avenue in Northwest Baltimore to Dundalk Avenue and Fort Holabird on the east side, it was at least a forty-minute drive. Molly Sallow and Grandma Jennie made it in thirty, drove their old Buick Special into the fort and stopped by the crowd of recruits.

"Get in the car," said Molly Sallow as she spotted her son in the crowd.

"I can't get in," he whispered hoarsely. Every eye at Fort Holabird seemed to be watching.

"Ronald, get in the car."

"Molly, you gonna get locked up," the grandmother cried.

"Get in the car, Ronald."

A big Marine sergeant appeared and asked, "What's the problem here?"

"I'm here to take my son home."

"Ma'am," said the sergeant, attempting an unaccustomed politeness, "he's in the Marine Corps. You can't take him home."

This seemed to stop her for a singular tick of the clock.

"Has he done everything he has to do to be in the Marine Corps?"

"Everything but swear his oath of allegiance."

"Then he's not officially in, is he?"

"I'm sorry, ma'am, but he's already signed his enlistment papers."

"Molly, you gonna get locked up," the grandmother cried again.

"Let me see the papers," Molly Sallow said.

The sergeant went away and returned a moment later. He handed Molly the enlistment papers.

This was a mistake. She clutched them in her hands, and she tore them and tore them, and then she scattered the papers all over the grounds of Fort Holabird. The sergeant said nothing at all. Molly Sallow turned to her son.

"Ronald," she said. "Get in the car."

Which he did, and no one in any uniform told him otherwise.

We had not yet learned to fear the thing that was coming in Vietnam. War still had some romance for us. The war that we knew was our fathers' war, and the only war that troubled us was the one that involved no soldiers, only guided missiles and bombs.

It was only a few years since I'd stood on the playground at Howard Park Elementary School, where my classmates had surrounded the girl named Martha and called her a commie. The moment came back to me in October of 1962, when John Kennedy announced the Cuban missile blockade.

"The commies," lamented a boy on the morning bus to City College. "They want to take over the world." He pointed to a row of printed advertisements just above the bus windows. In one dramatic picture, the Russian premier Nikita Khrushchev pounded his fist, as he had at the United Nations, and a headline declared, "We will bury you."

Now the burial day seemed to have arrived. President Kennedy, having been informed of Russian missiles in Cuba, told Khrushchev to remove them or risk nuclear war. The deadline was a Friday morning. At City College that day, the mood seemed somber, but occasionally puckish. The standard student conversation went like this:

"What are you gonna do if we hear the Russian bombers are coming?"

"I don't know about you, man, but I'm going over to Eastern."

The sexual bravado covered everyone's dread. The night before, when Kennedy had announced the confrontation, my family watched the speech on television. Then I made my own announcement.

"I'm not going to school tomorrow," I said.

"Why not?" said my father.

"What's the point?" I said.

My father shot me a look that said all conversation was closed. Never mind nuclear annihilation, there was probably some all-important French quiz to be passed. But the following morning, at the official hour of military confrontation, I cut an American history class with two of my classmates to listen to a radio broadcast of the news. If all history was about to end, why bother to attend a lecture about it?

The three of us sneaked into the little first-floor *Collegian* newspaper office and turned on the rock-and-roll station WCAO, fully expecting to hear the end of the world come over the radio. First came the sound of static: Had they begun by blowing up radio stations? Then we heard a voice: Little Richard's.

"Well, I saw Uncle John
with bald-headed Sally
He saw Aunt Mary coming
and he ducked back in the alley,
Oh, baby . . ."

Aunt Mary was coming, but the Russians were not. "If they're playing music, it means we're not at war," I said.

"Damn," said my friend Jerry Solomon. "It means we gotta go back to class."

Our history teacher never discussed this business about the end of the world. It wasn't listed in the curriculum. He covered World War II, and did it in the dry manner of many history teachers of that era. We were given names and dates to memorize, dry facts to be regurgitated back on test days and then forgotten the instant the test was over. There was never a mention of Nazi genocide, or of American military segregation, or of internment camps for Japanese Americans. I wondered what that war had been like for my father, and got no answers either from my history teacher, or from my father when I asked him.

"Who can remember?" he would say. If he saw John Kennedy on the television screen, my father would joke, "We served in the war together"— never mind that Kennedy was riding a PT boat in the Pacific and my father was riding bomb runs over Europe.

What I wanted was not heroic stories, but real connections. My father was connected to history the way my friend Ron Sallow had tried to become connected to it. My father was connected to the great American citizenship experience, which was the military and World War II. I did not yet connect his war with the Holocaust, or with John Kennedy's nuclear precipice, or with the body counts to come in Vietnam. I was simply reaching for my taste of mainstream America through him; I wanted to feel fully connected, and I did not quite.

My world at City College became the *Collegian*, the student newspaper that appeared every Friday morning of the school year. The paper attracted many extraordinarily bright boys, and me. I was trying to combine a vague interest in writing with a passion for sports. These other *Collegian* boys haunted bookstores and debated Marx and Freud when they were certain no menacing knuckle-draggers lurked nearby.

There was a fellow named Eddie Max, a *Collegian* managing editor known for correcting misinformation in school textbooks. "Yes, sir, Mr. Max," respectful teachers would say, having learned to take his word for it that the textbooks had it wrong. The *Collegian's* editor-in-chief, Victor Lieberman, corresponded with Bertrand Russell about nuclear disarmament, and published their exchanges in the paper. I understood almost none of it. A fellow named Robert Miller, who was my editor and drolly complimented my sports stories by calling them "very well typed," graduated City with me and, in the same time it took me to get my bachelor's degree from the University of Maryland he was earning not only his bachelor's from the University of Chicago but his Ph.D. from Princeton.

Most of these boys were in the A-course or Special College Prep sections. I was not. I was in a standard college prep homeroom with a diverse collection of boys whose sole common characteristic seemed to be a perverse pride in underachievement. We were fairly bright, but reluctant to work at it. To work was to risk the possibility of failure without the classic built-in excuse: "I didn't even study." In our crowd, studying was considered a form of cheating.

I felt caught between two worlds: the world of normal, rollercoaster adolescent drives, and these bookish wonks on the *Collegian,* who spent their idle moments wondering which Ivy League colleges were best suited to their needs.

As my involvement on the paper deepened, my days of rushing for the afternoon bus ended. Because the paper was published every week, those of us who worked on it stayed after school. All other students vanished, then all teachers and athletes and coaches, then all but the evening janitorial staff and some adults who arrived for evening English courses. The dinner hour arrived and departed, and we stayed. Darkness fell, and we stayed. We worked out of two tiny first-floor newspaper offices and a couple of nearby typing classrooms.

One winter night, Richard Bready, a pale, esthetic A-course student who wrote with a poet's sensitivity, strolled from the *Collegian* office into the school auditorium, where rehearsals had begun for the midyear class play. Backstage, he discovered makeup and a slight attack of whimsy. He applied great streaky gobs of the makeup to his face. He wore a maroon corduroy sports jacket, and tore away its pockets and left them dangling.

Then he headed for the room where the adult class was held. The students were first-generation Americans trying to learn English. Bready took on the hunchbacked posture of Quasimodo. He skipped into the room, face grotesque, clothing torn, body bent, arms dangling. He grunted. The adults turned and gasped. Bready grunted again. The teacher hollered and chased after Bready, who grunted once more and raced down the hall without ever losing his stride or his sense of character, cadaverous body bent over, feet skipping, arms flung this way and that, grunting like mad.

It was innocent adolescent fun, a group of guys descended from ethnically mixed backgrounds sharing a laugh over a group of newly arrived mixed ethnics. Only later did it hit us: These adults were the modern versions of our own grandparents, of those outsiders who had once arrived at the Locust Point piers, or worked the food stalls in Fells Point's Broadway Market and shouted across the aisles in their old Eastern European dialects. They were the newest versions of my great-grandmother Zlotte Strull changing her name to Jenny and sitting in her daughter Edith's night-school class, trying to learn English to make herself American.

In this time, many of us were oblivious to our own family histories, which were set aside in order to blend in. The Catholic John F. Kennedy had sworn to put his country before his religion. He had Jews in his White House cabinet who had taken the same vow. This generation of Americans was erasing its history of noticing our differences—except for color.

Race captured our sense of conscience. Negroes were psychological immigrants reaching for the full America. In the early 1960s Baltimore was a city attempting to put a congenial face on integration, and getting away with it only occasionally. It was this way across much of the state.

One night some of us from my neighborhood drove to the University of Maryland campus in College Park. Dennis Buchman was eighteen, the only one in the group old enough to drive. He was a freshman at Maryland. Barry

Director was there, and so were Steve Misler and Phil Rubinstein, who was fifteen but nearly ready to graduate high school. He was the smart one in the neighborhood.

Misler had a cherry bomb, a small version of a firecracker. As we stood near the school's big McKeldin Library, he tossed the cherry bomb into the emptiness of a grassy campus mall. It boomed loudly and lit up the night sky. We ran back to Dennis Buchman's car. A campus policeman was there.

"Follow me," he ordered.

We were kept for several hours at the campus police station, wondering what the penalty would be. Two police walked into the small room where we waited. Across a hallway we could see a row of cells.

"Oh, good," said a sergeant. "I see you picked up some Jews."

"Yeah," said the officer who had brought us in. "We'll have to do the same thing to them that we did to those niggers."

I glanced toward Barry Director to get his take on this. Across the South, they were turning dogs and firehoses against Negroes. There was a history of lynching; we had only tossed a cherry bomb, but these were anxious times in America.

But Barry could barely keep himself from laughing. He understood, instinctively, that the cops had overplayed their hand. We weren't Negroes! We were white people—even if we happened to be Jewish white people. Even in our adolescence, we understood that color meant everything. One of the police grabbed Steve Misler by his shirt collar, lifted him off his feet, and then let him go. They asked if we had any more cherry bombs. We said no. No charges were filed. They told us to go home, and make sure we didn't exceed any speed limits on the way. We left quickly, understanding we had been treated the way white teenagers were treated.

I wondered what might have happened to black guys in my class at City. Turhan Robinson was a student government leader. Mansfield "Sonny" Newsom, who sat in front of me, devoured several new library books each week. Sam Bishop, the strongest guy in the class, was also the gentlest. (Robinson graduated Morgan State University, rose to the rank of major in the U.S. Army, became a lawyer and assistant attorney general for Maryland. Newsom, lacking funds for college, made a career in the U.S. Navy and then created a successful computer business. Bishop graduated Morgan State and became a supervisor with Baltimore Gas and Electric.) What would those police have done with them?

In my neighborhood, Negroes had not yet moved in. In our free time, most of us met at our neighborhood schoolyard for pickup ballgames. But the neighborhood Jew-hater seemed increasingly agitated. Sometimes, after dark, he and the boy with the Nazi uniform disappeared. They went to Gwynn Oak Junction, where several cars would head down Liberty Heights Avenue toward the Ashburton Reservoir. The neighborhoods there had now changed almost completely.

The caravan of boys looked for Negroes walking alone in the dark. In their prowling, they carried guns and knives. They waved them out of their car windows. Then they chased their prey, sometimes in the cars and sometimes on foot, intending to spread the sense that no more movement up Liberty Heights Avenue would be tolerated.

Such incidents were never reported in the daily newspapers. They were not sufficiently dramatic, since nobody was killed. In our neighborhood, crosses were set afire at a nearby Jewish cemetery each Halloween by the Jew-hater and a few of his friends. This was seen as schoolboy prankishness, and not the thing later known as a hate crime.

One Sunday morning my father and I drove down Reisterstown Road to Cold Spring Lane, where we parked outside a church.

"One of my deals," my father said. This meant he was handling the property in a real-estate transaction. I looked through my window and saw a few people coming out of the church. It sounded, to my innocent ears, as if the church were being sold out from beneath the parishioners, who were being displaced at the whims of real-estate forces. I asked how such a thing could happen.

"What are you talking about?" my father said. "The neighborhood's changing. They're all moving somewhere else."

He did not imply any moral judgment. There was no talk of an exodus, for better or worse, or any off-hand *shvartzer* reference, or mention of white attitudes. Black families had reached this part of Northwest Baltimore and were now living along Cold Spring Lane, and white families were leaving. My father was simply showing me his piece of the real-estate action.

"How do these people feel about this?" I asked. My father shrugged. This wasn't about feelings, it was about real estate, and market forces, and social developments that simply *were*. He was showing me what he did for a living, and leaving me to interpret it on my own.

It was an awkward era. To the credit of the *Collegian*'s editors, the school paper covered Baltimore's changing race relations; to the credit of school administrators, they let us. In 1961 City's graduating class wished to hold a farewell sports dance at Gwynn Oak Amusement Park's Dixie Ballroom. Owners of the park said no. The park did not allow Negroes, not even if it meant turning hundreds of paying couples away from their doors. Gwynn Oak was picketed. So were restaurants and moviehouses.

Two years later Victor Lieberman paused in his correspondence with Bertrand Russell to cover one demonstration for the *Collegian*. He wrote about a group of students picketing a local restaurant, and about one black student who entered the place and was refused service. It was a remarkable piece of writing and reporting for a high school newspaper, with one drawback: The *Collegian* was not allowed to name the establishment refusing to serve black people. In the midst of a social revolution, that a business might suffer bad publicity for its lack of conscience was still unthinkable for those who ran the city's public schools.

As it happened, the business was the Mandell-Ballow Restaurant, on Reisterstown Road at the Hilltop Shopping Center. I went there sometimes with friends. My parents went with their friends. The atmosphere was congenial. I did not consider us racists in any way. We weren't vigilantes riding through Ashburton late at night; we weren't College Park campus cops issuing racial slurs. We weren't even the invisible people who kept the Buddy Deane television program segregated. I reveled in the City College experience, where almost everyone seemed to come from a minority background of some sort. Wasn't that the working model for the entire city? Didn't we see progress?

A decade earlier, there were no Negro taxicab drivers in the whole town. Now there were some. Only a few years earlier, no Negroes had been employed as salespeople in any of the big department stores downtown. Now there were some. Not many—but some. A few years earlier, Ford's Theatre—the only legitimate theater in town—would reluctantly allow blacks and whites to perform together on stage but would not allow them to sit together in the audience. Now they would. White liberals said things were certainly moving too slowly—but weren't there healthy signs? Blacks saw it another way: They needed jobs, not symbols.

The Jews felt they had gone further than anyone had. In 1954 the Baltimore Jewish Council drafted the Fair Employment Practices legislation prohibiting job discrimination. Two years later Baltimore became the first city below the Mason-Dixon Line to pass such a law. To liberal Jews, it said: We have a social conscience. When pickets marched to integrate Gwynn Oak Park, one of those arrested was Rabbi Israel Goldman, of the Chizuk Amuno Congregation.

But I heard adults in the neighborhood expressing grave concerns. They weren't prejudiced themselves, they always stressed—but they were afraid others would move away if Negroes moved nearby or ate at the same restaurants. Wasn't it enough that whites sympathized in their hearts? They wondered why events had to move so quickly, and asked why they had to be inconvenienced for somebody else's troubles? Across America in that time, the familiar phrase was: "You can't legislate morality"—you can't pass laws that will move people's hearts.

Then came a night in the spring of 1963, the night of the City College senior prom. About twenty of us—including some black classmates and their girlfriends—left the prom and went to Danny Dickman's, a spiffy restaurant on Charles Street. We were clothed in our tuxedoes and gowns, and in our innocence. We were stopped at the door. Negroes were not allowed.

I looked at Mansfield "Sonny" Newsom, who had sat directly in front of me for three years. Then, embarrassed, I looked away. I looked at Turhan Robinson, who was looking at his best friend, Gus Sitaris. They did not make eye contact. Behind the doorman, we saw nicely dressed people enjoying late dinners. And we stood there now at Charles and Eager Streets, all dressed up, and felt as if someone had pronounced us unclean, and unfit to be seen by respectable people.

"You can come in," a doorman said, gesturing toward the white couples. "But not them."

I felt the blood rush to my head. The doorman spoke politely, but he had a sense of tough-guy menace about him. All the empty, fatuous arguments about not rushing "too quickly" into integration, about "symbolic" triumphs, were translated into a simple emotion now: the humiliation of being declared a lower form of American citizen.

"What do you mean?" I asked.

"Listen, kid, don't give me a hard time," the doorman said. He glanced behind him, as though ready to summon reinforcements. "We don't allow colored."

Then I heard one of the white boys in our group mutter to another, "I don't want my prom night ruined. Why can't we go in and meet up with those guys later?"

Now arguments broke out over this notion: Did we owe it to ourselves to continue the party, and tough luck for the black guys? Did friendships count for nothing? Sonny and Turhan were quiet, and I wanted to place myself between them and this unseemliness. Gus Sitaris slipped away for a moment, found a telephone, and called home. The man at the door stood firm while a couple of white classmates argued about going inside. That seemed all wrong. The thing we had just gone through together, the years of public school, wasn't about marching to civil rights anthems; the lessons had always been implied. It was about different kinds of people going about their business in the same place, and discovering it was all right, and taking those lessons to the outside world. The problem was, we hadn't taken it very far into the outside world before now. We went to school, and then we went our separate ways. And now that we were extending the relationship, this was the outside world's response.

Then Gus Sitaris came back. There was food at his house, he said. We got back into our cars and drove to Northeast Baltimore. By the time we got there, Gus's parents had put out a table of Greek delicacies that took up one side of his club basement. "And some chopped liver," his mother said—in case the Jewish guys wanted any.

In a little while somebody put on some records. After a few songs, Sonny Newsom walked over to one of the white girls.

"Could I have this dance?" he said to her. They would take the *Buddy Deane Show* off the air for such a thought. But Sonny and the white girl danced slowly across the club basement, and nobody thought to raise an eyebrow. It was okay to cross such lines, as long as you did it in private. In the spring of 1963, that was considered great progress.

Charles A. "Dutch" Ruppersberger, the future
Baltimore County executive, pictured in the
1963 Baltimore City College yearbook. The
school drew its students from every neighborhood of the city. Not all of them were considered scholars. Courtesy of Dutch Ruppersberger

Nearly four decades later, C. A. "Dutch" Ruppersberger sat in his Baltimore
County executive office in Towson on a balmy summer morning. He remembered that era, and how that cosmopolitan mix had informed a political philosophy.

"You look at the schools today," he said. "We've lost that simple act of
learning things side by side."

In the city, segregation had returned; in the suburbs, there were signs of
something similar on the way. In Baltimore County, said Ruppersberger, the
overall African American population was somewhere between 20 and 30 percent. But the public school population was now nearing 50–50. The private
schools were getting fatter as the white public school parents became more
anxious. In the city, only about 13 percent of the public school kids were
white; all other whites had either moved to suburbia or found space in private schools.

"These kids don't understand what we had back then," he said. "It was the best time for integration. We didn't talk about somebody being Jewish or black. You might have started out feeling funny, but you wound up learning relationships. You worked through the rough spots. What's happened now is, you have segregation again. And that's sad. Because they become adults, and they don't know how to deal with each other.

"Sometimes," he said, "I'm dealing with an African American, and they'll say I'm playing the race card. And I'll say, 'What do you mean? Don't give me that race stuff.' People who haven't grown up with each other, they're intimidated by each other. Or they'll patronize each other. They can't work through the distance, because they didn't learn it when they were kids."

"I don't remember any brotherhood talks when we were at City," I said.

"Hell, no," Ruppersberger said. "You were just thrown in with guys. It's the way life is." He lived around Northeast Baltimore's Lake Avenue and the Alameda, all white, all gentile. At City he played football and lacrosse. "That's where I met the Jewish guys, playing lacrosse. And some of 'em had cars, and at lunchtime a bunch of us would go for rides. And weekends, they'd take me to their side of town to their parties. The biggest problem was Jewish fathers. I was different. I was gentile. If you were talking with their daughter, the girls would say, 'Oh, my father would never . . .'"

His voice trailed off. The dating of Jews and gentiles was still a rarity, still seen by some parents as a curse on their families. "It's kind of funny now," Ruppersberger said. He met his wife, the former Kay Murphy, at the Grace Methodist Church, Charles Street and Belvedere Avenue. The marriage has lasted three decades.

"At City, the big thing was the integration," he said. "I mean, I worked the student patrols, and this black guy comes into the school. He was from Carver or Douglass. And we get into a fight. So he says his group of guys is gonna get me after practice. And some of the black guys on our team heard about this, and they got behind me and walked me down to the bus after practice. I'm a big guy, I'm a white guy, but they're gonna protect me, see? It wasn't about race. It was about being part of the same thing, which was school, which was the same athletic team."

Those years on the *Collegian*, I covered sports and never wrote a word about race. And yet every story reflected life in the mix. One year I covered the track and cross-country teams. They were coached by Jerry Nathanson, who had delivered the impassioned lecture about the tragedy of body odor during World War II. It was part of Nathanson's persona: he was a salesman, and he sold a point of view to boys still in the market for one.

Each spring and fall he gathered his teams and delivered a lecture that seemed part of the City College coda. "The hell with color and religion," he said. "You're either a man, or you're not."

My friend Joel Kruh ran the two-mile event for Nathanson's track teams, and also ran cross-country. Most of his teammates were black. The distance runners worked out together, sometimes running in uniform through the streets near City to Clifton Park and back. As they ran, they talked. This simple act, considered so revolutionary in that era, led to friendships that extended beyond school.

On weekends, Joel went to parties with some of the black kids from the track team—Alvin Rawlings, Kenny Mason, Andy Bates, Bill Proctor, all standouts of their schoolboy era—and felt embraced.

"I felt like a brother," he said years later. The skinny, hyperactive kid from the old neighborhood was an attorney and political lobbyist now. We ate lunch at Attman's Deli, on East Baltimore's Lombard Street.

"The black guys were very protective of me," he said. "We'd go into Washington, or we'd go to house parties." He laughed. "As soon as we'd walk in, they'd yell, 'White boy coming in.' The parties were like our parties, except those guys could dance. To this day, when I go to a party, I'll yell, 'Get the white people off the dance floor.'"

We looked through the window of Attman's Deli. Across the street we could see the two remaining synagogues of nearby Lloyd Street, each barricaded against any possible intruders. The old bustle of Lombard Street was mostly a memory now. Most of the delis were gone. It was a sunny afternoon. On our side of Lombard Street, about forty yards west of Attman's, were the Flag House high-rise housing projects, home to several generations of black families, finally about to be imploded after a long, disastrous era of crime and drugs and splintered families.

In our time at City College we imagined a world where racial divisions would be healed and equality declared. In that same time, others insisted it would never work, that black people were not like whites. In our middle age, Joel and I recalled black classmates who were now political leaders, lawyers, teachers, professional people of all types whose values were the same as ours. The old segregationists merely pointed to the ruins of Lombard Street.

SIXTEEN

THE FORBIDDEN FRUIT

A marriage made in denominational heaven, this was not.

Gary Levin grew up in Northwest Baltimore, where his entire immediate world seemed to be Jewish. Joan Muth grew up in Northeast Baltimore, with an uncle who romped about the house, crying, "Watch out! Jew-boy's gonna get you." Gary was a Jew who imagined sexual conquest was as close as the nearest church dance, since reliable sources said gentile girls were easy. Joan came from a gentile family. She had a cousin in Delaware who lived next door to Jews and found their behavior remarkable.

"You know," the cousin confided, "they kiss the door."

The cousin referred to the *mezuzah*, the miniaturized casement for passages of Scripture that most Jews nail to their doorposts and some acknowledge with a kiss as they enter and leave. Joan Muth Levin told the story one spring afternoon with her husband, Gary, sitting across from her on their backyard deck in Hunt Valley, northern Baltimore County.

I glanced over at Gary, whose eyes twinkled behind his glasses as she told the story. In Baltimore, in our time of growing up, people from different backgrounds tended to live in separate worlds together. There were common denominators, such as the public schools. But we went home in different directions. Gary and I were roommates one year in college with a friend named Michael Wiener, who was half Jewish and half Catholic and dated a gentile girl named Brenda. He brought her to our apartment one evening as Gary and I sat in front of the television evening news eating dinner.

"This is Brenda," said Michael Wiener.

"What else do Jews eat?" said Brenda, as if stumbling onto the site of a strange civilization.

Wiener spent that spring semester committing himself to Catholicism. His father, U.S. Army Col. Leo Wiener, was Jewish. His mother, Sheila Wiener, believed she would suffer in the afterlife if her son did not commit himself fully to her religion.

Gary and I shrugged at his dilemma. Of all confusions in our lives, religion was not one. We were Jews from fully Jewish families. We had gone to Hebrew schools and had bar mitzvahs. We dated Jewish girls and joined a Jewish fraternity at the University of Maryland. We went to synagogue on the high holidays where we fretted reverently, like most people we knew, about the Baltimore Colts. Religious choice was no more an option than loyalty to our football team. We spent less time pondering Saturdays in synagogue than Sundays at Memorial Stadium. Our religious background was what it was. Our parents were Jewish, and each of us anticipated we would marry Jewish girls and raise Jewish children.

Nor did it occur to Joan Muth, of German-American, Presbyterian roots, that she would marry a Jew, convert to Judaism, and raise as a fully committed Jew a daughter Amy—who would then marry an Irish Catholic who cared not even slightly for any of the religious complexities that preceded his arrival on the scene, having few religious inclinations of his own.

So it sometimes goes in the American religious melting pot. In midcentury America the Jewish rate of intermarriage was about 5 percent; by century's turn, it was said to approach 50 percent. To American Jews, who number only about six million, this was cause for considerable anguish. Fewer than half the country's Jewish households reportedly belonged to synagogues, and religious school enrollment was only about half a million. America was about 2 percent Jewish, and every time there was intermarriage, even if the gentile spouse converted to Judaism, many Jews believed there was a loss to the culture.

"Joan knew," said Gary Levin, "that I wasn't gonna convert, and that I wanted my children to be Jewish. Culturally it mattered. Look, I don't buy into most religious stuff. I'm a rationalist, a skeptic. When I go to *shul,* once a year, it's a culture thing. I don't buy into any kind of revelatory beliefs— Christian, Jewish, whatever.

"You know," he said, gesturing toward Hunt Valley's nearby wooded greenery, "people like me are not gonna keep the culture going. I mean, look where I'm living. You don't see any other Jews here. But I do have a warm spot for what the culture has given me. The strength of family, the real important stuff, the strength of tradition."

He met Joan when she was working at Johns Hopkins Hospital. She had just ended a relationship with a Chinese doctor. His family cut it off. They did not want their son to marry a Caucasian. Each ethnic minority tries to hold onto the traces of its own history—and those who are eldest, and have the deepest investment in its culture, hold on tightest.

Joan moved on. She was a pale blonde with a quick sense of humor and a nimble mind. She grew up in a family with sickly parents who had no funds to send Joan or her identical twin sister, Jean, to college. But Joan had gone back to school over their young adult years, and was now the human resources director for an insurance company. Gary was retired after teaching English in the Baltimore area public schools. They met in 1969, and married in November of 1970. No one could have predicted such a union. Too much history was in the way, too many wary family members, too many neighborhoods wrapped inside ethnic wombs, preserving distance, cultivating suspicions—and not yet understanding the changes that were already beginning to unfold.

The Levins lived in the city's Forest Park section, remarkable for its overwhelming percentage of Jewish families. In elementary school Gary Levin had one or two gentile kids in his class. "They'd be like aliens, like they had just been dropped in," he said. "I knew there was a non-Jewish world somewhere out there, because you couldn't watch TV in December and not know

Joan and Gary Levin on their wedding day, November 22, 1970. Theirs was not a marriage made in religious heaven. Her roots were German; his were Jewish. They grew up in a Baltimore where the two did not often mix. *Courtesy of the Levin family*

that. But the gentile world still didn't touch me. It was just that entity out there. I'd say, 'Why are there Christmas shows on TV, but no shows on Chanukah?' My parents would tell me that most people in the world weren't Jewish. I'd see a celebrity on TV and say, 'Is he Jewish? Is he Jewish?'"

"*One of ours,*" Lionel Olesker would say. My father would strike a proud, proprietary note as Dinah Shore blew her weekly television kiss to America.

"*One of ours,*" my mother would say when Sid Caesar appeared on *Your Show of Shows.*

"Like Milton Berle," Gary said. "You know, the pride that one of your own was on television, and he was the biggest star in the country."

But the Jewish connection was never explicitly made. The gentiles had Christmas shows, and nightly sitcom families who went to church on Sundays, and Bishop Fulton J. Sheen's *Life Is Worth Living* show every week. They had Sunday morning religious services on television and radio. The Jews had Molly Goldberg. She was the only specific Jew, living with her family in the Bronx the way my parents had, calling across the alley to her neighbor, "Yoo-hoo, Mrs. Cohen," and Yiddishizing the English language: "So who's to know?" she would ask. "In the pot, put the chicken," she would declare backwards.

Beyond that, the television set that formed so much of the American culture seemed to belong exclusively to that greater gentile world slightly separate from our own. Our parents pointed out Jewish celebrities almost with a sense that these actors—Sid Caesar, Phil Silvers, Dinah Shore—were putting one over on America, that they were *passing* so that the bigger audience, the gentiles, would accept them and, by extension, us.

One winter night in my family's living room on Crawford Avenue we watched the quiz show *Twenty-one.* A middle-aged woman won a jackpot in the show's closing seconds. As she pranced off stage, she called exultantly, "Merry Christmas and a happy Chanukah to you all."

Shock waves crossed our living room. "Liney, did you hear that?" my mother cried. "She said, 'Happy Chanukah!'" My father sat speechless. In a sea of wintry Christmas specials, in a world of gentile programming, our mere existence had been acknowledged, and it had set off hallelujahs. I sensed my mother wanting to reach for the telephone, to call up relatives and friends, to notify the wire services and spread the good news. My father put down his newspaper and slapped his hands together. In the television set they said our name, and it hadn't set off a wave of pogroms. It was all right to say the word in the most public place in America.

Growing up in Parkville, in northeast Baltimore County, Joan Muth sensed none of this cultural division. Her family was American, and Presbyterian, and the two were part of the same whole.

"Christmas, to me, was a secular holiday," she said. "I didn't think, 'Oh, good, we can celebrate the birthday of our Lord.' I knew people who had birthday parties for Jesus, with birthday cakes. That was important to them, and I respect it. But to me, it seemed like a kind of national holiday."

Her parents rarely went to church. Her father, Russell Muth, was the youngest of seven children. He was stricken in the influenza epidemic of 1918 and survived with damaged lungs and a heart weakened over a lifetime of smoking cigarettes. He was an auto mechanic who drove a cab the last seven years of his life. Her mother, Alvera Muth, was the third oldest of nine children. She worked for the Singer Sewing Machine Company. They had a strong sense of doing the right thing. They worried: What will other people think?

"Like, if you didn't go to church on Sunday," Joan remembered. "There were certain things my mother wouldn't let us do on Sundays, like roller-skate. In the Puritan way my parents interpreted religious teaching, it was like, 'Thou shalt not have fun.'"

They sent her to a church retreat in her teens. Everyone had to stand up and talk about experiencing Christ. She found it intimidating. She thought some people were embellishing. She never expressed her own religious epiphany, because she felt none. She felt as if she were being put through a drill and wondered what it had to do with being a good person.

She remembered little sense of her family's roots. Her grandparents spoke German, but this was a secret language between the two of them. "Our sense of being culturally German," she said, "was my grandparents eating German foods like sauerbraten. But culturally, it didn't go much beyond that. My parents were American. When they talked about the war, they said, 'The Germans, the Japanese.' There was a distinction.

"It was my father's oldest sister's husband," she said, picking her way through the family maze, "who would chase one of the kids around the room, saying, 'Jew-boy's gonna get you.'"

"What did that say to you?" I asked.

She shook her head slowly. "There was a Jewish family in Parkville for a year or two," she said. "A brother and sister. And somebody would turn around and say, 'You know, they're Jewish.' I didn't know what that meant. And then my cousin in Delaware, telling me about the Jewish neighbors kissing the door. It sounded so absurd, so I didn't pursue it."

The Jews were somewhere on the other side of her consciousness. For the Levins, the gentiles were kept at a safe distance. Gary Levin's mother, Evelyn, was born in a small Polish town. She remembered pogroms. She remembered hiding under her mother's skirts. The family moved to America when she was eight. Her husband, Louis Levin, was born here but his parents were from Latvia and Russia and ran a little grocery store in the city's Bolton Hill neighborhood. They remembered Cossacks.

"For my parents," Gary Levin said, "the nature of their lives was, we can only depend on each other. They were products of their time. It was different for me. I grew up around all Jewish people, but there was assimilation in America, and nobody was threatening us. The anti-Semitism we faced was oblique, it bounced off. Once in a while, somebody called you a name, but . . ."

"But it was individual, not institutional," said Joan.

There were neighborhoods, such as Roland Park and Guilford, said to have mortgage covenants keeping out Jews and Catholics. These dated back to the close of the nineteenth century. There was the swim club with its legendary bigoted sign about Jews, blacks, and dogs, and country clubs with closed doors. But these were seen as sociological relics that were weirdly out of date to a generation born after the war who found friendships in the public schools and the athletic leagues and the scouting groups.

On Fernhill Avenue, where the Levins lived, Gary sat with a few buddies and listened to earnest talk about gentile girls. The common boyhood wisdom was: They weren't like Jewish girls. The Jewish girls echoed their parents' concerns about things sexual. The gentile girls were said to be wild. They were called *shiksas*. In Yiddish it translates simply as "gentile girl." But the use of the Yiddish implied something exotic, something just out of reach.

"*Shiksas*," he said, "were the forbidden fruit. That's what we talked about on Fernhill Avenue. And there was St. Ambrose Church, on lower Park Heights Avenue, and they were having an affair. We were eleven or twelve, and we all decided to go over there to lose our virginity."

"It was assumed," I said.

"Of course. Because gentile girls were everything that Jewish girls were not. That was the mythology. And one of the great things happened when I got to Poly."

Baltimore Polytechnic was the other great high school that drew boys from all over the city. What City College was to the humanities, Poly was to math and science. But City drew almost all of the Jewish boys who didn't go to Forest Park. Poly drew only a scattering of Jews. Gary was sports editor of the Poly *Press*.

"We had this guy on the football team, Wade Johnson," he said. "He didn't like me at first, but then I wrote something complimentary in the paper, so we became pretty good friends. And in my little Jewish crowd at Poly, we were always talking about these wild *shiksas,* and why couldn't Jewish girls be more like them?"

One day Wade Johnson approached him in the cafeteria. "Levin," he said, "how about setting me up with one of those wild Jewish girls?"

"Huh?"

"Come on, man, everybody knows they put out."

Gary could scarcely believe the conjunction of the two crucial words, "wild" and "Jewish." Never before in his experience had one followed the other. He felt a kind of epiphany, a disbelief that his classmate could be serious.

"How about it?" Johnson said. "I hear they're wild."

"Well," Gary replied, wanting to bathe in the waters of this wholly unanticipated sexual pool for at least a little while, and wanting some of it to splash over his own reputation, "let me think about it."

Sexual or not, the notion of interreligious dating was practically unthinkable. There were still roadblocks to simple friendship. One day a classmate asked, without apparent rancor, "How do you feel about going to hell?"

"What do you mean?" Gary asked.

"My minister says all Jews are going to hell for not accepting Christ." He had never heard this before, never heard about Jews being held responsible for Christ's killing.

One day, the first morning of a new school year, Levin sat behind a boy at Poly named Lambie. Behind Levin sat a boy named Morstein. The three followed each other alphabetically. When roll was called, Lambie snapped his head around.

"Oh, man," he said. "Two Jews behind me. Now I'll have to turn my desk around and never turn my back."

It was still a time of choosing up sides. Levin graduated Poly at midyear and went to his first class at the University of Maryland, in College Park, the morning after commencement. Poly was a racially integrated school. At Maryland he found a campus almost devoid of black students. One was Melvin Potillo, with whom he had attended Poly. When I arrived at Maryland I found Potillo in my dormitory, along with another black student, Ron Jones, who had taken the bus every day from his parents' home in West Baltimore, out Liberty Heights Avenue, to Forest Park High School.

Jones lived a few doors down from my room in Harford Hall, overlooking the main campus drive on U.S. Route 1. I was a journalism major and was assigned to write a feature on him. The angle? He was "a Negro on campus." That was remarkable enough for a story. He was an engineering major. So was Melvin Potillo, who was there the night I interviewed Jones, and started talking about the latest of the so-called southern Freedom Rides in which he had just taken part.

"Whoo-weee," Potillo laughed. He had a big gap between two front teeth. "You're sitting on that bus, and you got these white boys surrounding it, and you're thinking, 'Okay, baby, this is where I get into Non-violent Position Number One.' 'Cause, I'm looking to get my head busted in, you know, and they tutored us in the various positions."

He demonstrated the various self-defense postures, each a variation of some pathetic fetal position, each accompanied by comic whoops of pain. The pain was inevitable. His choice was sardonic laughter in place of rage. He mentioned firehoses and police dogs, but his stories constantly went for the punchline. I thought of the senior prom night I was turned away from the restaurant in Baltimore, a pebble in the ocean of Potillo's lifetime. Now he was saying life was difficult, life was unfair—but it would get better, he could see it happening.

Ron Jones wasn't so sure. "The South," he said, "will never be cracked in my lifetime."

"It won't?" I said.

"And maybe not the North," he said. "I was coaching a kid in my math class several times a week. One day we started talking about civil rights and stuff. He says to me, 'Don't you realize you're inferior?' That little pecker! I'm trying to get this complex shit into his brain, and he's calling me inferior. You know, all Mississippians don't live in the South."

"That's just one guy, isn't it?"

"Yeah," he said softly. "And what about this place? You think that guy's alone?"

In my dormitory, Harford Hall, just past the school's main entrance overlooking U.S. Route 1, there were three or four Negroes; in many dormitories, there were none. In those days I would bump into Jake Oliver once in a while. In a sea of white faces, there he suddenly was. On such a white campus, it seemed odd to bump into him—as though all other black people from my past had been left behind in Baltimore. Our talk was pleasant but superficial. I had no idea how isolated he felt. I only thought: This isn't Mississippi. No one stands in the schoolhouse door here the way the governor of Alabama did when he fought racial integration. Here we had Negroes on campus, and no conflicts appearing on the evening news, so this must be a good thing. Jake shared his unhappiness strictly with black friends, and I was too dim to imagine how he felt.

One night in the spring of 1964 the presidential election came to College Park. Lyndon Johnson was running for election, but one of Maryland's U.S. senators, Daniel Brewster, was running as his surrogate in the state primary. His opponent was George Wallace, the segregationist governor of Alabama. Brewster stood in front of the McKeldin Library, where a crowd of a few hundred students gathered and cheered politely. An hour later, Wallace spoke inside the Cole Fieldhouse, the gymnasium where Maryland's basketball team had just finished another dispiriting season with an all-white team in the all-white Atlantic Coast Conference.

Wallace drew some heckling. "I don't hate the nigrah," he declared. "This is a constitutional issue." The hecklers were drowned out. In a crowd of about a thousand people, the Kappa Alpha fraternity, with roots in the deep South, had gathered. They roared over Wallace's best lines and waved a large Confederate flag. That night, the television news was filled with lingering shots of their thrilled reaction to Wallace.

Such moments set something off in Jake Oliver's brain, and in Ron Jones's. For Oliver the words of Martin Luther King now sounded too soft, too placating. He needed someone younger and more muscular. He found Eldridge Cleaver and Bobby Seale, and then he found Stokely Carmichael. And Ron Jones found a deeper sense of isolation.

I went to his room later that night, wondering about the Wallace reaction.

"Society," said Jones, "has just put up all these barriers."

He had turned down an academic scholarship from the all-Negro Morgan State College in Baltimore to come to College Park. He said it prepared him to compete in a white world. He lived in a room at one end of the dormitory's second-floor hallway, by himself at first, because there was an odd number of Negroes in the dorm and no one had yet broached the unwritten interracial rooming barrier.

"Wallace was speaking for a lot of people," he said.

"Not for everybody," I said.

In our uneasiness the two of us changed the subject. In a few minutes I left his room and walked back to my own. In my first two years at Maryland I roomed with a fellow from Aberdeen named Joe DiPersio.

"Say something in Italian, Joe," somebody would say.

"Spaghetti," Joe replied. "That's the only Italian I know."

He said it comically, but it sounded poignant. He was willfully cut off from his own history. He seemed to be saying, I'm just an American; let up on the other stuff. He delighted in playing his guitar and singing Kingston Trio songs. The Kingston Trio was put together by Ted Venetoulis's brother, who made his name Nik Venet to sound less Greek. The group was good-natured and homogenized American. Joe DiPersio and I roomed for two years and recognized we had all the important adolescent things in common—sports, a complete knowledge of rock-and-roll lyrics, which we regularly sang during late-night bull sessions in the room—and we never had a discussion about our religious or ethnic roots. In fact, in that time of our lives, neither of us cared to dwell on them, lest they divide us in any way.

In College Park, there were unwritten divisions. Blacks felt isolated from whites. Whites seemed barely to note their existence. Fraternities and sororities divided themselves by religion. Girls were cloistered enough that they had to be in their dormitories, safe from boys, by eleven at night. And we were beginning to divide ourselves over Vietnam.

At first, we noticed the demonstrations on television. In my third year of college, when I shared an off-campus apartment with Michael Wiener and Gary Levin, we saw people our age burn their draft cards in crowds protesting the war.

Instinctively, we thought they were traitors. If America was at war, it was our job to back our country. We still had visions of the last big war, which we remembered not as Korea but World War II. That was *our* war, the war we had watched on movie screens, the war fought by our fathers. Since we still saw ourselves as young people at school, and saw our fathers as grown men, we imagined all wars were fought by grown men.

Then it began to dawn on us: This war would be ours. Wiener knew there was no getting out of it. As a colonel's son, he had no choice. Levin was preparing to teach school, and wondered if this would defer him. I went home to Baltimore one weekend and saw a buddy who lived down the street named Rodger Snyder.

"I'm going in," he said. He was a couple of years younger than I. He'd graduated Milford Mill High School but seemed unsure what to do next. We threw a football back and forth in the street in front of my parents' new house near Randallstown, in northwest Baltimore County, where the suburban exodus had taken them.

"What about Vietnam?" I asked.

"I want to be a paratrooper or a Green Beret," he said. That was the elite fighting force. Rodger wore thick glasses. He was pale and blond and skinny enough to count every rib in his chest when he took off his shirt.

"You gonna go?" he asked.

I hoped the war would end before I graduated. I hoped the North Vietnamese would come to their senses and understand they could not win against mighty America. I only wanted to go to ballgames and write newspaper stories about them. I had a bad back and went to my Uncle Dick for chiropractic treatments, and wondered vaguely if this might keep the Army away from me. I did not want to be seen as unpatriotic. I knew that my father had served in the Army Air Force, and saw his experience as a measure of my family's full American citizenship. I remembered hand-grenade debates on the playground at Howard Park Elementary School. I remembered stories of the boys from my parents' neighborhood in the Bronx going off to the fighting. But this war didn't sound like my father's war, and I was part of a generation that did not necessarily burn draft cards—but searched with increasing anxiety for ways to get out of the war without looking like draft-dodgers.

Gary Levin was protected—for a while, at least—by teaching. Michael Wiener trained as a medical officer at a base somewhere in Texas. In my last full year of college, I shared an apartment in Adelphi, a few miles off campus, with three fellows who followed the war news and reacted the same way.

"I think I have high blood pressure," Jim Goldman said one evening as the four of us thought about our prospects. He was short, curly-haired, and shaped like Buddha. He wound up in the Navy.

"I've got my knee," said Gerry Schechter. He made it sound like a prized possession. He'd been hurt playing high school football and underwent surgery. He limped across the living room and looked out the window. Across the street was a cemetery whose hundreds of headstones could be seen by the light of the moon. Gerry was nicknamed "Chester," since surgery left him with a gait like the actor in TV's *Gunsmoke*. He faced a lifetime of knee troubles. At that moment, we envied him such good fortune and did not know that one of our group would be buried in that nearby cemetery before long.

"I've got really flat feet," said Bob Mayers, who shared a bedroom with me.

"They don't care about flat feet," I said.

"They don't?" he said. Mayers's outward attitude toward all troubles was a cavalier declaration: "So, fuck it." But it masked the same confusion and dread and vulnerability we all felt over Vietnam.

We still remembered the old war movies and the recycled *Life* magazine photos. But this war insisted on telling itself in the present tense. Instead of heroic old World War II photos—cleared by the censors, doctored by editors, dated by weeks, effects muted by never showing American casualties—this was a nightly procession of American kids getting blown up on television. Mike Wiener's girlfriend Brenda had asked, What else do Jews eat? We were eating the same as everyone else who watched the nightly news: a helping of filmed catastrophe with our main course.

This wasn't the way we were supposed to go to war. Where were the shots of beautiful French girls tossing roses at our liberating boys in their jeeps? Where were the chocolate bars for Yank infantry men to hand out to grateful youngsters? These kids didn't look grateful. Who were they? This was somebody else's war, and somebody else's movie. These were people we knew nothing about, who didn't know our movies and didn't know how grateful they were supposed to be, and didn't share the vision we had of ourselves as saviors of oppressed people everywhere. If they weren't going to be grateful and act out their parts in our generation's version of the great old war movies, then what was the point? Freedom and democracy? Democracy could take care of itself. It was far bigger than any gesture we might be able to make, especially if we were about to be reduced to the size of bodies small enough to fit inside TV screens when they pulled us out of some godforsaken rice paddy.

"So, fuck it," Bob Mayers said. He made it sound cavalier, but it wasn't his attitude at all. A year later he began losing himself behind a veil of drugs, and a year after that he began to flunk out of school.

Increasingly, as I approached graduation, I wondered if my back would keep me out of the war, and then felt guilty for wondering about it. My father hadn't looked for excuses. His generation had kids with bad backs and flat feet and went off to war anyway.

"Maybe I should think about the Air Force," I said one evening. I was home from school for the weekend, and my father and I watched the evening news. Every night there were scenes of bloodied American boys, doing their bit, carried out of jungles on stretchers.

"Maybe," my father said. We had never talked about Vietnam, but he knew I had registered for the draft. We shared the same confusions. He remembered a time when people rushed to enlistment centers. Now, whatever questions he had, he didn't want to pass them to his oldest son. He was cynical about Washington, but he had a sense of duty.

"You flew," I said, bracing for the familiar brush-off. "It's safer up there, isn't it?"

He turned off the television news and talked about lying in bed before dawn in the last year of his war. He was stationed in Foggia, Italy, at an airbase shared by the Americans and the British. He would wait for the sound of an officer's footsteps on the gravel outside his barracks. The officer would come to awaken everyone for the day's bombing missions.

"Pretty scary?" I asked.

"We lost some guys," he said. This was more than he had said before. He remembered St. Valentine's Day of 1945. I felt as if a door was opening. My father was a tail gunner. He remembered his copilot, a fellow named George Peck. My father had just turned twenty-two. I was now twenty-one. My father said there was flak bursting outside Peck's cockpit window. From the kitchen, we heard my mother's voice, calling us to dinner. My father escaped to another subject.

My mother said she had bumped into Rodger Snyder's mother. Rodger was in Vietnam now, fighting in some jungle. I told her Michael Wiener was headed there. My mother said Dolores Snyder couldn't sleep at night from worrying about Rodger. She had managed to talk him out of trying to be a Green Beret, but he'd joined the paratroopers instead. It was crazy; Rodger was always afraid of heights, and now he was parachuting into jungles, part of the 101st Airborne Division in Vietnam. He would jump out of planes before the infantry arrived, getting some idea how treacherous things might be for the others. Already he'd been awarded several medals.

One night Gary Levin and I drove to College Park, where Bob Mayers roomed with a couple of friends. We shot pool for a while. Mayers was a natural shot, a gifted athlete, and a hit with girls who fell for his blue eyes. Also, he was a slob. The year we had roomed, he had half-eaten sandwiches lying on the floor for weeks at a time, and abandoned clothing everywhere.

"Even by your standards," I said, "this apartment's a pigsty."

But something else was going on. He seemed personally dissolute, undone, eyes bloodshot. He was in and out of school, feeling pressured by the draft, turning increasingly to drugs. One night he'd driven to the railroad line near campus while on LSD and laid down on the tracks.

"What are you talking about?" I said. "Suicide?"

"I just wanted to hear the sound of the train," he said. He understood the madness of that moment, but the drugs were his withdrawal. He was a decent student whose grades had now gone completely south. And the Army was watching every college for its flunk-outs, because the war would not go away and the draft was escalating.

One winter afternoon, my mother called. Rodger Snyder had telephoned his mother at five-thirty in the morning. Rodger's mother was a wreck. She was certain that Rodger was not coming home from Vietnam, and told everyone in the family. Now he had called ship-to-shore, near Bangkok, to say that he had survived seven months of parachuting into jungles and didn't have a scratch, and he was coming home in three weeks.

"Be extra careful," his father, Sidney, shouted into the phone. "Extra careful."

Rodger started to say something back, but his voice faded, the signal was gone, and his family sat there in the silence for a moment. Then his mother made preparations for his homecoming. She bought him a little television set for his bedroom and a new bedspread. She framed a photograph of his girlfriend. A few days later, Mrs. Snyder took an afternoon nap and woke up screaming. She said she heard Rodger calling her through the house. She telephoned her daughter Patty.

Rodger Snyder, "the kid from up the street," survived a year of ferocious action in Vietnam's jungles before a heart-wrenching telephone call to his worried family in Baltimore. *Courtesy of the Snyder family*

"Your brother's not coming home," she said.

"Mom," said Patty, "he's coming home. You've got to calm yourself."

Dolores Snyder hung up the phone, and ten minutes later heard her doorbell ring. She opened the door and saw an Army lieutenant standing in the cold.

"No," she cried. "Go away. Just go away."

But the soldier just stood there in the cold. The Army said Rodger was standing in a field somewhere in a place called Qui Nonh. They never cleared up the rest of it: a shot from some trees, or a small explosive. The details made no difference. He was gone.

A military motorcycle brigade led the procession to Arlington National Cemetery, in Virginia, on a snowy February afternoon when the tears froze on the faces of mourners. Everyone expressed great sorrow for his family. A bugler played "Taps," and a rabbi said, "I wish it could have been me, I'm three times his age."

In Baltimore, and in College Park, we heard more war stories—how to avoid it. Everyone had appointments with psychiatrists, psychologists, podiatrists, with osteopaths, with chiropractors, with surgeons of all types. Nobody went for actual surgery—merely for doctors' notes indicating surgical possibilities in the event of too much strain of some kind.

Almost everyone I knew—of draft age—hated the war. But many of us weren't certain why. There were a hundred legitimate reasons to hate it, but none quite nullified our suspicions of self-indulgence, the nauseating sense of guilt that it might be our own lack of courage behind our arguments. We could make every legitimate argument against it. It was a dreadful war, and it shouldn't have been ours, and our national leaders kept it going by lying about it. But we were a generation raised on stories of war heroes, and on the notion of soldiering as a gesture of paying dues for full membership in the country.

I had begun working at the *Baltimore News-American,* a Hearst paper that trumpeted the war effort. I waited for my draft notice. Gary Levin, teaching school, wondered if his deferment would hold out. He took graduate courses at Johns Hopkins University at night.

In one class he met a woman. The friendship became a romance. The woman was a blonde divorcée, a gentile. The course was called "The Death of God." As the relationship blossomed, Levin fretted about it. How would he tell his parents? He had a cousin who dated an Italian boy and stunned the entire family by marrying him. She had broken a taboo. Gary decided to speak to his mother.

"I'm seeing a gentile girl," he said. "It could get serious."

He saw a flash of pain cross his mother's face.

"I met her in my course at Hopkins. She's real smart. I was thinking of bringing her here to meet you."

"I don't want to meet her," said Evelyn Levin. She was upset. She still remembered pogroms, she remembered hiding under her mother's skirts. Her son was talking about The Other. "You're an adult, and I can't tell you what to do, but I don't approve and I don't know how I would handle it."

He did not tell his father. The relationship with the woman lasted about a year and then faded. Now he was teaching at Northern Senior High. One night a neighbor had a small party and invited Gary. Joan Muth was there.

She worked in an isotope laboratory at Johns Hopkins Hospital. In the lab were people from Japan and India, Pakistan and Dutch South Africa and Israel. She was fascinated by other cultures, and luxuriated in this mix. She took night courses and read books on comparative religions. Sometimes people from the lab had dinners where everyone brought a native dish and talked about their countries.

She hadn't attended church regularly since childhood, but decided to try Sunday services. One morning, the minister talked of the difference between Catholicism and Christianity. The title of his sermon was: "Victim or Victor?" He said the Catholics saw Christ as a victim on a cross but that Protestants saw him as having risen.

"This," she thought to herself, "is not a major issue for me."

But she went back again. This time she heard a sermon about souls predetermined to go to heaven or hell. She walked out of church that day thinking, "I'm done, see ya." She did not go back again.

At work she had telephone conversations with a resident at the hospital. It turned out he was a Presbyterian, like Joan. The conversations led to a date. The man turned out to be Chinese. He was born and raised in America. A relationship developed.

"He doesn't even look Chinese," said Joan's mother, trying to make the best of things.

"Mom, what are you talking about? He's as Chinese-looking as could be."

Then the man's parents found out about Joan. "They don't know what to make of it," he told her. He was politely ending the relationship. This was America, and it was nice to meet different people, but distinctions still had to be made.

When Joan arrived at the party at Gary Levin's neighbor's, she and Gary hit it off immediately. She invited him to a gathering at her house the following week. Later, he took her to College Park for a football game. Bob

Mayers was there, still in school but failing all of his courses, his life falling apart. That winter, Gary called his mother.

"I'm dating somebody who's not Jewish," he said. His mother reacted differently this time. She knew that he lived among gentiles, and worked among them, and did not come to Northwest Baltimore for dates. The odds did not favor a Jewish relationship.

"I want to bring her for Sunday breakfast," he said. His parents kept kosher. They had two sets of dishes, one for dairy and one for meat. Once, years earlier, when they had sneaked crabs into their home, his parents worried that Cantor Kotlowitz, who lived next door, might smell the crabs and know that they had broken the ancient dietary laws. They were, like some Jews, kosher inside their home but occasionally unkosher when they ate out. To eat crabs in their home was one thing; to invite their son's gentile girlfriend was a far more traumatic event.

Evelyn Levin was fine. Franny Levin, Gary's younger sister, was fine. His father, the most amiable and accommodating of men, could not look at Joan. It was the Jewish version of Nick Filipides' Greek father, refusing to look at a girl when told she was not Greek. It was generations of distance, and suspicions, and unnamed fears and unfocused grudges having nothing to do with individuals. It was the distance of the unknown. Louis Levin showed no anger, and felt none. He simply could not cope, and could neither look at Joan nor talk to her.

"It's not you," Gary explained to her when they left. "A taboo is being broken, and he doesn't know how to cope with it."

They began to talk about marriage, but not about religion. Gary would not convert, and wanted Joan to make the grand gesture. He felt hypocritical. He thought, Who am I, this cultural Jew who hates to go to synagogue, asking her to convert? So they didn't talk about it for months. He took her to services at a Reform synagogue. She liked the emphasis on humanism instead of ritual. She heard a rabbi say, "I'm not sure there is any entity such as God. Maybe God is something inside of us," and she thought, Somebody's thinking about this, and not just mouthing platitudes.

"My family had mixed reaction," she remembered. "My mother didn't have a frame of reference. My sister, Jean, said, 'If he's a good person, that's what's important.'"

Another relative said, "It's one of the Ten Commandments, it's the Christian thing to take in a Jew."

"It was the Jews who got the Ten Commandments," Joan said.

"It was?" the relative said.

Gary talked with his parents, and Joan talked with hers. Neither talked of religion with the future in-laws. Each acted as proxy for the other. When they finally talked, specifically, about conversion, Gary said to Joan, "I think it would be a problem if you don't convert."

She had gone to synagogue and listened to sermons. She had read books. She knew that her parents had gone to church out of obligation and not spirituality. She knew there were people in Gary's family who would not accept her as a Jew but might embrace her anyway. All her life, she had thought of Jesus Christ as a good man, a mortal man, with humanistic ideas. She believed human beings used him as a dividing force over stories whose veracity no one could ever prove. She liked what she saw as a Jewish emphasis on learning. She saw conversion as an approach to the world, and to humanity. She looked at the man who was asking her to change her religion, and saw someone with whom she could spend a lifetime.

"I don't have a problem," she said.

Thirty years later, she sat at a table facing her husband and smiled wryly as she remembered those words. They sounded a little businesslike. But she looked at Gary with such tenderness, and he looked back at her with such affection, and it was a marriage that had transcended everything: religion, and family misgivings, and all of the business that sometimes keeps people apart who might love each other dearly.

SEVENTEEN
THE RIOTS

On the day that Tommy D'Alesandro III became mayor of Baltimore, he won 555 of the city of Baltimore's polling places. This was considered quite good, since the city only had 555. It was also about as good as the news got for the next four years.

As the ballots arrived on election night, D'Alesandro remembered his father's first mayoral election in 1947, and the celebrations in Little Italy. Kids from St. Leo's spontaneously ran to the school that night to grab musical instruments and parade happily about, while roaring people filled the neighborhood's narrow streets. When his parents arrived home from their victory announcement, it seemed like V-J Day all over again. "Going crazy!" D'Alesandro recalled. "Going crazy!" It felt like an entire community's acceptance into the fullness of America.

Now, on the night of his own mayoral election two decades later, Tommy the younger drove his mother home from his victory party to the same corner house at Albemarle and Fawn in Little Italy. This time the streets were empty. Not a drum banged, not a cheer rose from a single throat. D'Alesandro kissed his mother goodnight, and then he drove himself home to the Northwest Baltimore neighborhood where he lived on the other side of town.

And this, too, was a kind of victory. There was no wild celebration in Little Italy, for this was merely a sweet political victory but no longer the declaration of full citizenship. Such a thing had long since arrived, thanks to years of Big Tommy as mayor, and Young Tommy in the city council, and political friendships across all manner of ethnic lines.

But the empty streets that night in Little Italy were also an omen of the years to come. People learned to stay home after dark. Four months into D'Alesandro's term, a sniper's bullet took Dr. Martin Luther King's life in Memphis. It was Thursday, April 4, 1968. D'Alesandro was eating dinner with Louis Azrael, the gray-haired, professorial columnist of the *News-American,* when they heard about King.

"Tommy, you'll have trouble now," said Azrael.

D'Alesandro was thirty-eight years old and had been groomed for this job since adolescence. He thought Azrael was mistaken. He considered Martin Luther King a friend, and he believed black people in Baltimore trusted him as a progressive mayor. He had a record, and his father before him had a record. When his father was mayor, he built low-income housing projects. Some, the Flag House apartments, were located between Little Italy and Lombard Street's Corned Beef Row.

"You can't do that," Tommy the elder had been told. "The colored will move in."

Politicians said this to him, and businesspeople, and neighbors in Little Italy and those around Lombard Street. D'Alesandro walked away from them all. He knew the names people had called Italians, and remembered years earlier when he had first walked neighborhoods outside of Little Italy.

He mentioned other low-income housing projects. One was Latrobe Homes, where my family lived for four years. "White people," he said. Black families surrounded the Latrobe projects, but did not yet live in the projects themselves. "These projects I am building," D'Alesandro said, "are for poor white families."

But he knew. He understood the inevitability, and also understood where history was going. The new projects were white for a while, and tilted increasingly as the first black families moved in, and by 1968 they were all black. Tommy the younger knew his father had taken the heat for this, but maybe such a history worked in his favor now and the city might stay calm.

Still, in the hours after King's assassination, he called his police commissioner to City Hall. He called black community leaders as well. He needed to know, the way a mayor can never find out on his own, what the danger level was in the city's black communities.

The city stayed quiet that night. D'Alesandro breathed a little easier and computed his political capital. In his years on the city council, he had introduced plenty of civil rights legislation. "You're a bum," white voices said when he did this. That was the polite language. As council president, he had reached into black communities the way almost nobody else at City Hall ever had. Maybe Theodore McKeldin, the all-embracing liberal Republican, could match him. But that was it. D'Alesandro remembered dinners, scores of them, where he was the only white person in the room. There were rallies on West Baltimore's Pennsylvania Avenue where he was the only white among hundreds of blacks. When he ran for mayor, he won 93 percent of the black vote. He appointed George Russell as the first black on the city's board of estimates, and made him his city solicitor. He appointed the first black fire commissioner, Marion Bascomb. He appointed the first blacks to the zoning board and the parks board. He was friends with Colonel William "Box" Harris, the highest-ranking black police officer, who had headed Martin Luther King's security detail when King visited Baltimore a few years earlier.

D'Alesandro had gone to the Lord Baltimore Hotel that night. He handed King the keys to the city. King took D'Alesandro by the shoulders. "Tommy," he called him. D'Alesandro was struck by his friendliness, and by his insights. King had been well briefed on the city's problems. He asked only for fairness. They spoke for two hours.

Now, when D'Alesandro heard the news that King had been shot, he felt he had lost a friend. Surely, this counted for something. Surely, the city's blacks understood the goodness in his heart and realized his political struggles.

Then came news that Washington was on fire. D'Alesandro turned on the television. He saw rioting in what seemed like every big American city but Baltimore. At three o'clock the next afternoon, a Friday, he went to Annapolis and met with Governor Spiro Agnew and National Guard General George Gelston.

"If we can make it to Sunday morning, when the ministers can talk in church, we'll be okay," D'Alesandro said. He drove back to Baltimore and tried to stick to his normal schedule. On Gay Street, on the city's east side, a pamphlet was circulated to business owners. In honor of Dr. King, it said, close your stores. The same kind of warning had circulated in Washington before it exploded. At five-thirty that evening a rock was thrown through a store window, and the riots of 1968 began in Baltimore.

D'Alesandro was in the war room at police headquarters when it happened. He heard reports but could see neither the rioters in front of him nor the hundreds of fires set along decayed inner-city blocks where poverty was ingrained and bitterness so deep that King's assassination was seen not only as enormous tragedy but as reason to vent entire lifetimes of rage.

Into the police war room came a major named Armstrong who had driven through the inner city and seen the trouble. It was D'Alesandro's moment of truth. In Armstrong's stunned face the mayor saw the disaster that had arrived. "Get me the governor on the telephone," D'Alesandro said. His heart sank. He asked Agnew to send in the Maryland National Guard. He called Joseph Califano, who was President Lyndon Johnson's liaison to the cities, and asked for federal troops. Then D'Alesandro went on Baltimore television and talked about what a terrible thing had happened to a man, Dr. King, who had been his friend, and he appealed for calm.

It was all too late. City police were overwhelmed, and so were hundreds of state police and National Guardsmen. They presented a show of force but could not stop massive burning and looting. Thousands of people filled the streets in a rage that sometimes turned to freaky carnival. More than a thousand fires burned, and nearly 5,000 people were arrested over four days. Hundreds of businesses were burned out, thousands looted, hundreds of people injured, and six killed.

In an hour of quiet General Gelston took D'Alesandro for a jeep ride. It was seven-thirty Sunday morning. They went to Gay Street and North Avenue. There were thousands of people already in the streets, but they were momentarily calm. D'Alesandro saw the ruins of his city and saw belligerence that hadn't yet been spent. He shuddered over the damage. He telephoned Governor Agnew again and said, "You'd better call the president. We need federal troops." On the other end of the line, Agnew seethed. By five-thirty that afternoon, the first of 5,000 troops from the 82nd Airborne Division arrived, and the city began to quiet down.

When Michele Winder heard the news of King's assassination, she was far from Baltimore. She recalled John Kennedy's assassination, and relived those awful emotions, and felt them more deeply because she knew that King spoke specifically for her.

She was there the day King delivered his famous speech in Washington. She and her mother had moved there that summer, and girlfriends from her old neighborhood in West Baltimore came to their apartment and stayed over. Her mother cooked for everybody. They went to King's speech to take part in the changing of the world. "This liberating thing," she called it. "I don't know if there are words to describe it, just so many people standing in the sunlight and embracing."

But now it was nearly five years later, and it felt longer than that. The world had changed in many ways, but not enough. When she heard the news of King's death, she was living in North Carolina, seeing that a community could be not only black but prideful and fairly prosperous. She heard voices extolling strength in separatism. And she wondered if King had been right. Was peaceful integration possible, or even desirable?

When Jake Oliver heard the news, it felt like confirmation. He thought King had asked America for justice when he should have demanded it. The assassination was a tragedy, but for black people who were coming of age, full of energy, full of fire, King seemed yesterday's news. They didn't want to be bullied the way their parents had. Oliver's heroes were the Black Panthers like Huey Newton and Eldridge Cleaver, and the uncompromising Stokely Carmichael and Hubert Geroid "Rap" Brown.

"The words," Oliver remembered years later. "The magic of Stokely's words, which ignited my whole generation." He still seemed awed by it. "It was like setting the whole world on fire. It was, like, when George Wallace stood in the courthouse door—or that night he spoke down in College Park—Stokely was the black confrontation for Wallace's image. It was, like, he's not gonna get away with that, because here's one of our guys, and he's just as tough as Wallace. And then Huey standing there with his gun, and then you listen to Cleve articulate the imagery of what Huey was projecting, and the person orchestrating was Stokely. He was igniting an entire generation. It was magic."

When I heard the news of King's assassination, and the beginning of riots around the country, I turned on the television and watched the *CBS Evening News*. In his nightly commentary, Eric Sevareid said King wanted integration but now the nation would find it hard to remember his legacy. There was too much fire standing in the way. Rhetorical fire, he meant. He mentioned Stokely Carmichael. Sevareid called Carmichael "a direct descendant of Hitler."

I turned off the television and drove into downtown Baltimore, to the third-floor offices of the *News-American,* where I had begun full-time work after graduating college several months earlier. The place felt like the last tattered remnants of Hildy Johnson's *Front Page.* I anticipated a newsroom full of clattering typewriters and editors dispatching reporters out to cover stories of the thing that had hit so many cities and was now certain to arrive here.

Instead, there was nothing. The nightside crew was taking obits, typing up early reports from the police districts, and handling telephone calls from readers. One wanted help on his income taxes, and another phoned to inform everyone of a flying saucer hovering over his home: the usual gentle lunacy. The newsroom had a drugged, sleepy feel to it. Outside, the city was still digesting the assassination news, and nothing incendiary had happened.

"Typical Baltimore Negroes," a voice muttered.

It was Byron Roberts, a rewrite man who had worked on a few Washington newspapers, where he showed a talent for both writing and drinking. The second outdid the first. He had drunk himself out of employment and come to Baltimore. The *News-American* had its share of such types: smart, talented throwbacks who imagined the romance of newspaper work included excessive alcohol. They'd paid the price professionally. Roberts was sleek, handsome, and bright. Gig Young could have played him in the movies.

"What do you mean?" I said. We stood near the copy desk, a half-oval rim where copy paper was sent up a conveyor belt to a fourth-floor composing room of linotype machines and hot metal.

"Every other Negro in the country's rioting, and these goddamn people are still sleeping," Roberts said.

"Stokely Carmichael," I said, remembering Eric Sevareid's phrase and wanting to mark myself as an insightful fellow. "He's a direct descendant of Hitler."

Roberts eyed me warily. "How old did you say you were?" he asked.

"Twenty-two."

He withered me with a pitying stare. "Didn't they teach you anything in that college you went to?"

I felt my face flush. Roberts guided me to a nearby elevator, and we walked down South Street toward the harbor. He was thirty-eight, which seemed pretty old, but he was considered cool. As a young man, he'd fought in Korea. He'd been married a few times, and divorced, and joked about it.

"All my wives had the same first name," he said once.

"What's that?"

"Plaintiff," he explained.

One morning in the newsroom, for no discernible reason, he'd looked up from his typewriter and announced he was going to run for mayor. He had no money, and not a political connection in the world. Everybody told him he was crazy, he could never get elected.

"I know," he said, "but this way, when I die, the obituaries will all have to say, 'Byron Roberts, former candidate for mayor of Baltimore...'"

Later, he changed his mind and decided to run for a city council seat. He went to the city's board of elections to fill out all the proper papers.

"That'll be a fifty-dollar filing fee," an election official said.

"What have you got that's cheaper?" Roberts asked.

When the spirit moved him, he could swing. Now, as we reached the bottom of South Street, we walked into a little corner saloon across from an abandoned waterfront area. A dozen years later the area would become a tourist mecca called Harborplace. In the spring of 1968 it could only be called an eyesore. Downtown had a malignant, abandoned look. Roberts ordered a stiff drink, and then several more until his speech went sloshy and his mood darkened. He was an urbane man talking to an empty boy.

"You liked Martin Luther King?" he said.

"Well, yeah."

He snorted. King appealed to people's sense of conscience, he said, and white people weren't going to give up anything based on conscience. They had to be scared into it. Unless there was a riot, there was no reason for whites to give up anything. He asked if I was counting on somebody's good intentions to make things better—or was I like those others upstairs?

He meant some of the old guard at the newspaper. The country was divided on so many things—Vietnam and race and politics—and the newspaper's city room sometimes seemed its dividing line. Police radios sat atop desks in the middle of the newsroom, where a city editor named Eddie Ballard listened between bursts of static for reports of violent crimes he could turn into headlines.

"Got a good one on the west side," somebody would say. A good one meant a homicide. Ballard would listen for the specific neighborhood.

"Nah," he would growl. "Just another nigger shooting."

Then he would glance across the newsroom to see if Lee Lassiter or Jack Hodge or John Robinson, three token blacks on the staff, had overheard him.

Black Baltimoreans lived outside the paper's radar and its sentiments. Blacks appeared on its pages only when they committed a crime on a slow news day, or scored a touchdown for the Colts. No black people served in Vietnam, at least not so that the paper noticed. None came to life in charming childhood photographs displayed in the paper, the way white kids were. None seemed part of the city's great ethnic tapestry. Nor, in the *News-American*'s coverage, did black people ever find discrimination in real estate offices or banks or employment offices. And none, in the paper's awareness, lived in squalid neighborhoods where they seethed over the differences between their lives and the lives in white America. The paper had no reporters covering such neighborhoods, and thus had no sense of the thing that was coming.

"Fear," Byron Roberts said that night, speaking through his drink, "is the only way to get these white people motivated."

"Fear?" I said. "Who could live like that?"

"Could you live like these fuckin' people do?" he asked.

Some of his words made sense, and some simply had the sound of good drama. I wanted to tell him that I knew black people. I thought this would mark me as a sympathetic fellow. But then I realized I didn't know any black people anymore. The last time I had been with a lot of them was high school, five years earlier, which was a fine time, a time when I thought we had all agreed we liked each other and that Martin Luther King had set the national tone: Good hearts could unite all good people.

The riots arrived the next night. The city's blacks watched television like everybody else, and then they went outside. It seemed like the primal howl of generations. I found myself, with a *News-American* photographer named John Davis, a few blocks from my family's old apartment in the Latrobe housing projects. The last whites had moved out some years earlier. Nobody here waited submissively to play in any white boys' games, to hear "catch a nigger by his toe" and pretend not to notice. These folks were furious. There were buildings burning everywhere and sullen, angry people all over the place. I took courage only because so many police were moving through the area.

When Davis and I slipped through the city later, there were places where crowds raced through streets like a wave that might never stop. They huddled together as they ran. They ran through tear gas intended to choke them into submission, through shattered glass covering entire streets, through the screech of sirens. Behind them were burned-out buildings with twisted girders piercing through the shells, and smoke that burned everybody's eyes and sometimes, when television cameras came near, they chanted: "Long live the King. Long live the King." And sometimes they just tried to hide merchandise they were hauling out of stores whose windows and doors they had smashed before setting them afire.

On East Lombard Street, on the block of little delicatessens, a sniper somewhere in the nearby Flag House public high-rise fired bullets down. Those were Tommy the elder's projects. In his Little Italy two blocks away, some neighborhood men went to rooftops with weapons to stop any blacks who might venture near. On Lombard Street, all stores were closed, Attman's and Tulkoff's and Pastore's Grocery. Yankelove the slayer of fresh chickens was nowhere to be seen. They had all stayed home, or barricaded themselves at their business places with guns to protect their livelihoods.

When the sniper started firing from the Flag House high-rise, I was next to Eddie Fenton, a puffy, breathless, overweight radio reporter who carried a large tape recorder on his back. "Get down," the police hollered at him. Everybody ducked behind cars. "I'm down as far as I can get," Fenton bellowed back, leaning on one knee. "If they hit me, they hit me."

When twilight fell, and the police stopped curfew breakers, the dialogue was always the same. The kids said they were going to their mothers; they said they were coming from their fathers. No one had two parents in the same place. They looked like kids I had once known. I thought about Michele Winder, and wondered if she was somewhere safe. I thought about Jake Oliver, walking in a crowd of white kids in College Park a few years earlier, so alone. I thought about Sonny Newsom and Turhan Robinson, and the night we'd been turned away at the restaurant. The rejections and the ostracism of so many lives had finally translated to this horror.

I wrote down what I saw and telephoned it to rewrite people back in the newsroom. I could hear people hollering at each other in the background there, and they could hear the sound of fire engines and police behind me.

On the second evening of the riots, I went back to the Latrobe housing projects. On spring nights such as this, they'd once kept the doors of the Church of St. James wide open by the side of Abbott Court. Worshippers would straggle in and out. Once in a while, I remembered, a wedding would spill into the street.

Now the big front doors were locked, and a priest behind them answered when I knocked. He did not open the door. I asked if we could talk for a moment. He said the church was closed for the night. I said I wanted to talk about the terrible thing that was happening. He offered a homily from the Scriptures. I looked up Aisquith Street and saw the row of mournful little rowhouses a block away where the colored women had greeted me on mornings I walked to School Number Twenty with Billy McKnight.

"*Why don't their kids go to our school?*" I asked.

"*Niggers don't go to our school,*" said Billy.

The priest would not open the doors of the church. Later I drove back to the newsroom and read a column written by the sports editor, John Steadman. He wrote, "You look in the faces of Negro friends and tell them your heart is heavy. Do they realize the depth of the sincerity, the profound grief you try to express over Martin Luther King?" He wrote, "It's an indictment upon us all that there was ever a division between races." He wrote, "That we were born white was only a matter of heritage. We have never been faced with the indignities and sorrow the Negro knows. Therefore, there is only compassion for the Negro and regrets for the troubles, the denials which have been placed in his way. . . . Now, more than ever, we must be our brother's keeper."

That he wrote such a column was remarkable; that he wrote it for a newspaper so openly dismissive of blacks, and so secretly contemptuous, seemed miraculous. He stood alone. Over the course of the riots, all other sports columnists wrote about the Orioles' prospects for the upcoming season. Steadman wrote about race. The home run and the pitching staff meant nothing if they did not translate to the human condition.

His heart was an open book. He had the eyebrows of an evangelical preacher and a soft touch for the down-and-out and the oddball character. He wrote about the town's sports heroes, but also those such as Mister Diz, the racetrack tout; and Balls Maggio who made a living rescuing tennis balls from the Jones Falls.

He'd hired me as a college intern two years earlier and assigned me sports stories that were only coincidentally about sports: about a weightlifter who had overcome childhood polio; about Aunt Mary Dobkin, a crippled woman who ran sports teams for poor kids; about a high school football player named Fred Sturm who was paralyzed in a practice but refused to give up. When I graduated college, and wanted to write about the world outside of sports, he made certain there was an opening for me on the paper's city desk.

When I read his column on the riots, I walked into the sports office and found him chafing over a follow-up.

"I think you wrote a great piece," I said.

"Good days and bad," he said. It was a standard line, the closest this humble man ever came to bragging. "Got anything I could use tomorrow?"

"What about the ballclubs?" I said. "Do the Orioles play ball as if nothing's happened?" The baseball season was opening in a couple of days. Tommy D'Alesandro wanted to throw out the first ball. Many argued against it. They said it would look frivolous in such an angry time. Call off baseball for a while, they said. D'Alesandro said no, the city had to move on and the ballpark was our common meeting ground.

"I remember when Buddy Young first arrived in town," Steadman said. Young was the first Baltimore Colts star, the man who later warned Lenny Moore about segregation in Westminster. Young came out of the locker room one day and two men in blackface were there to mock him.

"Buddy thought, 'What am I coming to here, a minstrel show?'" Steadman said. "But he had to be bigger than that."

"Do these players understand that they're role models for everybody?" I asked.

"I don't know," John said. "The Orioles didn't have many black players for a long time. The Colts mix on the field, but they go their separate ways afterwards. I remember Alan Ameche telling me one time, 'We never appreciated what the black guys went through.'" Ameche was the one who approached Lenny Moore on the field in Dallas, after the humiliation of separate hotels.

Steadman remembered a hotel banquet in Baltimore a few years earlier, attended by George Preston Marshall, the owner of the Washington Redskins. His club was professional football's last segregationist holdout. One of the evening's speakers was a black man. Afterwards, Marshall found Steadman.

"I'm never coming back here," Marshall thundered. "Never, ever again. To have a nigger speaking. You don't bring those kinds of people up here to speak to an audience. Those are the kind of people you use to clean out the toilet in your bathroom."

"He said that?" I asked Steadman.

"That's exactly what he said. It was Lenny Moore he objected to."

"And then we wonder how we reach a thing like this," I said, motioning outside. I told him I'd gone back to my old neighborhood and found locked doors at the Church of St. James.

"The old Tenth Ward," said another voice. It was Bob Blatchley, a reporter who'd grown up around Greenmount Avenue and Barclay Street, not far from the projects. He and Steadman were both Irish Catholics. The old Tenth Ward was one of the original pockets of Irish Catholics in Baltimore.

Like me, Blatchley had been hired by Steadman as a sports writer, but eventually found it confining and moved on to news. He had a cigarette dangling from his lower lip, his tie askew, and his belly gently overhung his belt as a kind of campaign ribbon to late nights in bars. Blatchley looked a little like Jimmy Breslin and talked like a guy who understood human weakness in everyone, including himself. He understood context. Everybody came from something. When discriminatory talk of any kind filtered through the newsroom, he waved a disparaging hand—no words, just a hand, which signaled no patience for such drivel.

"My father," Blatchley said one day, "was the youngest of six in a family almost devastated by alcohol. His oldest sister got through it all right, she married a bookmaker." He grunted comically. "My mother's side of the family was total Irish party people, but they could drink and dance and have a good time, and still go to work the next day." Another laugh rumbled up from his chest. He was just old enough to remember big family parties at the plumbers' union hall on Harford Avenue when his uncles came home from World War II. "Gunther Beer by the keg, and Four Roses on all the tables, and baloney sandwiches and potato salad," he said. "My grandmother was eighty-seven and asking for a beer on her deathbed. On Ilchester Avenue."

The attitude was: Who am I to look down on somebody else? In the American mix, everyone has flaws, so live and let live. Such an attitude begins in the schoolrooms and the playgrounds when we throw children together. Nobody has to make great speeches about it; nearness is all. As adults, you begin to find a voice, and from this comes the healthy give-and-take, and a new kind of comic competition. *You think your people were crazy? Let me tell you about my people.*

Blatchley grew up in a rowhouse. "All you needed was rosary beads and your own shot glass," he laughed. "It was mostly Irish and some Italian and a few Germans. See, you didn't grow up in a neighborhood, you grew up in a parish. Mine was St. Ann's, Greenmount and Twenty-second. We lived in my grandfather's basement for a while, but then my father got a G.I. loan after the war and we moved north." He nodded his head slowly. "I always said, it's just like the Irish, they get the price of a second set of underwear, and they move north."

Blatchley and I would hang out with Joe Nawrozki, who'd grown up in Polish East Baltimore. What the three of us had in common was formative years in city neighborhoods, and the great mixing in the public schools, and newspaper lives that began because John Steadman had hired us. What Nawrozki and Blatchley had in common was military service.

"The great equalizer," Blatchley called the Army. "You're thrown in with black guys, and with guys from Appalachia with teeth so bad that they got 'em all pulled at once and they're walking around with gauze in their mouth. That's how the Army did it. You were thrown in with these guys. It was the great equalizer."

Nawrozki had served in Vietnam. I was working in the sports office the day he came back to the paper and John Steadman wrote a column about his return: "Our GI Joe Returns from the War."

"How was it?" Steadman asked.

"Pretty rough," Nawrozki said softly. "A lot of guys get shook up bad."

Some of the older fellows on the paper chuckled among themselves when they heard this. They'd served in World War II, and set aside their memories of the things that had frightened them. They thought this generation was soft. Some of these kids didn't want to go to war, and those who came back complained about it. If Nawrozki noticed their reaction, he never let on. The country was just beginning to understand the depth of the Vietnam catastrophe. In the newsroom, though, lines were already being drawn.

It was a Hearst paper, and Hearst trumpeted the war. Those who opposed it were called traitors. The paper ran thunderous editorials calling for more men and more weapons. John Steadman, remembering World War II, saw Muhammad Ali dodge the draft and wrote columns blasting him. "Muhammad Ali Shames Our War Dead." Steadman saw this war the same way he'd seen World War II: Young men served when the country called; nobody was supposed to question the details. A conservative organization called the Valley Forge Foundation, citing the Ali columns, honored him as its man of the year. Byron Roberts, remembering his own fighting in Korea, and hating the Vietnam War, reflected on the Valley Forge award. "Every time it snows, Steadman's feet bleed," he said. This war was making good men turn on each other.

One night I went to see Bob Mayers, who was flunking out at the University of Maryland. On campus, a crowd of more than a thousand students protested the war. They held candles in the dark and sat on a grassy slope near the college president's home. National Guard troops in riot gear confronted them, and a nine o'clock curfew was set. Mayers had no sense of politics—but this war was beyond politics, it was the shadow over everyone's lives.

In front of the big crowd stood Edwin Warfield III, a major general in full military uniform. "Somebody's gonna get killed here," Mayers said. Warfield told the big crowd to go home or face arrest. He had rows of troops behind

The Four Horsemen of the *News American:* Michael Olesker, John Steadman, Bob Blatchley, and Joe Nawrozki. Steadman, the newspaper's sports editor, started the others in their newspaper careers. And it was Steadman who wrote a remarkable column in the midst of the 1968 riots.

him with clubs and gas masks that gave the scene an eerie, science-fiction feel. Who were these strange, threatening creatures? The moment was ripe for something dreadful to happen, the way it was happening on campuses around the country. Go home, Warfield told the crowd again.

Then another voice, high-pitched, unexpectedly split the air: "Leave us alone. Go away. Please don't hurt us."

The cry was bigger than everything. It was bigger than all show of weapons, all gas masks, and all endless debate about the war. It was a boy on the grass with a candle in his hand. Like all the others, he was just a kid about to get his head busted in by his fellow countrymen for declaring himself against war.

General Warfield stood there for a moment. He needed a response. He needed something that showed his authority, that confirmed the state's right to establish its curfew, but one that didn't make a tense moment worse. And then, as in a movie scene, there came singing in the crowd:

"*All we are saying*
Is give peace a chance . . ."

"We are asking you to disperse," Warfield said. He said it quickly, before the singing got too loud and the moment too emotional, before it could touch any of his own troops. "We happen to believe in peace as much as you do."

"Then join us," somebody in the crowd hollered. And then this became a chant: "Join us. Join us."

Warfield said nothing. He was a veteran of World War II, a man whose plane had been hit over Japan. He'd kept it in the air for nearly an hour and then bailed out over the Pacific. He floated in the ocean's vastness for four days until rescuers found him. He knew war in ways that few of these kids ever would. His generation hadn't questioned the politics of their moment. They'd signed on because everybody else was signing on. They believed in the country. Some of the boys didn't come back. And others came back, and they had families, and now some of those kids were sitting there in the grass. Warfield understood the legacy. These were the children of his comrades. These were the kids whose future they'd been trying to protect a quarter-century earlier.

Now he looked into the crowd, and he said, "We are your brothers."

The air itself seemed stunned for a moment. *We are your brothers.* He meant all these National Guardsmen barely out of school themselves, who were just as confused by the endless war, and just as scared of it—but were threatening to bash in the skulls of these kids.

"We are your brothers," he said again.

The tension eased a little The students did not move, but Warfield had sent a signal to everyone: let's be as civilized as we can. Many in the crowd dispersed. Some were arrested. But Warfield told officers, loud enough to be overheard, "Without roughing 'em up."

The moment expired, but the war went on. Bob Mayers and I left campus, and a few days later he left on a plane for the Spanish island of Ibiza. Two weeks later I was standing in the kitchen when a call came from Gary Levin. Bobby Mayers, he said somberly. I didn't remember anyone calling him "Bobby" before that. Then he stopped. Bob had gotten deeper into the drugs, and grown more dissolute and worried about the draft. And now there was a report from Spain, and conflicting stories involving drugs, involving Spanish police, involving roundups of American college students. The report was that Bob had run to the edge of a steep cliff and just kept running.

He was buried in the cemetery across from our old apartment a few miles from campus. His mother and father and his sister, stunned and silent, watched his coffin lowered into the ground. A girlfriend sobbed. Some of the old crowd from college was there, and we left the cemetery talking about Bob, and about the war and its iron grip on our lives.

One morning my draft notice arrived. Greetings from the president of the United States, it said, issuing orders to report to my draft board. I drove out to my parents' house and told them I would be going for my Army physical in a few weeks. My father sat in the living room with a newspaper on his lap. Neither one of us mentioned the word *Vietnam*.

"I remember the day we heard about Pearl Harbor," he said. He told the story about shooting pool with Bernie Mayer when they heard the news on the radio. They looked at each other blankly; they had no idea where it was. They were both eighteen years old, and the next day they were signing up for the fight. Nearly thirty years had gone by.

"Does it seem that long?" I asked.

"Sometimes it seems like yesterday, and sometimes it's like a story I read somewhere," my father said. "People lined up to give blood, to do whatever they could do right away. It was something that caught you up, and you couldn't come down."

"Not like today," I said.

"No," he said.

He'd finally gotten overseas around Christmas of 1944, and flew the first of eighteen bomb runs about six weeks later. "Sometimes," he said, "we'd fly up to eight hundred miles before we got to the bomb site, and then we'd have to fight our way out."

"Those must have been happy trips back," I said.

"Not really," he said softly. "We were exhausted."

"Yes, but alive."

"But spent," he said. "It took so much out of you. The tension was unreal."

He had never talked this way before. So many times I had tried to get him to talk about his war and he had brushed it off. My concept of his war came from heroic movies, from tales of sweet homecomings. I had taken my father's silence as a gesture of modesty. Whatever his role, he seemed to imply, it wasn't worth talking about. A man did what he had to do, and then put it behind him and kept quiet about it.

"You started talking one night about a mission," I said. "The flak bursting outside the copilot's window."

The copilot's name was George Peck. He was a kid, like my father. It was St. Valentine's Day of 1945, so my father had marked his twenty-second birthday four weeks earlier. He said it was his group's first combat mission together, and they were hit by fire from below. Shrapnel burst outside of Peck's window. Peck threw up his arm in a gesture of self-defense. The shrapnel burst through, shattering the window, his wrist, his flak helmet, and it sheared off the top of Peck's head.

In the next seat, the pilot was knocked out by the blast. In the level above, the engineer, looking down, lost control and screamed into the plane's radio so shrilly that it came out as incomprehensible static. In the back of the plane, men scrambled about as shrapnel burst through walls near them.

My father remembered sunlight shining through holes in the plane where the shrapnel had hit. In the cockpit, the engineer and the navigator struggled frantically with the corpse of young George Peck. They were still flying in formation, but Peck had to be pulled from his seat so that someone could slip in and help fly the plane.

"The scene that stays with me," my father said, "when we landed, the medics pulled the poor guy out of the plane head-first." His voice lowered to a whisper. As the medics pulled his limp body, George Peck's head lolled back, and everything that had once been inside spilled out of the top and fell to the airstrip and lay there in front of everyone.

So there, I thought. You wanted to hear about your father's war, and now you have. And it wasn't stirring tales of the boys in the old neighborhood in the Bronx signing up after Pearl Harbor, not soldiers kissing grateful young ladies in the celebrations of Times Square, and not my father's sweet homecoming that misty Atlantic City afternoon—but a kid my own age with his head blown off and his brains spilled onto an airstrip far from home and his family. My father hadn't merely been modest all those years; he was shielding his son from the reality of his war. And now, I wanted only to protect my father from his memory.

"You were one of the lucky ones," I said. "You came back alive."

My father started remembering those who did not. He remembered names, and the hometowns that went with each of the names. For years after the war, he said, he and his surviving crew members stayed in touch, sent cards each Christmas. But they had long since lost contact.

"What did you do after that mission?" I said.

"We were back up in the air the next morning," he said.

Now I had my own war. I left my parents' house, and a few weeks later drove to an old post office building on Reisterstown Road, in Baltimore County, where about a hundred other draftees gathered in a dank room. I knew plenty of them from high school days. We were a mix of kids laughing to cover nervousness, many of us united by one thing. We had letters.

"I got one from my doctor," said a grinning boy, holding it up with two hands, "says I only have one arm."

"Asthma," another declared triumphantly, showing off his note.

"They can't take me," said a fellow named Mitchell Bober, whom I'd known for nearly a decade. "I'm legally blind."

I had letters of my own, one from my Uncle Dick stating honestly that I'd been getting regular chiropractic treatments from him for several years for a bad back and, for good measure, a letter from an orthopedic surgeon who'd examined me and suggested surgery for a variety of back problems. But I knew the Army was hungry for bodies, and I supposed I could serve if I were pushed. I didn't like this war, and didn't like the lies surrounding it. But my father hadn't liked his war, either.

We rode an old bus to Fort Holabird and saw some of the devastation still remaining from the riots. "Looks like Hanoi, don't it?" one boy muttered. We arrived on a sunny morning and found thousands of boys going through grim, hurry-up proceedings. There was a vast industry in the healthy bodies of young men. Some marched around in their underwear, and others stood in a circle where they dropped their shorts and spread the cheeks of their buttocks for examining doctors. Some stood in lines in front of eye charts. Some met with psychiatrists. Some seemed utterly lost, as though awaiting word from some authority figure that a mistake had been made, that they could go home and not come back again.

Dozens of us were ushered into a large room where we sat at desks and were told to wait. The door was closed. The glad war cry of medical excuses filled the room again. "They can't take me," Mitchell Bober once again assured everyone. "I'm legally blind." Then an older man, maybe forty, decked out in an officer's uniform, walked in and ordered quiet. Some people ignored him.

"Quiet down," the officer barked again. But a few strands of whispers could still be heard.

"If I hear one more sound," the officer snapped now, each measured word dropping like a hammer, "you're all shipping out to Vietnam today."

The place went silent as a tomb. He had struck at the heart of the matter. No one quite believed him, but no one wanted to test him either. We were sitting in a rickety old wooden building in East Baltimore, a block from comforting Dundalk Avenue with traffic and pizza carryouts and houses where children skipped off to school the way we had only a few years earlier—but we were utterly removed from all of that now.

The day became a blur: physical tests, sanity tests, presentation of every desperate letter to every surly Army physician who suspected each note was a fiction. When the final reckoning came, there were two long lines leading to desks where officers waited to pronounce our future. Mitchell Bober stood next to me. "They'll never take me," he said. "I'm legally blind."

I thought about my father's generation going off to war. All these boys in line with me—hadn't they grown up with the same stories? If we had all turned away from them, what did it tell us? That an entire generation was gutless and self-absorbed? Or that this war was wrong, and should not be fought, and we had all figured it out?

I didn't know, and so I left it in the Army's hands. I stood before a cranky uniformed doctor with an impenetrable Southern accent who examined my papers and then looked up at me, not at all happily.

"You're perm'ly 'squalifahd," he said.

The key word was a linguistic blur. I could make "permanently" out of "perm'ly," but what was the rest of it? Had he said "qualified" or "disqualified?" Had he declared me fit for military duty, or freed me to live out the rest of my natural life?

"Excuse me," I said. "Did you say 'disqualified?' "

"Perm'ly 'squalifahd," he said again.

I didn't want to be a pest, but I didn't want to make a serious mistake by leaving and getting shot for desertion.

"I'm sorry," I said again. "Did you say 'disqualified?' "

Now the officer glared at me. It was a glare not unlike the man who had threatened us earlier in the day, a dark, baleful look that said, "If you ask me one more time, I'm sending your pathetic ass to Vietnam this minute."

"You're perm'ly 'squalifahd," he said again.

I decided to take a chance. It sounded close enough to "disqualified" that I could always claim misinterpretation if they put me in front of a court-martial, or a firing squad. And so I exited, clinging to my papers, floating rapturously out to Dundalk Avenue on the other side of the fort.

The last sound I heard was Mitchell Bober's voice, hollering at his doctor, "You can't take me. I'm legally blind." Bober, later unsatisfied with a tour of Vietnam, instead served two.

I found my way back to the *News-American*. On my way to a telephone to break the giddy news to my family I saw John Steadman.

"John," I said, bursting with relief, "I just got declared 'permanently disqualified' by the Army."

"Gee, that's too bad," he said. "It would have been a great experience."

I suddenly remembered where I was: in a newsroom owned by the Hearst Corporation, which trumpeted the war, surrounded by men who had served in World War II, speaking to a man I respected deeply who thought Vietnam was a solemn patriotic duty.

"I know," I muttered in a puny voice, at once ashamed of myself and massively relieved. "I know."

In the aftermath of the riots of 1968, the city of Baltimore came undone. Whatever racial alliances had been made were now reevaluated; whatever friendships established, reconsidered. A new set of rules would have to be written. The suburban exodus set off a decade earlier by racial uneasiness took on a frantic quality after the riots. White families disappeared as though fleeing earthquakes. Public schools shakily integrated for about a decade now became all black. City businesses were sold or simply abandoned. The melting pot oozed from all sides.

A lot of it was racial antagonism, but then it was attached to other things: the burgeoning narcotics trade, and the crime that grew out of it. Some of the new addicts were kids who had picked up the habit in Vietnam, and some were hopeless people simply retreating from reality. Many were poor, and in Baltimore the great percentage was black.

The drug trade hit a community called Cherry Hill with a particular vengeance. The neighborhood was located in South Baltimore, cut off from much of the city by the Hanover Street Bridge. It was built after World War II and had been stable and secure for years.

But now many of its young men were strung out on heroin, and the strongest of them tried to get off of it. They knocked on the doors of the city's drug clinics. The clinics all were filled. I followed them as they took one brushoff after another. They picketed City Hall, and then they picketed the State House. Nobody in power seemed to notice. They went to the State Drug Abuse Authority, and the Inner City Community Mental Health Program, always with the same words: Please help us get off the drugs. The pleas were ignored.

One summer evening I went to St. Veronica's Church on Cherry Hill Road. A couple of Josephite priests, Richard Wagner and Paul Banet, were trying to help. They'd coaxed a few city health officials to the church to meet with some of the addicts. "We just want to lead better lives," one said. His tone was part plaintive, part thinly veiled anger. The health officials, happy to be inside a church, expressed sympathy but said their agencies were broke. Their message was: We understand your problem, and thank you for not cutting our throats. And, if you have a problem, take it to someone who has influence instead of a mere job title.

One afternoon, fed up, the Cherry Hill guys walked unannounced into a meeting of state health officials, middle-aged white men in suits unaccustomed to sharing a boardroom with ticked-off young black men in dark glasses, some with open shirts and undone shoelaces, all with no illusions that they had anything going for them but their physical presence.

"This is an emergency," said a fellow named Charles "Butch" Johnson from Cherry Hill. He'd been one of the first blacks at Baltimore Polytechnic in the 1950s, full of hope, full of assurance that the city was changing. And everything in his life had fallen away with the drugs.

The white bureaucrats, seated around a long table, nodded their heads to show their sympathy. "We've got an epidemic in Cherry Hill," Johnson said. "A drug epidemic. We're asking you for a program to help us."

"We want to help you," said the head of one city agency. "We're just not set up for a program right now. We can't afford it."

"We have nothing, either," said a state drug official. He was nice about it, but immovable, and was followed by a series of men equally nice, equally nervous, and equally immovable. They all expressed the desire to help. But they all lacked money, and they all mentioned red tape that was impossible to cut through for any sort of emergency funding.

"Well, then," a fellow named James "Nose" Barnes said angrily, "we're gonna have to cut through some of that red tape."

"That's right," said a guy named Martinez Banks, who had walked to the meeting on crutches. His feet were swollen from heroin injections. His arms had long since run out of available veins. Around the table the benevolent smiles on bureaucrats' faces froze.

"Give 'em one riot," said Banks, "and you'll cut all the red tape so fast your head will spin."

He had said the magic word: *riot*. It was two years since the Martin Luther King riots, and no one's memory had faded. And not a single health official around the big table raised one squeaky voice.

"Listen, man," said Butch Johnson, "if that shopping center in Cherry Hill gets burned down, you're gonna have the governor asking why. Then you'll be coming up with all kinds of money for some jive-ass study to find out why. Well, we're telling you why before we do it. We need a program."

Then an amazing thing happened. In an instant, the state administrator raised an index finger in the air. "Hey, you know," he said brightly, as though this had never before occurred to him, "we might be able to get some available funding for an interim program."

"Yes, you're right," said a city official, turning to him. "We could put through a request for Safe Streets Act money, and . . ."

I remembered Byron Roberts's words the night that the riots didn't quite begin on time. "Fear," he said, "is the only way to get these white people motivated." But this left an important question unanswered: Could any community live by fear—and still call itself a community? Cherry Hill got itself a multipurpose health center a few years later, including a drug treatment program. William Donald Schaefer, running for a first term as mayor, made it a campaign project. But white city bureaucrats, having been cornered once, later learned new ways to hide from all those sneaking in from the streets.

Twenty years later, a newly elected mayor named Kurt L. Schmoke would propose a whole new way to fight drugs. Treat them like a health problem and not merely as a crime, he said. It was precisely what the addicts from Cherry Hill had been saying. By Schmoke's time, though, a problem with perhaps 10,000 Baltimore addicts had become a catastrophe of nearly 60,000 addicts. Neighborhoods were gutted not only by race but by junkies picking at the rotting carcasses of entire city blocks, separated not only from mainstream America, but from most civilized norms.

Tommy D'Alesandro retired from politics when his term ended. The common belief was that the riots killed everything for him. He insisted otherwise, claiming it was economics. He had a large family to raise, and being mayor of Baltimore simply did not pay enough.

So his city council president, William Donald Schaefer, ran for mayor. His opponent was George L. Russell, first appointed to political office by D'Alesandro and then appointed the first black judge on what was then called the city's Supreme Bench.

I followed both men around that summer. Schaefer was nervous and uncomfortable in public. Russell was smart, poised, and elegant. As the city neared Election Day, I met with Tom White, the *News-American*'s executive editor.

"Russell," I said, "is a much more impressive guy."

"Absolutely," White agreed.

"So the paper will endorse him?"

"Oh, of course not," said White. "If we did that, we'd lose 5,000 subscribers."

Schaefer turned out to be a four-term mayor credited with reviving the city; Russell left public life for a distinguished private law practice. The city spent the rest of the century attempting to recover and reinvent itself in the shadow of the riots and the narcotics revolution that drove everyone farther apart.

EIGHTEEN
"YOU GOTTA MARRY IN THE FAITH"

In the enduring heat of the era's racial antagonism, Spiro Agnew helped pass the torch to a new generation.

He was governor of Maryland by the time of the riots, a man in the midst of a series of political reinventions. He called himself a city Democrat until he realized his political ambitions were going nowhere, and so reinvented himself as a suburban Republican. He called himself Ted instead of Spiro, and Agnew instead of Anagnostopoulos. And he called himself a moderate until it no longer suited his needs, and then he became the darling of the American hard-right. He was, as they say, adaptive to circumstances.

"He was a product of that suburban culture," Tommy D'Alesandro III said years later. "Here was a guy from an ethnic family, who knew all about that desire to fit in. He's a Rockefeller liberal, which means he understands cities and little tight-knit neighborhoods. But then he sees what's happening in the suburbs. He sees all these people running from the city, and he figures that's his ticket. Politically, he forgot where he came from."

When he ran for Baltimore County executive in 1962, Agnew still called himself a political moderate. The future attack dog for Richard Nixon had not yet been invented, nor had the man who would excoriate Baltimore's black leaders after the 1968 riots. When he ran for governor two years before that, Agnew let voters invent a man who wasn't there.

His opponent that year was George P. Mahoney, whose campaign slogan was: "Your home is your castle—Protect it." Everybody knew what it meant. It was a call to choose up sides by race. It said: Don't let those black people move into your neighborhood and threaten your home the way they have threatened so many other people's. Through that long campaign summer, many waited for Agnew to repudiate such language. He never did. But he danced around the issue delicately enough that it looked like gentlemanly discretion, a desire not to participate in any unseemliness. Voters could fill in the silence with anything they wanted. Next to Mahoney, Agnew looked like Benjamin Disraeli.

That image died with the Martin Luther King riots.

In their ashes, Agnew still burned. He summoned about a hundred of the city's black leaders. They were respected community healers, judges, political figures, neighborhood organizers, ministers. There were none of the thunderers, the Stokely Carmichael types whom Agnew loathed. These were moderate people.

"You ran," he told them. A chill went through the room. He was the governor of Maryland, and they were people who had spent their lives struggling to accommodate themselves to a system created and run by white men. They had embraced the same values—hard work, strong families—that white people had embraced, and devoted their lives to appealing to the country's sense of conscience: Give us a fair shot. And Agnew was telling them they had all caved in to militants. He said they were frightened of being called "Mr. Charlie's Boy" and "Uncle Tom." He said they should never have let this thing happen—as if they possessed some mystical control of the streets. As if they alone might have calmed generations of pent-up rage. As if their grief wasn't profound enough over King's death. As if Agnew, and generations of insensitive, foot-dragging politicians before him, weren't the ones who had created this moment.

And there was implicit subtext to what he said: You blacks could have stopped the riots because you're black, too; you all know each other, you speak the same language and do those secret handshakes and speak that secret language. He was implying that they had an agenda—threatening, sinister—that made them different kinds of Americans from everyone else.

And this was as remarkable as anything he had said aloud. Agnew misplaced his own history. He was the son of a Depression-era Greek immigrant who worked hard his whole life. His father ran some little restaurants. He sold vegetables. He had moved to Northwest Baltimore's Forest Park neighborhood to fully Americanize his family. It wasn't easy. And now his son had forgotten completely the lesson that every ethnic minority comes to learn in the melting pot: Others will define you by the chosen stereotype, and will isolate you, if you let them. Agnew was doing to these blacks what others had done to his own people.

Ten minutes into the speech, half the crowd walked out of the room. More followed. "If you want to talk to us like ladies and gentlemen, Mr. Governor, we'll stay and listen," one man shouted over his shoulder. Agnew never lifted his head from his prepared text. By the time he finished talking, maybe thirty people were left in the room.

When Mayor Tommy D'Alesandro III heard about the speech that afternoon, he felt the blood drain from his body. It sounded like an overture to more trouble. "We gotta hold a press conference," he told aides. Agnew was sitting safely in Annapolis, but D'Alesandro was wading through rubble in Baltimore. When reporters arrived, he said, "This is a bad time to say what the governor said. Most of the people reject the extreme aspects of both sides." The city had calmed itself, and he did not want it to start up again. He was careful to call the riots "disturbances." The moment demanded delicacy. "Let's not fight among ourselves," he said.

Agnew, ruminating over the reaction, told aides, "I probably committed political suicide." Then he found out he was wrong. Telephone calls arrived at the State House. In the first hours, about 125 calls came, all from white people, and all but three of them supportive. Then came a wire signed by fifty Baltimore police praising him for "the guts to bring it out in the open." Across America, many saw him as a stand-up guy, speaking truth to what they saw as increasing black power, and finally standing up to blacks whose incessant demands had now escalated into the dreadful riots. In those first days after the speech, there were scores of telegrams supporting his language, and his sentiments, and then the news made its way to a place where Richard Nixon was listening.

The moment made Agnew. Nixon, searching about for a vice-president, told himself: This is my kind of tough guy. In the so-called Southern strategy that took electoral votes from states historically Democratic, Nixon used Agnew as a symbol: This was the man who stood up to those scary blacks. Spiro Agnew became the respectable personification of America's racial fault line. He wasn't George Wallace standing in a schoolhouse door, or Lester Maddox spitting racial epithets. He was a man in a tailored suit, with every hair nailed into place, speaking to America from the highest places and saying it was all right to criticize by race.

And in Baltimore County, where Agnew had gotten his political start, where white people were running in their postriot fears, Dale Anderson, the man who had replaced him as county executive, saw all of this and knew what to do with it. Anderson opened his arms to whites and sent up every signal he could that blacks were not welcome. The county was 93 percent white, and stayed that way for years. Anderson refined the use of code words. He said there would be no low-cost housing in his county. He turned away millions of dollars in federal grants rather than build any—because, as everyone believed, this would bring poor people to the county, and poor people would probably be black. When a U.S. civil rights commission studied county housing and racial policies, they described Baltimore County as a "white noose" strangling the city.

And then both men met disgrace.

In a crowded federal courtroom, Spiro Agnew pleaded *nolo contendere*— no contest—to charges that he had taken bribes throughout his career, including the years of his vice-presidency. And, two years later, in another room in that same courthouse, Dale Anderson would be found guilty of extortion and tax evasion.

Into this came Ted Venetoulis. He was a Greek American running for

Agnew's old Baltimore County office, with memories of Agnew still vivid in everyone's mind. Venetoulis was a liberal running in an anxious and racially conservative jurisdiction. But he was a newcomer who had no taint of corruption.

"Agnew made us very unhappy," Venetoulis remembered one morning years later. "He was one of ours, and we knew some of what he'd gone through to get there. We knew he had shortened his name from Anagnostopoulos. We worried about the ethnic thing when I started running, and then we started hearing comments. 'We don't need another Greek named "Ted" in that office,' that kind of thing. I heard that through the campaign, and my staff heard it."

It took Venetoulis back to East Baltimore's Highlandtown, to years when he wanted to be taken for an American and not a Greek, when he just wanted to fit in. And now these voices were saying: No matter what—no matter how you immerse yourself in a community, no matter how hard you work or how noble your intentions—you are still identified as The Other. Had the country learned nothing from the divisiveness of the riots? Did we still insist on choosing up sides by ethnic background?

It was still a time when language had to be carefully parsed. "The Greek stuff was tough to hear," Venetoulis said, "but then there was more than that. I was born and raised in the city, and the voters knew my closeness to Mayor Schaefer. What did that mean? That I was gonna make the county into the new version of the city? That carried all the racial overtones. We knew that words had hidden meanings. 'Urban renewal,' for example. We knew this was considered a very ugly word, that it meant federal money, which meant race. So you went after the same things, but you learned to use a different language, a different set of code words."

What mattered more than race, and more than ethnicity, in that season of corruption exposed in federal courtrooms, was the desire for reform. Agnew and Anderson were embarrassments not to be repeated. Marvin Mandel was on his way to his own legal trials, and so was Joseph Alton, the Anne Arundel County executive. Alton and Dale Anderson wound up in the same federal prison. Alton was repentant, while Anderson insisted he was innocent. When he heard Alton apologize, Anderson snarled, "Joe, they sent you to the wrong kind of goddamned institution."

But Venetoulis was clean. He was smart, sophisticated, and charmed everybody he met. He had hair like a Kennedy, and a face like a koala bear, and energy to burn. He was an ethnic who mixed with other ethnics, a Greek living among the Jews in northwest Baltimore County's Pikesville area. That was an American image, a melting-pot image, for voters who didn't want to think of themselves as bigots just because they were nervous about black people. Look at us, they could tell themselves, we're not prejudiced, we're voting for a minority. It's our kind of minority, a mirror of the America we used to hear about from our parents: those coming off the boats with tags on their overcoats, those working hard to make a better life for their kids, those marching in the I Am an American parades through the old rowhouse neighborhoods.

In his election as Baltimore County executive, Venetoulis carried liberal Pikesville wards by 12-to-1 margins. He took conservative Dundalk by 10-to-1 margins. He romped into office, the first Baltimore County executive born and raised in the city. The man he defeated? George P. Mahoney, whose "your home is your castle" motto was now perceived as a bad-taste reminder of attitudes that had preceded the 1968 riots and still, several years later, hung over everyone's heads. Nobody had the stomach for such a thing happening again. Mahoney was the man who had convinced people Spiro Agnew was a moderate.

And now Agnew was disgraced. On the evening of his resignation from the vice-presidency, having watched his moment in history implode, Agnew gathered his family about him. He decided he would not go into hiding. Where in the world could he hide? Instead, he took everyone to Sabatino's Restaurant in Little Italy.

Joe Canzane saw him first. Canzane still owned the place, but would sell it a few years later to his nephew, Vince Culotta. Agnew had been coming to Sabatino's for years. When he saw Canzane that evening, he smiled wanly.

"Joe," said Agnew, "you need any help around here? 'cause I'm out of a job."

"Sit down," said Canzane, putting a consoling arm around the disgraced man. "Have something to eat."

No one at dinner discussed the events of the day. The maitre d' at Sabatino's was Al Isella, the legendary bookmaker. He and Agnew knew each other because the Agnews dined regularly at Sabatino's. Also, they shared a certain history. Earlier that day, while Agnew was copping his plea in a federal courtroom on Calvert Street, Isella was directly across the street, dealing with justice in a municipal courtroom, where he was found guilty of taking bets on horseraces.

In Isella's case it was not such a big deal. In the course of a sixty-year career taking bets on horses and football games and street numbers, Isella was arrested so many times he lost count. The night that the Baltimore Orioles' Cal Ripken broke Lou Gehrig's consecutive game streak, the magic number was flashed on the scoreboard: 2,131. Isella's attorney, Richard Karceski, was in the ballpark that night and puckishly asked a man next to him, "How come they're flashing the number of times Al's been arrested?"

Isella knew Agnew the way he knew scores of politicians, judges, and police: When they wanted to let their hair down a little, here was a colorful lawbreaker—but it was only the gambling laws. Who was getting hurt? Thus, he had judges who placed bets with him. One issued Al a court summons on the very day he slipped him a wager on a horse. When Isella appeared in court one time, he heard the government prosecutor mention she liked the Orioles. "Hon," said Al, sitting at the defense table, "any time you need Orioles tickets, you just let me know." On another gambling rap, when a judge threatened to throw him into jail for speaking out of turn, Isella hollered across the courtroom, "Big deal, so I'll go to jail. So I won't have to spend so much on Christmas presents." When a member of Maryland's highest court, the Court of Appeals, had difficulty getting a relative into a prominent college, he mentioned it to Isella. Al called a highly placed contact, who made the right connection for the boy. Henceforth, the judge referred to Isella, whose own education got no farther than grade school, as the Dean.

Sometimes Isella had politicians offer him advice. He told friends that Governor Marvin Mandel had come to Sabatino's and told him, "Stay off the phones in this place. The cops are tapping you." Listeners tended to roll their eyes when they heard Al tell that story.

One day, though, in a conversation at Marvin Mandel's office, I mentioned Isella's name to him.

"Sure, I know him," Mandel said. "Are you kidding? I'm the one who warned him to stop taking bets over the telephone because the state police had his line tapped. Down at Sabatino's. They had the phone tapped because he was using it to take bets. He called me one day and said, 'You haven't been down for a while.' I said, 'Tell you what, I'll be down tonight and tell you why.' I got there and told him, 'That goddamned telephone's tapped over there.' They went through the ceiling at Sabatino's. Al went around the corner to a phone booth and used that until they tapped that, too."

The notion was remarkable: the governor of Maryland tipping off a career gambler about an investigation from his own state police—but it was Mandel's signal of Larger Truths. He'd had his own legal problems by this time. And now, he was saying, there are laws among friends that transcend the petty misdemeanors of police districts. It was Mandel and Isella, or it was Mandel and Irv Kovens. Friendship was all.

"You know about Al the night that Spiro Agnew copped his plea, don't you?" I asked Mandel.

"Agnew?" said Mandel. "Don't you know, I'm the guy who told him he was going down?"

Mandel heard about it from a well-connected friend. This was before anyone knew Agnew was under investigation. The very idea would have seemed absurd. Agnew was the impeccable picture of law and order. Mandel's friend said federal prosecutors had given three of Agnew's pals immunity to testify about payoffs that stretched over years. Mandel called Agnew in Washington.

"Ted, are you busy today?" the governor of Maryland asked the vice-president of the United States.

"What's the matter?" said Agnew.

"It's pretty important I come over to see you. As a friend, that's all."

"I'll cancel my appointments," said Agnew.

Years later, Mandel remembered, "I told him, 'I don't know what your friends might know, but the feds are giving three of them immunity.' Agnew said, 'Nah, it can't happen, it's not gonna happen.' I said, 'Why do you say that?' I figured he'd say, 'Because I haven't done anything wrong.' But he said, 'Because I have an agreement with the president and the attorney general that there'll be no immunity in my case.' Just like that. He said, 'I'll check it out immediately, but I'm not concerned because I have that agreement.' He called me back at five-thirty that afternoon."

"You know what?" Mandel remembered Agnew saying. "You're right. They're double-crossing me. They're giving immunity."

And he knew why. Nixon imagined Agnew would slake everyone's appetite for scandal in high places, no matter the implications of a thing called Watergate. He figured the country wouldn't have the stomach to pursue a president after losing a vice-president.

So now, on the night of his historic courtroom humiliation, Agnew took his family to Sabatino's Restaurant, where he met Al Isella, who had plowed through his own little courtroom drama that day. Isella was found guilty of taking bets on horses. He paid a fine, and lived to get himself arrested scores more times.

"Hey, Governor," Al cried when he saw Agnew. "I see they got you today."

Agnew braced himself, imagining the first in a lifetime of such encounters.

"What the hell," said Isella, "they got me, too. Don't worry about it, boss, it don't mean a thing."

The irony was lost on no one that evening: the one man, pursued by police for the crime of taking amiable sports bets; the other, seemingly the straightest of men, caught with his hands under the table, pursued for the rest of his life only by history.

Agnew thereafter slipped off to California, and Isella could be found each day at Sabatino's, at the heart of a lunchtime group that drifted in from various parts of town. They were irrepressible street guys whose lunchtime conversations were conducted at high octave. They rose and fell and overlapped. The men talked about ballgames and card games. They analyzed politics and crap games and point spreads. When women joined the group, each man became Cary Grant. Charm was in full bloom.

At a corner table, an ex-vice squad cop named George "Puddin'" Barry, a dead-ringer for Jackie Gleason's sidekick Art Carney, deciding to imitate pickpockets he had once arrested, slipped his hand into the front pants pocket of the burly roofer John Vicchio.

"Get your hand out of my pocket," Vicchio declared.

"I'm just trying to make change," explained Puddin'. Then, turning toward the door, he spotted the tile man Gus Hansen enter the restaurant with a young lady. Hansen was the son of a labor organizer. In the forties, his father had given pro-union speeches while his mother stood by with a gun in her purse in case things got out of hand. Hansen was now sixty-five years old. The young lady in his company now was perhaps twenty.

"What's a nice girl like you doing with him?" Puddin' called out happily.

"Hey, go easy on her," said Hansen. "She won me in a crap game."

While this went on, Clem Florio, professional horserace handicapper and ex-professional prizefighter, was giving his daily blessings to Franklin Roosevelt—"Where would we be without Social Security?"—and discoursing on inside politics, on New York Yankees baseball in the 1940s, on his sparring match with Jake LaMotta, and on his days hanging out with the great comic Lenny Bruce.

"Never mind that, I need a tip on a horse," said a guy named Bo. Bo got the nickname because he looked like the National Boh Beer mascot of years earlier. He was also famous for hiding his crap-game winnings under his toupee. In his youth Bo had a spotty record with the cops, starting with the time he and a couple of buddies did a little shoplifting. The buddies got caught. They squealed on Bo. The cops came to the house and told Bo's father, an immigrant, what had happened. The father let loose with a real good smack across Bo's face.

"Let this be a lesson," the father said.

"What do you mean?" Bo said.

"Always," said the father, "steal by yourself."

Across the Sabatino's lunchtime table, a guy called Puerto Rican Mike was telling his troubles to Al Isella. Puerto Rican Mike was not from Puerto Rico, nor even descended from Puerto Ricans.

"Why is he called Puerto Rican Mike?" a visitor asked one day.

"Because," explained an ex-beer salesman named Bill Benson, "everybody thinks he looks like Ricky Ricardo." Never mind that Ricky Ricardo was from Cuba, and not Puerto Rico—to everyone, he was Puerto Rican Mike. The big problem for Puerto Rican Mike was a woman he knew.

"She can't get off of the dope," he said, "and I don't know what to do with her."

"What do you mean you don't know?" Isella hollered at him. "Shoot her while she's sleeping."

He talked like that. It blew off steam for everybody, and the moment passed harmlessly. The lunches were always invigorating because they brought in people from all over town. This meant everybody in the room wasn't just like everybody else; it felt like a legitimate slice of America. The lunchtime gatherings were a window into a city's street-corner culture, and into its shifting and frequently good-natured ethnic give and take.

Isella, for example, had spent decades in the bookmaking business, mostly associating with Jews. An old federal prosecutor had dubbed the city's gambling rackets the Kosher Nostra. Over the years the Italian Isella's professional pals were Jews such as Julius Salisbury, the so-called lord of Baltimore's Block, who escaped federal prison by fleeing to Canada in the bottom of a horse van; Robert "Fifi" London, the bail bondsman and numbers racketeer; Nookie Brown, known to God as Daniel Brozowsky and to everyone else as Nookie the Bookie; and Philip "Pacey" Silbert. Years earlier, Pacey had been stopped by a uniformed policeman while holding betting slips. Reacting instinctively, he reached into his pocket and dropped a twenty-dollar bill onto the sidewalk.

"Excuse me, officer," said Pacey, looking to pay his way out of this slight pickle in the traditional manner. "Did you drop that twenty-dollar bill on the ground?"

"Not me," said the cop. "I dropped a fifty."

Nookie Brown had his own run-ins with the police. Once a year or so, the cops would kick in the door of his apartment to grab his numbers slips. One time, Nookie wasn't home but his sister was sitting in the living room when they arrived. The sister got very frightened.

Nookie hiked himself up to his full five-feet-five inches and walked into the Northwestern District, where he confronted the desk sergeant.

"Please," said Nookie, handing the sergeant a key to his front door, "next time you're coming, just use this."

Julius Salisbury and Fifi London avoided police by discussing their business dealings each evening on the telephone. They assumed the phones were tapped. Therefore, they counted up the business of the day in Yiddish.

Isella worked with all of these Jewish gamblers, and had been friendly with the gangster Meyer Lansky. One Saturday morning in the 1950s, the two men drove along Collins Avenue in Miami Beach. Al was behind the wheel. As they stopped for a red light, Lansky saw a man in a dark suit on the corner. He ducked below window level as though anticipating gunplay.

"Get this car out of here," he said.

"I got a red light," Isella said.

"Get it out of here," Lansky said through clenched teeth.

Isella ran the light. "What's the matter?" he asked.

"That guy on the corner," Lansky said darkly. "That was my rabbi. I'm not supposed to ride in a car on Saturdays."

Isella told the story without any comic intent. Lansky was a Jew, and Al was relating this as a sign that he knew Lansky well enough to have learned his sense of religious faith. The assimilation process worked everywhere, including the places people weren't supposed to know about.

"Why did you always work with the Jews?" I asked him.

"Because they were the only ones who wanted to deal with us," he said.

By "us," he included the East Baltimore city councilman Dominic "Mimi" DiPietro, a third-grade dropout but postdoctoral professor of the malaprop. To Mimi, the trouble with the court system was too much "flea bargaining." He thought coffee came from "coffee urinals." When his brother underwent intestinal surgery, Mimi declared, "They must have removed four feet of testicle from him." Also, in his own life, he dealt regularly with Jews—in gambling ventures he shared with Isella and in politics.

Once DiPietro helped Maryland governor Harry Hughes campaign along Highlandtown's Eastern Avenue commercial district. When they reached Goldberg's Shoe Store, Mimi hollered inside, "Hey, you Jews, come out and meet the governor."

When DiPietro's city council pal Clarence Du Burns ran against Kurt L. Schmoke for mayor of Baltimore, Mimi backed Burns. Their alliance was touching. Here were two east-side old-timers, Mimi and Du, an Italian and a black, raised in a time of ethnic antipathy and suspiciousness, who had bonded politically and personally. "A lot of people don't know it," Burns would say, "but I'm Italian. Now, you take Mimi. He's Italian by way of being born in Italy. I'm Italian by way of Belair Market," where he had worked years earlier at the Palmisano food stall.

But, in Burns's race for mayor against Schmoke, Mimi took their alliance one unfortunate step further. Burns, he told reporters without the slightest self-consciousness, understood poor people's needs better than Schmoke because Schmoke had lived with "rich Jews" up in "Jewtown."

When his remarks were reported in the *Baltimore Sun,* the newspaper ripped him. The remark embarrassed, or angered, everybody in town. Mimi sat in his City Hall office with his head in his hands. Everybody who knew him, he said, knew he had nothing against the Jews. It was just the way people in his generation sometimes talked.

"I got people calling my wife on the phone now and saying, 'How can you sleep with that dumb guinea who makes such remarks?'" he said.

"Who's making those kinds of calls?" he was asked.

"Other guineas," he said.

The words meant nothing to him; they were just identifiers, not disparagements. In a few minutes, the telephone rang again.

"You dumb guinea bastard," the man on the other end shouted.

"I know, I know," said Mimi. Then the man on the other end said, "Forget about it, I know you didn't mean anything." It was Irv Kovens, the Jewish political boss.

That night, unannounced, Mimi went to a *shiva* house where the veteran television broadcaster Richard Sher's family was mourning the death of Sher's mother, Lillian. Mimi stood in the doorway for a moment while a room filled with people went silent. The newspapers were full of his "Jewtown" remark.

"You know I would never do anything to hurt youse people," he told Sher's family.

"It's all right," a stunned Sher said, trying to console him.

"I'm sorry I talk like that," DiPietro said a little later. "I take a dying oath I didn't mean nothing by it. That's how I talk is all. I wanted to cut my tongue out when I realized people were hurt."

In America, there are fault lines everywhere. When we wish to assimilate, when we wish to befriend those who live in our community instead of holding them at arm's length, there is a difference between private and public language. In private, the differences become a comic gag line, a sign that we have transcended public politeness and reached intimacy. In public the unwritten rule is: Never give an opening to a bigot.

The Gang That Couldn't Eat Straight gathers at Sabatino's Restaurant in Little Italy. *Back row, left to right,* Michael Olesker, Al Isella, Joe Pizza, Walter Blimlein, George "Puddin'" Barry, Gus Hansen, Vince Culotta, John Vicchio. *Front, left to right,* Clem Florio, John Pica Sr., Lynn Hoffman. The restaurant became a gathering spot for "all known characters."

That notion of reaching beyond the old borders resonated with Vince Culotta when he bought Sabatino's Restaurant from his uncle, Joe Canzane. The neighborhood was Italian, but it represented something more to an entire city struggling to hold on. In the modern blandness of suburban tract housing and shopping malls, Little Italy became a link to yesterday. It was still there after so many of the old enclaves had vanished. It was a community of Italians, but it beckoned to everyone—with restaurants, with its lingering street-corner culture, with bocci ball all evening long—because it was also a nostalgic touchstone. It was a symbol for all who remembered their own family stories of American arrivals and rowhouse intimacy and dialects that landed between English and something else. The neighborhood became a city's collective memory for things that had gotten away.

"That's the thing," Vince Culotta said one summer evening, glancing beyond the restaurant's front door to crowds on the sidewalk outside. "People don't just come down here to eat. There's something else to it. I mean, you can eat anywhere. But you can't invent this kind of neighborhood."

It was a restaurant colony by century's turn, but it had a feel that reminded people of something left behind, of people living in close quarters, full of generous spirits. In a time when many communities turned inward with the coming of twilight, and hid behind locked doors, Little Italy seemed comfortable in its own skin.

One day at the Sabatino's lunchtime table, John Pica showed up with his daughter, Maria. She remembered the day she was married. The wedding, at St. Leo's Church, was six weeks after the royal wedding of Charles and Diana of Great Britain. All of Little Italy seemed to turn out for Maria Pica.

"What girl doesn't want a wedding day like mine?" she laughed. "Frankie Babusci got the Department of Public Works to wash the streets for me. You think Princess Di had it any better than that? Then there's police on every corner. And the limousine pulls off Eastern Avenue into Little Italy, and all up and down Exeter Street there's little old ladies sitting on their beach chairs waving at us. I get out of the car and walk to the balcony, and my father says, 'Wave to 'em, hon.' I tell you, Princess Di couldn't have felt better than that."

Her eyes twinkled at the memory. "Of course," she said, "that's the wedding my father didn't want me to have." It was the one where John Pica told his daughter, "You gotta marry in the faith—a Catholic or a Jew."

"What's that all about?" I asked Pica. "The Jewish-Italian thing?"

"Nobody else wanted us," he said. It precisely echoed Al Isella's words. "We'd fill out a *minyan* for them," a quorum for religious services. "Sometimes at the synagogue on Lombard Street, they needed us to sit *shiva*."

"What do you mean, 'Nobody else wanted us'?" I said.

"They didn't want to associate with us," Pica said.

"But why?"

"Just 'cause we were Jews and Italians," he said.

But such a notion seemed long ago and far away from this convivial lunchtime table. The mix was rich and yeasty and good-natured. For all of the American fault lines—the racial divisions exploited by some politicians, the arrivals of new minorities struggling with the language—there were millions of those who once felt like outsiders, but had discovered other outsiders, and together found the nation's sentimental heart.

NINETEEN

GOD IN PROTECTIVE CUSTODY

On Conkling Street in East Baltimore early one humid spring evening, a lady with pin curlers in her hair pushed opened her screen door and let loose a holler to carry past rowhouse marble steps, past neighbors perched on lawn chairs on the sidewalk, past parked cars, and past a large printed sign on a wall of Our Lady of Pompeii School reading "Bingo—Air Conditioned," all the way up to Tommy's Lounge, where several of the local men stood outside.

"Izzat Fat Frankie onna corner?" the lady called.

"Who wants to know, hon?" one of the men called back. He had an ear cocked to the first inning of an Orioles game coming through a nearby living-room window.

"The love of his life," the lady at the screen door half a block away hollered back.

"Fat Frankie ain't here, hon," said the guy, "but he loves you, too."

Romeo and Juliet, it was not. But it had a tongue-in-cheek Highlandtown romantic comedy feel to it, a tacit understanding that they were in on the joke. They were survivors of generational changes in the history of the city of Baltimore, and the keepers of a way of life: of rowhouse intimacy, of roots dug deep into a community, and of working-class street patois so affectionately identified with these neighborhoods that it sometimes slipped into cheerful self-parody.

This was the East Baltimore that Barbara Mikulski and Ted Venetoulis remembered warmly, but not uncritically. They remembered its comforts, but also its walls—and the reasons for those walls. The Poles were here, and the Greeks were over there; and over here the Lithuanians, and the Germans over there, each in a specific place, each nurturing insecurities, each looking to protect its own kind—until their children, born in this country, eager to mix, instinctively reached across the old borders.

Now there were others added to the old mix, and they overlapped, and much of the old self-consciousness was gone—among whites. And the newest mix came together on this spring night on Conkling Street, at Our Lady of Pompeii High School, whose seniors were graduating in services held at the church next door to their classrooms.

I sat near Christopher Russo, the school principal, and the Reverend Luigi Esposito, who led a Mass. The church overflowed. By the front doors, it was tough to tell which people standing in the aisle were related to graduates and which ones were simply neighbors from Conkling Street who slipped in to enjoy the moment. They'd seen a lot of these kids grow up, and they also remembered their own moments in cap and gown in this very place.

In Highlandtown, though, some of the eternal truths had changed. The kids were all encouraged to graduate high school now; years earlier, many routinely dropped out for jobs at Sparrows Point's steel mills, or at Esskay's meat-packing plant. But those jobs were gone, the victims of time and a changing marketplace. Most of these kids were now looking at community colleges. This rarely occurred to previous generations. Years earlier, a young person's dramatic move meant leaving the parents' old rowhouse for a place around the corner or down the block. But sometimes they went farther now. And when they left, newcomers moved onto these streets.

"Watch this," Christopher Russo whispered.

As they opened the Mass before graduation ceremonies, half a dozen seniors marched to a podium to read homilies. They had varying skin tones. They read the homilies in their families' native tongues—not only English, and not only the Eastern European languages long familiar to East Baltimore, but the not-so-familiar Spanish and Arabic. One meditation contained a prayer chanted in Hebrew. It felt as if a whole world had descended gracefully into Highlandtown.

Father Esposito looked at the graduates and then he gazed across the rows of their people sitting behind them. "I can see different generations of the same family I've baptized," he said.

The Mass, and the commencement ceremony that followed, lasted a few hours. And then, to the strains of "Pomp and Circumstance," a few dozen graduates marched up the church's center aisle and out the front doors onto Conkling Street. It was dark now, but streetlights shined on neighborhood people perched on front stoops. When the kids reached the sidewalk, they looked around for a moment: *What do we do now?* And then came the answer: happy whoops of abandon from one voice, and then more and more voices. In their caps and gowns, the new graduates danced about in the street and hooted delightedly, and the crowded little street answered back. From rowhouse front doors and cement steps came calls of congratulations. From second-floor bedroom windows, women leaned on their elbows and cried out, "Way to go, hon." There were cheers all the way down from Zanino's Funeral Home, a block away, where a couple of ladies pushed baby carriages on the sidewalk, and hoarse cries echoed back from some of the guys still standing in front of Tommy's Lounge, who quit listening to the Orioles for a moment. And a couple of police cars on the block flashed their roof lights, maybe just for the hell of it.

It felt like a neighborhood is supposed to feel, like a collection of people whose lives are intertwined. It looked like an assimilationist's dream of things finally working out, of the melting pot at full delicious bubble.

But it was also, in East Baltimore, a time of Expedito "Pedro" Lugo.

Lugo was a teenage boy beaten with a couple of baseball bats until his skull was fractured. He clung to life through medical technology. Lugo was Latino, and his assailants three African American teenagers. They found him walking through Patterson Park after dark. The park had always been East Baltimore's great embracer, with its ballfields and swimming pool, its ice rink and its lush acres of grass. Now it was a place to act out blind rage. The incident set loose waves of fear in East Baltimore—and voices of bitterness.

A generation earlier black people could not venture into these neighborhoods. They might get their faces rearranged. In some white city neighborhoods, the great voices of liberalism spoke of peaceful integration but quietly slipped away to suburbia at the first sighting of black families; in white East Baltimore, amid much grumbling, amid much slanderous insult, many had nevertheless stayed and tried to work things through. Some didn't have the money for suburbia; others simply declared themselves immovable. This was their home, after all; why should they go anywhere? But the beating of Pedro Lugo rekindled old racial fears, and old anger, and not even kids dancing in the street after a high school graduation could cover it up.

A few days after the beating I went to Lombard Street in East Baltimore and bumped into a young woman named Debbie Prestianni. She had a pit bull on a leash and stroked the top of its head. In a few minutes, she said, the kids would be coming out of Hampstead Hill Middle School.

"I want them to see the dog's teeth," she said. The dog was called Zeus. The school kids were called unprintable names. Prestianni perspired freely on a day not hot enough for perspiring. She stood outside a place called Willie's Auto Body with a young man named Paul Cook.

"These kids tried to set a couch on fire right around the corner," Cook said. "They yell at old people. They bust bottles all through the alleys." He hesitated for a moment, weighing a thought in his brain. "Is it racist for me to say that?" he asked.

I walked to Baltimore and Ellwood Streets a few blocks away as the Hampstead Hill afternoon school bell rang. The neighborhood was mostly white, but a lot of the school kids were black, and they flooded the narrow streets on their way home. The newspapers were filled with stories about troubles here. The beating of Pedro Lugo had become a symbol of unresolved tensions and set loose all sorts of residual, holdover accusations about race. As the kids bounced their way along each block, white residents stood in their doorways, watching for trouble. Uniformed police hovered about. The residents all had war stories: about kids walking atop cars, about trash randomly tossed in the street, about groups of big kids picking on smaller ones.

Much of the talk was racial. Everything was preceded by a phrase: "I'm not racist, but . . ." And this was the trap that they felt: They had stayed when others had run; they had hung in despite increased crime, despite trouble in the schools, despite waves of drug traffic; and now, if they dared to complain, their words were characterized as the rantings of racists.

I remembered the neighborhood from years earlier, when there were some demonstrations around Patterson Park against blacks who wanted to move in. Now the offspring of those blacks walked these streets, and some of them carried stories handed down from previous generations and held onto their parents' assumptions: that this was still a haven of racism, still a place where no blacks were welcome, and that it paid to have a chip on your shoulder.

A few days later I went to the city's Eastern District Court and met a woman named Betty Gleaves. Her son, Andre Flythe, was one of the accused assailants of Pedro Lugo. The doctors said Lugo had been transferred from Johns Hopkins Hospital to Montebello State Hospital. He would survive, but he would have to relearn simple motor skills that had been beaten out of him by the baseball bats.

Betty Gleaves had come to court to see her son. She never got the chance. The state's attorney's office decided not to let him out of his cell. Instead, someone in court recited an indictment number in a monotone voice, and a charge of attempted first-degree murder against Andre Flythe was read into the record, and when it was over, Gleaves walked into the busy hall outside.

She had the weight of the world on her, and tried not to show it. It was not merely that her son was an accused assailant; he was now being blamed for renewed racial tension in a mixed community trying to work things out, in a city where a thousand people moved away every month of every year.

She called her son timid. I thought about the baseball bat against Pedro Lugo's skull. She said Andre was shy. I mentioned Lugo's name. She said the other boys tended to pick on her son, who was nineteen years old and six-feet-three. I asked about the beating.

"To me, I can't picture him doing it," Betty Gleaves said. This was not precisely a denial.

"Are you saying he's innocent?" I asked.

"He said he was there when the boy was beat up," Gleaves said. She looked around the crowded courthouse corridor, as though seeking an exit. "But he said he didn't do any of the beating. I don't know whether he's lying to me or not, but my son is a timid kind of boy. People beat him up, not him beating up other people. He doesn't get in this kind of trouble."

"He's never been in trouble?" she was asked.

"Stealing cars," said Andre Flythe's mother. "But that's all."

That afternoon, I drove to St. Elizabeth's Roman Catholic School, across the street from Patterson Park. Dick Gatto was there. He was principal of the school, cheerful, curly-haired, a sensitive man who understood the neighborhood's changes. The Lugo incident terrified him. The kids coming out of Hampstead Hill Middle School, on the other side of the park, worried him. Gatto had moved up his school's closing afternoon bell half an hour just so his students could get home before the Hampstead Hill kids were released. St. Elizabeth's, once all white, was now about one-third black. Gatto said there were seven incidents where his students were beaten up by Hampstead Hill kids. The attackers were black.

"Racial?" he was asked.

"Look at this," he said. We had walked out of St. Elizabeth's and strolled into Patterson Park. Gatto swept a hand across the landscape. On a playground, children ran about, oblivious to all variety of skin color. On a basketball court, white and black teenagers played, and so did youngsters in the nearby swimming pool.

"To make this racial is not only untrue," he said, "it's an avoidance of the problem." He watched kids happily shooting water pistols at each other under a bright sun. "People here have come to an agreement," he said. "They've learned to live with one another. Look, who wants to be hassling all the time with your neighbors? But you look at the beating of Pedro Lugo, and you look at the Hampstead Hill school situation, and you see where everything's going astray. The city has such an opportunity here to say, 'Look at East Baltimore. Look how well it works.'"

His words hung in the air for a long moment. You can look at skin color and issue indictments of a race of people, he was saying—and it gets us nowhere. Or you can examine the individuals in each case, and leave skin color to the bigots. I thought Gatto sounded more hopeful than realistic.

I went back to Hampstead Hill Middle School in time for the afternoon bell. There were police all over the place, as they had been since the Lugo beating set off so many emotions in the neighborhood. A police helicopter fluttered overhead.

"How long will you be here?" I asked a uniformed officer. "Till it stops?"

"Till it stops being in the newspaper," he said.

The neighborhood was tense, but the police were not. To them it was routine business. But it was years after all manner of civil rights gestures were supposed to have removed us from such tensions, years since the neighborhood had been integrated. And now, all along this block, nervous white residents stood in their doorways, bracing themselves for the afternoon's onslaught of youngsters.

"It's not racial per se," one white policeman said. He looked around to see who was listening. "It's life. It's kids having a good time but acting out too far. But it's perceived to be racial. There's all these white people who see all these dark faces coming out of the school and walking down these streets. The movement of all those kids is gonna be annoying. It's gonna be scary sometimes. But I haven't seen one race specifically targeting another just because of race."

Another white cop nodded his head. The two of them seemed as hopeful as Dick Gatto. The second officer knew the area beyond professional duty. He'd grown up on these very streets.

"Used to be," he said, "if a kid did something bad, one of the neighbors would holler at him. They'd say, 'I know your mother.' And that's all you had to hear. You knew you were in trouble. But you can't say that now. The kids are coming in from different neighborhoods, and nobody around here knows their mothers."

When the afternoon school bell rang a few moments later, swarms of kids raced down Ellwood Street. Most were black. From front doorways, white adults watched—as did more uniformed police, and a couple of television news crews with cameras and microphones.

An African American girl, maybe thirteen years old, took in the whole scene as she strolled home. "We got the police and the news media," she said. "And we got the helicopters. What kind of goofy people are scared of us?"

A moment later, another girl called to a woman standing nervously behind her screen door, "Are you a prisoner in your own home?" Her tone was mocking, grandly comical. It was a white girl. She was mimicking overblown language she had heard on the television news programs. She was saying: Stop getting caught up in your own overblown language; this is kids' stuff.

Maybe the cops were right. It wasn't racial. It was just some kids who hadn't picked up all of the garments of civilization yet. But the neighbors were also right. They felt intimidated by these kids. Where was their sense of respect? Where were responsible parents making certain these kids behaved? And where had all the yesterdays gone, when they might have hollered at them, "I know your mother," and been assured that all would be well.

Maybe Dick Gatto had been right, too: People had come to an agreement; they were working it out. It was always messy in the melting pot, but we didn't have to attribute racial motives to it. And maybe this, too, would be worked out.

And then, as I reached my car, I looked toward Lombard Street and saw the young woman with the pit bull, and she was showing the dog's teeth. And I remembered Pedro Lugo.

One raw November morning in 1991, I went back to the Latrobe housing projects and stood in the extended shadows of those two towers of morality from my youth: the steeple of the Church of St. James, and the lookout tower of the Maryland Penitentiary, each hovering over Abbott Court.

From the look of things, the prison had claimed more souls than the church. Its cells had been filled, and then refilled, for years; but the church, a pillar of this neighborhood since 1865, was struggling to stay alive.

I approached Abbott Court the way any of its former children might: remembering the innocent past, remembering the operatic cries of the iceman, and children ducking behind freshly washed linens hung on laundry lines in our afternoon games of war. I remembered peering out of our kitchen window at the evening sunsets, and my mother explaining, "Sometimes you don't need money for the most beautiful things." At the Church of St. James across from our courtyard, I remembered weddings on sweet humid evenings when the bridal party came spilling out the front door.

But now I found God placed in protective custody.

A high metal fence with barbed wire across its top surrounded the old church. God was kept behind lock and key. Ancient stained-glass windows were now shattered, and window panes were missing. I remembered the last time I had been here, in the midst of the 1968 riots, when a voice behind the big church doors delivered a homily but refused to show a face.

I stood there on hilly Aisquith Street, just above the Institute of Notre Dame, and looked at Abbott Court across the street. Never a garden community, it was now a catastrophe. In a damp morning breeze, clumps of trash blew about randomly in the courtyard, and metal screen doors flapped on their hinges. Graffiti covered red-brick walls. The trash dumpsters were still there, but some people had simply dumped their garbage in the street at the base of the big cans rather than toss it inside, a gesture that seemed either breathtakingly lazy or contemptuous of all rules of civility.

Around the corner from the church front, I found a rectory and rang a bell by a locked gate: one more fence, one more roll of barbed wire across its top offered protection from the outside world. A man opened one door but remained behind a locked screen door.

"You know how kids are," he said. "They throw rocks and stones."

"Is that what happened to the stained-glass windows in the church?"

"That's what happened. Plus the air conditioner," he said. "And the copper rainspouts."

"What do you mean?"

"Stole them," he said. He shrugged his shoulders and would not give his name. In the morning mist I tried to make myself look miserable to get inside the warmth of the rectory. The man inside did not budge. He stood there behind his two doors, behind this protective fence, behind this jagged barbed wire. He said he did not know when, or if, the fence might ever come down.

"This church," I said. "It goes back to the last century, doesn't it?"

"Oh, it ain't that church no more," he said. "Was St. James. Not no more."

Now it was called the Urban Bible Fellowship Church. It felt as if God had been placed in a witness protection program, and the name of His very house altered for disguise. The man at the rectory said the new congregation had nearly seventy-five parishioners. Seventy-five? I remembered Sunday mornings four decades earlier when the sidewalk outside the church overflowed. The church was big and Gothic. I remembered a time when its mere presence seemed to dominate the neighborhood, like a mother hovering over her extended family. Now its doors were locked, as though she was covering her eyes not to see what had happened to her own children.

I walked back around the corner to Aisquith Street, and down to the Institute of Notre Dame next door. Girls in school uniforms raced through a hallway, chattering at high and happy volume. An administrator, Joan Rizicka, shushed them without noticeable effect.

"Yes, the church," she said. "It's very sad. We used to have the church for our girls. We had Masses there, and school ceremonies. But now, with all this vandalism . . ."

Her voice trailed off. This was the place where Nancy D'Alesandro had first ventured out of Little Italy; it was Barbara Mikulski's school when she took the bus here from Highlandtown. They were the descendants of immigrants venturing into Greater America. Now parents drove their cars up to the front door, cautiously deposited their daughters, and pulled back to the front door when each school day ended.

I walked across Aisquith Street and counted thirty-two apartment doors in Abbott Court. On thirteen of them, the metal screen doors were missing, or had their tops or bottoms ripped out. A man stuck his head through one of the doorways.

"Where did all the doors go?" I asked.

"Cheap screen doors," he said.

He chuckled sardonically. I walked to the far end of the courtyard, to 1103 Abbott Court, and knocked on the door of my family's old walk-up apartment for the first time in four decades. The current family's name was Barnes. The rooms seemed smaller than I remembered. I looked through the kitchen window and remembered magnificent sunsets. There were six people living here now, where once there had been my parents and me. When my brother Mitchell was born, we found the place confining enough to move out, though we had no money to move. Now the place had to fit a family larger than ours.

Kenneth Barnes sat in a living room chair with a diploma hanging on the wall behind him. Hagerstown Community College, it said. Barnes said he had not worked in eighteen months. He was black. In my time there were no blacks in the projects, only on the rundown streets all around them. Now all of the residents were black. Many were on welfare, and most had only one adult living here.

I thought about a morning three years earlier, when President George Bush had sent U.S. Housing Secretary Jack Kemp to these projects to proclaim a new day. For about a year the government moved everyone out of the projects' 700 units, and poured in millions of dollars in refurbishing, and then moved everyone back in.

And now, three years later, it was once more a disaster.

Whom to blame? The damned government, which turned its back on such housing projects for years, and then tried to catch up with one blast of overdue money? But look what had happened once they'd spent it. Whom to blame? The American economy, which created community colleges for people like Kenneth Barnes, who had graduated but now gone eighteen months without work? But whose fault was that? Barnes's, or construction outfits balky when it came to hiring minorities? Or was it something else?

This being the American reflex, the question came back to race. And I remembered Dick Gatto at St. Elizabeth's School, and those uniformed cops outside of Hampstead Hill Middle School. They were there in the middle of it, watching blacks and whites sometimes irritating the hell out of each other, and issuing their warnings: This is about many things, but don't make it about race when it isn't.

And on this dreary November morning in Abbott Court, all I had to search was my own history here. This was the courtyard where children had once romped happily, but alcoholic fathers had beaten them when the mood stirred them. There was trash cluttered around the big dumpsters, but the kids in my time had used garbage cans for bedding down. "Trash pickers," they had called one another when reaching for a slur that hit close to home. There were junkies stealing from a church now—but I remembered that ruined old wino on the church sidewalk years ago. When he tossed his last remaining money into the gutter, that swarm of us—grunting, frantic, mauling at each other—scrambled for his few coins as the old man crashed face-first to the sidewalk. There was trash all over the place now, but it was all over the place in my time, too.

These were black people now, but they were white then. They were poor people then, and poor now. Abbott Court, and the Latrobe housing project, would never be a garden spot so much as a waystation, a stopover place on the way to some place better.

The choice was still the essential American choice: to define those who lived there by their race, and therefore declare them The Other; or to see them in their individuality, and in their transition, as those looking for something better, and sometimes stumbling and falling before they got there.

One balmy May morning in 1994 I went to the old Garrison Junior High School, in Northwest Baltimore, in search of a postscript to history. The country was marking the fortieth anniversary of the U.S. Supreme Court decision to desegregate the nation's schools. I went looking for remnants of the journey taken by Michele Winder and Jake Oliver and me, and the rest of the first public-school generation of the full America. But most traces of our experience had vanished long ago.

We arrived at Garrison in September of 1957, three years after the high court's decision, and found a school roughly three-quarters white. When we left three years later, it was roughly 60 percent white. In the spring of 1994, there were 1,815 students at Garrison, and not one child was white. At Forest Park High School a block away, there were 879 students. Two were white. There were almost no white families remaining in the surrounding neighborhoods, nor had there been many for more than two decades.

Officially, integration was still the policy of the public schools. In the city of Baltimore, though, it was unofficially irrelevant. No one spoke the word and imagined it had anything to do with the thing written into law forty years earlier. It was just a word, and not a fact of life, not with so many white families having fled that, in a city roughly 60 percent black, its public schools were now 87 percent black, and its high schools 89 percent black.

A few days before I drove to Garrison, I had gone through my high school yearbook from Baltimore City College. I counted faces by skin color. Of roughly 800 boys in my senior class, about 500 were white. Now, thirty-six years later, there were fewer than 500 white high school seniors in the entire public school system of the city of Baltimore. Here, the melting pot was not even a rumor.

At Garrison I glanced into a third-floor classroom where Michele and Jake and I had fumbled with Mrs. Jacobson's ninth-grade algebra lessons. Now a teacher had written on a blackboard: ". . . to graph a linear equation in two variables by solving the equation for y and making a table of at least three solutions . . ."

To someone who hadn't puzzled over such language in many years, it looked like a pretty serious problem. Inside other classrooms, the kids seemed attentive and their teachers authoritative. The rooms and hallways were clean and well lighted. It was now a time when some African Americans were declaring, "You see? We don't need integration to be educated." I wondered what Thurgood Marshall might have replied. That was not his historic plea before the U.S. Supreme Court.

In the school office a young black woman named Paula Washington, who was Garrison's assistant principal, answered a few questions but seemed ill at ease. Those who worked in the city schools were accustomed to incoming flak about academics. But these questions seemed irrelevant. They were about race. She seemed to imply: What did race have to do with anything?

"I know these kids are getting a good education," she said softly.

"But is it the kind of education we used to talk about?" I said. "Something beyond academics, something about people getting to understand each other?"

Then I realized: She was too young to remember the nation's brief flirtation with integration. The look on her face said she had read about it, or heard about it from somebody, but it didn't quite register as an experience in her own life. If she saw value in an integrated environment, she did not make the argument. Her students came to school, and lived their lives, without white people—and found such a fact simply a fact.

"I don't know," she said, "if there's any kind of connection with white people in their lives."

I walked out of her office a little later and strolled the school's narrow hallways. Down one flight of steps was the cafeteria. I could still remember the smell of sticky buns and mashed potatoes with gravy. And I remembered a moment: Claude "Henny" Young standing on a table and belting out a Ray Charles number that sent the entire fifth-period lunch into spontaneous sing-along.

"*Baby, what I say,*

Baby, what I say right now . . ."

Such fun! Such unselfconscious joy in the very mix of voices, and the sense that we were all joining up to put one over on those uptight adults who ran the school, and all other distinctions were immaterial!

The broad education experience was different then. Once a year they trotted out the brotherhood lectures, which gave an official imprint to good intentions. National Brotherhood Week they called it. But it seemed superfluous. The rest of the time, everybody was left to figure things out on our own and we were succeeding fairly well: we were different, yes, but we had certain things in common, and we could build on them. Otherwise, what was the country all about?

When I walked outside to the old blacktop punchball diamonds, they were still there, and I remembered the great mixing bowl of the ballgames. *"Could not hit the punchball,"* Jake Oliver still lamented comically. No, but the games themselves were a starting point when the two of us had reconnected years after the fact. We had things in common we could talk about: the ballgames, the drudgery of algebra lessons, and the memory of a girl named Michele Winder.

When Michele and I caught up with each other forty years after we'd graduated and gone our separate ways, we sat in a deserted area of the Bibelot Book Store at the Village of Cross Keys, in Northwest Baltimore, one cold March afternoon. She lived nearby, in this largely white part of town, in an integrated apartment building.

"I guess that much has changed, anyway," I said.

"Yes," she agreed. She seemed sweet but wary. Maybe it was the setting. I wanted to talk about race, and any stranger could wander past and eavesdrop. So I started gently. I mentioned funny classmates; she remembered going to the cafeteria each day and hoping to find a friendly face. I mentioned boring teachers; but she remembered a teacher's racist remarks. I thought our little era had been the beginning of America's coming to grips with a conscience, but she wondered if the journey had been worth it. The air seemed chillier.

She talked then about the message of Malcolm X—not the Muslim religious doctrine, but the notion of racial separation—and how it contrasted with the loneliness she had felt before she heard his words. "In the so-called integration thing," she called that long-ago time. She sounded as sweet and considerate as ever, and I sensed no hostility when she said it. This loneliness was something she had gone through years ago, she was saying. I waited for the comforting wrap-up: we were adults now, educated, middle class, and had become cosmopolitan people who lived in the full America.

"And I'm thinking," she went on slowly, "you know, 'The separation, this is okay. Why do we have to integrate?' What Malcolm said was being fused in my head. To me, I think this is better, more realistic." She had switched tenses on me. She'd moved from *was* to *is.* I felt a small physical shock, as though the air itself had punched me. I waited for a last-moment update, some addendum to the previous statement.

"So I kind of still embrace that," she said. Her voice was even softer now. She had the gentle, almost apologetic tones of a girlfriend confessing she had fallen in love with another guy. I wanted her to say school integration had been the beginning of her grand American journey, the beginning of an entire generation's sense of full belonging, the same way it had been for me. And she seemed to know that I wanted her to say it. But she could not.

"I think it's a cool thing," she said, "because look at the negatives that came out of integration, all the people left behind, all the ghettos, losing the cultural base in neighborhoods."

"You're not saying you're anti-white," I said, "you're saying it's a comfort level." I wanted to hear her say that those school days meant something important to all of us, that at least we had grown up with good intentions, that the journey had its endearments. But I didn't want to put words into her mouth.

"It's comfort, it just makes sense," she said. She looked uneasy. "I guess it's a comfort level."

"It sounds," I said, "like you're saying it's never gonna work."

She heaved a sigh and looked like a person caught between her convictions and the instinctive kindness of not wanting to hurt someone she had once known.

"I'm not saying it's not gonna work," she said. "But I just think there are so many people reaching out for the wrong reasons. If somebody wants to integrate, yeah."

"You live in an integrated building."

"If you want to break barriers, okay," she said. "But what I saw in the South, the movers and shakers, the movement in general, the leadership . . ."

"My concern," I said, "when we segregate ourselves, suspicions grow. Antagonisms. Rather than look at each other as individuals, we're just a repertory company of racial clichés. And it's an excuse for those in power, who are usually white, to look out for their own. And that divides us."

"I don't know," she said. "I saw black-owned businesses. I saw banks in the South. I got this huge big picture of what we can achieve. I'm not saying segregated. But the integration piece, I found people moving away from their cultural roots, trying to embrace a part of something else, and not embracing and loving and being who we are and working from that. If you want to do that other thing, that's fine, too. But do it for the right reasons. I saw the interracial thing. It was people thinking they're moving into something better, thinking they were moving into this other thing. My whole life, with my children, and the loneliness again."

"You've mentioned that loneliness," I said. "You mean cultural loneliness?"

"I saw it with my children in integrated schools. They felt isolated. In Reston, Virginia. You don't have your black friends living next door to you. There are blacks in Reston, but they're spread around. I'll never forget going to my daughter's school. Boy, I tell you."

She sighed again. It seemed to contain memories of her own history: at Garrison Junior High, at Forest Park Senior High, at cafeterias and at movie theaters and who knew where else?

"It was so chaotic at lunchtime," she said. "The black kids would run up to each other, and they'd explode in this chatter, this thing where you could see it was the only opportunity to taste each other, to smell each other, to touch each other."

She was talking about her kids in Reston, but it might have been herself forty years earlier in Baltimore. The journey never ends, it only repeats itself. Each succeeding generation tries to work things out in its own way. And our generation's way hadn't worked for Michele. We walked silently out of the book store into a late-afternoon chill, two strangers looking across a forty-year distance and finding only traces of each other.

"I had the feeling," I said, "that you were holding back on some of your thoughts in there. As though you didn't want to offend me."

"I thought you might have had a preconceived overview for this book you're writing."

"No," I said. "This is what I mean by 'the journey.' Figuring out what's important enough to hold on to."

At century's turn integration seemed a romantic but bygone notion for many former believers. For many blacks, "community control" had replaced integration as a goal; for many whites, such a notion was a relief: it said that blacks no longer wanted in. But if that was the case, weren't they separating themselves not only from whites but from mainstream political power and money?

I thought again about the muddiness of the dream of Martin Luther King: It wasn't about being color-blind. It was about an equal chance. It was about integration, but that didn't mean obliteration of all differences. And Malcolm was the natural balance to King. Each was a vision of where we might go—and the country, one person at a time, had to find a comfortable place somewhere in between.

And then there was Lenny Moore.

In his football youth, his Colts were Baltimore's secular religion. And remained so, until the dreadful snowy night in March of 1984 when the Mayflower moving vans sneaked them out of town while everyone was sleeping. The town mourned the loss for the next decade, first begging the corporate gods of professional football for the return of the old team, and then groveling for any new one.

And in those wasteland years, the old Colts legends were recalled, and trotted out in public, and grew even more beloved in their retirement than they had been in their swift and rugged youth. Now we remembered only the touchdowns and not the fumbles; Unitas throwing to Berry and Moore was recalled, as in a dream, but not Robert Irsay and his bluster; now the past seemed awash not only in victories, but in delirious throngs united behind their happy band of brothers.

Many of the old Colts had never moved from Baltimore. John Unitas had his Golden Arm restaurant on York Road for a long time, and Art Donovan his Valley Country Club in suburban Towson. Jim Mutscheller had his in-

Lenny Moore and former Coach Weeb Ewbank embrace. Ewbank coached the
Colts during both the greatest years of Moore's Hall of Fame football career and
the moment of his greatest public humiliation. *Courtesy of the Moore family*

surance business and Jim Parker his liquor store at Liberty Heights Avenue
and Garrison Boulevard. Ordell Braase had a nightclub, and Lenny Moore
worked with troubled kids for the Department of Juvenile Services.

The city fathers would round them all up from time to time as reminders
of their football days and as symbols to the football overlords that a glorious history existed in Baltimore, and such glad times could be brought to

life once again. When the league seemed to pay little attention, grander steps were taken: an exhibition football game at packed Memorial Stadium for a meaningless preseason contest between two out-of-town teams; fundraising dinners in overflowing banquet halls; and enormous gatherings at the city's Inner Harbor, where the old ballplayers would gimp their way onto stage to say a few words to enthralled crowds.

When they cheered Art Donovan at a rally one sunlit day at the harbor, he leaned into a microphone and said, "You'd better sit down before I start crying. I came down to Baltimore forty-two years ago and told my mother, 'I'll be back in two weeks.' Forty-two years later, I'm still here."

It was precisely what the crowd wanted to hear: Donovan shared their heartache, he was part of Baltimore. And, unlike the Colts, he wasn't going anywhere else. The memory of the team now transcended athletic triumph and loss. The Colts were a reminder of lost innocence. The generation that had cheered them remembered the good times and put aside all memories that did not seem to fit.

One night, a few thousand people gathered for dinner at Martin's West, a huge banquet hall in the Woodlawn area of Baltimore County. Old game highlights were shown on a movie screen, and some of the Colts shared reminiscences with the crowd. I hung around afterwards with a few of the old ballplayers, who were clearly moved by the outpouring of affection, and by memories of each other in their youth.

"I watched that film for twenty minutes," Ordell Braase said to Art Donovan, "and I haven't seen you make a tackle yet."

"I made one back at St. Michael's," Donovan laughed. "I think they still have a picture of it there."

Sisto Averno laughed with him. He was the old lineman who had tried out with Donovan in the team's first summer training camp in Westminster. "The modern players don't have what we had," he said. "They got the money, that's all. Me, I got 4,000 bucks and played both ways." Clem Crowe coached the team in those early days. "One week, I went to Crowe and said, 'I can't play. I separated my shoulder.' He said, 'Which one?' I said, 'The right one.' He said, 'Hit 'em with your left.'"

"That's the way it was," Lenny Moore said. "I started at $10,000 six years after you, and I was the number one draft choice, man."

"I was number one the next year," said Jim Parker. "I got $12,500." He remembered the general manager, Don Kellett. "He handed me 1,500 one-dollar bills," Parker said. "He said, 'Look at this, son.' My wife said, 'Take it, fool.' We went to the Belvedere Hotel and put all the bills in the bathtub to look at them."

In the little group of ballplayers, everyone laughed at the memory of their mutual innocence. "Twelve thousand, five hundred," said Donovan. "That's more than the entire payroll in 1950, and Tittle got half of that." Tittle was Y. A. Tittle, the quarterback.

"And they had to send us out to hustle season tickets," said Jim Mutscheller. "They had three-dollar tickets on the fifty-yard line in the upper deck. Today you'd have to mortgage your house for tickets like that."

"Money was tight," Jim Parker laughed. "When I got my liquor store, a guy came into my place and said, 'Hey, some white boy just took six Schlitzes, let's call the police.' I said, 'Nah, he's a friend of ours.'"

"Yeah," said Artie Donovan, "I never did pay you for that six-pack I took."

Around the little group, everyone laughed appreciatively. Look, they were saying, how much fun we had, and look what friendships we have shared across so many years.

When I looked at Lenny Moore, though, I saw a wistfulness. Not just that day, but others. He joined in the laughter, and he never complained. But he was holding things inside. I didn't yet know about the humiliations of Westminster and Dallas, and the downtown Baltimore movie theater where he was turned away, and so many other slights. I looked at these men in their middle age, so comfortable with each other, and assumed it had always been that way.

It was not. And the time came when Moore decided to get it out of his system. The ballplayers had one of their private team reunions at Bill Pellington's pub, the Iron Horse, in Timonium. Pellington was a ferocious linebacker in Moore's era. He was nicknamed the Iron Horse for his brute strength and his terror tactics. Art Donovan maintained, "Pellington was so dirty, he should have been thrown out of every game he ever played in." Off the field, though, Lenny Moore thought Pellington was a man who had changed over the years.

In their playing days, there was an incident. "Almost a little riot," Moore remembered. In their training camp locker room at Western Maryland College, Pellington and Big Daddy Lipscomb had exchanged words. Lipscomb shoved Pellington, who swung back. As the two large men grappled, their teammates seemed to move into position.

"I'll never forget it," Moore said. "Everybody's shifting, see? And it became black-white. I could see the way the groups were shifting as to who was gonna do what. Johnny Sample's near me, and he's getting ready to do something, and here's a group of white guys lined together, and everybody's getting with their own sides. Thank God the coaches came in. But you could tell, the way it was weaving, it was gonna be black-white.

"The funny thing is, during Pellington's last years, I saw a deep mellowing, a deep mellowing. He was changed, I think, by his kids. Because they were hanging around black youngsters in the schools."

Then came the night at Pellington's Iron Horse Pub. The mood was jovial, the drinking substantial, and before the evening got too late, Moore decided to leave. He was wary. He remembered other reunions, where one or two fellows had drunk too much, and their talk became caustic.

"I'm ready," Moore told his wife.

"Don't go, Lenny," somebody said.

"Say a few words, Sput," somebody else said. "We're all gonna say a few words."

So Moore stood there as the room quieted down. He looked across the weathered faces of his teammates. They were becoming old men now, who had once known the cheering of crowds, who had been there at a nation's crossroads and served not only as athletes but as implicit symbols of the American melting pot to a community that only knew what it saw on the playing field.

"You know, it's a funny thing," Moore said. He saw Unitas sitting a few feet away, and the defensive back Bobby Boyd not far from him. There was Donovan with a beer in his hand, and Pellington and Parker and Braase.

"We don't know each other," Moore said. It was nearly four decades since these men had become his teammates. "It's a funny thing how much we adore each other. Truthfully, honestly, sincerely love each other. I mean, in that locker room. I mean, we put on those pads, and the joking and the acting like kids. We just bonded, man. But, come five o'clock, after the game, and we'd go back to that separation thing."

He looked at Unitas again, and at Weeb Ewbank sitting near him. Ewbank was the coach who had brought them all together in their legendary years. Nobody said a word. Moore thought of Westminster and Dallas and all the small hurts, and he wondered why no one, in all the years that followed, had ever mentioned the humiliations of that time. He thought of nights when the white fellows went one way and he and Big Daddy went to Pennsylvania Avenue in West Baltimore.

"You know what?" Moore said. "We're older guys now, and it's a shame. All these years were just wasted years. It's not your fault, and it's not my fault. It was society's fault. But we wasted all these years." He was a man opening his heart now, proclaiming his isolation, letting them know that he had been hurt, and then hurt again when no one seemed to notice his hurt.

"We don't know each other," he said softly. "I don't know you, and you don't know me. What a sad commentary this is. It's a damn shame. All these wasted years, and we've never come to really be friends, to know each other. I'm sorry. Never been to each other's homes. Never did anything socially, unless it was one of those team functions." He was conscious of the room's complete silence. "We went through the wars with each other, and we don't even know each other."

And in that silence, he turned and walked to the door. And has never heard a teammate, black or white, mention it since that night.

TWENTY

O'MALLEY'S MARCH

There's a young man at the harbor
And he stares across the sea
With his family all around him
Gripping fears of what might be.
Before he leaves to save his future
He wipes the tears so she can see,
Finally turns to kiss his mother,
"Wait for me."

The young man at the harbor was named Martin O'Malley. In the 1870s he left a place called Clombur, in Irish farm country called Kilmilkeen. This O'Malley was the great-grandfather of another Martin O'Malley, who would become the mayor of Baltimore, Maryland, 130 years later and was so moved by his imaginings of the immigrant great-grandfather's journey that he put his story to song.

So we come full cycle: the yearning to reach America and partake of all of its possibilities; and then the desire, by those born here later, to find out how the journey started, and discover what was left behind.

The mayor of Baltimore kept a sign on a wall above his City Hall desk: "No Irish Need Apply." This was the stark American rejection slip that appeared in countless windows early in the twentieth century, announcing to the Irish that they were not wanted, and signifying to everyone else that there was something different about these people, something to be avoided.

The modern Martin O'Malley was born in 1963, the year of John Kennedy's assassination. O'Malley was quick to mention the connection, letting a listener construct the political symmetry. He had an eye for narrative and an instinct for the telling moment. The emotional implication of this connection: Here was Kennedy's torch passed to a new generation.

By the time of O'Malley's birth, the bigotry against the Irish had been relegated to a period piece. The old "No Irish" sign was something recalled by elders and passed down to children—"Nobody wanted us," they said, echoing the eternal cry of all ethnic outsiders. But O'Malley kept the sign over his desk as a reminder of history, and as a sardonic joke. A lot of people hadn't wanted him to apply for the job of mayor. He was a white man in a mostly black city. White people had monopolized power for too long, and now it was supposed to be somebody else's turn.

But the American journey is never that simple. The country is about the mix, and the freedom to move about in it, or America is no different than any other place. O'Malley never knew the slights of his great-grandfather's generation, but he still felt the power of their rejection and was moved by it. He grew up in a house with John Kennedy memorabilia and with framed photographs of Martin Luther King as well. He remembered his father telling him once, "I think, if I had been born poor and black in this country, they would have had to lock me up for a very long time." The father thus gave birth to a son's social conscience.

Martin O'Malley had never seen the first American O'Malley, but the image reached him. It moved him as deeply as the photograph I had of my great-grandfather Max Strull in that Lower East Side sweatshop, or Barbara Mikulski imagining the loneliness of the ocean voyage of her forebears—or Jake Oliver's first sight of the picture of Emmett Till at the end of a hanging rope.

We are pulled in many directions. We want to belong, and we strive for the full citizenship. But there comes a time when we want to know about our uniqueness, about the people who made it easier for us, and what they had to overcome to make us who we are.

One day the moment arrived for O'Malley. In his early thirties, he was already a city councilman from Northeast Baltimore. He was married to Katie O'Malley, a Baltimore County prosecutor and daughter of Maryland's attorney general, J. Joseph Curran Jr., who was himself part of an extended Irish political family. There were two small O'Malley children—and another to come—and one O'Malley band, called O'Malley's Irish March, for which O'Malley was lead singer.

He wanted to know where all of this started. He thought of his great-grandfather as a man "who had slipped out of a blank page." He wanted something inscribed on the page. So he telephoned his father, Thomas O'Malley, a lawyer in the Washington suburbs of Montgomery County.

"Wouldn't it be nice to know where we came from?" Martin O'Malley asked his father. "How about, you kick in 500 bucks, and I'll kick in 500, and we'll send it off to genealogy people over there and find out where we're from?"

"I have no interest in that," said Thomas O'Malley.

"What do you mean?" said his son.

"I don't keep in touch with my living relatives," said the father. "Why would I want to go digging up dead ones?"

"Don't you feel the need to know?" asked the son.

"No," said his father. "Call your mother. Goodbye."

Instead, O'Malley wrote letters. He knew that the great-grandfather had landed in Pittsburgh and died there. O'Malley located his death certificate. The old man's parents were Thomas O'Malley and Nellie Burke O'Malley, who lived and died in the Kilmilkeen area, in Clombur. There were fifteen Thomas O'Malleys there. Martin O'Malley began eliminating them by dint of birthdays, marriages, dates of death. He was left with one, and imagined he had his man.

Then, early in his mayoral term, as O'Malley flew to Europe on a business trip, he opened some of his mail. It was two o'clock in the morning, and the plane was flying over Ireland. There was a letter from Ireland, from a pub owner in the village of Clombur near Kilmilkeen. O'Malley thought, "This guy's gonna try to shake me down for a few bucks."

But the letter mentioned his forebears' roots, and asked only if O'Malley might write a piece for the local parish bulletin for its Christmas edition. From Amsterdam where he landed, O'Malley called his wife and had her pull up the name of the pub on the Internet. Sure enough, there was a picture of the letter writer holding up a bottle of Guinness Beer, and he had another fellow with him, the lead singer in an Irish band, whom O'Malley had met when the band visited America.

More letters followed. Then, in September of 2000, O'Malley took his wife and two young daughters to Ireland, to the place where his great-grandfather had left home and, in O'Malley's musical imaginings, had whispered to his mother, "Wait for me." The visit felt like the belated fulfillment of a promise made by one generation on behalf of another.

In a village pub a visiting priest brought O'Malley and his wife copies of birth and death records. A few minutes later, a man and his sister, not much older than O'Malley, arrived from Kilmilkeen: Thomas and Therese O'Malley. They were the mayor's cousins. Thomas O'Malley was a high school teacher who had done a genealogy study of the Kilmilkeen O'Malleys dating back to 1773. He knew about O'Malley soldiers and farmers and Irish battles and O'Malley connections to them.

"I don't think this Martin O'Malley is the one you're looking for," he said.

The mayor of Baltimore felt all the air leave his body.

"We only had one O'Malley emigrate," said Thomas O'Malley. "Most of the O'Malleys had their own land. They were remote enough from the English power, and they got through the famine without a whole lot of people having to emigrate. The only one who left in the 1870s went to England."

"You know," said Martin O'Malley, "I could never find this written anywhere, but my father vaguely remembered that he went to England before coming to America."

And with that Thomas O'Malley of Kilmilkeen said, "He didn't settle in Pittsburgh, Pennsylvania, did he?"

"He did," said Martin O'Malley. "And there's 250 O'Malleys in Pittsburgh to this day because of him."

Now Thomas O'Malley looked at his sister. "Therese," he said, "get out the picture of 'Question Mark' O'Malley that we got from the old fellow's album."

He pulled out a big photograph, with a cardboard backing, of a well-dressed man with a high-collar shirt and a gold chain. The picture seemed late nineteenth-century vintage. It came from an old album, with about twenty photographs in it. A genealogical researcher had identified every one but this.

The first American Martin O'Malley, out of Kilmilkeen, Ireland. When the mayor of Baltimore reached into his family's past, he found his great-grandfather's photograph in an Irish pub in the hands of cousins he had never known. *Courtesy of the O'Malley family*

"My great-grandfather," Martin O'Malley of Baltimore said now. He sat in a little restaurant called Café Hon, in the working-class Hampden neighborhood of Baltimore, after returning from Ireland. "He had this big old mustache, and eyes and hair and nose just like my dad. The bottom of the picture said, 'Stanton Photography Studios, Forbes Avenue, Pittsburgh, Pa.' And I looked at these cousins, and Thomas O'Malley said, 'Jesus, it gives me the chills.'"

The great-grandfather had sent the photograph back to his family from Pittsburgh. When he left Ireland, he worked for a while as a miner in New Castle, England, and then sailed to America, where he worked in the coalmines of Pennsylvania. Then he moved to Brisbee, Arizona, where he fought the great Indian warrior Geronimo.

The morning after their arrival in Ireland, Thomas O'Malley took his American cousins to a little church in Kilmilkeen where the first Martin O'Malley would have been baptized. By the church was a graveyard, with many of the tombstones carved in Irish and some not marked at all.

"Those are famine graves," Thomas O'Malley explained. "People died so quickly that they just didn't do the carving of stones."

Then Thomas O'Malley took the American O'Malleys to the former home of the nineteenth-century Thomas O'Malley—the brother of Mayor O'Malley's great-grandfather. The mayor left a pendant there that had belonged to his great-grandfather, the young man at the harbor who sings, "Wait for me." It felt like the keeping of a promise.

"How he must have waited for his brother to return for so long," said this Thomas O'Malley.

Heading back to America, Mayor O'Malley sent Thomas an e-mail: "I still have to steer around that sad, tearful, empty space that opens in my heart every time I leave Ireland. My cynical ever-new American nature always tries to laugh the feeling off as corny sentimentality; but my Irish spirit and being senses a very deep, real, and serious thing—Genetic memory? Genetic loss of memory? Genetic memory of loss?"

When O'Malley returned to Baltimore and told stories of his trip, he seemed awed. This history clearly mattered to him: the Irish part, and the Catholic part, and the part that ties him to a young man saying goodbye to his mother at a harbor.

"But it didn't seem to move your father the same way," I said. "Why does it move you?"

"I don't know," he said. He drank a cup of iced coffee and mentioned lingering jet lag. He'd flown back to Baltimore less than two days earlier. "With a lot of immigrants to this country, there's a certain time when they ran away from being Irish, or being anything. Being Catholic was a handicap. With assimilation, there comes security. My father probably told me about the 'No Irish Need Apply' signs."

Security came from assimilation, and from jobs. Martin O'Malley's father went to law school on the G.I. Bill. A lawyer would never have to worry about signs telling the Irish to go away. Thomas O'Malley was in his father's home, in Pittsburgh, when the telephone rang. A friend told him he had passed the bar exam. O'Malley walked onto a little front porch where his father smoked a cigar.

"I did it," said the son to his father. "I passed the bar."

He was the first lawyer in the family. His father said nothing for a moment. He puffed on his cigar, and then said, "They will never take that away from you."

"Interesting, isn't it?" Martin O'Malley said now. "'They will never take that away from you.'"

"What does that say to you?" I asked.

"I think it underscored the sense of mission, and the sense of vulnerability," he said. He seemed to have been waiting for such a question, for the words charged out of him. "What I'm sure of," he said, "is what my grandfather and my great-grandfather had imprinted on them, an imprint of 800 years of oppression, where priests were hunted down like dogs and you weren't allowed to worship in your own church, or own land, or own a horse worth more than three pounds. All of that stuff. And it underscores how it continued to play out on this side of the Atlantic, and how everyone knew they were just one boat ride away from that world, and that deprivation and starvation and being treated like dogs."

The past stays with us, and sometimes drives us. O'Malley's mother, Barbara, had an Irish grandfather, but her background is mostly German. Her father, Joseph Suelzer, was a county chairman of the Democratic Party in Fort Wayne, Indiana, and once won ten dollars in a poker game from Harry Truman. She worked in political campaigns before she was old enough to vote. Thomas O'Malley's father was a ward leader on the North Side of Pittsburgh, an Irish Catholic ghetto. Family legend had it that they were the first Democratic club to recruit black membership.

Barbara Suelzer and Thomas O'Malley met when she worked as a committeewoman for the Young Democrats, and he was practicing law. They attended one of John Kennedy's inaugural balls. Politics was in the blood. Martin O'Malley was a toddler when his mother taught him to lead cheers for Hubert Humphrey. In grade school he walked through his Bethesda, Maryland, neighborhood handing out brochures for a friend of his father's who was running for Montgomery County executive.

The O'Malley children, November 1970 (*left to right*): Eileen holding Paul; Patrick; Martin, the future mayor of Baltimore; and Bridget holding Peter. For Martin, the passions of politics and Irish music and his family roots were quite a distance in the future. *Courtesy of the O'Malley family*

There were no black people in his neighborhood, and only a few in grade school. Then, in the ninth grade, O'Malley began riding a commuter train each day to Gonzaga High School in Washington, D.C. The school was located next to the K Street Projects, where students trudged each day past a mission for homeless men. They were lined up every morning when O'Malley arrived, and lined up again when he left in the afternoon. The line never went away. The ruined faces of the men moved O'Malley, who connected them with his father's feeling about Martin Luther King and with stories he was beginning to digest about the Irish.

At Gonzaga he played defensive back for the football team. "I like to hit people," he said. Before each game the football coach blasted Irish rock music into the locker room to pump up the team. O'Malley learned to play the guitar and the pennywhistle and joined an Irish band. In the house his mother played Clancy Brothers records. O'Malley paid attention to the words.

"You ask," O'Malley said, "if my parents were assimilationist. Well, they were never not Irish, and they were never not American. So I was aware of being Irish, without ever feeling marginalized."

That was surely more a condition of his age, and the country's shifting sensitivities, than of the history of the Irish experience in America and its Catholic connection.

Baltimore's Irish roots go back to the town's own infancy. The city was established in 1729, on land bought from the Carroll family, who had themselves come from Ireland. The Carrolls produced Bishop John Carroll, the first Catholic bishop in America; Daniel Carroll, who signed the U.S. Constitution; and Charles Carroll of Carrollton, who may have been the wealthiest man in America in his time and was the last surviving signer of the Declaration of Independence.

In the eighteenth century American political power still lay in the hands of a small number of privileged white men. In Baltimore, in order to vote you had to own property. By the early nineteenth century, though white males were allowed to vote, city elections were marked by violence. Much of it was directed at immigrants—often against Irish Catholics.

Most of the city's Irish lived in its southern precincts: Canton and Fells Point, Locust Point and the neighborhoods around the B&O Railroad yards in Southwest Baltimore. In the mid-1840s, many Irish immigrants found work at the B&O Mt. Clare yards, about a mile west of downtown. As the Irish potato famine worsened, their numbers grew so large that a Catholic parish was founded and a group of Irish nuns—the Sisters of Mercy—settled in the area to teach the children of the railroad workers and provide social services to the new arrivals.

By the end of the century, though, the Irish were moving north, especially along York Road, and over the years they dispersed so much that no thoroughly Irish neighborhoods had remained in Baltimore for years by the time Martin O'Malley arrived.

He studied political science and English at Catholic University, volunteered for Gary Hart's presidential campaign in 1984, then went to the University of Maryland Law School in Baltimore. "The cheapest one I could find," he said. He won his first city council seat at twenty-eight and held it for eight years, representing Northeast Baltimore's racial mosaic. He made it a point to have black political allies. One was a young council member from West Baltimore named Lawrence Bell, who became council president and heir apparent to be mayor. In the high-profile O'Malley-Bell alliance, many saw hopeful signs not only of racial harmony but of visible political role models for the city. Some called them Batman and Robin.

But theirs was an isolated model. In the last years of the twentieth century, the nineteen-member city council was heavily black, and sometimes contentious. A battle over new district lines brought out the worst in its members. There was also a fractious hearing when O'Malley attempted to question the city's housing commissioner, Daniel P. Henson. "Maybe the councilman would like to meet me in an alley," Henson erupted at a packed City Hall gathering. Behind him, several of Henson's large henchmen jumped to their feet to echo the challenge.

By the summer of 1999, as he pondered such pitiful behavior, and the city's continuing decay, O'Malley began to think seriously of running for mayor.

That was the summer that Felix Guevara reached for his little piece of American justice—and seemed to have his hand slapped away.

It was six months since the night he trudged home along East Baltimore's Gough Street from his dishwashing job and had his money taken by the uniformed policeman Dorian Martin. In those six months nothing had happened to Martin. He gave prosecutors one story, and then a different one. The prosecutors found both stories fraudulent, but not particularly worth their concern. In a city with 300 homicides each year, one man's loss of $300—a man who made his living washing dishes, who wasn't yet a citizen, who had never learned to speak English and hadn't a single political connection—was not considered top priority.

So they proposed a deal to Martin, and he was prepared to take it. Pay a small fine, endure a brief probation, and then fade away. There would be no prison time. Martin would pay a small restitution to Hector Portillo and Garcillia Roy, the other two men he had preyed upon because, like Guevara, they were Latinos who could not speak English, and thus were believed unlikely to complain.

The plea bargain offer was revealed in the *Baltimore Sun*. When Angelo Solera saw it, he fumed. He had been fuming since the winter night he saw Guevara's story scrawled on the wall of a little Fells Point restaurant and stalked out to find Guevara. "Don't give in to the bastards," he said. Now, in his apartment, he picked up his telephone and heard the voice of a television news reporter who remembered him from the early days of the case. Solera spoke English. For television, this made him a spokesman of convenience for the Latino community. He was asked, do you have any reaction to the plea bargain story?

"You better believe it," he said. "We're gonna demonstrate. We'll be outside the courthouse tomorrow."

Then a second call came: another TV reporter. Again, Solera puffed himself up and talked of demonstrations for justice. Great throngs of people marched through his imagination. They were crying for America to open its heart. Then Solera hung up the telephone, and he thought, "What have you done? You don't know what you're talking about. Where are you going to get demonstrators?" He wanted to call the television stations back and say, "I didn't mean it."

Instead, he went to a Home Depot store and bought cardboard for signs. He stayed up late that night and wrote words on the cardboard: "Justice Now." He called a few friends for help. He imagined the city's Latinos would invoke the modern American method of all public dissidence. If you can't fight City Hall, you summon TV cameras and reporters, and you stage your grievance with sufficient drama to embarrass every authority figure in sight. The friends said they would try to help. But they were working people, and this was the heart of the workday.

At noon the next day, Solera parked his car near the front of the courthouse and got out. Nobody was there. He ran a hand through his cropped thinning hair and thought, "I'm gonna look like a fool." Television crews were slowly setting up. Solera nervously held up a sign and saw a familiar face. Then he saw another. "Grab a sign," he hollered.

Within minutes, on this humid summer day on downtown Baltimore's Calvert Street courthouse corridor, a dozen or so people marched in a circle. On television, it looked closer to thirty. Their faces were self-consciously grim and determined, mirror images of those on television screens who had staged their own versions of ethnic grievance over the years.

"*Que queremos?*" Solera cried out.

"*Justicia,*" a chorus cried back for the television cameras.

"What do we want?"

"Justice."

After a few minutes, Solera slipped out of the circle of marchers and waited until all television cameras and microphones pointed at him. Demonstrators circled directly behind him for maximum visual effect.

"An injustice to the victims," he declared. He gestured toward the big courthouse behind him. "Every time, they work out a deal. How many times are they going to do this? At some point, you say, 'Enough is enough, this is a slap in the face.'"

His ruddy skin perspired in the midday heat. In a few minutes the TV news crews packed up their equipment and went away, and so the demonstrators left moments later, imagining their efforts had meant nothing. They did not yet know it, but they had won. A city judge overruled the plea bargain arrangement, and prosecutors decided to bring criminal charges against Dorian Martin. It was, by the standards of the city, a small case. But its details—the uniformed cop, the helpless immigrant turning to America for justice—had resonated through the halls where justice and politics came together.

In that heated time, Martin O'Malley came up against his conscience.

In eight frustrating years on the city council he had watched Baltimore come undone. The city's first elected African American mayor, Kurt L. Schmoke, had entered City Hall twelve years earlier to the blast of trumpets but would leave to the mutterings of disappointment. Things had not worked out. The city's murder rate, and its narcotics traffic, were among the worst in the nation. People fled some neighborhoods so frantically that thousands of homes were simply left behind to become vacant, rotting shooting galleries for junkies and eyesores for entire blocks. Trash piled inside them, and rats followed. The decay built on itself, and the housing commissioner sneered at all who questioned his policies. Meanwhile, the schools had turned out a generation of illiterates, despite the mayor's poignant municipal slogan: "The City That Reads."

And many who remained in the city were choosing up sides strictly by race.

Four years earlier, Schmoke had run for reelection against Mary Pat Clarke, the white city council president, a staunch liberal on race. Both she and Schmoke were products of the same midcentury civil rights struggle for racial equality. And yet, in the minds of many whites, Schmoke ran his final campaign as an overt appeal to vote by racial preference—and the results, across the city, seemed to reflect it. In many black neighborhoods, Schmoke received upwards of 90 percent of the vote; in white neighborhoods, Clarke got more than 90 percent. Four years later, with Schmoke ready to bow out of office for a private law practice, there were two major candidates for mayor of Baltimore, both African American: the city council president, O'Malley's old ally, Lawrence Bell; and a former councilman, Carl Stokes.

O'Malley believed neither man could handle the job. Bell was a slender young man who did not appear to have eaten solid food for much of his adult life, nor did he seem to have lived much of a life outside politics. In his late thirties, he was single, emotionally unattached, and lived in an apartment over his father's dental office. Meanwhile, Stokes had been caught shaving the truth about his academic history and could not raise money for a decent campaign. When O'Malley looked in the mirror, he saw the only one he believed capable of running the city. But then came the struggle with his conscience.

"Should a white man do this?" he asked himself. "Am I only doing it because I can take advantage of a split African American vote?" Then he thought, "To say that you can't run for office because of your color is a different sort of bigotry from saying, 'I won't *vote* for somebody because of color'—but it's still bigotry."

He told his wife what he was thinking. Katie O'Malley, daughter of the state's attorney general, niece of three generations of council members, professional prosecutor, student of the political game, told her husband he had lost all sense of perspective.

"You can't," she said. She mentioned the city's 60 percent black majority. "They call it representative democracy for a reason," she said.

"What are you saying?" her husband asked. "That people aren't fair enough to vote for a candidate who's the best person?"

"They're gonna call you a racist," said Katie O'Malley.

"It's not what they call you," said Martin O'Malley. "It's what you answer to."

He called Gary Hart, in whose presidential campaign he had worked. "Take some time alone," Hart said. "Separate your ambitions from your convictions. Because when the going gets rough, your ambitions won't sustain you. Only your convictions will."

O'Malley took the words to heart but also wondered how the city had gotten to this mindset. He was questioning his own conscience, but examining America's as well. Did we still believe in the melting pot, or were we only a collection of disparate people who would always keep each other at a distance and always measure each other by our differences? He came from a family where the civil rights movement was likened to a crusade. Had that been naïve? In his family, where Martin Luther King was treasured, the parallels of suffering had always been drawn between the Irish experience and the African American experience. Was it not enough to have a good heart? In the modern, cynical America, had we kissed off such notions so that it was now important only to have the right skin?

O'Malley telephoned Howard "Pete" Rawlings, a black state delegate respected by blacks in his home district and by whites in powerful positions of business and politics.

"I think I'm gonna run," he said.

"I admire your guts," said Rawlings. "Stephanie thinks very highly of you." He meant Stephanie Rawlings, his daughter, who served with O'Malley on the city council. "But I'm leaning toward Stokes."

Then, a week later, Rawlings unexpectedly called him back. "Come talk to a few people," he said. When O'Malley arrived, Rawlings had Furlong Baldwin and Calman "Buddy" Zamoiski in the room. Baldwin was one of the town's most prominent bankers; Zamoiski was a big businessman. This was politics, but it was also a political melting pot. In an earlier era Tommy D'Alesandro had walked into such a room and been turned away simply for having an Italian name. Now, two old-line white powerbrokers had been brought in by a black politician to look over the new white guy. Baldwin and Zamoiski both had access to money, and to persuasive people. Rawlings, still leaning toward Stokes, nevertheless wanted to consider becoming the first diplomatic bridge across the racial divide. But he knew the troubles he would bring on himself if he did.

O'Malley saw one other person in the room, a woman with a polling firm who held on her lap a large book of numbers saying he had no shot in a race for mayor.

"Maybe we can fast-forward this a little," O'Malley said. "I'll take it for granted that your numbers say I can't win." In fact, they showed O'Malley with 7 percent of the vote. Lawrence Bell was far ahead. "Well, I did my own poll. You think I'd be dumb enough to get into this without doing my own poll?"

He looked at Rawlings and thought he was holding back a smile. "Tell me," said O'Malley, "what your poll says about public safety and open-air drug markets."

"People don't identify those issues with you," said the woman from the polling company.

"They will," said O'Malley.

"What about race?" somebody asked.

"I'm doing this," said O'Malley, "with a great amount of personal peace."

"But you can't win," said Furlong Baldwin.

"I'm gonna win," said O'Malley.

And Pete Rawlings, silent for the moment, thought, "He's a cocky little bastard."

At home, O'Malley called an old ally, Joan Carter Conway. She was a state senator now, but several years earlier O'Malley had helped her win a council seat that had always been held by white men.

"They'll call you racist if you run," Conway said. She wasn't telling him what do; she only wanted him to anticipate the inevitable. He was going against the grain of history. Kurt Schmoke was the first child of the American civil rights movement to be elected mayor. Too many people had invested too much emotion in his candidacy, and in the very idea of a black person running the city, and controlling jobs and money and power, and then passing the job to another black person.

But there was another side of it. Schmoke was also a product of that narrow window when the city's schools had been genuinely integrated. He'd gone to high school at Baltimore City College, where he quarterbacked the football team. He had joined a mostly white organization, the Lancers Boys

Club, where he'd been taken under the wing of its advisor, Judge Robert Hammerman; went to Yale and to Harvard Law School; won a Rhodes Scholarship. And then, against all expectations, he had spent twelve years as mayor without saying a word about racial cooperation, without appointing any white people to high-profile positions except police commissioner, and then capped his tenure with a final campaign that had discomfitted so many people.

Now, four years later, as O'Malley wondered if old notions of racial cooperation had been damaged beyond repair, Stephanie Rawlings approached her father.

"O'Malley's a good man," she said.

"What are you telling me?" said Pete Rawlings.

His daughter replied, "Not to support him because he's white defies everything our whole family's ever been about."

The words moved Rawlings. His daughter had held onto ideals learned in her youth, and she was now giving them back to her father. The old dream still existed. Rawlings decided to meet with O'Malley again but this time laid out a list of assurances he would need: African American inclusion on the city's board of estimates, in the mayor's cabinet, in minority business contracts. If he was going to help put a white person back into the mayor's office, he would make certain there would be no housecleaning of blacks.

"I was gonna do all these things anyway," O'Malley said.

On a sunny Tuesday morning, June 24, 1999, at the corner of Harford Road and the Alameda in northeast Baltimore, O'Malley officially announced his candidacy. In his first breath he declared himself a product of an "integrated and hopeful" district. In case anybody missed the sentiment, he took another breath and invoked the phrase "working-class families of this city, black and white."

It was a city of the full American mix, he was saying. Think of our common journey. Think of something deeper than skin color, something more profound than appeals to bitterness, something beyond all of the name-calling and mutual suspiciousness that had replaced the old civil rights coalitions.

Then he held his breath. Pete Rawlings decided to announce his endorsement on the morning of August 8 on the steps of the city's War Memorial, across a large plaza facing City Hall. The night before, a nervous

O'Malley telephoned Rawlings. "I hear the uglies are coming tomorrow," O'Malley said. There were rumors that Bell's supporters were going to harass Rawlings.

"Let's rent a hotel, we'll get a room," O'Malley said. That way they could control the environment, keep out any troublemakers. This wasn't just a political endorsement on the line, it was an implicit statement about American ideals, about renewing a commitment to a thing that seemed to have slipped away.

"Well, frankly," Rawlings replied slowly, his deep voice rumbling, "this isn't your event. It's my event. If you want to come, you can come. If you don't feel you're up to it, you don't have to come."

O'Malley felt a little shiver of relief run through him. Rawlings was the old pro. He understood what was about to happen. With reporters and television cameras there, the more Bell's people acted out, the greater would be the public revulsion.

"I want them to see the people Lawrence has surrounded himself with," said Rawlings.

The next day, everyone did. The city witnessed an act of political vandalism. As Rawlings walked across sunlit War Memorial Plaza, about fifty people followed close behind and shouted epithets at him. They were young black men and women, aimless and broke, pulled off of street corners by Bell supporters, handed a few dollars, driven by bus to War Memorial Plaza, and told to shout at Rawlings. But the attack was led by Julius Henson and Robert Clay, two of Bell's campaign leaders.

As Rawlings marched across the plaza, he never broke stride and never seemed perturbed by the cries. He looked like a fellow about to be beaten up by thugs but never seemed even slightly intimidated. Bell's supporters looked like scroungy dogs yapping at a gentleman out for a stroll. This was exactly what Rawlings had anticipated. When he reached the microphones in front of the War Memorial building, he said, "We are not here to support the best black candidate, and . . ." And then his words were swallowed in another sound.

"We want Bell," cried Bell's gang. They stood directly in front of Rawlings, their faces nearly against his, calling so loudly and repeatedly that Rawlings could not hear his own voice. But microphones and cameras picked up everything.

". . . and we are not here to support the best white candidate," Rawlings said. The Bell forces were so close to him, and so loud, that their voices seemed to have a physical solidity. "We want Bell," they cried. Behind them, Henson and Clay hollered, "Pump it up, pump it up."

"We are here," said Rawlings, never for an instant losing his outward composure, "to support the best candidate for mayor of our city, and that person is Martin O'Malley."

The Bell forces continued to chant. Beyond the act of political thuggery, it was an attempt to blot out reality in the most primitive and misguided way—as though, to drown out Rawlings's words on this single morning, in a single downtown location, they might stop voters from ever finding out the news. And, more, it was an attempt to paint Rawlings as a traitor to his own race, to tell a majority black electorate to stick with its own kind.

But Rawlings was not the only black politician there that morning. Stephanie Rawlings was there, clutching her father's hand as they walked off together when it was over. And O'Malley's old friend, State Senator Joan Carter Conway, also showed up after a long struggle with her own conscience. "Martin brought me to the political table," she said, remembering how he'd helped her win her council seat. "This city's drowning. When you're drowning, and somebody puts out a hand to pull you out, you don't say, 'Go away, I'm waiting for a black hand.'"

Rawlings had been right; the city was appalled at the display, and the poll numbers began to turn. And the more Bell turned to race, the more they continued to turn. At a Druid Hill Park rally, he told black supporters they should only vote for "people who look like us." His poll numbers dropped dramatically. Then two of his insiders were caught printing racist literature. The poll numbers now plummeted like something thrown from a building.

In the city of Baltimore, overwhelmingly Democratic, the election was essentially settled on Tuesday, September 14, 1999, in the primary balloting. At fifteen minutes before ten o'clock that night, O'Malley reached for precinct returns he had jotted on a note pad.

"Listen to this," he said to a telephone caller. Each syllable he uttered seemed to perform a little pirouette; each word sprang wondrously along the telephone wire. "St. Ambrose School," he said. It was an African American precinct—and he'd gotten nearly a third of their votes. Edmondson High School, he said. Another black precinct, and another third of the vote—and he'd beaten Bell there. Northwood Elementary, with all black voters—and O'Malley had gotten nearly half the vote there.

"What's going to shock people," he said, "is the racial turnover all over town."

When the ballots were all counted, he had gotten 53 percent of the overall vote in a city more than 60 percent African American. And the candidate whose campaign had been most racially divisive, and who had seemed like the sure winner only months earlier, finished a distant and pathetic third.

For that moment in the city of Baltimore, there were political considerations more compelling than race.

And finally there came the call for Felix Guevara.

He stood at the little bend of that dank courthouse corridor, hemmed in by so many people, hearing so many voices hollering at him in a language he did not understand, looking utterly overwhelmed, and longing for El Salvador.

"I want to go back," he said in Spanish.

"Don't give in to the bastards," said Angelo Solera.

Guevara wore his sweatshirt with "United States of America" on the front. America was the new house he lived in—but maybe not for long. When the voice from the courtroom door called his name, he took a deep breath and came out of his corner like a fighter who knows he is about to be hurt. He walked into a courtroom the size of an arena and looked even smaller than he had looked in the hall. He seemed overwhelmed, as if taking the full measure of his circumstances for the first time. When he glanced across the room to the defense table on his right, he saw Dorian Martin, who had taken his money. Martin looked enormous. Behind him, Guevara saw a few Latino friends huddled together on the dark brown courtroom benches. They lived here, they worked here—but there was still the question: As first-generation arrivals from someplace else, was this their country? When, precisely, does such a moment arrive?

For Guevara, this was not the moment of citizenship, but of simple justice. Against all instinct, he had listened to the imprecations of his friends and taken this case as far as he could. Now he wondered: Would American justice be just another version of El Salvador's? And he saw Judge Clifton J. Gordy enter and call his court to order.

Gordy was a tall, graying African American man, fifty-three years old. He had grown up on a farm near the small town of Delmar on Maryland's Eastern Shore. After early morning farm chores, he walked to a school where every child was black. In high school he took a bus to nearby Salisbury. Every youngster in the school was black. Then he went to the University of Maryland, Eastern Shore, where almost everyone was black. It wasn't until he reached law school at the University of Maryland in downtown Baltimore that he saw a white face inside a school.

"Never had a white classmate," he said one afternoon, reclining on a chair in his chambers. "We had our little world, and they had theirs." He had grown up in the aftermath of the Supreme Court decision outlawing public school segregation, and it had meant nothing in his world. He was still in school when Hubert Geroid "Rap" Brown came to the Eastern Shore and instigated national headlines with inflammatory talk about segregation. And this had not changed the schools either.

"Never saw a white child, and never knew the difference," Gordy said. "You understand, I am philosophically opposed to any kind of segregation. But there was something protective about being with my own kind all my life."

And there was the American dilemma. We are comfortable with our own kind—but who are our own kind? Is it people who share our religious beliefs, or skin color, or national background? Yes, certainly. But, if these were the sole measure of comfort, then what was the point of America? When we stayed with our own, were we ordaining distance from all others?

Felix Guevara's case touched many people because he had reached for America in the most humble ways—working three jobs, sending money home to his family in El Salvador, following the journey of so many who had come before him—and had been treated so harshly by a protector of that classic route.

Now, in court, he strained to comprehend what was happening. He heard words and more words and understood none of them, and caught only pieces of the translations whispered in his ear. Before him, Dorian Martin's defense attorney, Warren A. Brown, striding across the big courtroom, attempted to break apart the core of Guevara's case.

"The state will tell you that this man doesn't speak English," said Brown. "That's not true." Guevara's translator, Dorothy Katzenstein, whispered the words in his ear. Brown walked toward Guevara. He seemed to be stalking him. "He speaks English when he wants to," said Brown. Now he stood over the skinny Guevara, who was leaning close to Katzenstein, and he hollered at him.

"You know more English than that, man," said Brown. "Come on. Answer me. You know what I'm saying."

Guevara stared blankly. Brown was heading directly into the symbolism of the moment: This wasn't about a poor little immigrant; this fellow Guevara had been here for half a dozen years. Surely, he had learned to speak English. Surely, he had made up this story about Dorian Martin picking on him just because he couldn't speak English. Surely, Brown was saying, this man was no more vulnerable than anyone else in this courtroom. "Answer me," Brown said. Guevara said nothing. Brown finally turned away in disgust.

The next day, when the policeman Martin took the witness stand, he claimed it had all been a misunderstanding. He said Guevara had disrespected him, had waved a wad of bills in his face and taunted him in English. Martin, changing his story one more time, claimed he had snatched the bills away in an instant of anger. The jury knew nothing about his other two Latino victims.

"In poor judgment," Martin said, "I snatched the money and in one motion, all at once, I put it in my pocket. At that moment, my radio went off." He said he had driven away on an emergency call, but later returned to look for Guevara, who was gone.

So it went. The trial took two days, and then the jury deliberated for just two hours. They found Martin guilty of theft and of misconduct in office. Felix Guevara, in his hour of triumph, took little solace. Would there be a significant penalty, he worried, or would Martin be free to come after him?

Three weeks later came the answer. On the morning of Martin's sentencing, Guevara stood in the courthouse hallway with a man named Miguel Rivera, a Latino community activist.

"He didn't want to do this," Rivera said. "We said, 'You've got to do this. This is not El Salvador, this is America.' He says, 'What if this man doesn't go to jail?'"

"I am afraid," Guevara said in Spanish. He seemed to shrink into that little corner of the courthouse hallway where he stood at the start of trial. He was still that lost soul in *The House I Live In,* wondering why so many people were hollering at him. He was a man wanting to go home—but uncertain where in the world home was.

"People don't seem to understand, we're outsiders," he said. "They don't know what that is like to be an outsider."

He was wrong. He did not yet understand. We are a nation of outsiders, cultural mutts caught between wanting to belong to the crowd and clinging to the pieces that fully define us: the family tales told around kitchen tables, the rituals and cultural tics and belief systems, and the sense of sacrifice made generations earlier, sometimes on the other side of an ocean, to get to this place and time.

In a presentencing gesture for leniency, Dorian Martin brought in a character witness named Robert Gault. He was a civilian who had once been stopped by Martin but did not have his money taken by him. Here, Martin was implying, was proof that he was an honest man. If he took from Guevara, surely he could take from anyone.

Judge Gordy asked Gault, "Are you a native-born American?"

"Yes."

"And you do speak English?"

"Yes."

"That's all," the judge said.

For there it was, the simple distinction for all to perceive: the language, and the vulnerability, of the outsider. When Felix Guevara took the stand that day he said in Spanish, "I am far from my country, where I had fear of police people. I work at three jobs, and I am fearful I could be killed. I work until one in the morning. I hope there will be good justice."

At his defense table Dorian Martin shook his head. He knew the game was up. Minutes later, when Judge Gordy asked Martin to stand for sentencing, he could not look the judge in the eye. Gordy called Martin's act "a putrid stain on the shield of the Baltimore police." Felix Guevara leaned close to Dorothy Katzenstein, who translated the judge's words. Guevara's eyes widened.

"Six months in jail," said Gordy, "and one year of probation."

And then it was over. Two police pulled Dorian Martin's huge arms behind his back, slipped handcuffs over his wrists, and then they took him away so that Felix Guevara did not have to be afraid anymore. A few minutes later, Guevara, smiling with relief, walked out of the dank courthouse and stood in the sunlight.

He seemed different now. Before, he was weighted down by his troubles and his fears. Now he seemed a man carrying history. He had become a tiny sliver of it. He was the newest version of an endless American story. He was a little man named Max Strull, leaving Latvia for that Lower East Side sweatshop in New York with only a head full of Yiddish to communicate. He was the same as Barbara Mikulski's people, finding a port city called Baltimore from somewhere in Poland, and reaching across the town's ethnic barriers for their American daughter. He was the first American Tommy D'Alesandro, scuffling through his days so that his children might leave the neighborhood and go anywhere at all—even to City Hall, or the U.S. Congress, or the White House to shake hands with a president who was named Franklin Delano Roosevelt.

My great-grandmother Zlotte Strull knew that man. She came here from Russia, and she called him Franklin Delano Rosenfeld to embrace him. Sometimes, she could feel America return her embrace.